A Birder's Guide

to

Southeastern

Arizona

By Richard Cachor Taylor

Based on his complete revision in 1995
and subsequent updates in 1997 and 1999

Original version by James A. Lane, 1965
Revised by Harold Holt, 1983

ABA/Lane Birdfinding Guide Series

Library of Congress Control Number: 2004116666

ISBN Number: 1-878788-22-1

Fifth Edition

1 2 3 4 5 6 7 8

Printed in the United States of America

Publisher

American Birding Association, Inc.

Production Editor

Virginia Maynard

Maps

Virginia Maynard, using CorelDRAW, version 8

Cover Photograph

Elegant Trogon
Paul Zimmerman

Back Cover Photograph

Montezuma Quail
C. Allan Morgan

Illustrations

Georges Dremeaux, Narca Moore-Craig, Terry O'Nele, David Sibley, Gail Diane Yovanovich

Distributed by

American Birding Association Sales
P.O. Box 6599
Colorado Springs, CO 80934 USA
phone: 800-634-7736 or 719-578-0607
fax: 800-590-2473 or 719-578-9705
email: *abasales@abasales.com*
website: www.americanbirding.org/abasales

A SPECIAL NOTE

Like all books that attempt to describe
the avian dynamics of Southeastern Arizona,
this book owes much to *The Birds of Arizona*, 1964,
by Allan Phillips, Joe Marshall, and Gale Monson,
and the subsequent
Annotated Checklist of the Birds of Arizona, 1981,
by Monson and Phillips.
These works are the foundation
of our knowledge
of the status and distribution
of the avifauna in this state.
They have made this book possible.

FOREWORD

After my first visit to Southeastern Arizona fifteen years ago, I knew I would return. I have lived or visited there every year since. Because of my intense interest in the area, friends often asked me to plan their visits. I started writing itineraries for them. Each year these get more detailed and numerous. Someone suggested I write a book. . .

— Jim Lane, 1965

These words were written for the preface of the very first edition of a little book entitled *A Bird Watcher's Guide to Southeastern Arizona* by the late James A. Lane (1926–1987). Jim dedicated most of his adult life to helping others find and enjoy the birds of all of North America. During the last two decades of his life he wrote or co-authored seven books in his popular regional *Birder's Guide* series. The first of Jim's guides was for Southeastern Arizona. It was a charming little book containing 46 pages, modest by today's standards, but a very real accomplishment in 1965. For the rest of his life, Southeastern Arizona remained Jim Lane's favorite place to bird in North America.

Soon after Jim Lane met Harold Holt in 1972, the two teamed up to co-author a Colorado birdfinding guide. Although Jim was also leading tours for the Massachusetts Audubon Society, he managed to revise the Southeastern Arizona book twice, once in 1974 and again in 1977. Meanwhile, Harold had assumed responsibility for distribution of the Lane Guides, and in 1982 he began updating all of the books. The Southeastern Arizona birdfinding guide was revised by Harold Holt in 1983, 1984, and 1986.

Jim Lane, the father of the popular modern North American birdfinding guide, was honored at the 1986 Tucson Convention with the American Birding Association's Ludlow Griscom Award for his outstanding contributions to the birding world. At the same time Jim's health was gradually failing. The North American birding community lost a great path-finder in March of 1987, but Jim's legacy continues in what have come to be known among birders as "The Lane Guides."

After Jim Lane's death, Harold Holt updated his late friend's Southeastern Arizona birdfinding guide twice, in 1988 and again in 1989.

In 1990, the American Birding Association assumed the on-going responsibility for keeping the Lane Guide series current and for adding new titles to the ABA *Birdfinding Guides*. Major new editions in an innovative format have now appeared for all but one of the books in the original Lane series.

In 1995, the ABA asked Richard Cachor Taylor to revise *A Birder's Guide to Southeastern Arizona*. Rick is a local birder with a lifetime of first-hand experience in the region, and he is also the author of *Trogons of the Arizona Borderlands*, based on a research project that he launched in 1977. Not only did Rick build on the considerable contributions of Jim Lane and Harold Holt, and capture the spirit of Jim's intentions in this book, but Rick also added extensively to the depth and coverage of the book. [Rick's 1995 edition was updated in 1997 and 1999, primarily with revised bar graphs and expanded specialties accounts.]

It is hoped that this new version of the Southeastern Arizona guide will earn the same kind of reception as previous editions by Jim Lane and Harold Holt, that it will enable birders to thoroughly enjoy the birding potential in Southeastern Arizona, and that users of the book will continue to make suggestions for improving future editions.

Paul J. Baicich

Editor, ABA Birdfinding Guide Series, July 1995

Editor's Note to the Spring 1999 Reprint

The third printing of Rick Taylor's *A Birder's Guide to Southeastern Arizona* contains material not included in the first (August 1995) or second (July 1997) printings of this 4th edition of the book. If you compare this volume with the earlier printings, you will find 16 additional pages to accommodate an expanded *Birds of Southeastern Arizona Bar Graph* section, offering birders easily comparable information about all species recorded for the area. Species accounts have been updated also, and much other inforamtion information has been updated to reflect current conditions. The small corner of Arizona covered by this guide is constantly undergoing important changes—old "hotspots" give way to new ones, created partly by birds' natural movements, partly by changing access, and habitat changes, such as the recent development of Sweetwater Wetlands in Tucson. The sum of these changes led ABA to issue this expanded and revised reprint of the guide.

On December 22, 1998, the birding world, and particularly the American Birding Association, lost a steadfast and treasured friend when Harold R. Holt passed away. This Southeastern Arizona guide was one of Harold's favorites in the Lane Guide series.

Cindy Lippincott

Editor, ABA Birdfinding Guide Series, April 1999

Editor's Note to the 2005 Edition

This second edition of Rick Taylor's *A Birder's Guide to Southeastern Arizona* revises his first edition to include completely updated and expanded Bar Graphs and Specialties Accounts, as well as the most current information on all of the birding sites. Rick has also added several new stops on the Southeastern Arizona birding circuit, and has updated all of the maps. We hope that birders will continue to enjoy Rick's engaging prose, and will share his obvious joy in exploring the birdlife of this special region of the continent.

Virginia Maynard

Editor, ABA Birdfinding Guide Series, January 2005

ACKNOWLEDGMENTS

The list of birders to whom I am indebted for the information contained in these pages is long. I am especially grateful to the hundreds of birders with whom I've shared the oases, deserts, valleys, canyons, and mountains of this beautiful and bird-rich area. This book owes much to their companionship and their insights. It would have been impossible to write it without their help.

At the same time, this book is very much the outgrowth of the pioneer work done by the late Jim Lane and subsequently by the late Harold Holt. All those who helped Jim and Harold in the past versions of this birdfinding guide should be recognized: Larry Balch, Janice Bezore, Jewel Bezore, Steve Bezore, Barbara Berton, Edward Chalif, Edna Chamness, Peter Christensen, Hal Coss, Mary Dodd, Bill Harrison, Wes Hetrick, Gary Kirkreit, LaVona Holt, Glenn Isaacson, Billie Lane, Cebina Lane, Kent Nelson, Ray Olson, Carroll Peabody, Joan Peabody, Edna Phelps, George Pilling, Noble Proctor, Eleanor Pugh, Vincent Roth, Doug Salyar, Fletcher Sillick, Larry Smith, Tom Southerland, Rich Stallcup, Jolan Truan, Bernard Weiderman, Hugh Willoughby, Bob Witzeman, and Fern Zimmerman.

Since I first undertook this project in the fall of 1994, a number of people who deserve special mention have made concrete suggestions or contributed information. I would like to take this opportunity to express my deep appreciation to the following friends and fellow birders: Sandy Anderson, Mary Jo Ballator, Robin Baxter, Tom and Edith Beatty, Chris Benesh, Barbara Bickel, Tom and Debbie Collazo, Jeffrey Cooper, Troy Corman, Alan Craig, Doug Danforth, Louie Dombroski, Shawneen Finnegan, Tony Godfrey, Clive Green, Mary Jean Hage, Stuart Healy, Rich Hoyer, Dave Jasper, Kenn Kaufman, Lynn Hassler Kaufman, Karen Krebbs, Dave Krueper, Paul Lehman, Jackie and Winston Lewis, Katherine Lunsford, Terry McEneaney, Bill Maynard, Scott Mills, Gale Monson, Narca Moore-Craig, Arnie Moorhouse, Bob Morse, Jack Murray, Marion Paton, the late Wally Paton, Jeff Price, Rick Romea, Gary Rosenberg, Will Russell, Jay Schnell, Wayne Shifflett, the late Robert T. Smith, the late Walter and Sally Spofford, Dave Stejskal, Mark Stevenson, Lynne Taylor, Dave Thayer, Thea Ulen, Jack Whetstone, Sheri Williamson, and Tom Wood.

I would also like to thank Georges Dremeaux, Narca Moore-Craig, Terry O'Nele, David A. Sibley, and Gail Diane Yovanovich for their illustrations, and Paul Zimmerman and C. Allan Morgan for their cover photos. Cindy Lippincott supplied the maps and black-and-white photographs for the first edition. Bob Berman and Eric Taylor provided the computer expertise necessary to bring the bar graphs and mileage chart to life. The guide would be neither as attractive nor as user-friendly without these superb graphics and visual devices.

I owe a special debt of gratitude to those people who improved the text immeasurably with their editorial patience and expertise. Every word of the first edition was carefully scrutinized for accuracy and precision by Barbara Bickel, Cindy Lippincott, and Hugh Willoughby. Paul Baicich, as series editor, helped to bring disparate elements of the first edition together. This book would not be as good without their encouragement and teamwork.

The second edition was edited by Virginia Maynard, who also updated and revised the original maps. Bob Berman was once again instrumental in designing the bar graphs. Bill Bickel and Cindy Lippincott provided attractive black-and-white photographs. Lynne Taylor once again transcribed mileages, kept notes, and provided material encouragement both in the field and in the office. Finally, special mention is owed to Barbara Bickel, who undertook both research and editing responsibilities for every chapter of my rough drafts.

This second edition of *A Birder's Guide to Southeastern Arizona* would not be as accurate nor as easy to use without the help and friendship of all of these people. They have my heartfelt thanks.

Rick Taylor

Tucson, Arizona

January 2005

TABLE OF CONTENTS

Painted Redstart
Narca Moore-Craig

INTRODUCTION

Southeastern Arizona is one of the most exciting regions for birding in North America. More than 400 species occur here annually, and 514 species have been recorded. That is more kinds of birds than any other land-bounded area of comparable size in the United States. In fact, only Texas, California, and Florida have state lists that exceed the total list for the 15,000-square-mile area encompassed by Southeastern Arizona. Of these birds, 36 species are not regular anywhere else in the U.S., and another 40-plus are confined to the zone along the U.S. border with Mexico.

Not only is the birding exceptional, the scenery is spectacular. If Sabino Canyon, Sonoita Creek, Cave Creek Canyon, or any of the other southeastern Arizona beauty spots were found in any other state, they would be declared scenic wonders and set aside as national parks. Where else in the United States would you take time out from watching such dazzling birds as a Magnificent Hummingbird, a Red-faced Warbler, or a Varied Bunting to simply enjoy the scenery?

GEOGRAPHY

Southeastern Arizona is usually defined as that part of the state lying south and east of Tucson, plus the Altar and Avra Valleys west of the city. Geologically, Southeastern Arizona belongs to the Basin and Range Province, a region of comparatively small mountains oriented on a north-south axis, separated by broad alluvial valleys. Elevations range from 1,500 feet at Picacho Reservoir to 9,796 feet on the summit of Chiricahua Peak near the New Mexico border.

The drainage system of the region is equally complex and also deceptive, since most of the water flows underground. Two rivers flow north, two flow south, and a system of streams goes nowhere. Running north are the Santa Cruz and the San Pedro Rivers. The Santa Cruz rises in the San Rafael Valley east of Nogales, swings south into Mexico, makes a big loop back into Arizona, and then flows northward through Tucson. The San Pedro is born in a low pass that barely separates it from the Río Sonora in Mexico. Sycamore Canyon on the west and Guadalupe Canyon on the Arizona-New Mexico border in the east harbor south-flowing streams at the headwaters of Mexico's Río de

1

la Concepción and Río Yaqui, respectively. The Sulphur Springs Valley collects a number of streams that dead-end in a large alkali basin called Willcox Playa. But there is no land barrier whatsoever between the Sulphur Springs Valley and the Río Bavispe in Sonora.

Clearly, watercourses serve as a direct conduit for tropical birds to enter Southeastern Arizona. Since 1950, Short-tailed Hawk, Buff-collared Nightjar, Violet-crowned Hummingbird, Green Kingfisher, Thick-billed Kingbird, Rufous-capped Warbler, Flame-colored Tanager, and Streak-backed Oriole have all nested successfully. And since 1990, the list of valley and canyon vagrants has included Ruddy Ground-Dove, Cinnamon Hummingbird, Blue Mockingbird, Crescent-chested and Fan-tailed Warblers, and Black-vented Oriole.

BIOMES AND LIFE ZONES

Just as important as the rivers for the birdwatcher, these 15,000 square miles also contain the terminae of four major biogeographical regions, or biomes: the Rocky Mountains, the Chihuahuan Desert, the Sonoran Desert, and the Sierra Madre Mountains. Each contributes a unique flora and bird fauna to Southeastern Arizona.

On the north end of the region, the Santa Catalina and Rincon Mountains mark the southern limits of the Rocky Mountain Biome. These ranges are largely composed of granite and gneiss. Vegetation is similar to that of the Mogollon Rim in Central Arizona. Both Corkbark Fir and Mountain Chickadee find their southernmost outpost in the Santa Catalina Mountains.

The Chihuahuan Desert from the southeast extends fingers of thornscrub and desert grassland as far west as the eastern flank of the Whetstone Mountains, particularly in areas of limestone soil. This desert is characterized by Whitethorn Acacia, Tarbush, and Soaptree Yucca (the New Mexico state flower), and is the preferred habitat of Scaled Quail and Chihuahuan Raven.

The Sonoran Desert follows low-lying valleys into the vicinity of Tucson. Saguaro Cactus—whose large, showy white blossom is the Arizona state flower—both delimits and symbolizes the Sonoran Desert Biome. Saguaros can't withstand more than 24 hours of continuous frost. The range of the Saguaro-nesting race of the widespread Purple Martin most nearly conforms to boundaries of the Sonoran Desert in Arizona. Gila Woodpecker, the architect responsible for the majority of the nest holes in Saguaro, also follows the desert rivers upstream to exploit the cottonwood groves in the valleys southeast of Tucson.

Of special interest to the birder are the northernmost outliers of the Sierra Madre Occidental of Mexico. From west to east along 150 miles of the frontier with Sonora, the border ranges are represented by the Atascosa (ah-tah-SKO-sah), Santa Rita, Huachuca (wah-CHEW-cah), and Chiricahua (cheery-CAH-wah) Mountains. Each of these four ranges is isolated by surrounding desertscrub or desert grassland. Madrean pine-oak woodland cloaks the mid-elevations of all four of the mountain islands, and provides a habitat not found elsewhere in the entire United States. This is the home of the only breeding Elegant Trogons north of Mexico.

Each biome has a somewhat different group of plants and animals. Combined, they make a long list. In addition to over 500 species of birds, there are some 30 fishes, 20 amphibians, 79 reptiles, 102 mammals, and about 2,500 plants. No one has counted the insects, but bugwatchers—especially butterfly-watchers—find Southeastern Arizona an entomologist's paradise. An incredible 253 species of butterflies and skippers have been recorded in this corner of Arizona.

Southeastern Arizona can be further stratified into life zones and biotic communities. Climbing from the desert at Tucson (2,300 feet) to the boreal spruce forest on top Chiricahua Peak (9,796 feet), one crosses five life zones: Lower Sonoran, Upper Sonoran, Transition, Canadian, and Hudsonian. The corresponding plant communities for each life zone are: Chihuahuan or Sonoran desertscrub, interior chaparral or Madrean oak-pine woodland, Ponderosa Pine forest, Douglas-fir/aspen forest, and, at the highest elevations in the Chiricahua Mountains, Hudsonian stands of Engelmann Spruce, the southernmost spruce in North America.

The life-zone concept was first described by C. Hart Merriam, based on his floristic studies in Arizona near the turn of the twentieth century, when he realized that for each 1,000-foot gain in elevation, the vegetative change was equivalent to a journey north of 300 miles. In Southeastern Arizona the temperature decreases an average of four degrees every thousand feet of elevation increase. Since cold air cannot hold moisture as well as hot air, average annual precipitation increases approximately four inches per thousand feet. Consequently the 5,000 feet of vertical elevation change on a trip from the hot, dry mesquite thickets at Portal to the cool, moist spruce groves on Chiricahua Peak is roughly equivalent to a 1,500-mile change in latitude. For his pioneer work in describing how elevation, temperature, and moisture combine to create distinctive plant and animal communities, Merriam is generally regarded as the founder of the modern science of ecology.

Both life zones and biomes have many applications for today's birder. First and foremost, if the temperature is a pleasant 75 degrees Fahrenheit in Tucson, it will probably be a frigid 50 degrees at the 8,500-foot-elevation Ski Valley in the nearby Santa Catalina Mountains. Birders will also find that certain species are restricted to certain life zones. Cactus Wrens live in the Lower Sonoran Life Zone, in both the Chihuahuan and Sonoran Deserts. But to locate a Sierra Madrean species such as a Blue-throated Hummingbird, a birder must explore the Upper Sonoran Life Zone in the border ranges. Areas such as Madera Canyon in the Santa Rita Mountains and Ramsey Canyon in the Huachuca Mountains fall within the appropriate biome and life zone for Blue-throated Hummingbird.

Together, these life zones and biomes create a rich mosaic of habitats unmatched for diversity anywhere else in the United States. Understanding how they interact will help birders pinpoint the locations of the species they hope to find.

WEATHER

Sunshine is the most constant weather feature here. A day without sunshine in Arizona is the exception. The lowlands in the southeast corner receive approximately 300 days of sun per year. From November until May, this abundance of sun makes almost every day a perfect day in Tucson. Of course, there is that one little stretch from mid-May through October when the word "desert" takes on special significance. Most birders will want to follow the birds up into the mountains during the prolonged desert heat wave.

Mid-summer highs around Tucson average 100 degrees Fahrenheit or more during the day, and it does not cool off much below 80 at night. The low humidity helps, but temperatures at or above the century mark are never comfortable—no matter how zealously the natives extol the virtues of "dry heat." On the other hand, the mountains are quite comfortable in summer, especially when the rains begin. After the onset of the monsoons, daily highs in Madera, Ramsey, and Cave Creek Canyons seldom run above the low 80s, and are frequently cooler.

Southeastern Arizona is a land of summer rains, usually commencing in early July—July 3 is the average date for Tucson—and ending in mid-September. The summer monsoon "officially" begins when the dewpoint in Tucson averages 54 degrees or more for three consecutive days. The earliest onset of the monsoon was June 17, 2000, and the latest recorded start date was July 25, 1987. Some years, however, the area experiences what local wags refer to as a "nonsoon," when the rains simply fail to materialize.

In normal years almost two-thirds of the annual precipitation occurs in the three summer months, when moist air from the Gulf of Mexico moves northwestward into the area. Crossing the high mountains the air rises and forms huge cumulus clouds. Every afternoon these clouds mushroom over the peaks, and then drift over the surrounding countryside, often accompanied by intense lightning, thunderclaps, and downpours. The showers are so concentrated that natives jest that you can stand at the edge of the rain and wash your hands without getting wet.

During the summer rainy season, the nights and mornings are ideal. As a rule, it rains only during the afternoon, and then only for *siesta* hour. Since these showers are both cool and refreshing, you will soon be looking forward to them.

During late summer and early fall, storms called *chubascos* occasionally arrive from the southwest out of the Sea of Cortéz, and it may rain all night. These storms are typically the outer fringes of tropical hurricanes, and can produce unusual birds. Almost-annual late-summer sightings of Magnificent Frigatebird over Tucson are a consequence of the *chubasco* phenomenon.

Winter rains generally occur about once a month, and seldom last more than a day or two. Most desert winter days are balmy, and the nights are cool, not frigid. But maximum temperatures in the higher mountains are apt to be 20 to 30 degrees cooler than in the adjacent valleys.

WHEN TO COME

Southeastern Arizona has plenty to offer birders every month of the year. With enough skill and luck, you may discover an exotic species such as Plain-capped Starthroat, Blue Mockingbird, or Flame-colored Tanager that all U.S. birders covet for their life list. But even many of the expected species have charisma. Month by month, some of the prime attractions are:

January: Bendire's, Crissal, and Curve-billed Thrashers burst into full song, often from exposed perches. Mountain Plovers and Ruddy Ground-Doves are easier to locate this month than any other time of the year. Some Anna's Hummingbirds are already fledging young in Tucson. The "Wings Over Willcox" birding festival celebrates Sandhill Cranes and 14 species of raptors wintering in the Sulphur Springs Valley.

February: Numbers and species of ducks and geese peak. Inca Doves, Great Horned Owls, and Curve-billed Thrashers begin to nest. The first Tree Swallows pass through as they migrate north. Male Yellow-rumped Warblers assume nuptial plumage, although they remain in the lowlands, thousands of feet below their summer territories on the mountain tops. South and west of Tucson, Mexican Gold Poppies and Parry's Penstemons begin to daub the desert in shades of molten gold and hot pink.

March: Common Black-Hawk, Gray Hawk, and Zone-tailed Hawk—the three Southwest specialty raptors—arrive almost simultaneously. Hummingbirds increase from sparse to common as the month progresses, and the population of Vermilion Flycatchers multiplies ten-fold. Lucy's Warblers and Painted Redstarts enter the southeast corner en masse. Cottonwoods leaf out in all the valleys.

April: Early in the month Flammulated and Elf Owls join resident Western and Whiskered Screech-Owls in nightly choruses. Virginia's, Grace's, and Red-faced Warblers arrive. After mid-month the first Elegant Trogons begin to set up territories in Madera, Garden, Cave Creek, and other canyons in the border ranges. Desert mesquite trees put on their new leaves just as the Sierra Madrean oaks in the foothills drop their somber brown-and-orange foliage and begin to bud.

May: Common Poorwills in the deserts, Buff-collared Nightjars in thornscrub, and Whip-poor-wills in the mountains fill the hours before dawn and after dusk with their unique calls. Sulphur-bellied Flycatchers and Purple Martins arrive all the way from South America. Rose-throated Becards commence knitting their enormous, globe-shaped nests, using materials salvaged from the preceding year's nursery. Many birds are nesting and the first fledglings begin to appear. Canyon streams are now trimmed with the nodding blossoms of showy Golden Columbine. "The Festival of the Hummingbirds" birding event is held in Tucson.

June: Most Yellow-billed Cuckoos, Varied Buntings, and Five-striped Sparrows finally arrive. This is the best month to look for a vagrant Yellow Grosbeak from Mexico. Fruiting Saguaro Cacti attract White-winged Doves and a host of other Sonoran Desert species. By the end of the month the first male Rufous Hummingbirds will have begun the migration south. This is the hottest month, but distant lightning flashes on the southern horizon in Mexico herald the approach of the life-giving, mid-summer monsoons.

July: The onset of the rainy season initiates the breeding season for Montezuma Quail, and Botteri's and Cassin's Sparrows. Painted Redstarts and Western Tanagers launch their second clutches. Baby birds are everywhere. Owls stop calling and seem to disappear altogether by the end of the month. The mountains turn green, and the wildflowers that transform southern Arizona into hummingbird heaven begin to blossom.

August: Hummingbird numbers and diversity reach their peaks for the year, augmented by new fledglings, southward migrants, and late-arriving rarities from Mexico. This last group includes much sought-after White-eared, Berylline, Violet-crowned, and Lucifer Hummingbirds, and Plain-capped Starthroat. Families of Elegant Trogons are silent but conspicuous as they move through the border canyons. By the end of the month most *Myiarchus* and Sulphur-bellied Flycatchers have vanished. This is the best month to search for Aztec Thrush. The "Southwest Wings Birding Festival" is held in Bisbee.

September: Astonishing numbers of Red-tails, Swainson Hawks, and American Kestrels seem to cap every post and pole. Hordes of migrating shorebirds transform sewage lagoons into *de facto* estuaries. Lines of Western Kingbirds perch on valley electric wires like clothespins. Early wintering species include Northern Harrier, Cedar Waxwing, and Green-tailed Towhee. This is the greenest month of the year, and if the rains have been generous, the valley grasslands may be belly-deep in sunflowers.

October: Before the end of the month, most of the 20,000 or more Sandhill Cranes will assume their winter quarters in the Sulphur Springs Valley. Joining them is a scattering of brightly-plumaged Ferruginous Hawks. White-winged Doves become scarce around Tucson and other towns farther east. Red-naped Sapsuckers invade the canyons, orchards, and isolated valley groves. Aspens turn gold on the peaks.

November: Most of the winter birds have arrived. The early-morning carols of Townsend's Solitaires flute over the juniper woodlands. In some years, Eared Quetzals may descend into South Fork Cave Creek or Ramsey Canyon just as the Bigtooth Maples reach their peak autumn colors. Depending on the winter, flocks of Mountain Bluebirds in the valleys can number from a handful to several hundred.

December: Christmas Bird Count teams always discover some goodies, either on the count itself, or earlier in the month while scouting. Locations are pinpointed in the San Rafael Valley for Bald Eagle, Sprague's Pipit, Baird's Sparrow, and McCown's Longspur. "Regular" rarities such as Rufous-backed Robin, Black-throated Blue Warbler, and Streak-backed Oriole turn up almost every year, and occasionally true vagrants such as Red-headed Woodpecker or Blue Mockingbird are also discovered. December in Southeastern Arizona offers some the year's most exciting birding!

WHAT TO WEAR

Western apparel is generally informal, and casual attire is acceptable nearly anywhere. Shorts, blue jeans, or tough slacks are the order of the day for birding. T-shirts are both cool and socially acceptable, but long sleeves are suggested for early mornings in shady mountain canyons, and are a necessity for those who burn easily. Don't forget a warm jacket or sweater. The nights can be chilly, especially on spring owl prowls. When it clouds over in the rarified air above 8,000 feet in Rustler Park or on top Mount Lemmon, temperatures may plummet to below 50 degrees at high noon, even in mid-summer. Winter fronts can hold daily highs down to below 50 degrees throughout Southeastern Arizona. A windy November day spent sorting through sparrow flocks in the Sulphur Springs Valley can feel like the Arctic. Long underwear, gloves, and a wool cap will all be welcome. Vast areas of the southeastern corner lie above 5,000 feet in elevation, where the thin air can change from scorching to cold in a few scant minutes. Be prepared for sudden shifts in the weather.

If you expect to hike or take prolonged bird walks, wear the appropriate foot gear. This may translate into lightweight boots or tough walking shoes for the field, and an extra pair of house shoes in your duffel. Dinner while wearing a clean, dry pair of shoes just seems to taste better!

WHAT TO BRING

This is the skin-cancer capital of the U.S.—do not forget a brimmed hat. The short-pants and T-shirt set have a special self-obligation to invest in sun block rated SPF-15 or higher. Lip balm is a good idea for anyone. And remember to carry water with you on any bird walk. Experts calculate that you should drink at least two quarts of water a day during the Arizona summer, a full gallon for those exercising outdoors. (You will absolutely need that full gallon if you intend to chase Five-striped Sparrows down near the border in Sycamore Canyon.)

Mosquitoes and other biting insects are seldom a problem, but some people attract what few there are. If you know you are one of these people, dose yourself with insect repellent before every bird walk. For reasons doubtlessly related to the community of 600,000 souls who have put down roots here on the rim of the Sonoran Desert, the arid valleys surrounding Tucson frequently have more mosquitoes than the wet mountain canyons—especially in late summer. After the summer monsoons commence in July, there are also chiggers. The Patagonia-Sonoita Creek Preserve is the single worst location in Arizona for them, but chiggers occur along all the major lowland watercourses and in lower mountain canyons. To avoid the raised, itchy welts occasioned by chigger bites, simply stay out of tall grasses and weeds where chiggers lurk. If you must plunge into the rank undergrowth, dust your clothes with sulfur powder, or spray them with an aerosol repellent. Chigger season is over by the first of October.

Hummingbird aficionados arriving in late summer may want to bring an umbrella, poncho, or at least a water-repellent windbreaker. The likelihood of an August thunder shower is pretty good on any given day in the border ranges. Similarly, campers will need a tent with a rain fly.

This should go without saying, but *do not* attempt to cross flooded washes, streams, or rivers. Do not ignore warning signs or attempt to circumvent barriers erected for your protection. Don't be foolhardy. Water levels usually recede in a few hours, and it's not worth losing your vehicle, or even your life, just because you are in a hurry to see a Gray Hawk.

WHERE TO STAY

Many of the camping and lodging facilities are listed at the end of each route description. Additional lists of motels, etc., may be obtained from the chambers of commerce of the various cities or from the numerous travel guides, such as AAA. More details on camping sites and a forest map of the Coronado National Forest are available from the Recreation Staff, Coronado National Forest, 300 W. Congress, Tucson, AZ 85701.

Southeastern Arizona is ideal for camping. The weather is warm and usually dry. Biting insects are few, although the bloom of new, "benign" insects in the spring and summer are what makes this a birdwatcher's paradise. Newcomers to Southwest camping may worry about snakes; however, you will be lucky to find even one during your entire stay.

In recent years Black Bears have learned that campers in the high Chiricahuas carry food. A few bears have developed the unsavory habit of punching out the windshields of parked cars in Rustler Park, especially after dark, as they search for edible tidbits. Campers should be aware that simply locking up leftovers in the trunk may not be enough to deter a hungry Black Bear. Anyone camping in any mountain range in Southeastern Arizona should *never* sleep with food in the tent. Bear boxes are provided for storing food in higher-elevation campgrounds—use them! In 1996 there were two Black Bear attacks on teenage girls tent-camping in the Santa Catalina Mountains. An offending bear was shot, and the Forest Service began issuing citations to picnickers and summer-home owners who feed the bears.

CAMPGROUNDS

Location	Name	Elevation	Open
Tucson	Gilbert Ray (Tucson Mtns.)	3,000	All year
	Catalina State Park	3,000	All year
Santa Catalina Mountains	Molino Basin	4,500	Sep–May
	Prison Camp	4,800	All year
	Rose Canyon	7,000	Apr–Oct
	Spencer Canyon	8,000	Apr–Oct
Madera Canyon	Bog Springs	5,600	All year
Peña Blanca Lake	White Rock	4,000	All year
Nogales	Patagonia Lake State Park	4,050	All year
Parker Lake	Lakeview	5,400	All year
Huachuca Mountains	Reef Townsite	7,100	Feb–Nov
	Ramsey Vista	7,400	Feb–Nov
Chiricahua Mountains	Idlewild (Cave Creek)	5,000	Apr–Oct
	Stewart (Cave Creek)	5,050	All year
	Sunny Flats (Cave Creek)	5,150	All year
	Rustler Park	8,400	Apr–Nov
	West Turkey Creek	5,900	All year
Rucker Lake	Camp Rucker	5,600	All year
	Rucker Lake	6,300	All year
	Cypress Park	6,000	Mar–Oct
	Bathtub	6,050	All year
	Rucker Forest Camp	6,150	All year
Dragoon Mountains	Cochise Stronghold	5,000	All year

RESOURCES

An invaluable aid to resident and out-of-state birders alike is the Arizona/New Mexico BirdChat Listserve site hosted by the University of Arizona. Both rarities and regularly-occurring species are reported on a daily basis, and most contributors include a list of selected other species seen at the site. Type in http://listserv.arizona.edu/archives/birdwg05.html to access the current AZ/NM postings as well as the archives. If you wish to post messages to the list, instructions for subscribing can also be found at the above website.

All birders will benefit from a visit to the Tucson Audubon Society Nature Shop at the onset of their tour of Southeastern Arizona. Located at 300 E. University Boulevard, #120, Tucson, AZ 85705 (520-629-0510, www.tucson audubon.org), shop hours are 10:00 a.m. to 4:00 p.m., Monday through Saturday (closed on Monday during summer). This natural-history book store is among the finest in the state, and it also carries field guides, checklists, binoculars, feeders, and other birdwatching accessories. Among the services provided by TAS is a library that includes computer resources and a list of local bird guides, which they will furnish upon request. Interesting sightings are posted weekly on their bulletin board, or you can call 520-798-1005 for their taped rare bird alert information. To report unusual sightings to the RBA, call 520-696-4461 and press 3 when you hear the recorded message (you do not have to listen to the entire message).

The Nature Conservancy of Arizona has developed brochures that offer insight into the Aravaipa Canyon, Patagonia-Sonoita Creek, Ramsey Canyon, and Muleshoe Ranch Preserves, as well as information on preserve hours, parking regulations, and other rules. To obtain these brochures contact the Conservancy from 9:00 a.m. to 5:00 p.m., Monday through Friday, at 1510 E. Fort Lowell Road, Tucson, AZ 85719, 520-622-3861, www.nature.org/arizona.

The Southeastern Arizona Bird Observatory was founded in 1996 to promote the conservation of regional birds and bird habitat through research, monitoring, and public-education programs. Their field office is located in Banning Creek near Bisbee, 2 miles west of the Mule Mountain Tunnel off Highway 80, or 4.2 miles east of the junction with Highway 90 in Banning Creek. Motorhomes exceeding 20 feet or vehicles with trailers will need to park in the broad pullout here. Standard-sized vehicles may continue approximately 200 yards across a one-lane bridge on Hidden Meadow Road to a small, blue-and-white cabin with bird feeders. The bird feeders are open for public viewing every day throughout the year. To learn more about SABO's wide variety of programs check the website at www.sabo.org, write SABO at P.O. Box 5521, Bisbee, AZ 85603-5521, or call 520-432-1388.

Three birding festivals are held annually in Southeastern Arizona. On the third weekend of January the Willcox Chamber of Commerce sponsors "Wings Over Willcox," a celebration of the thousands of Sandhill Cranes that winter in the upper Sulphur Springs Valley. This area is also one of the most important wintering areas for birds of prey in the entire Southwest. To obtain more information contact the Willcox Chamber of Commerce at 800-200-2272 or 520-384-2272, website www.wingsoverwillcox.com.

In the first week of May "The Festival of Hummingbirds" takes place in Tucson. Aficionados from throughout the U. S. and many foreign countries meet to attend presentations, exhibits, and lectures on the ecology and conservation of this unique bird family. More information is available from the Hummingbird Society at 800-529-3699 or www.hummingbirdsociety.org.

In early August the town of Bisbee hosts the "Southwest Wings Birding Festival." Between the San Pedro River Valley and the neighboring Huachuca Mountains, participants are treated to an average of 12 species of hummingbirds and at least 100 other species of birds. Information on this exciting event can be obtained by calling the Southwest Wings Birding Festival information line at 800-946-4777 or visiting www.swwings.org. Activities at all three of these events include lectures, birding workshops, and numerous field trips.

SOME HELPFUL PUBLICATIONS

A free travel-information kit is available from the Arizona Office of Tourism through their website (www.arizonaguide.com) or by phone (866-275-5816). Excellent maps produced by the Coronado National Forest can be obtained by writing to the Recreation Staff, Coronado National Forest, 300 W. Congress, Tucson, AZ 85701. Maps are also available there for the Santa Catalina Mountains, the Nogales and Sierra Vista Ranger Districts, and the Chiricahua, Dragoon, and Peloncillo Mountains in the Douglas Ranger District at a cost of $6.00 each. Maps, checklists, and other information pertaining to the San Pedro River National Conservation Area are available by contacting the Bureau of Land Management, 1763 Paseo San Luis, Sierra Vista, AZ 85635; 520-458-3559. The *Arizona Atlas and Gazetteer* by DeLorme is available at book stores and convenience markets throughout the region as well as from ABA Sales, 800-634-7736.

Detailed topographic maps can be ordered from the U.S. Geological Survey, Denver, CO 80201. First write for the *Index to Arizona Maps*, for which there is no charge, and use that to pick the individual topo maps that you want. Hiking maps for the Santa Catalina, Santa Rita, Huachuca, and Chiricahua Mountains are available from Tucson Maps (3239 N. 1st Avenue, Tucson, AZ 85719; 800-473-1204 or 520-887-4234) or Summit Hut (5045 E. Speedway Boulevard, Tucson, AZ 85712; 520-325-1554; www.summithut. com).

You will need field guides that cover all of North America to identify the regularly occurring birds of Arizona, as well as the tropical rarities. Of special interest is *Finding Birds in Southeast Arizona*, published by the Tucson Audubon Society. The Tucson Audubon Society has also prepared a new, pocket-sized field checklist for Southeastern Arizona, which provides a general indication of the status of each bird species. To obtain a copy, send a self-addressed, stamped envelope and 50¢ to Tucson Audubon Society Nature Shop, 300 E. University Boulevard, #120, Tucson, AZ 85705.

Numerous publications cover the natural history and ecology of this region. Some of the better ones are listed in the reference section at the end of this book. Many of these can be obtained from ABA Sales, Box 6599, Colorado Springs, CO 80934, 800-634-7736. When you are in Tucson, try the Tucson Audubon Society Nature Shop, the Arizona-Sonora Desert Museum Gift Shop, or the visitor centers of Saguaro National Park, either east or west section.

Away from Tucson, natural-history bookstores located in some of the prime birding areas include the Santa Rita Lodge Gift Shop, Kazzam Nature Center in Patagonia, the Ramsey Canyon Preserve Bookstore, The San Pedro House at Highway 90 and the San Pedro River, Coronado National Memorial, Sierra Vista Ranger Station, Portal Store, U.S. Forest Service Portal Information Center, Southwestern Research Station Gift Shop, and Chiricahua National Monument.

REPORTING RARE BIRDS

While birding in Arizona, please report rare or unusual sightings to the Tucson Audubon Rare Bird Alert (520-696-4461; press 3 when you hear the recorded message—you don't need to listen to all the options). Written documentation to follow up your telephone report should be made to the regional editors of ABA-published *North American Birds* (by e-mail to Gary Rosenberg at ghrosenberg@comcast.net or to Mark Stevenson at drbdr@att.net, or by mail to P.O. Box 91856, Tucson, AZ 85752-1856). Reports on species on the Arizona Review List will be forwarded by the regional editors to the Arizona Bird Committee.

The Arizona Bird Committee (ABC) was created in 1972 to improve the quality of state bird records and to further our knowledge of bird distribution within Arizona. The committee would appreciate detailed descriptions to substantiate any sightings of accidental, rare, or otherwise unusual birds. Please send details to the *North American Birds* regional editors listed above. For your convenience, a sample ABC report form is included at the back of this book, or it can be downloaded directly from the ABC website (http:// ghrosenberg.home.comcast.net/index.html). Your detailed descriptions (preferably written at the time of sighting without reference to a field guide) will be circulated among the members of the ABC, who will evaluate the report. The committee's decisions on all reviewed records are published in the journal of the Western Field Ornithologists, *Western Birds*. Descriptions and supplementary material (photographs, sound recordings, etc.) as well as the committee's decisions are filed in the Department of Ecology at the University of Arizona.

Attracting Birds

Many birders have tried the various squeakers and calls that are sold to attract birds. After a few days the novelty wears off, and the squeakers become too much trouble to carry around. "Hissing-at-the-villain" or "pishing" through pursed lips is still the time-proven favorite for most birders, along with the sound made by sucking on the back of the hand—reminiscent of lover's lane on a moonlit night.

However, in the Southeastern Arizona border ranges, the sound that outdoes them all is the double toot of the Mexican form of the Northern Pygmy-Owl. No other noise will excite the birds of the mountains nearly as much, and your imitative toots can attract up to 15 species at once, although five is a more typical number. In valley riparian areas such as the San Pedro River and along Sonoita Creek, an imitation of the descending, bouncing-ball call of the Western Screech-Owl produces similar results. During the practice period, you may be ridiculed by your family or given odd glances by your neighbors, but when you have mastered replicating the calls of these owls, you will be an Arizona birdfinder extraordinaire.

If, however, you just cannot squeak, hiss, pish, or hoot, you can still attract birds with the judicious use of a tape-recorder or an MP3 player. Most birds, even flycatchers, will respond to an imitation of their calls. The big advantage of playbacks is that their use can save habitat by bringing the bird within range of the trail or road without the brush-smashing, flower-trampling search that an unseen singing bird may unwittingly incite. As soon as the bird appears, turn your device off. Territorial defense is a normal avian behavior and one must assume the bird feels it has vanquished the unseen invader when you stop the playback.

Remember, however, that any use of bird tapes is forbidden in both the Ramsey Canyon and Patagonia-Sonoita Creek Preserves, as well as in Garden, Scheelite, and Sawmill Canyons on Fort Huachuca, and in Madera Canyon and South Fork Cave Creek on the Coronado National Forest.

During the day, small birds can be attracted with owl calls. At night, the owls themselves can be coaxed into view by playing their respective calls (no fewer than 11 species of owls occur in the southeast corner of Arizona!). But birds are not hard of hearing. *Do not play the tapes loudly or continuously.* Most birds will come much closer if the tape is played softly, and this is particularly true of owls.

ARIZONA BIRDING BEHAVIOR

The American Birding Association's *Code of Birding Ethics* appears in the Appendix at the back of this book. Adhering to the ABA *Code of Birding Ethics* is particularly important in this heavily birded region. There are also some special concerns for birders in Southeastern Arizona:

1. Please respect the rights of landowners. Always ask permission before entering private property. Your trespass may result in the loss of visitation privileges for all future birders. Areas of private land are always indicated as such in the text.

2. Please drive slowly to ensure your own safety. Many of the access roads in Southeastern Arizona are not hard-surfaced, and dust clouds churned up by fast-moving cars endanger vehicles following behind, and the oncoming traffic as well.

3. Avoid abrupt stops that may lead to rear-end collisions, and never park in the road. This is extremely important in the small canyons of the border ranges, where blind curves and narrow roads are the rule.

4. During the summer rainy season or after heavy winter storms, make local inquiry before assuming any road is passable. Never enter flooded washes or streams.

5. Most of Southeastern Arizona is rangeland. Watch for cattle—especially at night. Even straight-aways are often intercepted by blind washes that may conceal either livestock or wildlife.

6. Remember that more nest failures can be directly attributed to photographic disturbance than from any other human cause. Canyon and river groves are often so narrow that it is impossible to set up either a blind or even a camera without attracting undue attention from other birders, who may be less sensitive to the moods of the bird than you are. Also remember that many birds simply cannot tolerate any prolonged attention. Above all, do not manipulate the actual nest or the surrounding vegetation.

7. Tape recordings, taped playbacks, and MP3 digital bird songs to lure rare birds into binocular range are inappropriate where a few birds may be exposed to a wholly unnatural onslaught of such devices at popular birdwatching locations. In Southeastern Arizona the use of tape recordings is prohibited at Madera Canyon in the Santa Rita Mountains, the Patagonia-Sonoita Creek Sanctuary, Ramsey Canyon Preserve and the Garden Canyon drainage in the Huachuca Mountains, and South Fork Cave Creek in the Chiricahua Mountains.

8. Please stay on trails and established routes. Plants grow back slowly in this arid environment, and if the tens of thousands of birders who visit Southeastern Arizona all broke branches and smashed low-growing vegetation in

pursuit of those tantalizingly hidden voices, we could easily destroy this fragile environment.

9. Some of the best locations for hummingbirds, as well as other species, are the private yards of a handful of selfless homeowners. These people not only provide food, water, and literally gallons of sugar water every day for the birds—as well as keep their numerous feeders clean—they often furnish birders with shady seating from which to watch the birds. Thousands of people visit these private residences each year. Please be sensitive to the other birders with whom you share the yard. Do not interfere with others by obstructing their views of the feeders, talking too loudly, or scaring the birds by approaching too close to the feeders. Photographers should pursue their hobby as inconspicuously and with the least amount of apparatus possible— and certainly without the use of flash. Please obey any posted hours or rules. Smoking is not permitted at any of these private residences. Never leave any litter and please do not picnic. Leave gates open if they were open when you arrived, and closed if they were closed when you arrived. Never block the driveway of the homeowner, and never park where it will affect adjacent landowners or local traffic. Do not trespass on the property of adjacent landowners, whether it is posted or not. The usual donation to the sugar fund is $1.00/visitor, and it's always okay to leave a bit more. That money offsets the cost of buying sugar and bird seed, replacing feeders, fixing lawn furniture, and the general maintenance that goes with opening your home to a horde of birders who can number in the thousands over the course of just one year. Above all, if she or he is present, always thank the host.

As the number of birders grows and the special joy of birdwatching in Southeastern Arizona is better publicized, these commonsense considerations have become essential.

HOW TO USE THIS BOOK

The purpose of this guide is to help visiting birders design a custom tour of Southeastern Arizona that suits their time, energy, and budgets. Resident birders in southeastern Arizona should also find directions to sites and bird status and locational information helpful.

The bird nomenclature in this book follows that of the American Ornithologists' Union (AOU) and the American Birding Association (ABA). Some recent name changes (including splits and lumps since the previous edition of this guide) are listed on page 17.

The book is divided into three major sections. The first section includes nine chapters describing nine primary locations; Chapter Ten, which concludes the first section, is devoted to 15 additional sites. Listed under the title of each trip are the total mileage and the minimum time recommended to cover the area. In some location descriptions, mileages are shown in parentheses. These represent the distance *from the last place mentioned* and *not* from the starting point. Whenever an outstanding site is mentioned, it is shown in **bold-faced** type. If you have a catholic taste in birds and wish to see the most species possible in a limited amount of time, stop only at bold-faced sites on the loop. Three of the sites where you will be hiking as well as birding are described by duplicate Tear-Out Trail Maps which are reproduced at the end of this book.

In the second section, under the heading of "Specialties of Southeastern Arizona," an effort has been made to give the status and to describe the habitat of every western, southwestern, and Mexican species presently known to occur regularly in Southeastern Arizona. Some more widespread species, Painted Bunting for example, are included when they are of special interest to local birders. With a few exceptions, at least three places are listed where each species has been found in the past. These sites are highly specific. *Please remember not to put undue pressure on an unusual species through prolonged observation or photography.*

The third section is a series of bar graphs representing all known birds that have occurred in the region, showing relative abundance for each month of the year, as well as habitat preference. A seasonal clock divided into four "pie wedges" tells which habitats birds are most likely to use when they are present. Briefly annotated checklists of the herpetofauna and mammals of Southeastern Arizona conclude the book.

Regardless of the length of your visit, I suggest a visit to the Arizona-Sonora Desert Museum at the outset of any trip. Here you will receive a solid introduction to the flora and fauna of the entire region and have an opportunity to study approximately 100 species of birds in captivity, as well as many wild birds ranging freely on the grounds. The Hummingbird Aviary features eight species of Southwest hummingbirds in a flower-filled garden.

To cover all the primary routes, allow at least two weeks. If you have less time, it's best to read all the trip descriptions and choose the ones that suit you best, according to the season and your most-desired birds. From April 1 through October 31, be sure to visit a valley riparian area such as Patagonia or the San Pedro River, and at least one of the three principal border ranges: the Santa Rita, the Huachuca, or the Chiricahua Mountains. The mountains are not particularly productive from November 1 through March 31, and the upper elevations may be closed by snow. During winter the deserts, grasslands, and valley riparian areas offer the best birding. Plan a trip to the grasslands in the San Rafael Valley or the Sulphur Springs Valley for hawks, sparrows, and longspurs.

It's impossible to savor all the delights of Southeastern Arizona birding on any one excursion. Different birds will quicken your pulse as the months change, and every year brings its new exotics, some of which may never have been seen before in the U.S. After your first visit, you'll understand why so many birders count Southeastern Arizona as their favorite birding destination in all of North America.

NOMENCLATURE CHANGES

Since the publication of the previous edition of this guide in 1999, several changes to English names for Southeastern Arizona birds have been adopted by the AOU and ABA. These are listed below.

PREVIOUS SPECIES NAME	CURRENT SPECIES NAME
Oldsquaw	Long-tailed Duck
Common Snipe	Wilson's Snipe
Rock Dove	Rock Pigeon
Strickland's Woodpecker	Arizona Woodpecker (Arizona Woodpecker split from Strickland's Woodpecker, which occurs in the highlands of Mexico)

In addition, the split of the Canada Goose "complex" in 2004 added a new species, Cackling Goose, to the checklist.

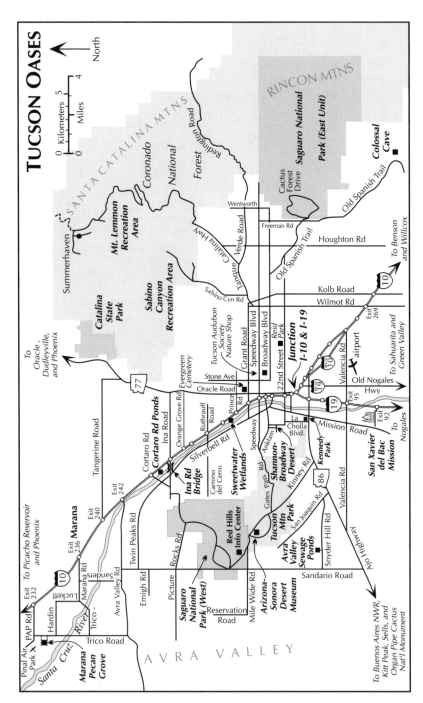

TUCSON OASES

North

0 Kilometers 5
0 Miles 4

SANTA CATALINA MTNS

RINCON MTNS

Coronado National Forest

Mt. Lemmon Recreation Area

Summerhaven

Saguaro National Park (East Unit)

Catalina State Park

Sabino Canyon Recreation Area

Redington Road

Cactus Forest Drive

Colossal Cave

Wentworth

Tanque Verde Road

Freeman Rd

Old Spanish Trail

Houghton Rd

To Benson and Willcox

Sabino Cyn Rd

Catalina Hwy

Kolb Road

Wilmot Rd

To Oracle, Dudleyville, and Phoenix

77

Evergreen Cemetery

Tucson Audubon Society Nature Shop

Grant Road

Speedway Blvd

Broadway Blvd

Reid Park

Exit 269

10

Stone Ave

Oracle Road

Orange Grove Rd

Ruthrauff Road

Prince Rd

22nd Street

Junction I-10 & I-19

Valencia Rd

airport

Exit 95

To Sahuarita and Green Valley

Cortaro Rd

Cortaro Rd Ponds

Ina Rd

Silverbell Rd

Speedway

Camino del Cerro

La Cholla Blvd

Mission Road

Old Nogales Hwy

19

Exit 92

To Nogales

Tangerine Road

Ina Rd Bridge

Sweetwater Wetlands

Ankiam Rd

Shannon-Broadway Desert

Kennedy Park

San Xavier del Bac Mission

Exit 242

Gates Pass Rd

Kinney Rd

86

Twin Peaks Rd

Rocks Rd

Red Hills Info Center

Tucson Mtn Park

San Joaquin Rd

Valencia Rd

Ajo Highway

Exit 240

Marana

Exit 236

Exit 232

Marana Rd

Sanders

Avra Valley Rd

Emigh Rd

Picture Rocks Rd

Mile Wide Rd

Saguaro National Park (West)

Arizona-Sonora Desert Museum

Avra Valley Sewage Ponds

Snyder Hill Rd

Sandario Road

To Picacho Reservoir and Phoenix

10

Pinal Air Park

PAP Rd

Hardin

Luckett

Trico Road

Trico - Marana Rd

Marana Pecan Grove

Santa Cruz River

Reservation Road

AVRA VALLEY

To Buenos Aires NWR, Kitt Peak, Sells, and Organ Pipe Cactus Nat'l Monument

CHAPTER 1

TUCSON OASES

THE ARIZONA-SONORA
DESERT MUSEUM LOOPS

This trip explores a series of oases—areas with trees and ornamental plantings and/or permanent water—that are magnets for both resident birds and migrants. En route it passes a neighborhood on the outskirts of Tucson that hosts a representative selection of the city's "backyard birds," as well as visiting the neighborhood "wilderness" in Tucson Mountain Park, and the western section of Saguaro (pronounced *Sah-WHA-row*) National Park. The highlight of the trip is the Arizona-Sonora Desert Museum, which features an excellent collection of plants and animals native to the Sonoran Desert. Many of the species are displayed in naturalistic enclosures that are true to their preferred habitats in the wild.

To conclude this loop birders can choose between the Marana Pecan Grove (also known as the Pinal Air Park Pecan Grove), a well-known vagrant trap north of the Tucson Mountains, or turn south to the Avra Valley Sewage Ponds (also known as Snyder Hill Road Sewage Ponds) for waterbirds, before continuing on to San Xavier del Bac Mission, founded by the Jesuits in 1700. Both the Pecan Grove and the Mission are most productive early in the morning, and birders may well choose to run either or both of these loops in reverse sequence.

ARIZONA-SONORA DESERT MUSEUM LOOP

(28 miles/one-half day to Arizona-Sonora Desert Museum)

The starting point is the intersection of Interstate 10 and St. Mary's Road in Tucson (take Exit 257 or Exit 258 and follow signs on the frontage road to West St. Mary's Road). Just 100 yards west of I-10, St. Mary's Road crosses the Santa Cruz River, which is one the major drainages in Southeastern Arizona. Ordinarily there is no surface flow unless you arrive on the heels of a storm. However, in October 1983 a mud-choked torrent closed the bridge for 24 hours and swept away other concrete spans 11 miles upstream at San Xavier Mission.

Continue straight west. St. Mary's turns into Anklam Road at Silverbell Road (1.0 mile) and passes Pima Community College (2.3 miles), then climbs over a rise to a public junior high school (0.5 mile) opposite the T-intersection with Shannon Road. Turn left (south) onto Shannon Road. Traffic is usually moderate in this westside neighborhood, and there is plenty of road shoulder to pull onto if you spot an interesting bird on the powerlines on the right. Park at the intersection with Broadway Boulevard (0.3 mile).

In early morning the **Shannon-Broadway Desert** intersection abounds with birds, but in the heat of the afternoon sun, not a single bird may be visible. Permanent residents include Gambel's Quail, Mourning Dove, Greater Roadrunner, Gilded Flicker, Gila and Ladder-backed Woodpeckers, Verdin, Cactus Wren, Curve-billed Thrasher, Black-tailed Gnatcatcher, Phainopepla, Northern Cardinal, Pyrrhuloxia, Canyon Towhee, Black-throated Sparrow, and House Finch. In summer watch for White-winged Dove, Elf Owl (night), Lesser Nighthawk (fluttering around the mercury vapor lights overhanging

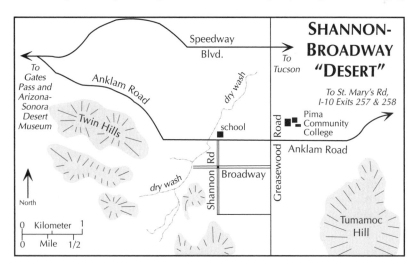

the intersection after dusk), Black-chinned Hummingbird, Ash-throated Fly-catcher, Purple Martin (especially in July and August), Bronzed Cowbird, and Scott's Oriole. In winter look for Anna's and Costa's Hummingbirds, Northern "Red-shafted" Flicker, Rock Wren, and White-crowned Sparrow.

In spite of a new housing development on the northwest corner and a huge student apartment complex on the southeast side, the Shannon-Broadway Desert remains one of the most reliable locations on the western perimeter of Tucson for Rufous-winged Sparrow. In 2004 there were at least three pairs within a few hundred yards of the intersection. This small, Chipping Sparrow look-alike differs in having a grayish eyebrow and a long, rounded tail. The rufous shoulder patch is usually concealed. Watch for it to sing from exposed perches in small trees. If walking all four cardinal directions at the intersection doesn't turn up a Rufous-winged, try 200 yards farther south on Shannon. One or two pairs usually nest in desert vegetation along the median. Alternatively, Rufous-wings also use the west (right) end of Broadway (0.2 mile), where the boulevard dead-ends at a large dry wash. This area is also good for Black-tailed Gnatcatchers year round, and Broad-billed and Costa's Hummingbirds in early spring. Both hummingbirds patronize the feeders in the trailer park on the south edge of Broadway.

Return to Anklam Road (0.5 mile) and turn left (west). Saguaro Cactus becomes common along Anklam as the road enters the foothills of the Tucson Mountains. In summer, this is an excellent place to see the desert race of the Purple Martin, which nests in Saguaro holes originally created by Gila Woodpeckers. Powerlines running north from just east of the intersection of Anklam and Speedway (2.1 miles) serve as an evening roost for thousands of Purple Martins in late August and September. After Anklam and Speedway merge and become Gates Pass Road, the pavement winds sinuously up to Gates Pass (2.7 miles; elevation 3,150 feet) and arcs steeply down into Avra Valley. Tucson Mountain Park may not match your image of either a mountain or a park, but it contains an excellent example of desert vegetation. Plant life is surprisingly lush and varied. Before trying to key out the shrubs and cacti, wait until you reach the Desert Museum, where the plants are labeled.

Two miles west of the pass, the road swings north of a cluster of buildings on the left. This is Old Tucson, a movie set inaugurated in 1939 that doubles as an amusement park for tourists. A sudden fire in April 1995 destroyed much of the facility, but a new Old Tucson re-opened in 1997. Gates Pass Road ends at Kinney Road (2.2 miles). Turn right (north) toward the Desert Museum. McCain Loop Road, the turnoff to the Gilbert Ray Campground, is on the left side (0.7 mile; $20 per night for RVs, $6 for tents). A pair of Great Horned Owls often nest in a Saguaro near the campground. In mid-winter Gilbert Ray is usually overflowing with "snowbirds"—seasonal human refugees from the cold northern latitudes of the U.S. and Canada.

Another 1.9 miles brings you to the **Arizona-Sonora Desert Museum** (13.3 miles from Tucson. The museum is open October–February from 8:30 a.m. to 5:00 p.m., and March–September from 7:30 a.m. to 5:00 p.m. November–April admission is $12 for ages 13 and older, $4 for children 6–12, and free under 6; May–October admission is $9 for ages 13 and older, $2 for children 6–12, and free under 6; 520-883-2702, www.desertmuseum.org). On Saturday evenings in summer (June–September), the Museum stays open until 9:00 p.m. for visitors to enjoy this special time in the desert. The word 'museum' hardly describes this institution. It is not a dusty assortment of artifacts and stuffed animals. The Desert Museum has earned an international reputation for both its outstanding collection and its imaginative presentation of the *living* plants and animals native to this region. Exhibits portray not only the Sonoran Desert, but also the Sierra Madre in northern Mexico, and the same "mountain islands" of Southeastern Arizona which are treated in this book. Since it opened in 1952, this combination zoological park, arboretum, and research facility has been wholly funded by private donations, membership support, and public admissions.

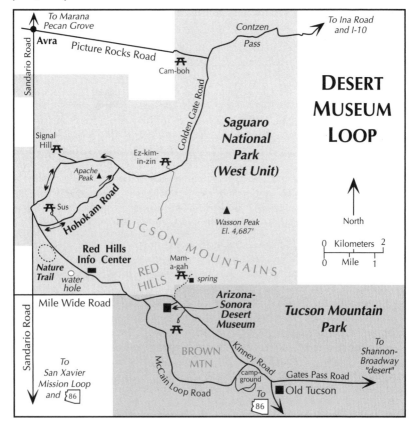

View of Arizona-Sonora Desert Museum grounds from the museum's entrance patio.
William S. Bickel

Learning about the native flora and fauna is easy at the Desert Museum because many of the plants, vertebrates, and even arthropods are displayed in naturalistic settings. Additionally, a cadre of docents—volunteer staff—are stationed at strategic points around the grounds to answer questions and explain the ecology of the exhibits. Birders will have a field day at the walk-in hummingbird and mixed-species aviaries, and at the wheel-shaped bird enclosures, especially when they see the Mexican species that appear in Arizona only as vagrants—or have yet to arrive. Both Military Macaws and Lilac-crowned Parrots are known to breed just 150 miles south of the border. Raptor free-flight demonstrations are scheduled at 10:30 a.m. and 1:30 p.m. from November to mid-April, offering museum visitors an opportunity to observe raptor behavior in a natural setting.

But wild birds hold their own here, too. All the "regular" desert species are present: Inca Dove, Gila Woodpecker, Cactus Wren, Verdin, Curve-billed Thrasher, Black-tailed Gnatcatcher, and Northern Cardinal. Owing to the lush plantings, the Desert Museum is also an excellent place to see Costa's Hummingbird (year round), Red-naped Sapsucker (primarily in the cottonwoods by the otter pool) during migration, Purple Martin in summer, Canyon Wren (using the artificial rock cliffs in the mountain island exhibit), Bronzed Cowbird in summer, and Hooded Oriole in summer. The "oasis effect" of tall trees in the desert also attracts the unexpected. Over the past decade the museum has played host to such surprise species as Black Vulture, Northern Saw-whet Owl, Lucifer Hummingbird, Sulphur-bellied Flycatcher, Rufous-backed Robin, and Indigo Bunting. In May 2004 an adult male Yellow Grosbeak attracted hundreds of birders during the week it was present.

Male Costa's Hummingbird at Salvia
Narca Moore-Craig

The tiny Costa's Hummingbird illustrates the dynamic impact of a desert oasis. Like the Inca Dove and the Curve-billed Thrasher, it has adapted to the harsh climate by nesting early in the spring. Formerly, after exploiting the peak desert flowering period between February and April, Costa's left the lowlands before the temperatures began to soar. Since the mid-1980s, however, Costa's Hummingbird has learned to take advantage of this man-made oasis habitat. Now Costa's is a year-round resident at the Arizona-Sonora Desert Museum, as well as in gardens in west Tucson.

Some of the mammals that live on or near the museum grounds include Kit Fox (night), Coyote, Rock Squirrel, Harris's Antelope Ground-Squirrel (chipmunk-like stripes), Desert Cottontail, and Desert Mule Deer. An excellent place to look for wildlife is across from the museum parking area in King Canyon. A parking area on the right (east) side of Kinney Road just past the museum entrance (0.1 mile north) marks the trailhead. It is a one-mile hike on an abandoned mining road to Mam-a-Gah ("Deer Dancer") Picnic Area. Here the trail intersects King Canyon at a point where water bubbles up in the wash. In winter this is a great place to watch for Cooper's Hawks, Rock and Canyon Wrens, Ruby-crowned Kinglet, Yellow-rumped and Orange-crowned Warblers, Green-tailed and Canyon Towhees, and Chipping and Black-chinned Sparrows. Petroglyphs just one-quarter mile downcanyon from the picnic area date back approximately 1,000 years.

To catch bird and wildlife activity at its peak, arrive as early as possible, especially in the summer. It takes no less than two hours to simply walk the grounds. If you plan to read exhibit materials, attend docent demonstrations, photograph the wildlife, or shop at the natural-history bookstore and gift shop, count on a minimum of four hours. Even then, it's hard to leave.

To continue the loop turn north (left) onto Kinney Road and proceed to the entrance of the western sector of Saguaro National Park (1.3 miles). At Mile Wide Road, stay right on Kinney Road to the modern Red Hills Information Center (0.9 mile; 520-733-5158) to look at the exhibits and to study the map showing the roads and trails in the park. You will also find a good selection of books dealing with local natural history.

This part of the park was acquired in 1961 to protect one of the best stands of Saguaros in the state. Three miles past the visitor center on Hohokam Road, there is a dense cactus "forest" that averages 15,000 to 20,000 Saguaros per square mile. This is also a fine area for other plants and for birds, especially during the peak of the flowering and nesting season in April. Phainopeplas are particularly abundant on the north end of the Tucson Mountains, and breeding Harris's Hawks occur here as well. The birds in Saguaro National Park are subjected to less human disturbance than in Tucson Mountain Park, because the average tourist seldom gets past the Desert Museum.

Except in mid-winter, reptiles are a common sight in the park. The usual lizards are Collared, Leopard, Side-blotched, Regal Horned, Desert Spiny, Western Whiptail, and the dainty little Zebra-tailed, which dashes across dirt roads waving its tail in the air. Most desert snakes are nocturnal. If you drive these roads at night, especially after a rain, you may spot such snakes as the Desert Patch-nosed, Glossy, Long-nosed, Saddle Leaf-nosed, Spotted Leaf-nosed, Banded Sand, or Western Diamondback Rattlesnake. Harmless and quite beneficial, the Sonoran Gopher Snake is probably the most abundant snake in the park.

This is decision time: It is a total of 22.5 miles northwest to the Marana Pecan Grove, the next route; alternatively it is 34.5 miles to complete the San Xavier Mission Loop as described later in this chapter. Or it is just 13.3 miles east on Golden Gate, Picture Rocks, and Ina Roads across the north end of the Tucson Mountains to Interstate 10 and Tucson. In summer take the scenic and shorter route back to Tucson. But in spring and fall migration and throughout winter, there is excellent birding along the way to either the Marana Pecan Grove or the San Xavier Mission.

MARANA PECAN GROVE LOOP

(65 miles/one day to Marana Pecan Grove)

To reach the Marana Pecan Grove (also known as Pinal Air Park Pecan Grove) from the Red Hills Information Center at Saguaro National Park, follow Kinney Road (northwest) to Sandario Road (1.7 miles), and then proceed right (north) on Sandario for 6.5 miles to Marana High School on the northwest corner of Emigh Road. Between late December and early March—when the bird sings—it may be worth the time to detour left on Emigh for remotely-possible Le Conte's Thrashers. Although Le Conte's have not been seen in this area in recent years, they could be anywhere along the road in the surrounding open creosote desert. Watch for them to sprint along on the ground, dodging between the shrubs like pale rodents with cocked tails.

To reach the Marana Pecan Grove continue due north on Sandario till it dead-ends at a T-junction with Avra Valley Road (3.6 miles). Turn left and proceed west to Trico Road (5.1 miles). Turn right here and follow Trico north, scanning for raptors. The area near the bridge over the Santa Cruz

River (5.4 miles) is especially productive during winter. Aside from dozens of light-morph and rare dark-morph Red-tailed Hawks, Northern Harriers, and American Kestrels, this is an excellent place to find a gorgeous White-tailed Kite and—some years—a Rough-legged Hawk.

The signed intersection with Hardin Road (0.6 mile) signals that you are approaching the south entrance to the **Marana Pecan Grove** (0.5 mile). Turn left onto the dirt road here and follow an abandoned concrete-lined irrigation ditch straight west toward the trees. Burrowing Owls are apt to sit motionless on the edge of the track anywhere between Trico Road and the grove (0.7 mile). In winter watch for possible Mountain Plovers in the bare fields.

The Marana Pecan Grove is private property, where birders have no acknowledged permission to bird from the owner. It isn't posted and there have been no problems, but to lose access—as has happened in other places— would be a major loss for the birding community. Birders must stay out of fields, away from machinery, leave gates as they were found, and stay out of the grove if cattle are present. Cows may or may not be obvious, but remember that farmers are very sensitive about having their livestock spooked, even when it's unintentional. This is such an important site that birders must be on their best behavior.

The grove of dead and dying trees is about 0.4-mile square, with a large, overgrown earthen irrigation canal along its western boundary. Surrounded by miles of bare fields and open desert, it's easy to see why the Marana Pecan Grove is an important resting area for migrating and wintering birds, as well as a magnet for vagrants passing through the Santa Cruz River Valley. Some of the regular wintering species include White-tailed Kite (resident in the nearby fields), Sharp-shinned and Cooper's Hawks, Inca Dove, Barn Owl, White-throated Swift (sometimes hundreds), Anna's and Costa's Hummingbirds (check the Tree Tobacco along the back irrigation canal), Gila and Ladder-backed Woodpeckers, Red-naped Sapsucker, Northern "Redshafted" Flicker, Black and Say's Phoebes, Vermilion Flycatcher, Horned Lark, Common Raven (a major roost), House Wren, Ruby-crowned Kinglet, Blacktailed Gnatcatcher, Bendire's Thrasher, Loggerhead Shrike, Orange-crowned and Yellow-rumped Warblers, Pyrrhuloxia, Abert's Towhee, Lark Bunting, Song and Lincoln's Sparrows, Red-winged and Brewer's Blackbirds, and Lesser Goldfinch.

The list of vagrants and rarities that have been found at the Marana Pecan Grove since 1992 is equally impressive. These include Zone-tailed Hawk, Crested Caracara, Mountain Plover, Ruddy Ground-Dove, Groove-billed Ani, Violet-crowned Hummingbird, Lewis's Woodpecker (most winters), Red-headed Woodpecker, Tropical Kingbird, Greater Pewee, Chestnutsided, Blackburnian, and Black-and-white Warblers, American Redstart, Harris's Sparrow, Painted Bunting, and Lawrence's Goldfinch (irruptive). In 1994 and 1995 a pair of Streak-backed Orioles attempted to nest here, but were foiled by summer winds. Arizona's first record of Northern Wheatear occurred here in late October 1996. In fact, a visit to the Marana Pecan Grove, especially in the fall, could produce the most exciting find of your entire trip to Southeastern Arizona.

The dirt track continues west past some pipe corrals, then turns north, parallel to a major ditch that usually contains water and is trimmed with rank vegetation. Locked gates, however, may prevent vehicle access to this west side of the grove. Another dirt road runs east from Trico Road through open fields to the north end of the orchard (0.6 mile). It is all wonderful birding. To return to Tucson, turn left (north) onto Trico Road until it deadends at Pinal Air Park Road (1.0 mile from north entrance of the Pecan Grove). Turn right. It is 2.2 miles east to Exit 232 on Interstate 10. Twenty-five miles south on the interstate will bring you back to the starting point at St. Mary's Road.

SAN XAVIER MISSION LOOP

(70 miles/one day to San Xavier Mission)

This extension of the basic tour begins with a return to Kinney Road from Saguaro National Park's Red Hills Information Center. Turn right (north) onto Kinney Road to Sandario Road (1.7 miles). At Sandario Road, turn left (south), and proceed to the intersection with Mile Wide Road (1.5 miles). The west end of Mile Wide has sporadically hosted Tucson's closest pair of Le Conte's Thrashers, although none have been reported since about 1990.

To check for this very rare and irregular species between late December and early March, as well as for Sage Thrasher and Sage Sparrow, turn right onto Mile Wide Road and follow the pavement down to the floor of Avra Valley. Barn Owls are occasionally found holed up under either the first bridge (1.5 miles) or the second bridge (1.5 miles/3.0 miles west of Sandario). Just beyond the first wooden bridge, a series of large Central Arizona Project recharge basins lie concealed behind huge earthen berms on the south side of Mile Wide, but at this writing there is no public access. Another recharge basin located about midway between the two bridges (mile 2.1–2.5) off the north side of the road may or may not have aggregations of waterfowl, waders, and larids, depending on whether or not it contains water. When the reservoir is full, the water is viewable from the road shoulder; do not cross the fence. Pavement ends at the second one-lane bridge, but Mile Wide Road continues to an L-intersection with Reservation Road (0.5 mile/3.5 miles west of Sandario). During winter the adjacent Sonoran desertscrub along the road sides is worth checking for both Sage Thrashers and Sage Sparrows. Winter raptors often include Northern Harrier and Prairie Falcon.

A rough and rutted powerline road runs due south through a pipe gate opposite the beginning of Reservation Road. This is an unsigned entrance to Cocoraque Ranch on the edge of Ironwood Forest National Monument, created in 2000. The ranch is State Trust Land, which means it is open only to those with a state hunting, fishing, or recreation license ($15 for an individual recreation license, $20 for a family; 520-628-5480). A short walk south on the powerline road into Cocoraque Ranch or north along Reservation Road could possibly yield Le Conte's Thrasher. Birders using taped playbacks should be aware that Crissal Thrashers respond vigorously to Le Conte's songs, and Crissals are common here in winter. Bendire's and Curve-billed Thrashers along Reservation Road mean that it is possible—although highly unlikely—to see all five species of regularly occurring Arizona thrashers in a single location.

Return to Sandario and continue south to Snyder Hill Road (6.0 miles). A conspicuous line of dying Eucalyptus trees on the right (west) side of Sandario, opposite the west end of Snyder Hill Road, merits investigation. Vagrant warblers are always a possibility here, and careful perusal of the few living trees may reveal one or more Great Horned Owls on concealed perches. The Eucalyptus row is only 0.35 mile long. A dirt road follows the trees on the north side, and a quick drive is usually worth the effort.

Cross Sandario and drive east on Snyder Hill Road, a wide, well-graded gravel road (*but be careful—after heavy rains Snyder Hill Road may be impassable*). The low-growing, mesquite-dominated desertscrub on either edge of the road is generally unproductive until the turnoff to the **Avra Valley Sewage Ponds** (also known as the Snyder Hill Road Sewage Ponds) on the left (north) side of the road (2.5 miles). The pavement on Snyder Hill begins 0.2 mile before the turnoff to the ponds, and a paved drive runs 100 yards to a chain-link gate into the facility, which is generally open from 7:30 a.m. to 2:00 p.m. seven days a week (520-578-7341). Visitors are asked to sign in at the office before birding. If the gate is locked, a dirt lane outside the fence that parallels the Snyder Hill Road offers a fair view of the quarter-mile-long South Pond. A spotting scope is helpful.

There are four major impoundments and a smaller pond lined in black plastic, with a total area of about 160 surface acres when all the ponds have water. Usually one or more of the ponds has been drained for renovation. The two largest ponds to the left or west side of the facility usually harbor the most waterfowl and shorebirds. The list of species that have been found here includes almost all of Southeastern Arizona's waterbirds. Eared Grebes are common in winter, and both Western and Clark's Grebes are occasional. Great Blue Herons are present year round, sometimes with Great and Snowy Egrets, and not infrequently with one or two dozen Black-crowned Night-Herons. Flocks of White-faced Ibis pass through during migration, as do large numbers of Least Sandpipers and smaller aggregations of Western and Baird's Sandpipers, Long-billed Dowitchers, and both Wilson's and Red-necked Phalaropes. There are typically one hundred to one thousand ducks on the ponds in the winter. Tiny insects in the air above the water are irresistible to Lesser Nighthawks at dawn and dusk throughout the summer; five or six species of swallows dine on the same items during migration. Spotted Sandpipers and American Pipits teeter down the shorelines in winter. Rarities are also attracted to the ponds. A presumed Cackling Goose arrived in December 2004, Reddish Egret has put in three appearances (in August 1996, July 1998, and late June and early July 2004), an Upland Sandpiper showed up in September 1998, single Elegant Terns were present in July 1990 and 2001, and Arizona's first Nelson's Sharp-tailed Sparrow was discovered in October 2003. The Avra Valley Sewage Ponds constitute the single most important stopover area for water-dependent species in the entire Tucson region.

Turn left (east) as you exit the ponds. Watch for Prairie Falcons perched on utility poles (winter) until Snyder Road dead-ends at San Joaquin (3.2 miles). Turn right (south) onto San Joaquin for a short distance until it, too, comes to a dead-end at Ajo Way (0.6 mile). Turn left (east) to return to Tucson or to continue this birding loop. Ajo Way cuts through a low pass on the south end of the Tucson Mountains before arriving at a traffic signal for La Cholla Boulevard (6.3 miles). If time is not tight, consider turning left (north) onto La Cholla to check out the five-acre lake in John F. Kennedy Park (0.1 mile). Anglers usually ring the lake every morning by 9:00, but this doesn't seem to discourage wintering waterfowl, and it has no impact on migrating swallows. Tree, Violet-green, Northern Rough-winged, Bank, Cliff, and Barn Swallows are all possible simultaneously in April. A lost Little Blue Heron put down here in late April 2004, joining a Snow Goose that forgot to migrate.

Back on Ajo Way at La Cholla Boulevard, continue east on Ajo Way to the next traffic light at Mission Road (0.4 mile). Turn right (south) here, and follow Mission Road onto Tohono O'odham Nation lands to San Xavier Road (5.6 miles). Glimpses of the white dome and accompanying towers of **San Xavier del Bac Mission** telegraph your approach to the T-intersection. Turn left (east) onto San Xavier Road. The mission is plainly visible ahead (0.6 mile). In the past decade tribal police have rather brusquely evicted birders from the road shoulder along this stretch of pavement, especially in the precincts of the cemetery. *Please respect the wish of the Tohono O'odham by continuing directly to the mission.*

San Xavier Mission was founded by Father Eusebio Kino in 1700, but work on the present structure did not begin until 1783. Kino selected this place known as Bac—or place where the river reappears—as the site for the first church in what became Arizona and California, simply because it had the largest concentration of Tohono O'odham in the Santa Cruz Valley. The year 1797 is usually given as the completion date, but it is evident from the parking lot that the east bell tower was never finished. Church historians have speculated that the padres continued to receive funds so long as they could claim that the edifice was still under construction.

The area on the east side of San Xavier Mission usually has the best birding. Follow the low wall back past the bookstore and gift shop north to the rear of the building. A long list of birds visits the mission grounds throughout the year. Regular clients are Gambel's Quail, Mourning and Inca Doves, Common Ground-Dove (in truth, uncommon), Cactus Wren, Northern Mockingbird, Curve-billed Thrasher, Northern Cardinal, Pyrrhuloxia, Canyon Towhee, Black-throated Sparrow, Great-tailed Grackle, Brown-headed Cowbird, and House Finch. In summer White-winged Doves are abundant, and a Ruddy Ground-Dove appeared during the winter of 1993–1994.

While birders may not enter private property across the road, winter is especially "birdy" in a desert plot just east of the low wall. From October through March watch for Sharp-shinned and Cooper's Hawks, Greater Roadrunner, Anna's Hummingbird, Gila and Ladder-backed Woodpeckers, Northern "Red-shafted" and Gilded Flickers, Verdin, Blue-gray and Black-tailed Gnatcatchers, Ruby-crowned Kinglet, Bendire's and Crissal Thrashers, Phainopepla, Green-tailed Towhee, and White-crowned Sparrow. Wintering Rock Wrens sing from the small knoll overlooking this little patch of desert.

During the cold months it is worth checking any conspicuous perch for Northern Harrier, Red-tailed Hawk, and American Kestrel. Most winters there are also sporadic sightings of Rough-legged Hawk and Prairie Falcon on isolated tree and utility pole perches. Among the other open-terrain winter residents are Killdeer, Say's Phoebe, Horned Lark, Common Raven, Mountain Bluebird (irruptive), Loggerhead Shrike, Lark Sparrow, Lark Bunting, and both Eastern and Western Meadowlarks. Don't forget to visit the mission itself before you leave. The interior reflects San Xavier's origins in the Spanish colonial period, and its ornate style will inspire your respect for the unknown Native American artists of centuries past. San Xavier Road turns south in front of the mission and soon ties into Community Road (0.25 mile). Turn left (east) onto Community Road. It is one mile to Interstate 19 (Exit 92) south of Tucson. Go under the freeway and turn left (north) to return to Tucson.

THE SANTA CRUZ RIVER IN WINTER

(28 miles/one-half day)

A series of ponds and marshes along the Santa Cruz River on the west side of Tucson provides some of the best winter birding in Southeastern Arizona. Aside from a generous supply of waterfowl and waders, the river is an important migratory corridor, and a wonderful location for birds of prey. Ordinarily these oases are not as productive in summer.

This trip begins at **Sweetwater Wetlands**. To locate these small, cattail-trimmed ponds take Interstate 10 six miles north of the junction of I-10 with I-19 to Prince Road (Exit 254) and turn left (west), moving into the far right lane to go under the overpass (the other two lanes are for left turns only). Cross the frontage road and continue 100 yards to a T-intersection. Turn right (north) onto Business Center Drive to River Park Road (0.2 mile).

Follow River Park Road for 0.5 mile as it curves to the right twice to loop around the business park, where it becomes Commerce Drive. Turn left (north) onto Benan Venture Drive to the T-intersection with Sweetwater Drive (0.2 mile). Turn left (west) onto Sweetwater Drive. (While these directions may sound complex, there are few places to get lost and the route basically parallels the freeway to the intersection with Sweetwater Drive.) The entrance to the facility is a short distance beyond (0.1 mile) on the left (south) side of the street at 2667 W. Sweetwater Drive. Sweetwater Wetlands is open from daybreak to 6:00 p.m., with an occasional weekday morning closure for mosquito abatement. If you find the facility closed, check back after 10:00 a.m. Created by the City of Tucson for water recharge and wildlife habitat in 1997, the Sweetwater Wetlands has proven a magnet for birds. Wintering species include Pied-billed Grebe, 10 or more species of ducks, Sora and Virginia Rail (especially conspicuous in spring), Common Moorhen, Black Phoebe, Vermilion Flycatcher, Marsh Wren, Ruby-crowned Kinglet, Orange-crowned and Yellow-rumped Warblers, Common Yellowthroat, Brewer's, Song, and Lincoln's Sparrows, Lark Bunting, and Yellow-headed Blackbird. In addition to Northern Harriers and Red-tailed Hawks, all four species of Arizona's falcons frequent Sweetwater during winter.

The resident raptor *du jour*, however, is the ever-present Harris's Hawk. Behaving as if sublimely unaware of humanity's existence, a family of these magnificent birds of prey alternates perches between the tall trees at Roger Road Sewage Ponds and the tall dead snags thoughtfully provided by the Sweetwater Wetlands development team. One or more are visible—and often audible—somewhere in the area all day long. They are apparently particularly fond of dining on the native cotton-rats that scuttle in and out of the cattail hedges. Other year-round residents include Inca Dove, Greater Roadrunner, Cactus Wren, and Abert's Towhee.

To bird Sweetwater, follow the concrete path past the restrooms and interpretative signs over a bridge and into the artificial marsh. The half-mile loop trail circles three small ponds. Three additional ponds lie west of the designated trail; however, two are currently signed as off-limits to the public. Some of the best birds discovered at Sweetwater to date include Least Grebe (intermittently present since 2000), Tricolored Heron, Greater Scaup, Common Goldeneye, Purple Gallinule, Ruddy Ground-Dove, and Chestnut-sided and Pine Warblers. From the berm along the south side of the ponds there is a view of four larger ponds with bare banks and very shallow water. Aside from hundreds of Northern Shovelers during winter, the ponds harbor lesser numbers of other waterfowl, as well as Black-necked Stilts in summer and White-faced Ibis in migration. Drinking water, restrooms, and a shade ramada are much-appreciated amenities provided by the City of Tucson, but it is the sheer number of birds at Sweetwater that makes any visit a pleasure.

On the north side of Sweetwater Drive lie the Pima County Roger Road Wastewater Treatment Ponds. Turn left (west) as you leave the

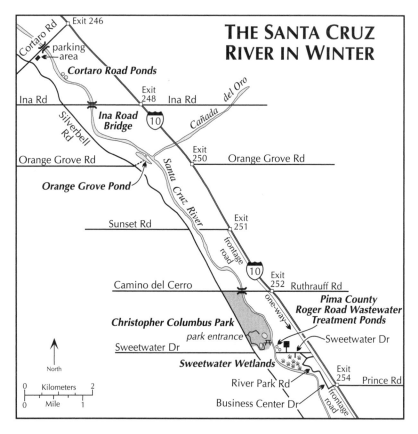

THE SANTA CRUZ RIVER IN WINTER

Exit 246
Cortaro Rd
parking area
Cortaro Road Ponds
Ina Rd
Exit 248   Ina Rd
del Oro
Ina Road Bridge (10)
Cañada
Silverbell Rd
Orange Grove Rd
Exit 250   Orange Grove Rd
Orange Grove Pond
Santa Cruz River
Sunset Rd
Exit 251
frontage road
(10)   Exit 252   Ruthrauff Rd
Camino del Cerro
one-way
Pima County Roger Road Wastewater Treatment Ponds
Christopher Columbus Park
park entrance
Sweetwater Dr
Sweetwater Dr
North
Sweetwater Wetlands
0   Kilometers   2
0   Mile   1
River Park Rd
Exit 254   Prince Rd
Business Center Dr
frontage road

Sweetwater Wetlands parking area, and turn right (north) at the visitor entrance to the **Roger Road Ponds** (0.2 mile). Continue 100 yards to the red-brick administration building and park in the slots marked for visitors off the left (west) end of the building. The Roger Road Ponds are open Monday through Friday from 7:30 a.m. to 3:30 p.m. Occasionally, when the national-security risk is elevated, these ponds are closed. Birders are asked to register at the office and to restrict their visit to the immediate vicinity of the two ponds. The ponds are located approximately 100 yards west of the office in a grove of tall pine and Eucalyptus trees.

From a birder's perspective, the Roger Road Ponds have benefited from the development of the Sweetwater Wetlands on the south side of the street. Owing to better coverage, Roger Road has recently earned a reputation as a vagrant trap. Some of the birds found here in the post-Sweetwater era include Varied Thrush and Prothonotary, Kentucky, and Hooded Warblers. It remains a reliable location for Harris's Hawk. In winter check the milling throng of Mallards and Northern Shovelers on the west pond for Wood Duck and both Blue-winged and Cinnamon Teal. During irruption years, Red Crossbills lurk in the pines.

The next stop is the north end of the River Loop. Follow Sweetwater Drive east to the frontage road and turn right (south). Turn left (east) onto Prince Road (0.7 mile), go under the overpass, and turn left (north) onto the freeway entrance ramp. Take I-10 northwest to Exit 246 (7.5 miles), and turn left (west) onto Cortaro Road. Follow Cortaro Road under the freeway overpass and continue to the bridge across the Santa Cruz River (0.5 mile). Immediately beyond the bridge on the left (south) side of Cortaro Road lies a small parking area. From here it is possible to foray upstream on the west bank of the Santa Cruz River approximately one-half mile to a series of old gravel pits in the riverbed known as **Cortaro Road Ponds**. Cortaro Road Ponds are probably the most reliable site for Canvasbacks near Tucson, and there are generally Cinnamon Teal and Gadwalls in the mix. Present in 1998 was a drake Eurasian Wigeon, and in 2000 Snow, Ross's, and Canada Geese all put in an appearance. More recently, Chestnut-sided Warbler in the winter of 2001–2002 and Harris's Sparrow and Orchard Oriole in early 2003 were found along this stretch of the Santa Cruz. A scope is useful to scan the ponds 100 to 400 yards away. Other primarily winter birds include Pied-billed and Eared Grebes, Great Blue and Green Herons, Black-necked Stilts, Greater Yellowlegs, Spotted Sandpipers, and Least Sandpipers. As many as 40 stilts may overwinter, and most winters they are joined by a Dunlin or two and several or more Long-billed Dowitchers, During mild winters also watch for White-throated Swifts and Northern Rough-winged Swallows. During irruption years, Lawrence's Goldfinches may be common.

A nice mixture of wintering hawks exploits the avian bounty along this comparatively quiet portion of the Santa Cruz. Omnipresent are Northern Harriers and Red-tailed Hawks. Also likely are Sharp-shinned and Cooper's Hawks, Harris's Hawk, and one or more falcons: American Kestrel, Merlin, Peregrine, or Prairie. Extremely rare in this western desert valley, a Bald Eagle agitated the ducks at Cortaro Road Ponds from December 1998 until its untimely demise in a powerline accident in February 2002.

Upon returning to your vehicle at the Cortaro Road Bridge continue west to the traffic signal at the intersection with Silverbell Road (0.5 mile). Turn left (south) onto Silverbell Road and drive to the four-way stop at Ina Road (1.0 mile). Turn left (east) again to **Ina Road Bridge** (0.3 mile). The best place to both park and bird is on the right (south) side immediately before the long concrete span. Traffic is often heavy on Ina Road, but a pedestrian walkway with a concrete barricade separating you from the thoroughfare creates a margin of psychological comfort as you scan for birds in the riverbed. Nonetheless, your scope will vibrate like a tuning fork every time a truck thunders by.

Ina Road Bridge is a suggested stop because every winter it produces a few good birds. Some of the vagrants that have occurred here in recent years include Brown Thrasher, Pine Warbler, American Redstart, and Fox Sparrow.

Often they are best observed from the center of the bridge itself. Even without rarities, however, there are nearly always plenty of birds. To the south, the river is braided and shallow, with numerous overgrown sandbars. Regularly occurring winter birds include Great Blue and Green Herons, Mallard, Northern Shoveler, Northern Harrier, Red-tailed Hawk, American Kestrel, Killdeer, Least Sandpiper, Wilson's Snipe, Anna's and Costa's (after December 15th) Hummingbirds (especially in the Tree Tobacco), Black and Say's Phoebes, all of Arizona's regular swallow species (primarily in migration), Loggerhead Shrike, European Starling, Cactus and Marsh Wrens, Horned Lark, American Pipit, Ruby-crowned Kinglet, Orange-crowned and Yellow-rumped Warblers, Common Yellowthroat, Abert's Towhee, Savannah, Song, and Lincoln's Sparrows, Red-winged and Brewer's Blackbirds, and Great-tailed Grackle. Almost any species mentioned for any location on the Santa Cruz River can and has turned up at the Ina Road Bridge.

Although there are no established trails after the first couple of hundred yards, it is possible—and a welcome relief from the traffic noise—to walk either upstream or downstream along the west side of the river. Downstream (north) are the Cortaro Road Ponds with Cinnamon Teal and other ducks, as well as Black-necked Stilts, Dunlin, Long-billed Dowitchers, and other shorebirds. Upstream (south) is better for vagrant passerines. Southeastern Arizona's first Le Conte's Sparrow was discovered 200 yards south of the bridge in December 2004. During invasion winters, Lawrence's Goldfinches are frequently found within the first quarter-mile either up or downstream.

The next important winter birding venue along the Santa Cruz is the **Orange Grove Pond**. Return to the four-way-stop intersection at Ina and Silverbell (0.3 mile) and turn left onto Silverbell Road. Just beyond a small bluff on the right look for a street sign for Orange Grove Road (1.5 miles), and turn left onto a short dirt track directly opposite Orange Grove Road. The little road ends in 75 yards at a rolling earthen levee that's heavily scarred with all-terrain-vehicle trails. *Be careful! To view Orange Grove Pond it is necessary to scramble to the top of the earthen embankment, and the interior wall is clearly steep and unstable. Do not approach the edge!*

Orange Grove Pond is an abandoned gravel quarry approximately one-quarter mile long and 100 yards wide. A scope is definitely an asset here. A cut on the east side formerly joined the pond to the Santa Cruz River and kept it full. Siltation closed the channel in 2002, but groundwater seems adequate to maintain at least some water in the pond. Judging from the regular occurrence of ducks such as Redhead, Ring-necked, Bufflehead, and Ruddy, Orange Grove Pond is probably one of the deepest bodies of water along the Santa Cruz. Hooded Merganser is occasional. As with all sites along the Santa Cruz River, however, Northern Shoveler tends to outnumber all other waterfowl species combined. Although the pond is ringed with plastic containers and other debris, a variety of birds is more likely to appear here than at other locations on the Santa Cruz. Throughout the winter, flotillas of Eared Grebes usually outnumber the resident Pied-bills, Western Grebe may be found, and both Double-crested and Neotropic Cormorants are sporadic. Either a Great Egret or a Snowy Egret is apt to overwinter, and Great Blue and Green Herons and Black-crowned Night-Herons are possible. Migrating Osprey may soar overhead, and Belted Kingfishers rest on the scattered perches available in the small trees and shrubs that have colonized the sheer walls of the pond. In the fall of 2001 a flock of 13 American White Pelicans settled in for a couple of weeks. In the winter of 2002–2003 a flock of approximately 100 Lawrence's Goldfinches were consistently using the river area just east of the pond. Esthetically speaking, Orange Grove Pond leaves a lot to be desired, but it generally adds a few species not seen elsewhere on a winter birding trip to the Santa Cruz.

The final stop along the river is, however, designed for a picnic. To close the loop, continue south on Silverbell Road past the traffic light at El Camino del Cerro (2.5 miles) to **Christopher Columbus Park** (0.8 mile). Turn left (east) here and follow the pavement to two small, artificial ponds known as Silverbell and Archer Lakes (0.2 mile). Drinking fountains, restrooms, tables, shade trees, and shade ramadas are available here. Although crowded with fishermen—especially on weekends—the ponds occasionally attract Greater White-fronted Goose or Greater Scaup among the resident feral waterfowl during winter. Southeastern Arizona's fourth record of a Blue-winged Warbler occurred in mid-March 1999 in the ribbon of cottonwood and willow trees fringing the Santa Cruz just east of the park. Silverbell Lake is almost directly west across the river from the Sweetwater Wetlands and Roger Road Ponds. Great Blue Herons, Cooper's, Harris's, and Red-tailed Hawks, Merlins, Peregrine and Prairie Falcons all apparently view the tall mesquite and tamarisk trees and the even taller utility poles and towers just south of Silverbell Lake as logical resting locations. If you failed to find a wintering Vermilion Flycatcher at Sweetwater Wetlands at the beginning of the loop, watch for the telltale spark of scarlet here.

Return to the traffic signal at El Camino del Cerro/Ruthrauff Road (0.8 mile) and turn right (east) to return to Interstate 10 (0.8 mile) at Exit 252.

CAMPGROUNDS, RESTAURANTS, AND ACCOMMODATIONS

Camping facilities are available at Gilbert Ray Campground in Tucson Mountain Park or at Catalina State Park nine miles north of Tucson off Highway 77. Motels and hotels are abundant in Tucson, particularly along I-10 and in "hotel row" —Tucson Boulevard north of Tucson International Airport.

Local-guide referrals for the Tucson area as well as all Southeastern Arizona are available from Tucson Audubon Society (300 E. University Boulevard, #120, Tucson, AZ 85705; 520-629-0510; www.tucson audubon.org).

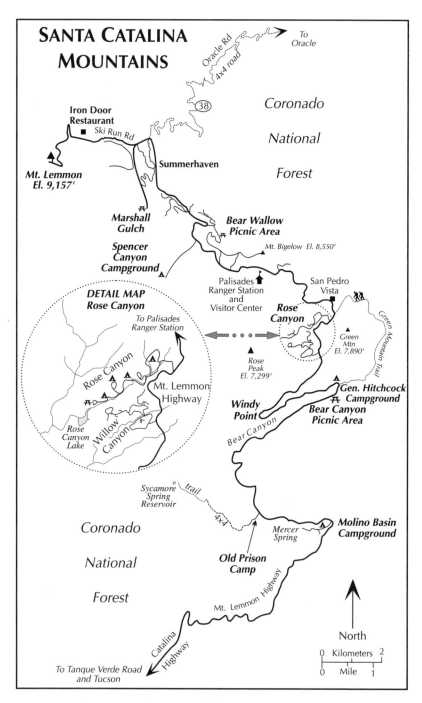

SANTA CATALINA MOUNTAINS

Oracle Rd
4x4 road
To Oracle

38

Coronado

National

Forest

Iron Door Restaurant
Ski Run Rd

Summerhaven

▲ **Mt. Lemmon El. 9,157'**

⛩ **Marshall Gulch**

Bear Wallow Picnic Area

Spencer Canyon Campground ▲

▲ Mt. Bigelow El. 8,550'

Palisades Ranger Station and Visitor Center

San Pedro Vista

Rose Canyon

Green Mountain Trail

DETAIL MAP Rose Canyon

To Palisades Ranger Station

Rose Canyon

Mt. Lemmon Highway

▲ Rose Peak El. 7,299'

▲ Green Mtn El. 7,890'

Rose Canyon Lake

Willow Canyon

▲ **Gen. Hitchcock Campground**
⛩ **Bear Canyon Picnic Area**

Windy Point

Bear Canyon

Sycamore Spring Reservoir

trail

4x4

Mercer Spring

Molino Basin Campground

Coronado

National

Forest

Mt. Lemmon Highway

Old Prison Camp

Catalina Highway

To Tanque Verde Road and Tucson

North

0 Kilometers 2
0 Mile 1

36

CHAPTER 2

SANTA CATALINA MOUNTAINS

For most visitors and many residents, the Santa Catalina Mountains are part of Tucson itself. Rising nearly 7,000 feet above the desert floor, the blue crest of the Catalinas completely dominates the northern Tucson skyline. The Saguaro-studded canyons that drain into the Tucson basin are the city's emblem, embedded in the public imagination and depicted in untold post-card and magazine images.

Two full days are required to bird all three areas described in this chapter. In summer the two lower areas, Sabino Canyon and Redington Pass, should each be visited as early as possible, both to avoid the heat of the day and to see the birds before they are disturbed by an awakening Tucson. The starting point for all three trips is the intersection of Tanque Verde Road and Sabino Canyon Road in northeast Tucson.

CATALINA HIGHWAY TO MOUNT LEMMON

(72 miles/one day)

The road from Tucson (El. 2,200 feet) up the south flank of the Santa Catalina Mountains to the top of Mount Lemmon (El. 9,157 feet) is one of the most spectacular in the United States. Birders will not only be impressed by the magnificent scenery and the sweeping vistas, but also by the tremendous diversity of plants and animals. The road climbs through five radically different life zones. Changes in the flora and fauna over the 35-mile trip up the mountain are equivalent to a journey from Mexico to Canada.

Stretching about 25 miles east-west and encompassing over 200 square miles, the Santa Catalinas are exceeded in size in southeastern Arizona only by the Chiricahua Mountains. Winter snowfall can be heavy. From November through March the highway is occasionally closed after major storms, or chains may be required above certain elevations. Even in summer the heights are far cooler than Tucson, and apt to be cold if skies are overcast. Always toss in a jacket for any trip to the top, and remember that summer monsoons may bring torrential cloudbursts. When in doubt call 520-547-7510 to check road conditions. Gasoline is not available on the Catalina Highway.

Sadly, since the summer of 2003 no account of the Santa Catalinas can avoid mention of the catastrophic Aspen Fire, a man-caused blaze that blackened approximately 85,000 acres all the way from the bottom to the top of the mountain. Aside from destroying over 300 homes around Summerhaven, high up in the headwaters of Sabino Canyon, all campgrounds and picnic areas along the Catalina Highway sustained some degree of damage. At this writing in September 2004 only Molino Basin, Prison Camp (Gordon Hirabayashi Recreation Site), Rose Canyon, and Spencer Canyon Campgrounds remain open, but birdwatching on a walk-in basis is still permitted in many of the areas. (More information about campground, road, and trail closures can be obtained by calling the Catalina Ranger District at 520-749-8700 or by checking their website at www.fs.fed.us/r3/coronado.) A late but wet summer rainy season in 2003 has already started the healing. Many oaks now have a corona of new leaves around the base, and a film of green annuals has spread over vast tracts of the mountain. Certain species of birds, Hairy Woodpeckers and Western Bluebirds for example, will undoubtedly benefit from the new habitat created by the fire.

The starting point for this tour is the intersection of Tanque Verde Road and Sabino Canyon Road in northeast Tucson. Continue straight ahead (east) on Tanque Verde Road to the Catalina Highway (2.5 miles). Turn left here. Leave early and try to avoid weekends. The Coronado National Forest, which administers this area, estimates the Santa Catalina Mountains receive no fewer than one million visitors per year.

You are in the Lower Sonoran Life Zone over the first stretch of the **Catalina Highway** as it crosses the desert to the base of the mountains (4.4 miles). Saguaro Cactus on the hillsides symbolize the Sonoran Desert, as do other plants such as Foothills Palo Verde, Ocotillo, and Brittlebush. Mileage markers erected by the U.S. Forest Service along the Catalina Highway are convenient indicators for the stops on this tour. Forest Service milepost 0 is set at 2,900-foot elevation at the base of the mountain.

As of 2004 completion of the Mount Lemmon Highway Reconstruction Project is expected by the end of 2005. Until then, delays and closures may occur Monday through Thursday between mileposts 11 and 16. The road is open with no construction delays from 6:00 a.m. Friday to 9:00 p.m. Sunday. Some parking areas within the construction zone may be temporarily closed. For more information, call the construction hotline at 520-751-9405. There is a Forest User Fee for the Santa Catalina Ranger District, payable at the fee station just beyond milepost 5 on the Catalina Highway. (Fees are $5/day, $10/week, or $20/year; Golden Eagle, Golden Age, or Golden Access cards accepted. National Parks Pass not accepted.) Permits purchased here are also good for Sabino Canyon and Madera Canyon in the Santa Rita Mountains and for National Forest fee areas in the Chiricahua Mountains. (Separate campground fees apply.) When the fee station is closed, there is a self-service pay station 0.5 mile ahead on the left at the Molino Basin Campground.

Initially the road climbs rapidly up the front range through gray-and-white banded gneiss formed 17–30 million years ago. Scenic pullouts over the next few miles offer a chance to see some of the typical birds that are more or less restricted to the Lower Sonoran Life Zone. Among these are Gambel's Quail, Gila Woodpecker, Verdin, Cactus Wren, Black-tailed Gnatcatcher, Curve-billed Thrasher, and Black-throated Sparrow.

Saguaros give way to Mexican Blue, Arizona White, and Emory Oaks as the road approaches **Molino Basin**, elevation 4,370 feet (5.5 miles). Mexican Blue Oak, with light bark and small, bluish leaves, is confined to Southeastern Arizona. Pale-barked Arizona White Oak has larger leaves than the Mexican Blue Oak. The leaves are fuzzy beneath with prominent venation, and the leaf color is always green. Emory Oak has dark green, holly-shaped leaves and dark, comparatively smooth bark. The habitat here is in the Upper Sonoran Life Zone, an area too cold for most cacti to colonize. Park at the fee station to look for oak-zone birds such as Acorn Woodpecker, Ash-throated Fly-catcher (summer), Western Scrub-Jay, Mexican Jay, Bridled Titmouse, Bush-tit, Bewick's and Rock Wrens, Black-throated Gray Warbler (summer), Can-yon Towhee, Rufous-crowned Sparrow, and Scott's Oriole (summer).

Specialty birds at Molino Basin are Crissal Thrasher and Black-chinned Sparrow. Both of these species are particularly fond of the dense, low- grow-ing thickets on the arid slopes which ecologists classify as Interior Chaparral. Pointleaf Manzanita, easily identified by its wine-red bark, is the dominant spe-cies in the chaparral belt. Alligator Juniper and Border Pinyon Pine are the small trees that polka-dot the brushy flanks of the mountain. The trail across the Catalina Highway from the fee station and restrooms is a good place to look for the thrasher and the sparrow.

Beyond Molino Basin the road enters the perimeter of the Aspen Fire. Most of the trees were consumed in the blaze, and almost all those that re-main have been scarred. As the pavement winds up the dry hillsides watch for Palmer Agaves, or "century plants," that blossom once during the life of the plant, usually in July and August, then die. The plants are actually only 10 to 25 years old when they flower. The thorn-fringed leaves of agaves form a com-pact rosette, and their large, bell-shaped, yellow flowers are borne on stalks that may reach 15 feet in height. Hummingbirds, woodpeckers, and orioles are attracted by the flowers. Both the stalk and the artichoke-like heart at the base of the plant were used as food by the Apaches. In Mexico agaves are cultivated to make a coarse thread called sisal, and in the manufacture of alcoholic beverages. Tequila is the most famous of the agave liquors.

As the road continues to ascend the main massif, a new oak becomes common. Silverleaf Oak is easily recognized by the white undersurface of its long, slender leaves. Silverleaf Oak grows on rocky, south-facing slopes for most of the remaining distance to the crest of the mountain range.

The Catalina Highway enters **Bear Canyon** at Milepost 10 (4.5 miles). Once again the character of the vegetation changes. Both shady and cool, Bear Canyon escaped the brunt of the fire. This is the home of the champion Arizona Cypress tree in the United States. It measures 20 feet in circumference at breast height and stands 93 feet tall. The north-facing slope of Bear Canyon hosts the most impressive stand of Arizona Cypress in the Santa Catalina Mountains. Aside from the beautifully symmetrical, blue-green foliage of the cypress trees, Bear Canyon also supports a stringer of Arizona Sycamore trees along the little stream, and a scattering of both Ponderosa and Chihuahua Pines. To explore the birding in Bear Canyon, park in any of the three picnic areas just beyond Milepost 11. Elevation here is 6,000 feet, approximately midway between the valley and the highest summit, as well as about halfway up the road to Mount Lemmon.

Warblers love Bear Canyon. In springtime it is not uncommon to hear the combined voices of Olive, Virginia's, "Audubon's" Yellow-rumped, Black-throated Gray, Grace's, and Red-faced Warblers, and Painted Redstart all contributing to the morning chorus. These songs are apt to be augmented by assorted chips and calls of migrating Townsend's, Hermit, and Wilson's Warblers until mid-May. Other birds of the tall timber in Bear Canyon include Band-tailed Pigeon, Flammulated Owl, Whip-poor-will, Acorn and Arizona Woodpeckers, Northern "Red-shafted" Flicker, Dusky-capped Flycatcher, Western Wood-Pewee, Plumbeous and Hutton's Vireos, Bewick's Wren, Hepatic Tanager, Spotted Towhee, and Yellow-eyed Junco.

The Catalina Highway re-enters the charred remains of the Aspen Fire burn soon after leaving Bear Canyon. At 6,623-foot-elevation Windy Point (2.9 miles) an enormous boulder on the left (south) side of the road offers a stupendous overlook of Bear Canyon in the foreground, backdropped by the Tucson Valley. Nowhere are the geological forces that wrought the Santa Catalinas more apparent. A volcano erupted below here some 70 million years ago with a force estimated to be one thousand times greater than the explosions that shook Mount St. Helens in 1980. More recently, owing to plate tectonics, the old volcano slid west off the rising granitic mountain and the Catalinas assumed much the shape we see today. Except in mid-winter—and on occasional sunny days even then—White-throated Swifts are common at Windy Point. Listen for the cascading songs of Canyon Wrens on the strange rock formations called "hoodoos" by geologists.

Red-faced Warbler
Narca Moore-Craig

A pass just before Milepost 16 (1.8 miles) marks the abrupt division between the burn and the Ponderosa Pine forest that dominates the uplands above 7,000 feet. While the fire singed the ground cover and saplings, most mature conifers were spared in this area of the Catalinas. Ponderosa Pine, the tree indicator of the Transition Life Zone, also signals a shift to a community of Rocky Mountain plant and animal species that is reflected in the avifauna. Some of the resident birds of this zone are Wild Turkey, Band-tailed Pigeon, Steller's and Mexican Jays, Common Raven, Mountain Chickadee, White-breasted and Pygmy Nuthatches, Brown Creeper, Western Bluebird, Olive Warbler (more common in summer), Yellow-eyed Junco, Red Crossbill (irregular), and Pine Siskin. In summer look for Zone-tailed Hawk, Peregrine

Falcon, Magnificent and Broad-tailed Hummingbirds, Greater Pewee, Violet-green Swallow, Virginia's (in oak thickets), Yellow-rumped, Grace's, and Red-faced Warblers, Hepatic Tanager, and Black-headed Grosbeak. Migration brings Anna's Hummingbirds at a surprisingly high elevation, as well as Townsend's and Hermit Warblers. Dark-eyed Juncos, especially "Grayheaded" and "Oregon," are common in winter.

There are three summer (April to October) recreation sites, Rose Canyon, Spencer Canyon, and Bear Wallow, that offer birders a springboard into this area. The popular **Rose Canyon Lake and Campground** (fee area, turnoff just after milepost 17, 1.3 miles) offers birders many of the same species listed below for Spencer Canyon and Bear Wallow. Walking the lower paved road that drops down through an open forest to the seven-acre impoundment (1.25 miles) can be very productive—except on summer weekends, when Tucson anglers take their recreation cheek-by-jowl as they whip the water into whitecaps in quest of elusive hatchery trout. But on summer weekdays, Red-faced Warblers are common along the little creek.

Spencer Canyon (4.3 miles), with far fewer visitors, is one of only two developed campgrounds in the upper Catalinas. The 1.2-mile descent to Turkey Track Campground (bear left at 0.8 mile) passes through Ponderosa Pine interspersed with Douglas-fir and Gambel Oak before entering the grassy area adjacent to the semi-permanent water in Spencer Creek itself. The lush growth here near the end of the road is especially good birding. During summer Red-faced Warblers gravitate to the oaks, and Olive Warblers can be found gleaning in the pine tops—even in winter. In winter also watch for Williamson's Sapsucker (uncommon), Cassin's Finch (irregular), and Red Crossbill (irregular). The introduced Abert's Tassel-eared Squirrel, Cliff Chipmunk, and Rock Squirrel frequent the campsites.

While Black Bear and Mountain Lion both roam the highlands, the only large mammal truly common in the upper Catalinas is the Coues subspecies of the White-tailed Deer. In this race bucks seldom weigh over 90 pounds, and does average under 70. Only the subspecies endemic to the Florida Keys is smaller than a Coues White-tailed Deer in North America.

Reptiles are also well represented in the high Santa Catalinas. Short-Horned Lizards, called "Horny Toads" by Tucson children, are relatively commonplace. Everything about Horned Lizards is designed to discourage predation. Their silver-dollar shape makes them difficult to swallow, as does their serrated lateral fringe, jagged dorsal scales, and the corona of "horns," which gives this species its name. Short-Horned Lizards also have the capacity to shoot blood from the corners of their eyes into the face of a would-be predator. Most important, their cryptic coloration and habitat of freezing before they're noticed make them extremely difficult to detect.

The Western "Arizona Black" Rattlesnake is a subspecies that occurs in the Ponderosa Pine belt of the Catalina and nearby Rincon Mountains. These

Rose Canyon (between the lake and campground),
Santa Cantalina Mountains.
William S. Bickel

beautiful reptiles may be almost solid black. This heat-absorbing adaptation probably allows the cold-blooded animals to remain active at high elevations for a longer period of the year.

A short distance beyond Spencer Canyon, **Bear Wallow** Recreation Site (0.8 mile) is set among the mixed conifers of the Canadian Life Zone. The Catalina Highway crosses the crest of the range just before Milepost 22. As it curves down a long, cool, north-facing slope into Bear Wallow Canyon, the Ponderosa Pine yields to a twilit forest of tall Douglas and White Firs. A lush broadleaf association features Gambel Oak, Bigtooth Maple, Box Elder, and Quaking Aspen, all competing for light along the tiny brook. Bracken Fern, Wild Raspberry, Red-osier Dogwood, and a host of wildflowers carpet the understory. While birdwatchers may hear no more than a cathedral-like hush in late October and November, it is hard not to recommend a pilgrimage to Bear Wallow in autumn. The fall colors in the afternoon alpenglow are simply superb.

Turn right onto the unpaved Bear Wallow Road to access the recreation site. Many of the same birds that occur in the Transition Life Zone also use the boreal forest at Bear Wallow. Numerous from Rose Canyon to the summit of Mount Lemmon, Mountain Chickadee is a perfect example of these ubiquitous birds of the forest. The Mountain Chickadees that frequently lead mixed flocks of small birds in the high Catalinas represent the southernmost population of their species in all of North America.

Other birds, Hermit Thrush and American Robin for example, are far more common in moist areas such as Bear Wallow. Deep-timber specialists to watch for in the Canadian Life Zone include Northern Goshawk, Spotted Owl, Hairy Woodpecker, Cordilleran Flycatcher, Warbling Vireo, Steller's Jay, Red-breasted Nuthatch, House Wren, Golden-crowned Kinglet, Western Tanager, and possibly Evening Grosbeak. Bear Wallow Road wanders up a shady canyon nearly a mile before it tops out on the backbone of the Santa Catalinas. Most of the undeveloped campsites (no fees) are located here. At mile 1.3 from the highway it merges with the Mt. Bigelow Road; stay left at the three-way junction (0.3 mile) and enjoy the boreal forest the remaining distance to 8,550-foot elevation Mt. Bigelow (1.2 mile). Substantially unaffected by the Aspen Fire, the 2.8-mile-long Bear Wallow/Mt. Bigelow Road meanders through the largest unbroken tract of forest to have survived the flames unscathed in the entire upper Santa Catalina Mountains. While the birds on the Mt. Bigelow Road are largely the same as those in Bear Wallow, the scenic majesty of the Santa Catalinas only becomes more evident as this well-graded but little-traveled road ascends to the parking area just below the summit. A U.S. Forest Service lookout tower shares the rocky top with several Tucson television and radio station transmitters.

After leaving Bear Wallow, the Catalina Highway lies just below the crest. One consequence of the Aspen Fire are numerous new roadside vistas of the

San Pedro River Valley over a vertical mile below. The old control road to Oracle that drops off the "back" (north) side of the mountain to the right is not recommended (2.5 miles). High clearance is a requirement, the road is 28 miles long, it's rough and dusty, and neither the scenery nor the birding can match the scenery or the birding along the paved Catalina Highway.

The major junction in the upper Santa Catalinas lies just beyond the Oracle Road intersection (0.1 mile). Curve left downhill to Summerhaven to see the worst of the devastation left behind by the 2003 holocaust. Miraculously, the post office, a café, and a few other buildings survived the flames, but hundreds of other structures were reduced to charred rubble. The residents of Summerhaven vow to re-build, but in fall 2004 there were few services available for birders. However, the Marshall Gulch Picnic Area (1.1 miles) re-opened in August 2004, and, unexpectedly, a pair of Common Black-Hawks apparently summered in this high-elevation canyon.

To complete this tour take the **Ski Run Road** at the Summerhaven intersection. In the absence of safe pullouts, there is little opportunity for birding until the 8,320-foot-elevation lodge (1.2 miles). Sugar-water feeders on the veranda at the Iron Door Restaurant afford birders all the genteel comforts one could wish for, as well as the possibility of a summering White-eared Hummingbird. By August these feeders are pinwheels of color. Among the regular species competing for a sip are Magnificent, Calliope, Broad-tailed, and Rufous Hummingbirds. Also watch for Zone-tailed Hawk, Steller's Jay, Common Raven, and American Robin winging across the ski bowl, while Yellow-eyed Juncos hop tamely among cars in the parking lot. In the summer of 2004 a pair of Short-tailed Hawks adopted the crest of the Santa Catalinas as a home, and Ski Valley seemed to be the nexus of the area they patrolled.

Unless deep snows have closed it, the paved road continues on to the very top of 9,157-foot-elevation Mount Lemmon (1.7 miles). Like the Bear Wallow/Mt. Bigelow Road, this last short, steep leg offers a unique opportunity to see breeding species typically confined to the deep forests of the Rocky Mountains farther north. On the penultimate curve below the summit, there is a stand of Corkbark Fir, probably marooned here since the last ice age, 11,000 years before the present. This cool, moist north-facing slope also hosts graceful sprays of Rocky Mountain Maple and deep groves of Quaking Aspen. Nesting species here are Cordilleran Flycatcher (summer), Golden-crowned Kinglet, and Pine Siskin.

Bracken-choked glades and meadows, often created artificially by early logging or construction activities, radiate from the summit of Mount Lemmon. Snowberry, Gooseberry, and Scouler Willow thickets fringing these clearings represent the last remnants of the relict habitat used by breeding Orange-crowned Warblers in the Santa Catalina Mountains. Since a damp, iris-trimmed patch near Summerhaven was bulldozed by developers in the early

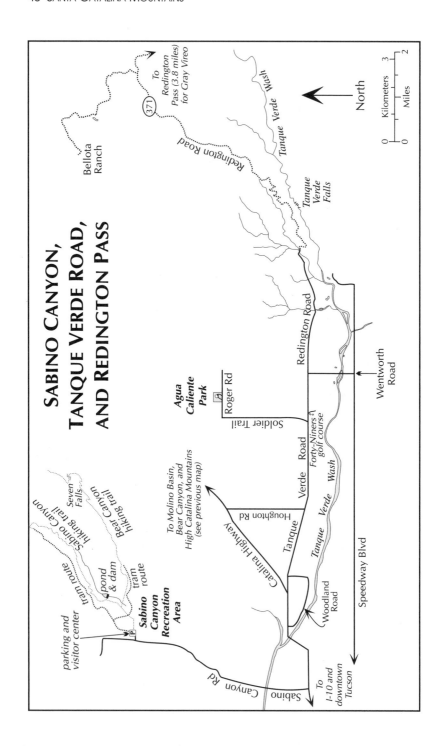

SABINO CANYON,
TANQUE VERDE ROAD,
AND REDINGTON PASS

1950s, there are no other known nesting locations for Orange-crowned Warblers in the range.

Mount Lemmon has no view from the summit. But a short trail (0.6 mile) leads to Lemmon Rock Lookout at 8,800 feet. As the path descends through a remnant burned-over forest of Ponderosa Pine, Southwestern White Pine, and Douglas-fir en route to the stupendous monolith on which the lookout perches, watch for Mountain Chickadees, Pygmy Nuthatches, Grace's (summer), Red-faced (summer), and Olive Warblers, Chipping Sparrows, Yellow-eyed Juncos, and Red Crossbills (irregular). The lookout itself seems to be balanced on a granite egg 1,500 feet above the 56,933-acre Pusch Ridge Wilderness Area. Lemmon Rock makes a tremendous observation dome from which to watch for Short-tailed, Zone-tailed, and Red-tailed Hawks, and Peregrine Falcons soaring by on the updrafts, while Tucson shimmers like a mirage in the desert heat over a vertical mile below.

SABINO CANYON
(9 miles/one-half day)

The starting point is the intersection of Sabino Canyon and Tanque Verde Roads. Turn left (north) onto Sabino (sah-BEE-no) Canyon Road and continue to the Sabino Canyon Recreation Area (4.5 miles).

At the entrance to the recreation area, turn right into the large parking lot. There is a Forest User Fee for the Santa Catalina Ranger District, including Sabino Canyon Recreation Area, payable at the booth as you enter the parking area. (Fees are $5/day, $10/week, or $20/year; Golden Eagle, Golden Age, or Golden Access cards accepted. National Parks Pass not accepted.) Permits purchased here are also good for Mount Lemmon and the Catalina Highway, for Madera Canyon in the Santa Rita Mountains, and for National Forest fee areas in the Chiricahua Mountains.

The small visitor center is open from 8:00 a.m. to 4:30 p.m. weekdays, and from 8:30 a.m. to 4:30 p.m. on weekends and holidays, closed Thanksgiving and Christmas. Birders will probably arrive before the Forest Service opens shop, but the facility provides an interesting and welcome rest stop when you return. Be sure to check the exhibits and inspect the book store. For more information call the Catalina Ranger District at 520-749-8700, or check the Sabino Canyon website (www.sabinocanyon.org).

Watch for Gambel's Quail, Greater Roadrunner, Cactus Wren, Northern Cardinal, and Pyrrhuloxia at the ticket booth by the tram stop. Tickets for the Sabino Canyon Shuttle cost $6 per adult, $2.50 for ages 3–12, and run hourly from 9:00-4:00 July through November, and every half hour, 9:00 to 4:30, December through June. The 45-minute ride takes you to the end of the Sabino Canyon Road (3.8 miles) and back again. A separate shuttle into Bear Canyon goes 2.5 miles to the Lower Bear Picnic Area and the Seven Falls Trailhead: $3 per adult, $1 for ages 3–12, hourly, 9:00 a.m. to 4:00 p.m. year round. Both shuttles allow you to disembark or board at any time. For more information call 520-749-2861.

The trams are contracted to a private firm, and the Sabino Canyon trip includes a narrated program over loudspeakers which will interest first-time visitors. Sabino Canyon is a picturesque spot where Saguaros march down to meet sparkling green Fremont Cottonwoods and Arizona Sycamores along a beautiful little stream, all against a backdrop of stupendous cliffs. The knife-like ridge that divides Sabino from Bear Canyon towers over 2,500 feet above.

Given its dramatic scenery and its proximity to Tucson, you can expect to share Sabino Canyon with other nature lovers. On a typical day Sabino receives 2,700 visitors. The Coronado National Forest estimates that annual visitation exceeds one million people. *Hint: birders should try to avoid weekends.*

To dodge the crowds and partake of a slice of the solitude that used to characterize Sabino, arrive early and plan to hike. Don't forget a water bottle —*the water in the stream is unsafe to drink.* A 2.2-mile loop hike, including Sabino Dam, takes birders through a variety of habitats. Leave from the far right (southeast) corner of the visitor center parking area. A wide trail parallels the Forest Service boundary fence for 0.4 mile to Bear Canyon Road. Follow Bear Canyon Road east for another 0.4 mile to a paved road junction near the restrooms at Bear Canyon tram stop number two, just short of Sabino Creek. (Shuttle-users should ride the Bear Canyon tram to this stop.) Turn left (north) here, following signs to Sabino Dam West. It is 0.3 mile to the end of the road at the Lower Sabino Picnic Area. A small, one-acre pond lies upstream behind a Civilian Conservation Corps rock-and-concrete dam. In spring and fall the large willows around the pond and elsewhere along the creek host many migrants. Oddities have occurred here over the years, including Purple Gallinule, Great Kiskadee, and Winter Wren. Southeastern Arizona's fourth record of Blue-headed Vireo put in a brief appearance here in October 2004.

Some of the resident birds to watch for are Cooper's Hawk, Red-tailed Hawk, Gambel's Quail, Mourning Dove, Greater Roadrunner, White-throated Swift, Gila and Ladder-backed Woodpeckers, Gilded Flicker, Northern Beardless-Tyrannulet, Black Phoebe, Common Raven, Verdin, Cactus, Canyon, and Rock Wrens (more common in winter), Black-tailed Gnatcatcher, Northern Mockingbird, Curve-billed Thrasher, Phainopepla, Black-throated Sparrow, House Finch, and Lesser Goldfinch.

In summer check the entrances of Saguaro Cactus cavities for sleeping Elf Owls. Also summering here are White-winged Dove, Lesser Nighthawk (dawn and dusk), Broad-billed and Black-chinned Hummingbirds, Ash-throated and Brown-crested Flycatchers, Bell's Vireo, Lucy's Warbler, Bronzed Cowbird, and Hooded and Scott's Orioles. In winter towees are numerous. It is possible to see Green-tailed, Spotted, Canyon, and Abert's Towhees all foraging practically simultaneously beneath a single picnic table in Lower Sabino on a winter morning. Black-chinned Sparrow is uncommon but regular in winter.

To complete the loop back to the visitor center, continue past the dam for 0.2 mile to a trail junction. Take the Bluff Trail 0.2 mile to join the Upper Sabino Canyon Road. From here, it is 0.6 mile left (southwest) to the visitor center and parking area. With extra time, you may detour to the right from here on Upper Sabino Canyon Road as it follows Sabino Creek for 3.2 miles. During sporadic winters American Dippers take advantage of the numerous cascades and falls along the stream. Check beneath bridges created by the CCC when Sabino Canyon Road was built in the 1930s.

TANQUE VERDE ROAD AND REDINGTON PASS

(54 miles/one day)

The first half of this trip visits a series of mesquite bosques and oases adjacent to Tanque Verde Road in northeast Tucson. Redington Pass, which divides the Santa Catalina from the Rincon Mountains, is the last half of the trip. Either part of the Tanque Verde Road/Redington Pass trip is perfect for a half-day outing. To begin the full tour or to do either half-day segment, turn east onto Tanque Verde Road at the intersection with Sabino Canyon Road.

Vermilion Flycatchers link all of the areas along Tanque Verde Road. The first locale to check for these brilliant red birds is **Woodland Road**, the first turnoff on the right (south) after Tanque Verde crosses the long bridge over Tanque Verde Wash (0.3 mile past the wash; 1.6 miles east of the starting point).

Real-estate prices are high along Woodland Road. These spacious properties are situated on the broad, level terrace just north of the stream, where silt deposition over the millennia has fostered deep, rich soils. A mesquite bosque—or woodland—formerly flourished along the banks of Tanque Verde Wash. Many grand old trees remain, some over 30 feet high. Homeowners have cleared others to create horse pastures. This is wonderful habitat for Vermilion Flycatchers. Other species to look for in this area of shade and pasture include American Kestrel, Gambel's Quail, White-winged (a few overwinter) and Mourning Doves, Greater Roadrunner, Lesser Nighthawk (summer), Gila Woodpecker, Gilded Flicker, Western Kingbird (summer), Barn Swallow (summer), Mountain Bluebird (irregular in winter), Northern Mockingbird, Cedar Waxwing (winter), Phainopepla, Orange-crowned Warbler (winter), Lucy's Warbler (summer), "Audubon's" Yellow-rumped Warbler (winter), Northern Cardinal, White-crowned Sparrow (winter), Great-tailed Grackle, House Finch, and Lesser Goldfinch. Unfortunately, European Starlings and House Sparrows are common. A pecan orchard (0.8 mile) halfway along Woodland is a convenient place to park and check for all of these birds. During winter watch for possible Lewis's Woodpeckers on conspicuous perches and Red-naped Sapsuckers on the trunks of the pecans.

Woodland Road, shaped like a horseshoe, rejoins Tanque Verde Road just 100 yards east of the turnoff to the Catalina Highway (1.6 mile). Turn right (east) onto Tanque Verde. The left (north) turnoff on Soldier Trail (3.4 miles) for **Agua Caliente Park** is well signed. Turn right (east) onto Roger Road (1.9 miles), then left (north) at the prominent entrance (0.5 mile) to access the parking area. Agua Caliente, Spanish for "warm water," refers to the perennial spring that feeds the main pond. A line of palm trees running east from the large pond leads to the nearby spring.

Roadrunner during Painted Lady irruption
Narca Moore-Craig

Surrounded by palms, cottonwoods, and tamarisk, this lovely 2.5-acre pond is a magnet for both waterfowl and desert species alike. Ordinarily a Great Blue Heron or a Green Heron is stalking the shallows, and a handful of dabblers and American Coots are plying the open water. Also watch for Wood Ducks here. This is one of the best places in the Tucson basin for Sora. Look for them along the edge of the tules that line most of the far side of the pond. Sometimes hundreds of roosting Red-winged Blackbirds blacken the cattails and the surrounding trees.

The tall trees at Agua Caliente provide excellent habitat for Great Horned Owls, as well as a variety of other birds. Both Broad-billed and Black-chinned Hummingbirds nest here, as do Northern Beardless-Tyrannulet, Vermilion Flycatcher, Bell's Vireo, Lucy's Warbler, Northern Cardinal, and Hooded Oriole. Most winters an Osprey is present. In the winter of 2001–2002 both a Brown Thrasher and an Ovenbird were skulking in the vicinity of the bridge on the east end of the main pond. Several additional small ponds are located just another 100 yards farther along the trail after the bridge. Dense brush along the edges of the trail is good for Green-tailed Towhee in winter, as well as an occasional Bobcat.

Soldier Trail rejoins Tanque Verde Road opposite the long, false-adobe fence of the Forty-Niners Golf Course. Turn left (east) to continue this trip. The entrance to the golf course (0.15 mile) is marked by enormous double pylons on either side, but unless you arrive very early, golfers will have flushed all the birds. Anyway, birders are not permitted on the paths after 8:00 a.m.

A better bet is to continue east to Wentworth Road (0.9 mile), and turn right (south) to access **Tanque Verde Wash** (0.6 mile). Park on the near bank for birding. *Do not attempt to cross Tanque Verde after heavy storms, if there are barriers in place, or if you have any doubt about the depth of the water.* One of the Sonoran Desert's regrettable but oft-repeated initiation rites for newcomers and the unwary is to drown their vehicles—and occasionally the occupants—in these normally "dry" desert rivers. Tanque Verde Wash consumes cars every year.

Once again the first bird you see as you exit your car may be a Vermilion Flycatcher. Check for it in the pasture on the left (east) side of the road. A barbed-wire fence cuts off access upstream, but the broad, sandy wash provides an open route west down Tanque Verde. Thick trees and brush along the banks may harbor summering Gila and Ladder-backed Woodpeckers, Gilded Flicker, Northern Beardless-Tyrannulet, Bell's Vireo, Lucy's Warbler, Yellow-breasted Chat, Summer Tanager, Blue Grosbeak, and Abert's Towhee. In winter search the same areas for Orange-crowned and Yellow-rumped Warblers, Green-tailed Towhee, and a variety of sparrows. White-crowns are usually the most abundant, but other wintering sparrows that occur here include Chipping, Brewer's, Black-chinned, Lark, Black-throated, Savannah, Fox (rare), Song, and White-throated (rare).

Tanque Verde is also perfect habitat for migrant warblers. The most common are MacGillivray's and Wilson's. Surprise Eastern vagrants such as Nashville, Northern Parula, Chestnut-sided, "Myrtle" Yellow-rumped, and Black-and-white Warblers, as well as American Redstart, have also occurred. A Magnolia Warbler was in the wash in October 2003. Years separate the sighting reports for some of these species.

Return to the pavement—now officially known as Redington Road—and consider how much time you have budgeted for this tour. To the left (west) lies Tucson (8.25 miles to the starting pointing at the intersection with Sabino Canyon Road). To the right (east) the pavement ends at a major tributary that feeds Tanque Verde Wash (2.8 miles). Steep, rocky, dusty, and wash-boarded, Redington Road snakes its way up to the pinyon-juniper woodland and interior chaparral of the Upper Sonoran Life Zone. **Redington Pass** has proven a reliable location for Gray Vireo (11.2 miles beyond the end of the pavement, 3.8 miles beyond the Bellota Ranch Road junction), an otherwise difficult-to-locate species in Southeastern Arizona.

If winter storms have closed the Catalina Highway, Redington Pass offers an access point to a new community of birds in the immediate vicinity of Tucson. Some of these include Acorn Woodpecker, Western Scrub- and Mexican Jays, both Bridled and Juniper Titmice, Bushtit, Blue-gray Gnatcatcher, Western and Mountain (irregular) Bluebirds, Crissal Thrasher, Spotted Towhee, and Black-chinned Sparrow. In summer additional species include Cassin's Kingbird, Plumbeous Vireo (more common than Gray Vireo), and Black-throated Gray Warbler.

Care is needed to distinguish Gray Vireo from the Plumbeous Vireo that breeds in Redington Pass. Neither species has any tinge of yellow. The bold white spectacles that join in a crisply demarcated line above the Plumbeous's bill, give the Plumbeous an acute, "scholastic" expression quite distinct from the vague, mild-looking face of the Gray Vireo. Note that the Gray has a thin eye ring that does not fuse on the forehead. Gray Vireo also lacks the heavy, double white wing bars of a Plumbeous. If you can't decide whether the wing bars are heavy or fine, it's a Plumbeous. At first glance, the brownish-gray wings of a Gray Vireo often do not seem to have wing bars at all. Unless you really are an expert on the songs of both species, don't make your call based on vocalizations. Variations in the song of Plumbeous account for almost all sound identifications of Gray Vireo in Southeastern Arizona.

It is about 22 miles back to the starting point in Tucson on the Redington/Tanque Verde Road.

CAMPGROUNDS, RESTAURANTS, AND ACCOMMODATIONS

There are four Forest Service campgrounds in the Santa Catalina Mountains. Molino Basin (4,500 feet) is open September to May. The Gordon Hirabayashi Recreation Site (also known as the Prison Camp; 5,000 feet) is open for camping year round. Rose Canyon (7,000 feet) and Spencer Canyon (8,000 feet) are summer-only (April to October) high-elevation campgrounds. Call the Catalina Ranger District at 520-749-8700 or visit their website at www.fs.fed.us/r3/coronado for additional information. Motels and hotels are abundant in Tucson.

Two restaurants continue service following the Aspen Fire. The Iron Door Restaurant (520-576-1321) in the Mount Lemmon Ski Valley has a full menu for lunch and offers breakfast on weekends. The Mount Lemmon Cafe in Summerhaven (520-576-1234) is open daily for lunch, opening earlier for breakfast throughout the summer and on winter weekends.

Local guide referrals for the Tucson area as well as all Southeastern Arizona are available from Tucson Audubon Society (300 E. University Boulevard #120, Tucson, AZ 85705; 520-629-0510; www.tucsonaudubon.org).

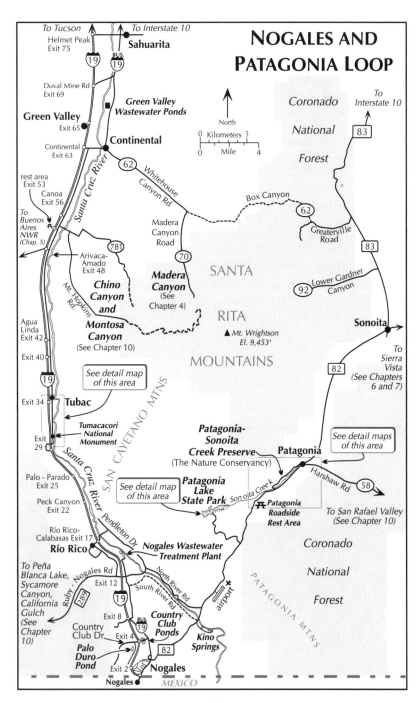

NOGALES AND PATAGONIA LOOP

To Tucson
Helmet Peak
Exit 75

To Interstate 10

Sahuarita

19 BUS. 19

Duval Mine Rd
Exit 69

Coronado

To
Interstate 10

Green Valley
Wastewater Ponds

National

83

Green Valley
Exit 65

Forest

Continental
Exit 63

Continental

North

0 Kilometers 5

0 Mile 4

62

Whitehouse Canyon Rd

Box Canyon

62

rest area
Exit 53

Canoa
Exit 56

To
Buenos
Aires
NWR
(Chap. 5)

Santa Cruz River

Madera
Canyon
Road

Greaterville
Road

83

781

Arivaca-
Amado
Exit 48

70

SANTA

92 Lower Gardner Canyon

Chino
Canyon
and

Madera
Canyon
(See
Chapter 4)

RITA

Sonoita

Agua
Linda
Exit 42

Mt. Hopkins Rd.

Montosa
Canyon
(See Chapter 10)

▲ Mt. Wrightson
El. 9,453'

To
Sierra
Vista
(See Chapters
6 and 7)

Exit 40

MOUNTAINS

82

19

See detail map
of this area

SAN CAYETANO MTNS

Exit 34

Tubac

Tumacacori
National
Monument

Patagonia-
Sonoita
Creek Preserve
(The Nature Conservancy)

Patagonia

See detail maps
of this area

Exit
29

Santa Cruz River

Palo - Parado
Exit 25

See detail map
of this area

Patagonia
Lake
State Park

Sonoita Creek

Harshaw Rd

58

Peck Canyon
Exit 22

Pendleton Dr.

Patagonia
Roadside
Rest Area

To San Rafael Valley
(See Chapter 10)

Río Rico-
Calabasas Exit 17

Río Rico

Nogales Wastewater
Treatment Plant

Coronado

To Peña
Blanca Lake,
Sycamore
Canyon,
California
Gulch
(See
Chapter
10)

Ruby - Nogales Rd

Nogales Rd

Exit 12

289

North River Rd

South River Rd

19

National

PATAGONIA MTNS

Forest

Exit 8

Country
Club Dr.

BUS. 19

Country
Club
Ponds

airport

Country
Club Dr.

Exit 4

Kino
Springs

Palo
Duro
Pond

Exit 2

82

Nogales

Nogales ●

MEXICO

54

CHAPTER 3

NOGALES AND PATAGONIA LOOP

(181 miles/two days)

This tour follows the green cottonwoods of the Santa Cruz River upstream (south) to Nogales, then loops around the south end of the Santa Rita Mountains to Patagonia at the verdant headwaters of Sonoita (*so-NOY-tah*) Creek. From here, the route crosses a lush grassland east of the Santa Ritas before dropping back to the desert at Tucson.

There are many good birding areas along the way, but the most outstanding are near Patagonia. Probably more rarities and vagrants are discovered annually in the vicinity of Patagonia than in any other area in Southeastern Arizona. To properly bird Patagonia Lake, the feeders at the Patons' home, The Nature Conservancy's Patagonia-Sonoita Creek Preserve, and the Patagonia Roadside Rest Area, plan to spend a night either here or in nearby Nogales. Patagonia is also the best place to begin a winter birding excursion out to the San Rafael Valley (Chapter 10).

From the starting point at the intersection of Interstates 10 and 19 in Tucson, go south on I-19 toward Nogales. *Note: this is the only highway in the United States signed in kilometers.* Exit numbers are useful, but they will not agree with a trip odometer on U.S. cars. Plans are underway, however, to revert to miles.

Much of Arizona's history in the 17th and 18th centuries occurred in the Santa Cruz River Valley. Visible on the right near the river crossing (6.0 miles) are the white dome and towers of San Xavier (*sahn-ah-VEER*) Mission, founded by Father Kino in 1700. (For details on birding the Mission, see Chapter 1.) Along the river on the left are irrigated pastures where once stood a forest of giant mesquite trees. Until 1945 the Santa Cruz flowed permanently above the ground through the San Xavier Reservation. This *bosque*, or wood-land, was the home of thousands of White-winged Doves and other birds, including Gray Hawks and Common Black-Hawks.

Steadily increasing demands on the upper watershed, as well as in Tucson, finally bled the river dry after World War II. There was a wholesale die-off of mesquite. With the trees went the wildlife. Members of the Tohono O'odham tribe chopped down the dead mesquite forest for firewood, and now only these blackened stumps remain. The death of the lower Santa Cruz River at Tucson is one of the saddest chapters in human-wildlife interactions in the 20th century in Southeastern Arizona.

For a preview of future changes, look ahead on the right at the huge and barren piles of tailings from a copper pit. Eventually much of the West may look like this if the mining industry continues to gouge the earth in search of copper, coal, and other ores without proper environmental safeguards. Several wells in Green Valley (16.2 miles) have been abandoned in recent years as a consequence of groundwater pollution from the mines.

As you continue south down the interstate you will pass the exits for two birding areas described later in the text. The first is Madera Canyon in the Santa Rita Mountains at Exit 63 for Continental (1.3 miles). Madera Canyon is featured in the next chapter. Canoa Interchange, Exit 56 (4.2 miles), is the departure point for the Chino and Montosa Canyons side trip, if you have the time or inclination (Chapter 10).

Exit 53, the Amado Roadside Rest Area (2.0 miles), provides an excellent introduction to the birds of the Santa Cruz River Valley. Featured here is nesting Rufous-winged Sparrow, a species largely confined to the lower Santa Cruz watershed as a breeding bird within Arizona and the United States. Listen for its distinctive *chip-chip-trill* song in the mesquite behind the shaded picnic tables. Other typical Sonoran desert birds here are Gila Woodpecker, Bell's Vireo (summer), Verdin, Cactus Wren, Curve-billed Thrasher, Pyrrhuloxia, and Black-throated Sparrow. The manager's house on the south end of the rest area is a miniature oasis with a small lawn and a few big willows. Birds to watch for here include Cooper's Hawk, Gambel's Quail, Vermilion Flycatcher, and—in summer—Lucy's Warbler, and both Hooded and Bullock's Orioles.

Exit 48 at Arivaca/Amado (5.3 miles) marks the beginning of the Arivaca Cienaga/Buenos Aires Wildlife Refuge Loop (Chapter 5). Next stop on this tour is the renowned artists' community at **Tubac**, Exit 34 (8.7 miles). Tubac began life as a *visita,* or part-time mission, established by the Jesuit padres in 1691. The Pima Revolt in 1751 led the Spanish to construct Arizona's first *presidio*—walled fortress—here in 1752. In 1775 Captain Juan Bautista de Anza left Tubac on the California expedition that gave rise to present-day San Francisco. A frequent target of Apache raids, Tubac was deserted several times before it was finally sacked and burned to the ground in 1849.

Two intrepid prospectors, Charles Poston and Henry Ehrenberg, re-stored life to the little hamlet in 1854. Arizona's first newspaper was printed here in 1858, and by 1859 the population was approximately 800. But over the next few turbulent decades the residents of Tubac fled to nearby Tucson again and again as Native Americans besieged their settlement. Continuous occu-pation of the site did not really begin until early in the 20th century. Now Tubac is an arts and crafts center, with a museum and a state historical park.

To bird Tubac leave I-19 at Exit 34, go under the freeway, and turn left (north) on the Frontage Road (0.6 mile). Follow the Frontage Road to the prominent entrance to the town (0.4 mile). Bear right around the boutiques that crowd the principal boulevard, and continue east until the pavement makes a right angle turn at Tubac Presidio State Historic Park (0.3 mile); park in the visitor center parking lot (museum admission $3). The trail begins across the street in the picnic area.

B irders should arrive early to hike the **Juan Bautista de Anza Trail**. The elevation of the Santa Cruz River at Tubac is only 3,200 feet, and most of the year the temperature climbs rapidly after sunrise. Except in win-ter, bird activity almost ceases after 10 a.m.

Vermilion Flycatchers are permanent residents in the picnic area at the trailhead. The 1.25 miles to the first river crossing offer a good cross-section of birding opportunities along the entire 4.5-mile-long path between Tubac Presidio and Tumacacori Mission. The trail threads in and out of a mesquite bosque and eventually reaches strands of Fremont Cottonwood on the river bank. Melting adobe walls near the beginning of the broad, well-signed trail are almost all that remain of the first two centuries of the town's history.

In summer watch for Gray Hawk, White-winged Dove, Yellow-billed Cuckoo, Broad-billed and Black-chinned Hummingbirds, Bell's Vireo, Lucy's Warbler, Yellow-breasted Chat, Summer Tanager, Blue Grosbeak, and Hooded and Bullock's Orioles. In winter look for Sharp-shinned and Coo-per's Hawks, Gray Flycatcher, Anna's and Costa's Hummingbirds, Red-naped Sapsucker, House Wren, Yellow-rumped Warbler, and a host of sparrows—especially Chippers, Savannahs, and White-crowns. Year-round residents in-clude Great Blue Heron, Mourning and Inca Doves, Gila Woodpecker, Gilded Flicker, Northern Beardless-Tyrannulet, Common Raven, Bewick's Wren, Phainopepla, Northern Cardinal, Pyrrhuloxia, Canyon and Abert's Towhees, and Lesser Goldfinch. This section of the Santa Cruz River is perhaps at its best during fall migration. From late September through October the cotton-woods host migrating flocks of Plumbeous and Warbling Vireos mixed with Orange-crowned, Black-throated Gray, and Yellow Warblers. Fields are alive with Lazuli Buntings, Blue Grosbeaks, and Lincoln's Sparrows.

Birders hiking the de Anza Trail should *plan on carrying plenty of water*, es-pecially in the summer; the water in the river is not potable. En route to Tumacacori the trail crosses the Santa Cruz several times, and walkers need to be prepared to wade. *Do not attempt to cross the river if the water is high.* This trail is located on an easement through private property; both camping and off-trail use are prohibited.

There is no need to re-enter the interstate to access Tumacacori. Simply stay on the Frontage Road south from the underpass road to the old church (2.4 miles). (If you elected not to visit Tubac, take Interstate 19 Exit 29 for Tumacacori 3.1 miles south of Tubac, cross under the freeway, and go north on the Frontage Road 0.7 mile.)

Tumacacori (*tuma-COCK-or-ee*) **National Monument** preserves one of the missions founded by the Jesuits in northern Mexico and southern Arizona some 300 years ago. Father Eusebio Kino built the first structure here in 1701, but the present adobe church probably dates from the Franciscan era in the 1790s. By the mid-19th century, under continuous pressure from the Apaches, the mission was abandoned. It came under the protection of the National Park Service in 1908.

To bird Tumacacori, park off the north (Tubac) end of the stuccoed adobe wall enclosing the ruins, and walk north up the Frontage Road (0.1 mile) to find the de Anza Trailhead at a gate in the fence. The first half-mile of the trail leads east to the Santa Cruz, where a wintering Rose-throated Becard and a Painted Redstart were discovered in early 2004. Then the route turns left (north) and follows the west bank of the river. The first crossing is another 0.75 mile downstream from the trailhead. It is a total of 4.5 miles to the end of the trail at Tubac. If you can budget a half-day for a hike, and if you can find someone who shares your interest in the area, the de Anza Trail makes a perfect place for a car-key swap at the midpoint. Or you can always ask a sympathetic spouse to wait for you at the far end. Birds here are the same as those mentioned above for Tubac.

To continue the main tour, follow the Frontage Road south from Tumacacori to the turnoff that leads under the freeway (0.7 mile), turn right, go under it, and turn left to access Interstate 19 (0.2 mile).

Río **Rico** (7.5 miles) at Exit 17 is usually the nearest location to Tucson for Tropical Kingbird (summer). Turn left (east) over the interstate and follow the pavement around a long curve north until the road turns right (east) and crosses the Santa Cruz River on a narrow bridge (0.5 mile). *Do not pause on the bridge; traffic is heavy on Río Rico and the approach is blind.* Just beyond the bridge the pavement divides on either side of a broad, bare median which provides a safe parking area overlooking pastures both north and south of the road. Small ponds are in the near (northeast) corners of the two large pastures on the south side of the road. During summer the Tropical Kingbirds tend to perch on the barbed wire along the right (south) side of the road, but don't neglect the small trees on the fenceline and tall weed stalks in the pastures. Other species to watch for in the floodplain here include Gray Hawk (summer), Ladder-backed Woodpecker, Northern Beardless-Tyrannulet,

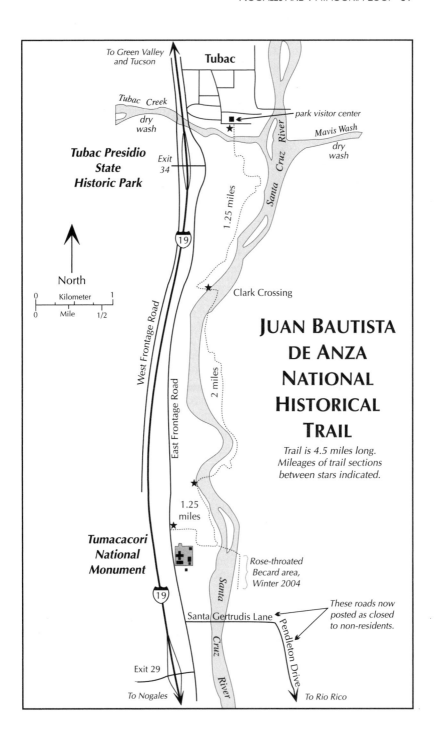

To Green Valley
and Tucson

Tubac

Tubac Creek
dry
wash

park visitor center

Mavis Wash
dry
wash

**Tubac Presidio
State
Historic Park**

Exit
34

Santa Cruz River

1.25 miles

North

| 0 | Kilometer | 1 |
| 0 | Mile | 1/2 |

19

Clark Crossing

West Frontage Road

East Frontage Road

2 miles

**JUAN BAUTISTA
DE ANZA
NATIONAL
HISTORICAL
TRAIL**

*Trail is 4.5 miles long.
Mileages of trail sections
between stars indicated.*

1.25
miles

**Tumacacori
National
Monument**

Rose-throated
Becard area,
Winter 2004

19

Santa Cruz River

Santa Gertrudis Lane

Pendleton Drive

These roads now
posted as closed
to non-residents.

Exit 29

To Nogales

To Rio Rico

Black Phoebe, Vermilion Flycatcher, Ash-throated and Brown-crested Fly-catchers (summer), Cassin's and Western Kingbirds (summer), Northern Rough-winged, Cliff, and Barn Swallows (summer), Verdin, Phainopepla, American Pipit (winter), Bell's Vireo (summer), Lucy's Warbler and Yellow-breasted Chat (summer), Summer Tanager (summer), Pyrrhuloxia, Blue Grosbeak (summer), Lazuli Bunting (primarily migration), Green-tailed (winter) and Abert's Towhees, Rufous-winged and Lark Sparrows, Bronzed Cowbirds (summer), Bullock's Oriole (summer), and Lesser Goldfinch. A Tricolored Heron was using a pond here in late July 2002, and an immature Roseate Spoonbill idled away late August and much of September 2004 at the same location. If the fields are flooded watch for Black-bellied Whistling-Ducks and White-faced Ibis in the wet furrows. Turn around at the intersection with Pendleton Drive (0.8 mile) to return to the freeway.

Continue south to access the **Nogales Sewage Ponds.** *Please note: the Nogales Sewage Ponds were closed for renovation in 2003, and in 2004 there was still no firm date when they would be re-opened. Leave Interstate 19 at Ruby Road, Exit 12 (10.6 miles from the Tumacacori Exit; 3.1 miles from Río Rico) and turn left to cross over to the Frontage Road (0.5 mile) on the east side. Turn left (north) and go to a group of warehouses on the right. Watch between the buildings for a small road on the right that crosses the railroad tracks (1.0 mile) and then jogs left to the sewage ponds (0.1 mile). The sign that formerly marked the turnoff was removed in 1993. You must register at the office for permission to bird around the ponds, and you must also sign-out when you leave. Before closing for renovations, this 90-acre facility was usually open daily from 7:00 a.m. to 4:00 p.m.*

The Nogales Sewage Ponds typically harbor one of the largest concentrations of wintering waterfowl in Southeastern Arizona. There are ordinarily no fewer than one thousand ducks on the 17 ponds from November through March; sometimes there are several times that number. While the smallest pond is only a couple of acres, the weedy overflow reservoir on the north end of the facility is a substantial 23 surface acres when full. A scope is definitely an asset here. Nogales often produces 15 or mores species of waterfowl in mid-winter.

The most abundant ducks are Mallard, Northern Pintail, Northern Shoveler, American Wigeon, and Ruddy Duck, but there are always a smattering of other species, too. These include all the teal, Gadwall, Canvasback, Redhead, Ring-necked Duck, and Lesser Scaup. Also usually present are one or a few Common Goldeneye, Bufflehead, or Common Merganser—or some other duck seemingly wholly misplaced in the arid Santa Cruz Valley. A gorgeous drake Eurasian Wigeon appeared at Nogales in January 1993 and stayed until mid-April. It, or another, wintered at Nogales the next several years.

Never dependable, Black-bellied Whistling-Ducks are also frequent visitors at the Nogales Sewage Ponds.

A wide spectrum of other birds enjoy the 50-plus acres of water at Nogales. This is one of the best locations in the southeast corner for a flock of Black Vultures year round, and a lone Turkey Vulture in winter. Also watch for Great Blue Heron, Northern Harrier (winter), Gray Hawk (summer), American Coot, Killdeer, Spotted Sandpiper (winter), Black Phoebe, six species of swallows (summer and migration), Common Raven, American Pipit (winter), Common Yellowthroat, Yellow-breasted Chat (summer), Bobolink (rare, migrant), Red-winged and Brewer's (winter) Blackbirds, and House Finch. Southeastern Arizona's third record of a White Ibis was present from early July through mid-September 1999.

Fluctuating water levels in the huge north reservoir create a series of mud flats, channels, and weedy vegetation perfect for waterbirds. Check the north pond for geese and ducks, egrets, White-faced Ibis, plovers, sandpipers, gulls, and terns.

Return to Ruby Road and cross back to the west side of the interstate. Peña Blanca Lake, Sycamore Canyon, and California Gulch (all described in Chapter 10) are located off Ruby Road to the west. To continue the Nogales/Patagonia tour, turn left (south) back onto Interstate 19. Move into the left lane to take the first Nogales off-ramp, Exit 8 (2.2 miles). You are now driving south on Grand Avenue (Business 19). Be prepared for an abrupt right turn at the first paved road on the right, Country Club Drive (1.0 mile).

This is an optional side trip to several small ponds. Country Club Ponds (aka Drive-In Theatre Ponds) are located on both sides of the road 0.2 mile west of Grand Avenue (Business 19). It is unsafe to park directly in front of the ponds. Park near the overpass for I-19 and walk back. Country Club Ponds are excellent for Virginia Rail. They even breed here. The ponds are also a good location for Sora for virtually the entire year except June. Vermilion Flycatchers and Yellow-rumped Warblers dart among the bare boughs of the willows throughout the winter.

Country Club Ponds would be a wonderful birding site if it were not for the murderous onslaught of commuter traffic throughout the day. Given the narrow shoulder, it is all too easy to image yourself splattered across the landscape like a crate of ripe tomatoes.

A better option is to continue under the overpass for Interstate 19 to the frontage road on the west side (0.5 mile). Go straight ahead at the first stop sign for the frontage road and proceed about 100 yards to a wide pullout on the right (north) across the road from **Palo Duro Pond**. The best viewing of this 250-yard-long golf course pond is from the north end, 50 yards south of Country Club Drive. To access the low dam, skirt the golf course; do not interfere with the golfers, even if it means walking through weeds. An overgrown trail-of-use out onto the dam on the north end offers views of the grassy golf course coming down to the water's edge on its west bank, along with mud flats bordered by reeds, drowned dead trees, and open water in the center. Watch for herons and egrets on the shoreline, shorebirds on the mud flats, Virginia Rail and Sora at the edge of the reeds, Neotropic and Double-crested Cormorants in the dead trees, and grebes and ducks in the open water. The line of willows overhanging the water on the east edge of the pond, parallel to the frontage road, is good for warblers and—sporadically—Green Kingfisher. An Osprey is frequently present during migration periods, either in the dead trees in the center of the pond or perched in big trees on the south end. Among the regular species found here are Pied-billed Grebe, Great Blue and Green Herons, Great Egret, Black-bellied Whistling-Duck, Gadwall (breeding), Cinnamon Teal, Black Phoebe, Bewick's Wren, Phainopepla, Common Yellowthroat, Song Sparrow, and Lesser Goldfinch. In summer watch for Gray Hawk, Cassin's and Western Kingbirds, Yellow Warbler, Yellow-breasted Chat, and Bullock's Oriole. Winter birds include Marsh Wren, Yellow-rumped Warbler, Green-tailed Towhee, and—occasionally—Lawrence's Goldfinch. Lazuli Bunting and Blue Grosbeak are common migrants. Among the surprises at Palo Duro have been a Tricolored Heron in August 2002 and again in October 2003, presumably the same Roseate Spoonbill that wound up at Río Rico in August 2004, and a Caspian Tern in May 2000.

There is also a pullout on the south end of Palo Duro Pond, but with a limited view of the water.

Retrace your route back on Country Club Drive, and turn right onto Grand Avenue (Business 19; 0.5 mile) to access Highway 82 in south Nogales (4.0 miles). Get into the right lane and cross the overpass above Grand Avenue (Business 19). The entrance to **Kino Springs** is on the right (south) side of Highway 82 at an elaborately landscaped junction with a stucco wall just west of the Santa Cruz River (4.3 miles).

It pays to watch for birds beginning just inside the turnoff, but *remember to pull completely off Kino Springs Road.* Rock Wrens breed on the rocky hill on the right (west) side of the pavement, and in spring occasionally sing from the stucco wall across the street. Varied Buntings (summer) also inhabit the rocky knoll. Sometimes male Varieds use the powerline on the left side of the pavement as a song perch. Watch for Black Vultures soaring overhead or awaiting updrafts on hillside boulders.

As the road swings away from the little hill, keep an eye peeled for Gray Hawks (summer) near the river. They often use the short utility poles for perches in this comparatively treeless stretch along the Santa Cruz. Other possibilities include Say's Phoebe, Western Kingbird (summer), and Blue Grosbeak (summer). A tall grove of cottonwoods on the left signals the first pond at Kino Springs (1.0 mile). There is ample room to park well off the pavement on either side of the road.

As a consequence of the prolonged drought that hit our area in the mid-1990s, there may not be any water at all in the first pond. It was entirely dry throughout most of 2003, and renovation efforts were underway in 2004. When the first pond is full, some of the birds to look for include Pied-billed Grebe, Great Blue Heron, Green Heron, Virginia Rail, Sora (primarily winter), American Coot, Belted Kingfisher (winter), Black Phoebe, Tropical Kingbird, Vermilion Flycatcher, Marsh Wren (winter), Common Yellowthroat, and Song and Swamp Sparrows (winter). Usually during winter, assuming there is water—and sometimes even in summer—there are a dozen or so ducks on the pond. The most common species are Northern Shoveler, Gadwall, American Wigeon, Ring-necked Duck, and Lesser Scaup, but almost any other duck can and has occurred here.

There are two distinct habitats at the first Kino pond. Each has its own subset of birds, but—as you can imagine—some species freely use both. This is especially true of the dry-land birds that are most common in the big Fremont Cottonwoods and Netleaf Hackberry trees that lie on the far (east) side of the pond. Some of the resident and summering birds to watch for here include Gray Hawk, Common Ground-Dove, Costa's Hummingbird, Gila and Ladder-backed Woodpeckers, Gilded Flicker, Northern Beardless-Tyrannulet, Brown-crested Flycatcher, Cassin's and Western Kingbirds, Verdin, Bushtit, White-breasted Nuthatch, Bewick's Wren, Curve-billed Thrasher, Phainopepla, Bell's Vireo, Lucy's and Yellow Warblers, Summer Tanager, Northern Cardinal, Lazuli and Varied Buntings, Abert's Towhee, Rufous-winged Sparrow (summer, irregular), Hooded and Bullock's Orioles, and Lesser Goldfinch. In winter and migration watch for Northern "Red- shafted" Flicker, Hammond's Flycatcher, Ruby-crowned Kinglet, Mountain Bluebird (irregular), Hermit Thrush, American Robin, Yellow-rumped "Audubon's" Warbler, Western Tanager, Chipping Sparrow, and American Goldfinch. Over the years the first pond area at Kino Springs has hosted many rarities, including Green Kingfisher, Thick-billed Kingbird, Rose-throated Becard, Rufous-backed Robin, and in October 2001, a male Black-throated Blue Warbler.

After birding the first pond area, continue on the road through the Kino Springs Golf Course to access the second pond area. As you pass through the greens you may see Greater Roadrunner, Say's Phoebe, and Western Kingbird (summer). On warm days in the winter a flock of American Wigeon may be grazing on the golf course in a compact flock that's bound to grab your attention. Turn right (0.85 mile) at the clubhouse and park here. Drop by the pro shop to request permission to bird around the pond area across the road. *Do not distract golfers and stay off the golf course itself.* Watch for a ridiculously self-important male Bronzed Cowbird patrolling the immaculately groomed lawn in front of the clubhouse throughout the summer. The trees and shrubbery surrounding the buildings and parking areas are also excellent for Yellow-billed Cuckoo (summer) and Thick-billed Kingbird (summer). In February and March 2003 two Eastern vagrants—a Yellow-bellied Sapsucker and a Palm Warbler—were working the pines and the lone cottonwood between the clubhouse and the pro shop.

Less than three miles from the Mexican border, the 3,700-foot-elevation golf course pond was formerly famous as the premier location for Tropical Kingbird in the United States. The same drought that afflicted the first pond, however, has also devastated the second. Although the pond was renovated, divided into a "split-level" pond, and refilled in 2004, most of the tall cottonwoods along the banks died. Cassin's and Western Kingbirds seem to have weathered the drought without any problems, but Tropical Kingbirds were decidedly scarce in 2002 and 2003. If you are fortunate enough to find a candidate kingbird, look for Tropical's distinctly greenish back, large bill, contrasty dark ear patch, and lack of a dark gray breast. The notched tail may not be visible. Most important, listen for the Tropical Kingbird's twittering, high-pitched song, quite distinct from the guttural *C'mere!* of a Cassin's or the querulous *What-a-deal-we've-got!* call of a Western Kingbird.

Formerly the caved-in old boat dock near the far end of the pond was the best place to look for ducks. Often a flock of Black-bellied Whistling-Ducks was resting on the opposite bank, and if the pond is ever filled again it's a good bet they'll return. From late April to mid-May 1990 the Kino Springs golf course pond hosted a Fulvous Whistling-Duck, strictly a vagrant to Southeastern Arizona. A hybrid Eurasian Wigeon wintered here at least three times in the early 1990s. This was also a reliable site for beautiful male Cinnamon Teal in winter.

Depending on water levels, the swallow flocks can be amazing. During the prolonged migration periods, it is not uncommon to detect five or six species in a single flock of 50 to 500 birds. Two Cave Swallows were even high-graded from one such mixed flock in August 1992. Remember to scan the banks for Green Heron, and check the trees for Gray Hawk (summer), Zone-tailed Hawk (summer), or a sleeping Great Horned Owl. Sometimes a flock of Black-crowned Night-Herons roosts in one of the trees on the far end of the lake.

Red-winged Blackbirds, Yellow-headed Blackbirds (erratic, but especially likely in winter), and Great-tailed Grackles are far more common at the golf course pond than at the first pond. Otherwise the bird lists for both ponds at Kino Springs are much the same. They should both be checked on any trip.

To continue this tour return to Highway 82 and prepare to turn right. *Look both ways.* The Kino Springs junction lies at the bottom of a steep hill on the left with a bridge to the right—traffic can be treacherous. Don't try to pull out onto Highway 82 unless it's clear for a long distance in both directions. After turning right (northeast) onto Highway 82, the road crosses the Santa Cruz River. Here again you may see a Gray Hawk, but remember that it's unsafe to stop or even slow down on the bridge or the curve beyond.

Black-bellied Whistling-Duck
Gail Diane Yovanovich

The next birding site is Nogales Airport (2.7 miles). This is an optional stop only, primarily for Botteri's and Cassin's Sparrows after the summer monsoons have begun. Turn right into the lush mesquite grassland at the airport entrance to find the sparrows.

The left (west) turnoff into **Patagonia Lake State Park** (3.8 miles) leads to a more important stop (see map on next page). This 265-acre lake on lower Sonoita Creek was constructed primarily for fishing and water-skiing in 1968. Since then, however, it has become Southeastern Arizona's only reliable location for Neotropic Cormorant. To find the cormorants follow the paved and winding road to the entrance station (3.9 miles), and then bear right 100 yards later near the bottom of the hill. From here the road runs almost

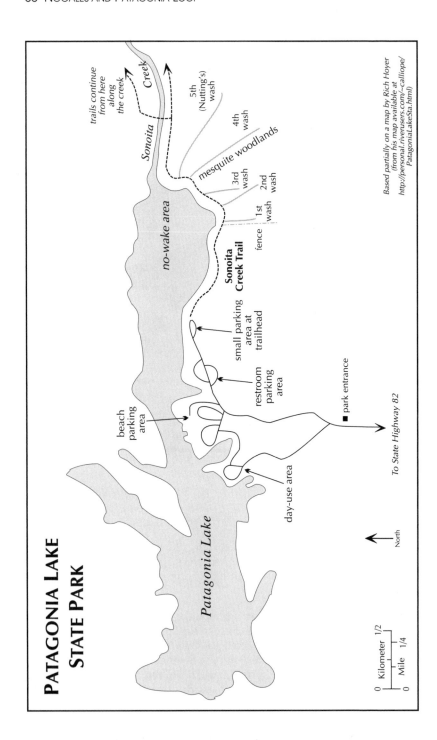

Patagonia Lake State Park

Patagonia Lake

Sonoita Creek

trails continue from here along the creek

5th (Nutting's) wash

4th wash

mesquite woodlands

3rd wash

2nd wash

1st wash

fence

Sonoita Creek Trail

no-wake area

small parking area at trailhead

restroom parking area

beach parking area

day-use area

■ park entrance

To State Highway 82

← North

0 Kilometer 1/2

0 Mile 1/4

Based partially on a map by Rich Hoyer (from his map available at http://personal.riverusers.com/~calliope/PatagoniaLakeSta.html)

straight east through the campground until it ends at the trailhead (0.4 mile). There are only four parking slots, which creates quite a problem on weekends, holidays, or if a rarity has been discovered. At present the *de facto* solution is to park back up the road at the restroom area (0.2 mile), or—if that's full—practically back at the turnoff in the day-use area. *Camp site parking slots, even if vacant, are off-limits for people with day-use permits.* The day-use fee is $7 per car. Day-use hours for non-campers are from 8:00 a.m. to 10:00 p.m. For more information call 520-287-6965. Adjacent Sonoita Creek State Natural Area offers birding walks as well as pontoon boat tours of the lake (520-287-2791).

Views of the "no-wake area" in the upper lake (where larger boats and water-skiing are prohibited) can be had by hiking approximately 50 yards up the trail to a bench. A second opening another 100 yards beyond offers a slightly different perspective. Since the lake is 2.5 miles long and nearly 0.5 mile wide, a scope is nearly essential. Both Double-crested and Neotropic Cormorants share the upper basin, and without a scope it's very difficult to distinguish between these species. One trick for identifying young cormorants at a distance is to remember that immature Neotropics are brown overall and immature Double-cresteds have off-white or pale gray chests. Distant adults, however, appear wholly black. In winter scan the lake carefully for Common Loon (especially near the dam), Pied-billed and Eared Grebes, and deep-water ducks such as Common Goldeneye, Bufflehead, and Common Merganser. Don't forget to check the trees. Osprey and Merlin are recorded during winter, and occasionally both Bald and Golden Eagles are present.

The 0.6-mile-long trail winds down to the backside of the reeds on the near (south) shoreline. With careful perusal in winter you might find Virginia Rail, Sora, Wilson's Snipe, Marsh Wren, Common Yellowthroat, and Swamp Sparrow slipping among the stems. In spring look for American and Least Bitterns. The wet, flat open edges are good for American Pipits in winter. Also in winter, the *Empidonax* genus is especially well represented at Patagonia Lake. Watch the edges of the trail for Hammond's, Dusky, and Gray Flycatchers. While Ash-throated Flycatcher is usually present in winter, the discovery of only the third Nutting's Flycatcher ever recorded in the U.S. created a flurry of visitation at Patagonia Lake from mid-December 1997 through February 1998. The Nutting's Flycatcher foraged actively in the mesquite woodland that flanks the trail before it reaches Sonoita Creek. In October 2002 a pair of Black-capped Gnatcatchers adopted the same area, bred successfully the following summer, and re-nested in 2004. Nearly every winter a Rufous-backed Robin uses the same mesquite bosque.

A herd of white cows also roams the precincts of upper Patagonia Lake. While no birders have been injured, occasionally, especially in spring, the cattle block the trail and are belligerent towards birders. Whenever possible, give them a wide berth.

For the intrepid who don't mind wading, or who have rubber boots, it is possible to cross Sonoita Creek and follow cow paths to an old road that stays on the north side of the canyon all the way to a ranch fence (about 1.0 mile). thornscrub on the hillsides in conjunction with foothill canyon groves create a subtropical habitat that is rare in Arizona. Irregular but potential species here are Ruddy Ground-Dove (winter), Violet-crowned Hummingbird (summer), Elegant Trogon (winter), Green Kingfisher (primarily winter), Eastern Phoebe (winter), Thick-billed Kingbird (summer), Rose-throated Becard (summer), Louisiana Waterthrush (winter), and Varied Bunting (summer). Many of these species are more commonly found and more easily accessed upstream a few miles at the Patagonia Roadside Area. Rock Wren and Green-tailed Towhee, however, are the regular winter fare.

The "best" bird ever recorded at Patagonia Lake was a male Black-vented Oriole in April 1991. Although a previous sighting was reported from Cave Creek Canyon in the Chiricahua Mountains 20 years earlier, a photograph of this second individual provided indisputable documentation. The oriole was eating oranges supplied by a camper.

Return to Highway 82 and turn left (north) to continue this tour. The next stop at the **Patagonia Roadside Rest Area** (3.2 miles) on the right (east) side of the highway is one of the most famous roadside birding areas in the world. At least two first records of birds in the United States have come from here: Black-capped Gnatcatcher in May 1971 and Yellow Grosbeak in June 1971. The first Rose-throated Becard seen in the twentieth century in Arizona was discovered along Sonoita Creek in September 1947. More "life-list" becards come from the little colony that presently lives along this section of Sonoita Creek than anywhere else in the United States.

The Patagonia Roadside Rest Area is no more than a 0.3-mile-long stretch of pavement that parallels Highway 82 at the base of a steep ridge. A lone concrete picnic table is set in a long, narrow island of cottonwood, ash, and walnut trees that divide the Rest Area from the road. Sonoita Creek itself lies on the opposite side of the highway. Birders should walk along the Rest Area road in search of summering Gray Hawk, White-winged Dove, Broad-billed and Black-chinned Hummingbirds, Cassin's and Thick-billed Kingbirds, Brown-crested Flycatcher, Northern Beardless-Tyrannulet, Phainopepla, Bell's Vireo, Summer Tanager, Pyrrhuloxia, Rufous-crowned Sparrow, and Hooded and Bullock's Orioles. Listen for the melodic, descending whistles of Canyon Wrens cascading down from the cliffs on the north end of the rest area, as well as for the excited chittering of White-throated Swifts, which nest in crevices in the same rocks.

The arid thornscrub on the hillside is excellent for Varied Buntings. Males typically sing from the highest available exposed perches. In 1969 Five-striped Sparrows were discovered breeding in this area, and by 1975 the population reached 25 birds. The following summer only four returned, and ultimately all the sparrows vanished. Nonetheless, the habitat seems perfect for Five-stripes, and sooner or later they will probably be back. Equally unpredictable, observations of Ferruginous Pygmy-Owl have been separated by calendar years since the first was detected in June 1975. Here, too, a Buff-collared Nightjar was calling in July 1975. The Roadside Rest Area is still producing tropical rarities: a Yellow Grosbeak spent four days at the Rest Area in June 1994, a Fan-tailed Warbler appeared in May 1997, a Black-capped Gnatcatcher was present in late May 1998, and a Yellow-green Vireo was singing in July 1999.

At a point directly across the highway opposite the north end of the Patagonia Roadside Rest Area, a trail-of-use created by birders drops down under the big Arizona Sycamore trees that grow along Sonoita Creek. Within 10 yards the trail encounters a tautly strung barbed-wire fence marking the property line of the Circle Z Guest Ranch. From there the path turns upstream and parallels the fence for approximately 150 yards. *Do not trespass on Circle Z Ranch property.*

This trail offers the best vantage points for seeing Rose-throated Becards. Almost any summer one or two pairs are in residence in the streamside sycamores. They nest in huge, loosely-woven, globular structures either hanging straight above the water, or dangling directly over the trail. Finding the nests is easy, but finding the occupants can take luck and patience. Listen for the their thin, high, shrill little cries that suddenly die off like a ricocheting BB shot. Rose-throated Becards ordinarily arrive in mid-May. They fledge their young by mid-August, and then disperse before departing in September. After the young leave the nest, the becards are as apt to be seen in the trees in the median between the highway and the Rest Area as in the riparian grove along Sonoita Creek.

Even if it's a slow day for becards, the canyon grove may be teeming with birds. This is one of the best places to see Gray Hawks, as well as Thick-billed Kingbirds. Other species to look for include Zone-tailed Hawk, Violet-crowned Hummingbird, Phainopepla, Lucy's and Yellow Warblers, Yellow-breasted Chat, and Lesser Goldfinch. Watch the far hillside for Collared Peccary (locally known as Javelina) and Desert Mule Deer, especially at daybreak. Both bird and mammal activity subsides after 10 a.m.

By now it's late enough for either lunch or supper (unless you drove straight through from Tucson, 63 miles). It may even be time to scout up lodging or a campground for the night. Drive on into Patagonia (4.2 miles). Although the population of Patagonia is only approximately 1,200, there are four restaurants, a grocery store, a nature shop, one RV park, two bed-and-breakfasts, and one small hotel. The town park on the right (east) side of Highway 82 offers a shady and tranquil area, a butterfly garden, restrooms, and a picnic tables. *No camping or picnicking is permitted in the Patagonia-Sonoita Creek Preserve.*

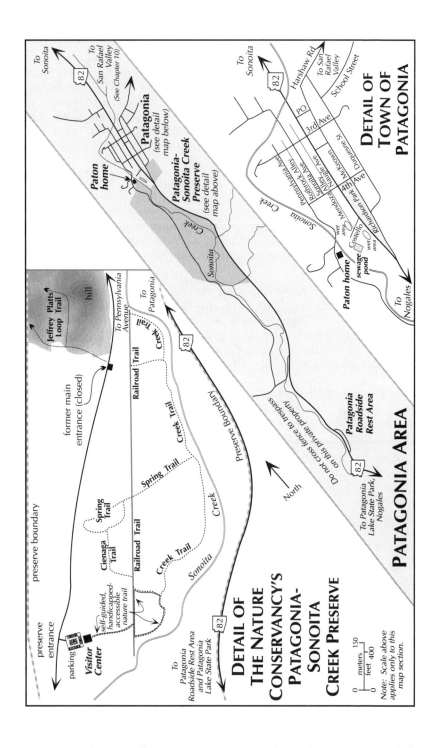

DETAIL OF
TOWN OF
PATAGONIA

PATAGONIA AREA

DETAIL OF
THE NATURE
CONSERVANCY'S
PATAGONIA-
SONOITA
CREEK PRESERVE

Note: Scale above
applies only to this
map section.

To continue this loop, turn left (west) off Highway 82 opposite the park restrooms onto 4th Avenue (there is a bar on the southwest corner of the intersection with the highway). Go two blocks and turn left (south) onto Pennsylvania Avenue. It will soon become a dirt road that crosses Sonoita Creek on a concrete-lined ford (0.2 mile from Highway 82). *Do not attempt to cross Sonoita Creek if barriers are in place or if the stream is obviously flash-flooding.*

The Patons' Home just beyond the ford offers birders a chance to observe many of the area's best birds from a chair. Noticing birders peering at his feeders from the roadway, the late Wally Paton and his wife, Marion, spontaneously invited any and all birders to enter their private property. Wally and Marion even put up a canvas awning complete with chairs for birders. In the summer of 1995 they constructed a recirculating waterfall to attract more birds. Although Wally passed away in 2002, Marion generously continues to welcome birders. This is a very special place and Marion Paton is truly a special person to share it so unselfishly.

Hummingbirds tend to be present all day long, even after activity dries up at the Patagonia Roadside Rest Area and the Patagonia-Sonoita Creek Preserve by mid-morning during the warmer months. The Patons' driveway is on the left side of the road 100 feet beyond the Sonoita Creek crossing. A sign on their chain-link fence says "Hummingbirders Welcome." If the two-car parking area at the entrance is full, continue another 75 yards and pull completely off the road under the shade of some big Arizona Cypress trees on either side of the road. *Please do not block the Patons' or the neighbors' driveways!* (Another sign on the fence directs visitors with handicapped plates or placards to feel free to park in the yard inside the fence. Do not park in a way that interferes with access by the residents.)

The Patons' home is far and away the most dependable site for Violet-crowned Hummingbird in the United States. Aside from Violet-crowns coming in at 10- to 20-minute intervals from March through September (and sometimes throughout the winter, too), other regular clients at their sugar-water feeders include Broad-billed, Black-chinned, and Anna's Hummingbirds. A few Costa's are present in spring, rare in summer and fall, and an occasional Lucifer may put in an appearance; Rufous Hummingbirds are uncommon in spring but common from July through September. Allen's are undoubtedly here in late summer, but only adult males can be safely separated in the field from Rufous, and adult male Allen's Hummingbirds are always scarce in Southeastern Arizona.

Plain-capped Starthroat is always a summer possibility anywhere in the Patagonia area, primarily from late June through late August. Starthroats exhibit a complex of characters that should render them inconfusable, but every year birders turn in erroneous reports from Patagonia. The distinct, elongated white oval on the lower back is duplicated by no other U.S. hummingbird. Only a female Magnificent can match the tremendously long bill of a

Starthroat, and she will never show a blackish throat (the lower, diamond-shaped gorget has a dull, orange-red iridescence that is seldom visible). Size alone should eliminate all other Patagonia hummingbirds, since neither Blue-throats nor Magnificents are apt to stray down to this 4,000-foot elevation locale.

To date there are only two acceptable records of Cinnamon Hummingbird in the U.S. The first was a bird was photographed at the Patons' home in July 1992. The Cinnamon is just another proof that this place is a magnet for hummingbirds; frequently it seems there are more hummers at the Paton feeders than any other place in the state of Arizona.

But not only hummingbirds frequent Marion Paton's property. Selected other visitors include Great Blue Heron, Black Vulture, Gray and Zone-tailed Hawks (summer), Gambel's Quail, Inca Dove, Yellow-billed Cuckoo (summer), Gila and Ladder-backed Woodpeckers, Northern Beardless-Tyrannulet (summer), Vermilion Flycatcher (summer), Thick-billed Kingbird (summer), Bewick's Wren, Bell's Vireo (summer), Lucy's Warbler (summer), Yellow-breasted Chat (summer), Northern Cardinal, Abert's Towhee, Song Sparrow, Bronzed Cowbird (summer), Hooded and Bullock's Orioles (summer), and Lesser Goldfinch. In winter watch for both Common and Ruddy Ground-Doves, White-winged Dove, House Wren, Hermit Thrush, Cedar Waxwing, Green-tailed Towhee, Lincoln's, White-throated (uncommon), and White-crowned Sparrows, Lazuli Bunting, Cassin's Finch, and Pine Siskin. An adult male Scarlet Tanager in the yard in eye-searing nuptial plumage in May 2002 is one of the few spring records for Southeastern Arizona.

It is best to visit the nearby **Patagonia-Sonoita Creek Preserve** as early as possible in the morning. The preserve is open Wednesday–Sunday, 7:30 a.m. to 4:00 p.m., October–March, and 6:30 a.m. to 4:00 p.m., April–September; the preserve is closed on Thanksgiving, Christmas, and New Year's Day. A fee of $5/person ($3 for Nature Conservancy members) for a seven-day pass is collected at the visitor center (520-394-2400).

Partially to comply with visitation hours, but—more importantly—because the birding can be superb, many local birders work the upper (north) section of the preserve from the road that bounds its west edge. Sonoita Creek swings close to a bluff at the north boundary of the Preserve (0.3 mile), juxtaposing a mature Fremont Cottonwood gallery forest on the left side of the road with desertscrub dominated by Velvet Mesquite on the right. This is the area of the road where Arizona's third Crescent-chested Warbler was discovered in September 1992. After spending the whole winter of 1992–1993 essentially between the preserve and the Patons', in all probability the same bird returned to the same area again for an encore performance over the winter of 1993–1994. The Crescent-chested Warbler was almost always seen in mixed flocks with Bridled Titmice and Yellow-rumped Warblers. *Park completely off the road if you bird this area, and do not enter the preserve here.*

Vermilion Flycatcher
Narca Moore-Craig

It's worth the effort to walk all the way through this ecological bottleneck to the former main entrance to the preserve (0.4 mile). In summer there is almost invariably a pair of Gray Hawks nesting in the closed area across the stream. This is also a favorite haunt for Gilded Flicker, Northern Beardless-Tyrannulet, Olive-sided (migration), Dusky-capped (summer), and Brown-crested (summer) Flycatchers, Bridled Titmouse, Rufous-backed Robin (rare, winter), Yellow (summer) and Yellow-rumped (winter) Warblers, and Yellow-breasted Chat (summer).

Bell's Vireo, Cactus Wren, Verdin, Curve-billed Thrasher, Rufous-crowned Sparrow, Varied Bunting (summer), and Blue Grosbeak (summer), as well as other desert species, are likely in the thornscrub on the right hillside across from the old main entrance. The Jeffrey Platts Trail, a 3-mile loop that begins here, accesses the hilly area northwest of the preserve. Species are much the same as those found along the road, but without the interruption of motorized traffic.

A new visitor center was dedicated in February 1996 on the 30th anniversary of the preserve. It is located on the south end of the Patagonia-Sonoita Creek Preserve (0.5 mile; see map). When The Nature Conservancy of Arizona purchased this property in 1966 it contained only 312 acres; today some 750 acres are permanently protected from development. Visitors are requested to obey a set of rules designed to perpetuate the unique wildlife and plant resource at Patagonia. *Birders must stay on established trails.*

Other environmental safeguards include bans against smoking, picnicking and camping, swimming and wading, hunting and fishing, and bicycling and horse-backing. *Additionally no tape-players or radios are permitted and no pets are allowed inside the preserve.*

This lush oasis attracts an abundance of birds at all seasons, including many rare and exotic species. One of the flashiest has to be the Vermilion Flycatcher, which is common in summer and fairly common in winter. Other birds to look for include Gambel's Quail, Common Ground-Dove, Greater Roadrunner, Western Screech-Owl, Great Horned Owl, Acorn, Gila, and Ladder-backed Woodpeckers, Gilded and Northern "Red-shafted" Flickers, Black and Say's Phoebes, Mexican Jay, Bridled Titmouse, Verdin, Bushtit, White-breasted Nuthatch, Bewick's Wren, Eastern Bluebird, Phainopepla, Northern Cardinal, Canyon and Abert's Towhees, Song Sparrow, and Lesser Goldfinch.

In summer watch for White-winged Dove, Yellow-billed Cuckoo, Elf Owl, Lesser Nighthawk, Common Poorwill, Broad-billed and Black-chinned Hummingbirds, Northern Beardless-Tyrannulet, Cassin's, Thick-billed, and Western Kingbirds, Dusky-capped and Brown-crested Flycatchers, Bell's Vireo, Lucy's (especially in mesquite) and Yellow (especially in cottonwoods) Warblers, Yellow-breasted Chat, Summer Tanager, Blue Grosbeak, Lazuli and Indigo Buntings (rare), Bronzed Cowbird, and Hooded and Bullock's Orioles. Most years there are three pairs of Gray Hawks raising young on the Preserve. Although Rose-throated Becards have nested in the big cottonwoods on the north end, your chances of finding one of these tropical specialties are best in the previously described sycamores near the Patagonia Roadside Rest Area.

In winter look for Red-naped Sapsuckers, Ruby-crowned Kinglets, American Pipits, Plumbeous Vireo (uncommon), Orange-crowned and "Audubon's" Yellow-rumped Warblers, Green-tailed Towhee, "Oregon" and "Gray-headed" Dark-eyed Juncos, and White-crowned and Lincoln's Sparrows, and—during irruption years—Lawrence's Goldfinch (rare). Green

Kingfisher sightings usually come from the north Railroad Trail bridge abutment and are more common in winter than in summer.

The Creek Trail is the best preserve path for passage *Empidonax* flycatchers. Willow and Pacific-slope are strictly migrants, but a few Hammond's, Dusky, and Gray Flycatchers may pass the entire winter in the thickets that border Sonoita Creek. In December 1992 a Yellow-bellied Flycatcher was detected on the annual Christmas Bird Count. Only the second accepted record of this Eastern species in Arizona, the bird lingered until the spring of 1993.

Probably the most frequently seen mammal on the preserve is the beautiful, silvery-tailed Arizona Gray Squirrel. Other wildlife species found at Patagonia include Sonoran Opossum, Raccoon, Coati, Ringtail, Spotted, Striped, Hooded, and Hog-nosed Skunks, Gray Fox, Coyote, Bobcat, Rock Squirrel, Harris's Antelope Ground Squirrel, Antelope and Black-tailed Jackrabbits, Desert Cottontail, and White-tailed Deer. Many of the mammals are nocturnal and difficult to observe.

Several species of birds are more common farther south along the road than on the preserve. As you approach the rocky, normally dry stream crossing at Temporal Gulch (0.3 mile), be especially alert for Common Ground-Doves. The wash itself may harbor Rock Wrens. *Do not attempt to cross Temporal Wash if it is flooded.*

Soon a series of low, scenic rocky outcrops flank the right (west) side of the road. Aside from both Rock and Canyon Wrens, this is the best area for Zone-tailed Hawk and Thick-billed Kingbirds. The area on the left (east) side of the road is private property and posted no trespassing. This stretch of the road is also worth walking. Arizona's first record of an Eastern Towhee occurred here during the winter of 1999–2000. More recently, a Yellow-throated Vireo sang from the road edge in the same vicinity in late August 2004. *Do not cross the fenceline. Do not stop and block this narrow, winding road. Park completely off the road.*

Make a left turn at the major intersection with Salero Road (1.3 mile). In 200 yards Salero Road crosses Sonoita Creek at a sandy ford unsuited for low-slung cars. This is the area where the first Blue Mockingbird recorded in the United States was found in December 1991. As a consequence of a few thoughtless birders who trespassed, the Circle Z Guest Ranch now asks birders *not* to stop at the ford area. A couple of hundred yards beyond, Salero Road ends at Highway 82 on the east side of Sonoita Creek (0.3 mile).

Turn right (south) if you care to make a second pass at the nearby Patagonia Roadside Rest Area (0.9 mile). To continue to the final birding area at Patagonia turn left (north) and drive to the first street on the left (unsigned, dirt Costello Road) as you enter town on Highway 82 (3.3 miles). Go 25 yards to the junction with Mendoza Alley on the right, and park here where service vehicles will have no trouble avoiding your car. The Patagonia Sewage Pond is directly in front of you.

When there is water in the pond, there is usually only one species of waterfowl present: Black-bellied Whistling-Duck. You can see them on the far (south) half of the pond by standing at the gate and looking to the left. *Visitors are not allowed inside.* The tall cottonwoods between Highway 82 and the far end of the pond support Patagonia's only Great Blue Heron rookery. A dozen or so nests are visible in the upper third of the trees. Wet, reedy patches on both sides of the entrance drive are good for wintering Virginia Rail, Sora, and Swamp Sparrows. The Patagonia Sewage Pond area was a favorite of the Crescent-chested Warbler for the two winters it was present. Equally intriguing, what would constitute Arizona's first record of White-collared Seedeater, if accepted, spent two weeks here in January 1998.

Exit the Patagonia Sewage Pond by going up Mendoza Alley, keeping an eye peeled for any small doves. A small flock of Ruddy Ground-Doves spent the winter of 1992–1993 in downtown Patagonia, primarily in the vacant lot north of the Big Steer Bar off Main Street, but also here in Mendoza Alley. Patagonia must be the only town in the United States that can boast of Ruddy Ground-Doves—not gangs—hanging out in its alleys. Turn right on 4th Avenue (0.2 mile) and go 50 yards to return to Highway 82, and turn left (north).

Nearby Harshaw Canyon affords birders in Patagonia a chance to see Montezuma Quail, Golden Eagle, Sulphur-bellied Flycatcher, and Eastern Bluebird. Directions and a more complete description are in the San Rafael Valley section of Chapter 10.

Leaving Patagonia on Highway 82, you soon climb into the Sonoita Grasslands, which turn lawn-green after the monsoons drench the landscape in July and August. A sign on the left (west) is all that remains to mark the site of old Camp Crittenden (9.3 miles), established in 1867 and deactivated in 1873. Camp Crittenden was abandoned because the soldiers living there contracted malaria. Its desertion tells something about how marshy this area was before the drought of 1892. By the time the rains finally returned cattle had grazed the grasses to mineral soil, and subsequent erosion cut the channel in which Sonoita Creek still runs today. Working near Camp Crittenden, the indefatigable Army surgeon Elliot Coues collected the type specimen for the small subspecies of Whitetail Deer that bears his name. "Coues' Flycatcher," the old name for Greater Pewee, formerly honored this pioneer ornithologist of the American Southwest.

The little settlement of Sonoita (2.9 miles) is in the heart of the grassland. Here Golden Eagle, Loggerhead Shrike, Say's Phoebe, Horned Lark, Grasshopper Sparrow, and Eastern Meadowlark are common throughout the year. Swainson's Hawks are summer residents, and Northern Harriers and Prairie Falcons occupy the sweeping prairie in winter.

To sample the birds of the **Sonoita Grasslands** simply continue straight ahead (east) on Highway 82 at the only intersection in downtown Sonoita. A substantial gravel pile on the left (north) side of the road (0.9 mile) just beyond the last buildings offers a convenient place to park. When they are singing in late summer, this is usually a sure-fire stake-out for Cassin's Sparrows. Scan the fencelines on both sides of the highway for Grasshopper Sparrows. If none are evident, wait until the highway is entirely clear of traffic, then watch for any small bird on the lower three strands of barbed wire as you continue driving east. The trick is to find a bird near a safe pullout. East of Sonoita, until the road climbs out of the grassy headwaters of Cienaga Creek (6.5 miles), most of Highway 82 has no shoulder whatsoever. This is a truck route—*if you stop here, park completely off the pavement.* Other summer residents include Common Nighthawk (very local in Southeastern Arizona) and Western Kingbird.

Vast flocks of sparrows move onto the Sonoita Grasslands in winter. Most are Brewer's, Vesper, Savannah, and Lark, but there may be longspurs, too. Chestnut-collared are far and away the most common species of longspur in the Sonoita Grasslands, but McCown's is also possible. Watch for a small, unsigned dirt track (2.8 miles) adjacent to a cattle guard (now fenced) on the right (south) side of Highway 82 just 3.8 miles east of Sonoita. Part of the Empire-Cienaga Resource Conservation Area (South Unit) managed by the Bureau of Land Management, this area of the Sonoita Grassland has proven reliable for Sprague's Pipit and Baird's Sparrow, as well as longspurs. The Baird's are most common in the grassy swales on the left (east) side of the dirt track. Flocks of Chestnut-collared Longspurs flit up in both the swales and along the road. Often the best look at the longspurs occurs when the birds alight on the road in front of your vehicle. (Birders visiting the Empire-Cienaga from points east will find the turnoff on the left side of the road 15.0 miles west of the junction of Highways 82 and 90, just 0.3 mile beyond the well-signed entrance to the Empire-Cienaga RCA North Unit.)

A herd of Pronghorn has been introduced into the Empire-Cienaga Resource Conservation Area on the left (north) side of Highway 82. Watch for these speedsters in the tall grasses at the bottom of the swales. Sometimes a small group of Pronghorns rest or browse, oblivious of curious human onlookers, within a 100 yards of the highway. A quarter-mile remove, however, is more typical.

To visit the Huachuca Mountains (Chapter 6) or the San Pedro Valley (Chapter 7), continue on Highway 82 to the Highway 90 intersection, then turn right (south) toward Sierra Vista (32.5 miles from Sonoita). To complete this loop, return to Sonoita and go right (north) on Highway 83.

Lower Gardner Canyon, to the left of Highway 83, can be a good birding spot. The road to Gardner turns off west at the bottom of the first steep hill (4.1 miles). Cassin's and Botteri's Sparrows can be heard singing in July and

August in the Sacaton grasslands just off the highway. The next four miles of broad, grassy canyon where the road stays in the bottom is a good place to look for Montezuma Quail. University of Arizona researchers working with trained dogs estimated that there were 40 adult quail per square mile in this area in the early 1960s, and that figure is probably still accurate today.

The road continues up to pine-oak woodland, but beyond the ranch (7.5 miles) it becomes very rough and rocky. The left fork (9.0 miles) goes another five miles to a basin in upper Gardner Canyon. The right fork lasts a comparable distance before dead-ending in upper Cave Canyon. *You should not attempt to drive to the road-ends in either Gardner or Cave Canyon without high clearance and four-wheel-drive.* Elegant Trogons summer high up in both of these seldom visited drainages, and an Eared Quetzal was found using upper Gardner Canyon in August 1991.

Back on Highway 83, continue northward. At the Greaterville Road (3.8 miles), you can choose how to end this tour. To return to the starting point in Tucson, go straight ahead (north) on Highway 83 to Interstate 10 (17.2 miles), then west on I-10 (21.3 miles). If you plan to visit Madera Canyon, the Greaterville Road cuts off about 60 miles of travel. You should be aware, however, that after the pavement ends (3.1 miles), the Greaterville Road turns into a rough, rocky, steep, narrow, and washboarded track in Box Canyon before it rejoins the pavement leading up to Madera from Continental (10.8 miles). *Do not attempt to pull a trailer over the Greaterville Road.*

The birding in Box Canyon is often quite rewarding. Among the summer birds are Broad-billed, Lucifer, and Costa's Hummingbirds, Northern Beardless-Tyrannulet, Bell's Vireo, Rock and Canyon Wrens, Rufous-crowned Sparrow, and Varied Bunting. Golden Eagles are resident. A Black-capped Gnatcatcher was seen in Box Canyon in August 2003.

CAMPGROUNDS, RESTAURANTS, AND ACCOMMODATIONS

Lodging and services are available along the Interstate 19 corridor between Tucson and Nogales, including Tubac Golf Resort (P.O. Box 1297, Tubac, AZ 85646, 800-848-7893) with a one-mile birding trail along the Santa Cruz River, in addition to birding packages, accommodations, and a restaurant, and at Río Rico Resort (1069 Camino Caralampi, Río Rico, AZ 85648, 800-288-4746).

A fee campground is available at Patagonia Lake State Park (HC2 Box 273, Nogales, AZ 85621; 520-287-6965). Non-hook-up sites are $15 per night, hook-up sites are $22, and the gate is locked at 10:00 p.m. and opened at 4:00 a.m. Patagonia RV Park, P.O. Box 768, Patagonia, AZ 85624; 520-394-2491, is located on Harshaw Road on the outskirts of Patagonia.

Gas, groceries, four restaurants, and other services are available in the little town of Patagonia. In Patagonia the Western-flavor Stage Stop Inn (P.O.

Box 273, Patagonia, AZ 85624; 520-394-2211) has a good restaurant and is only a half-mile from the Patagonia-Sonoita Creek Preserve.

Among the many bed-and-breakfast establishments, those catering to birders include Duquesne House B&B, 357 Duquesne Avenue, Patagonia, AZ 85624, 520-394-2732; The Black Dove B&B, 576 Gringo Avenue, Patagonia, AZ 85624, 520-394-2080; Tierra de Los Sueños B&B, 3 S. Harshaw Creek Road, Patagonia, AZ 85724, 520-394-0095.

Two guest ranches are also available: Circle Z Guest Ranch, P.O. Box 194, Patagonia, AZ 85624; 520-287-2091; and Crown C Ranch, P.O. Box 507, Sonoita, AZ 85637; 520-455-5739.

Services are also available in Sonoita. The 18-room Sonoita Inn opened in 1998 at the crossroads of Highways 82 and 83 (P.O. Box 99, Sonoita, AZ 85637; 520-455-5935). The Old Benton Place B&B (P.O. Box 129, Sonoita, AZ 85637; 520-455-9303) welcomes birders.

A visitor's guide to the Patagonia/Sonoita area is available from the Patagonia Area Business Association (P.O. Box 241, Patagonia, AZ 85624; 520-394-0060). Additional information on other services and facilities in the area is available at www.patagoniaaz.com.

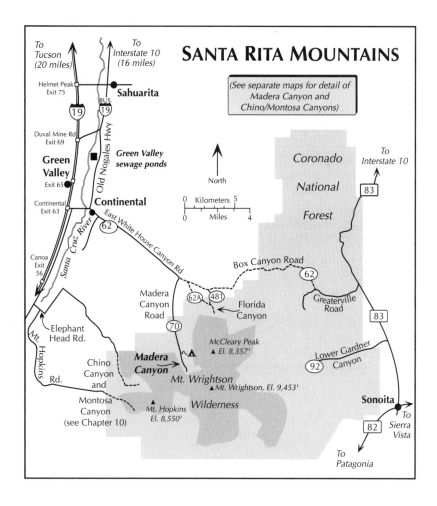

SANTA RITA MOUNTAINS

(See separate maps for detail of Madera Canyon and Chino/Montosa Canyons)

To Tucson (20 miles)

To Interstate 10 (16 miles)

Helmet Peak Exit 75

Sahuarita

BUS. 19

19

Old Nogales Hwy

Duval Mine Rd Exit 69

Green Valley Exit 65

Green Valley sewage ponds

North

0 Kilometers 5

0 Miles 4

Coronado National Forest

To Interstate 10

83

Continental Exit 63

Continental

62

East White House Canyon Rd

Santa Cruz River

Canoa Exit 56

Box Canyon Road

62

Greaterville Road

83

Madera Canyon Road

62A 481

Florida Canyon

Elephant Head Rd.

Mt. Hopkins Rd.

70

McCleary Peak ▲ El. 8,357'

Lower Gardner

92 Canyon

Chino Canyon and Montosa Canyon (see Chapter 10)

Madera Canyon ▲▲

Mt. Wrightson

▲ Mt. Wrightson, El. 9,453'

Sonoita

▲ Mt. Hopkins El. 8,550'

Wilderness

82

To Sierra Vista

To Patagonia

CHAPTER 4

SANTA RITA MOUNTAINS

(From Green Valley: 29 miles/one day)
(From Tucson: 76 miles/one day)

Madera Canyon in the Santa Rita Mountains is perhaps the best-known and most-often visited birding spot in Arizona, and with good reason. Most of the birds of Southeastern Arizona occur within 15 linear miles. Only an hour south of Tucson, Madera Canyon is the nearest and easiest place to see the full panoply of Sierra Madrean hummingbirds, Elegant Trogon, Sulphur-bellied Flycatcher, and other pine-oak woodland specialties confined to the border ranges. If you only have time to bird a single location in spring or summer, visit Madera Canyon.

The starting point for this tour is at the Continental Exit (Exit 63) on Interstate 19, 23.5 miles south of its junction with I-10 in Tucson. Turn left (east) to go under the freeway and continue to White House Canyon Road (1.4 mile), located halfway through a bend in the midst of a pecan grove. To follow the main tour, turn right (southeast) here.

In winter or with adequate time, an interesting side trip is to continue straight ahead on what soon becomes the Old Nogales Highway. This little-traveled lane runs north along an enormous pecan grove to a Pima County Department of Transportation maintenance yard on the left side of the highway (2.1 miles); this makes good place to park. A young male Red-headed Woodpecker took up residency in the work yard in November 1991. By the time it disappeared in May 1992, it had molted into full adult plumage. More recently a Lewis's Woodpecker and a Yellow-bellied Sapsucker were both present in the Continental Workyard itself and adjacent trees of the pecan orchard during the winters of 2001–2002, 2002–2003, and 2003–2004. *Trespassing into the pecan orchard is strictly prohibited.*

81

Entrance to Madera Canyon, Santa Rita Mountains
Richard Cachor Taylor

The perimeter trees at the maintenance area include the pecan grove and a hedgerow of mesquite. When the trees are bare in winter, watch for Orange-crowned (uncommon) and Yellow-rumped Warblers, Chipping, Brewer's, Vesper, Lark, Savannah, and White-crowned Sparrows, and Lesser, Lawrence's (irruptive), and American (uncommon) Goldfinches. A migrating Gray Vireo (rare) was detected here in late March 1992.

Continuing north on the Old Nogales Highway, the pavement now parallels an enormous artificial clearing. Keep an eye out for White-tailed Kites, which are occasionally seen along this stretch. Regularly-occurring winter raptors include Northern Harrier, Red-tailed Hawk, and American Kestrel. Gambel's Quail are common in this large grassland, as are Greater Roadrunners, wintering sparrows, Lark Buntings, and wintering Western Meadowlarks. The **Green Valley Wastewater Ponds** (1.9 miles) are also on the left (west) side of the pavement. A few McCown's Longspurs were using the area on the north side of the entrance drive to the Green Valley Wastewater Ponds in January and February 2004. Officially open from 7:00 a.m. to 3:00 p.m. everyday (and sometimes—mysteriously—not open), this is a quick stop for waterfowl and shorebirds in winter and migration. Park in the visitor lot by the new office building (0.3 mile) and sign in to bird the small ponds. A spotting scope will be useful here.

The shorebirds and ducks at Green Valley are neither as diverse nor as numerous as in Tucson or Nogales, but are far more convenient for birders in

Madera Canyon. Occasionally surprises turn up, such as a pair of Surf Scoters in October 2004 and a Red Phalarope in October 1993. And the little ponds are oddly good for raptors. Crested Caracara was recorded in November 1999. Every year produces sightings of Zone-tailed Hawk, Peregrine Falcon, and Merlin (winter). After birding the ponds, return to White House Road (3.0 miles) to continue the Santa Rita Mountain tour.

An interesting community of birds can be found in the immediate precincts of **Continental** (0.3 mile). These include Gambel's Quail, Phainopepla, Bell's Vireo, Lucy's Warbler, both Northern Cardinal and Pyrrhuloxia, Rufous-winged Sparrow, and Hooded Oriole. In summer, look for Ash-throated Flycatcher, Western Kingbird, and Blue Grosbeak, and, in winter, Sage Thrasher (irregular), Green-tailed Towhee, and Lincoln's Sparrow. Beginning with the winter of 2001–2002, a Lewis's Woodpecker has been a winter fixture on the tall utility poles by the café parking lot. From February–April 2001 a gorgeous male Magnolia Warbler could be found in the shrubbery in the curve of the road just beyond the railroad track. Excluding vagrants, all of these can also be found in Florida Wash, much closer to Madera. Unless you have more than one day to devote to this tour, I suggest you go straight to Madera Canyon.

Once the road leaves the Santa Cruz bottomlands at Continental, it swings left up onto a *bajada,* or alluvial apron of material washed down from the Santa Rita Mountains after they were formed over 75 million years ago. This broad, grassy steppe has been managed by the University of Arizona as the Santa Rita Experimental Range. The purple cactus with the large, flat pads is Santa Rita Prickly Pear, a much sought-after ornamental in Southwest landscaping. The purple one with the small, round stems is Staghorn Cholla (*CHO-yah*). The abundant, large, green cholla with the chains of green fruit is called Chain Fruit Cholla.

It is rumored that joints of the Chain Fruit Cholla can actually lunge out and stick themselves to you as you pass. This is, of course, not true, but it is hard to convince people who have had an unfortunate encounter with this species. The segments of this cholla are loosely attached because the plant's primary method of propagation is vegetative. When people or other mammals brush against the spines—even very lightly—the joint pins itself aboard. Potential new plants are thereby transported away from the parent. And that leads to an alternative name for the species—Jumping Cactus. Use a comb or a stick to remove the piece of cactus, should you find yourself the unwitting host of a future Chain Fruit Cholla.

Some of the birds to watch for in this desert grassland are Turkey Vulture, Red-tailed Hawk, Gambel's Quail, Greater Roadrunner, Say's Phoebe, Common Raven, Verdin, Cactus Wren, Curve-billed Thrasher, and House Finch. In winter, Chipping and White-crowned Sparrows are abundant.

The rare Antelope Jackrabbit, whose range barely extends into the United States, can sometimes be found here. It is larger and paler than the more common Black-tailed Jackrabbit, and has a habit of showing the white on its flanks as it bounds away. In addition to the hares, you may see Harris's Antelope Ground Squirrel. Like a chipmunk it has stripes on its sides, but unlike any true chipmunk it lacks facial stripes. Chipmunks do not occur in the Santa Rita Mountains.

To continue the main tour route from the junction of Box Canyon Road (7.0 miles), follow the pavement and turn right (south) toward the soaring blue pinnacles of the Santa Ritas. Box Canyon Road, leading east from this intersection, is the short-cut to Sonoita, Sierra Vista, and Patagonia, lopping off over 60 miles from the Tucson route. Be aware, however, that the first stretch to the pavement at the Greaterville Road (10.8 miles), is steep, narrow, and badly wash-boarded. The final link to Highway 83 (3.1 miles) is paved. *Vehicles pulling trailers should not use the Box Canyon Road.*

If you would like to visit the upper part of Florida Canyon as a side trip from this intersection, take unpaved Box Canyon Road (Road 62) to Road 62A (0.3 mile) which angles off to the right (east) through an area of tall grass, mesquite, and Ocotillo (*oh-co-TEA-yo*). Both Cassin's and Botteri's Sparrows inhabit the grassy flats before the road enters Box Canyon itself. The bright red flowers of the Ocotillo along the route attract Lucifer (rare), Black-chinned, and Costa's Hummingbirds from April to mid-May. This road joins Road 62 (1.8 miles) and continues up Florida Canyon to the Santa Rita Experimental Range Work Center (1.4 miles). The trailhead for the Florida Canyon Trail is located in the parking area. Wintering Black-chinned Sparrows can often be found near the start of the trail, and, since 2000, a male Elegant Trogon has been sighted sporadically during winter in the same area. During August 2000 a White-eyed Vireo was using the thicket at the entrance to the Work Center, and a Rufous-backed Robin was present there throughout the spring of 2003. *No trespassing is permitted onto the grounds of the Work Center.* Ordinarily, however, the birding is far better in Madera Canyon.

Continuing the main tour from the Box Canyon junction, the Madera Canyon Road passes over three one-lane bridges. Scan the road on the opposite side for fast-approaching traffic before committing yourself to crossing any of these bridges. *Don't even dream of slowing down or stopping on a bridge!* The third and final bridge (0.8 mile) crosses **Florida Wash**. There are convenient pullouts on both sides of the road just before the bridge, and a stile for crossing the barbed-wire fence on the left (east) side. Florida is pronounced *flow-REE-dah*, and means "full of flowers" in Spanish. A walk up or down this broad, perennially dry watercourse seldom produces many flowers, but you may encounter Gambel's Quail, Ladder-backed Woodpecker, Verdin, Cactus Wren, Curve-billed or Crissal Thrasher, Phainopepla, Northern Cardinal, Pyrrhuloxia, Canyon Towhee, and Black-throated Sparrow. In summer look

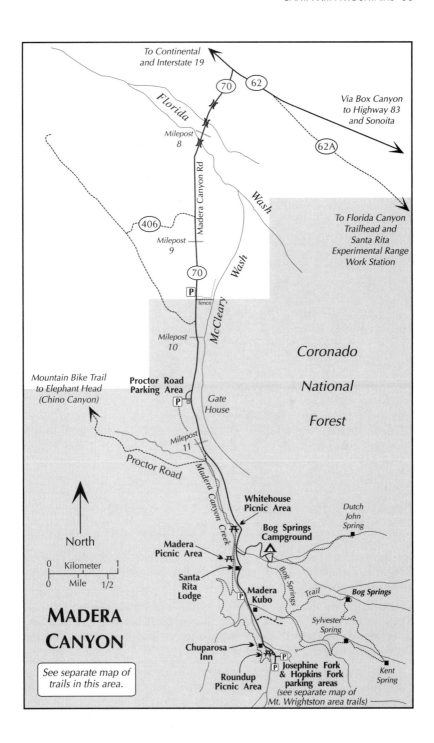

To Continental
and Interstate 19

Florida

(70) (62)

Via Box Canyon
to Highway 83
and Sonoita

Milepost
8

(62A)

Madera Canyon Rd

Wash

(406)

To Florida Canyon
Trailhead and
Santa Rita
Experimental Range
Work Station

Milepost
9

(70)

P

Fence

McCleary

Wash

Milepost
10

Coronado

Mountain Bike Trail
to Elephant Head
(Chino Canyon)

**Proctor Road
Parking Area**

National

P

Gate
House

Forest

Milepost
11

Proctor Road

Madera Canyon Creek

**Whitehouse
Picnic Area**

Dutch
John
Spring

North

**Bog Springs
Campground**

0 ___ Kilometer ___ 1

0 ___ Mile ___ 1/2

**Madera
Picnic Area**

**Santa
Rita
Lodge**

Bog Springs

Trail

Bog Springs

**Madera
Kubo**

P

Sylvester
Spring

**MADERA
CANYON**

**Chuparosa
Inn**

Kent
Spring

P

P

See separate map of
trails in this area.

**Roundup
Picnic Area**

**Josephine Fork
& Hopkins Fork
parking areas**
(see separate map of
Mt. Wrightston area trails)

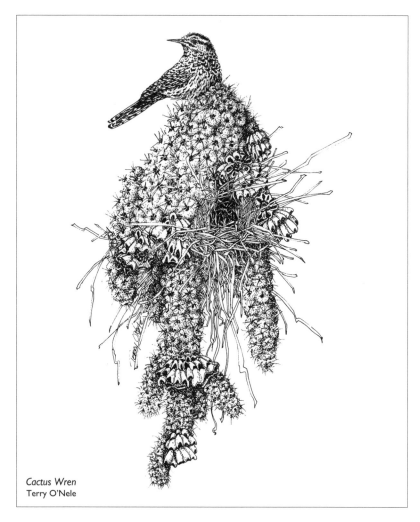

Cactus Wren
Terry O'Nele

for Black-chinned and Costa's (primarily spring) Hummingbirds, Northern Beardless-Tyrannulet, Ash-throated Flycatcher, Bell's Vireo, Lucy's Warbler, and Varied Bunting.

Florida Wash is also good for the highly local Rufous-winged Sparrow. The chestnut wing patch is hard to see on most birds, but its bright, clear song is very distinctive. Luckily, Rufous-winged Sparrow sings a lot. Listen for two or three opening chips followed by a trill.

The only other summer sparrows are Black-throated and Rufous-crowned, which also occur higher up where canyons enter the foothills. Rufous-crowned is superficially similar to the Rufous-winged, but Rufous-crowned Sparrow is a much huskier bird with a solid rusty crown, and a bold, black moustachial stripe. In winter, there are a number of other sparrows. Immature Chipping and White-crowneds could possibly be confused with Rufous-winged, but Chippers have notched tails and White-crowns of any age always show an orange bill.

Dense patches of mesquite and thornscrub along the streambed constitute prime Crissal Thrasher habitat. The bright rufous undertail coverts and strong malar stripe are good field marks, but be sure to note the bill shape and eye color. Curve-billed Thrasher, also common in Florida Wash, lacks the scythe-like bill of a Crissal and has a bright golden eye, not the dull iris of a Crissal Thrasher.

After crossing Florida Wash, the Madera Canyon Road runs arrow straight over the next several miles of desert grassland, as if aimed directly at the Smithsonian Astrophysical Observatory on top 8,585-foot-elevation Mt. Hopkins. The giant, multiple mirror telescope positioned on the summit of Mt. Hopkins in 1979 is the third-largest chunk of optical glass in the world. Use this opportunity to familiarize yourself with the topography of Madera. The 7,100-foot-high pass left (east) of the observatory is called Josephine Saddle. The massive volcanic dome all the way to the left (east) is Mt. Wrightson, at an elevation of 9,453 feet the highest point in the Santa Rita Mountains. With the highest and most expansive drainage area in the range, it is not surprising Madera is the best watered canyon in the Santa Ritas.

Continuing up the Madera Road above Florida Wash, Forest Road 406 (0.6 mile) enters on the right (west). Both Botteri's and Cassin's Sparrows nest along this dirt track during the rainy season in July and August. With some practice you may notice that Botteri's tends to look browner, but unless you manage a prolonged, full-frame scope view, it is best to separate the two by song. Botteri's sings a "rock-and-roll" jumble of short, hard notes; Cassin's song is composed of clear, long-drawn notes, infinitely poignant.

Farther up the canyon, you will come to a cattleguard (0.7 mile; 1.3 miles above the Florida Bridge). This was the famous Buff-collared Nightjar site in **McCleary Wash** (which is often erroneously referred to as Florida Wash). Unfortunately, Buff-collared Nightjars seemingly abandoned the site in 1995. Many other birds still use the area, however, and there's no telling when the nightjars may return. Park in the large pullout on the right (west) side of the Madera Canyon Road on the down-slope (north) side of the cattleguard. A cobbly, somewhat overgrown trail created by birders begins across the Madera Canyon Road from the parking area, passes through a wire gate (please shut it behind you), and parallels the fenceline 150 yards east to the edge of McCleary. A natural viewpoint between two large Ocotillos here overlooks the quarter-mile-wide floodplain of the big, dry drainage.

To try for the Buff-collared Nightjar plan to arrive soon after sundown to take a position. Don't forget a sweater. The cold air sinking from 8,357-foot-high

McCleary Peak off the north end of the Santa Rita crest can plunge temperatures over 20 degrees within a half-hour after sunset.

During the decade it was present, the nightjar was most apt to vocalize at late dusk between mid-April and June. In spite of a well-publicized etiquette that asked birders to refrain from playing tapes to attract the Buff-collareds, the pair of nightjars in McCleary Wash were probably exposed to more taped playbacks of their ascending, piano-like song than any other pair of birds in all Southeastern Arizona. The miracle was that they returned to nest every year after they were discovered at this site in 1985 through 1994. Like other over-taped species, however, they were soon "taped-out" and seldom respond to recordings of their song after the middle of May.

A powerful light is needed to scan McCleary Wash. Like Whip-poor-wills, Buff-collareds tend to hunt moths and other nocturnal insects from tree perches. Pan your light across the dead branches that project above the mesquites that fill the wash, and search for their glowing orange eyeshine. The Buff-collareds also tended to use the same perch for multiple sallies, and they only rested briefly between each foray. Common Poorwills, by contrast, most often use ground perches and generally do not return repeatedly to the same place.

There have always been more Common Poorwills at McCleary Wash than there ever were Buff-collared Nightjars. Skepticism is in order. When possible, use voice to separate the two species; but if the bird in question is silent, note that Buff-collared Nightjar has Whip-poor-will-like proportions, especially its long tail. Poorwills have comparatively short tails and a bull-headed jizz. The buffy hindcollar of this rare nightjar is difficult to discern at night without a good spotting scope.

There are many other reasons for an evening visit to McCleary Wash. Listen for the songs of both Botteri's and Cassin's Sparrows in the nearby desert grassland, and watch for Rufous-crowned Sparrow on the rocky brink of the ravine. Given the superb acoustics, you may even hear a herd of Desert Mule Deer walking along the far side of the wash before you pick out their soft gray shapes in the gathering dusk. As evening descends, the monotonous, tri-noted mimicry of Northern Mockingbird is the most typical bird song emanating from the dark thickets below. Check behind you for the fluttery flight of a Lesser Nighthawk (summer) over the grassland. The western sunsets over Baboquivari Peak, 40 miles away and the sacred peak of the Tohono O'odham nation, are invariably spectacular. Twenty-five miles due north, the lights of Tucson gradually appear at the base of the solid black silhouette of the Santa Catalina Mountains. The quavering, high-pitched wails and yips in the distance emanate from the original song-dog, the Coyote. Once the sky is fully dark, a Western Screech-Owl or a Great Horned Owl may join the evening chorus. With or without the Buff-collared Nightjar, this is one of Southeastern Arizona's most enjoyable birding spots.

Flocks of Mountain Bluebirds (irregular) are partial to the grasslands between the McCleary Wash parking area and **Proctor Road Parking Area** (1.2 miles) during some winters. In spring watch for a Common Raven nest on a telephone pole on the right (west) side of the road in the same area. On weekends and holidays all traffic is funneled through a fee station on the right (west) side of the Madera Canyon Road.

There is a Forest User Fee for the Nogales Ranger District; fees are $5/day, $10/week, or $20/year. (Golden Eagle, Golden Age, or Golden Access cards are accepted; National Parks Pass not accepted.) Permits purchased here are also good for Sabino Canyon and the Santa Catalina Mountains and for National Forest fee areas in the Chiricahua Mountains. (Separate campground fees apply.) When the fee station is closed, there is a self-service pay station 0.2 mile ahead on the right at the Proctor Road Parking Area.

The Proctor Road Parking Area is the trailhead for a paved and bridged Forest Service trail that follows lower Madera Creek upstream all the way to the Madera Picnic Area (1.3 miles). Walking at least part of this trail is suggested. In summer try to arrive before sunrise for the most activity. Birds at the Proctor Road Parking Area include Ash-throated Flycatcher, Verdin, Phainopepla, Northern Cardinal, and Blue Grosbeak. Look for Varied Bunting in the mesquite and Ocotillo thickets that edge the lot. A 50-yard-long interpretive trail drops down to a ramada off the northwest corner of the parking area that overlooks lower Madera where the stream leaves the foothills. At dusk throughout the summer the ramada provides an excellent vantage point to watch for Lesser Nighthawks.

But the best birding is along the stream. As the trail descends through dense oak and hackberry watch for Ladder-backed Woodpecker, Northern Beardless-Tyrannulet, Bell's Vireo, and Lucy's Warbler. The trail strikes the stream bottom near the old Proctor Road in 200 yards. In this area look for Black Phoebe, Cedar Waxwing (winter), Summer Tanager (summer), Lazuli Bunting (migration), Varied Bunting (summer), Lincoln's Sparrow (winter), Hooded Oriole (summer), and Lesser Goldfinch. The first U.S. record of Five-striped Sparrow came from the mouth of Madera Canyon in June 1957, although it has not been seen in this area since. Other vagrants of note include breeding Thick-billed Kingbirds from 1963 through 1965—and occasional recent sightings—and a Rose-throated Becard in May 1979. A lone Buff-collared Nightjar joined this list in June 2004.

During winter, Madera Creek above the Proctor Road crossing is one of the best rarity traps in the Santa Rita Mountains. Some years a Greater Pewee bivouacs between the ford and the Madera Picnic Area on the upper end of the trail. Most winters there are Olive Warblers and Painted Redstarts in the same area. Also in winter, a male Elegant Trogon has been annual along Madera Creek above Proctor Road since the winter of 2000–2001.

Proctor Road proper (0.2 mile beyond the paved parking area) is a rocky, rough, steep dirt track that crosses the stream (0.1 mile) and continues on as a four-wheel-drive route through a habitat of stunted oak and mesquite. It is a favorite with Tucson mountain-bikers. Since the birds are the same as those found in Florida Wash and at the Proctor Road Parking Area, it is suggested that you *not* wreck your car on this hot and dusty detour to nowhere.

The **Madera Picnic Area** (1.0 mile) on the right (west) side opposite the Bog Springs Campground junction represents a lush, new habitat to explore. From here to the end of the road, you will be in the Sierra Madrean pine-oak woodlands of the Upper Sonoran Life Zone. In a serendipitous and unusual overlap of geopolitical and ecological boundaries, Madera Canyon Road leaves Pima County and enters Santa Cruz County just 100 feet up the road. Elegant Trogon, Sulphur-bellied Flycatcher, and Painted Redstart are the summer birds of upper Madera Canyon.

The Madera Picnic Area can be a delightful place to bird, although on weekends you may have to share the place with 50 or more noisy non-birders. In summer, you should see Western Wood-Pewee, Painted Redstart, Hepatic Tanager, and Black-headed Grosbeak. The huge sycamores over the lower tables usually host a pair of nesting Sulphur-bellied Flycatchers, which can easily be located by their high-pitched, squeaky calls. At night, narcissistic Whip-poor-wills repeat their names from the shadows of the live oaks, and Common Poorwills do the same from positions on the oak hillside across the stream. In July 1993 a Yellow-throated Vireo spent most of the month grooming the picnic area trees.

A hike downstream from the picnic grounds can be productive in the early morning. The stillness is broken by the loud cries of Cassin's Kingbirds in the sycamores and by the trilling of Canyon Tree Frogs from the water. A pair of Black Phoebes calls *p-seee* from near their nest under the bridge. Listen for the loud whinnies of Arizona Woodpeckers keeping tabs on each other in the dense riparian woods. The west bank of the stream is also worth inspection. Look for Canyon Wrens on rocky ledges, and for Bewick's Wrens, Bushtits, and Rufous-crowned Sparrows among the Emory Oaks.

Three very similar *Myiarchus* flycatchers summer here, Dusky-capped, Ash-throated, and Brown-crested. Separating these three bushy-crested flycatchers seems difficult at first, but with sufficient practice comes mastery. The smallest is the Dusky-capped. This species has a dark crest, and a long, thin bill. Adults lack rufous in the tail, and its dying, *peeur* whistle is one of the characteristic sounds of Sierra Madrean pine-oak woodland. The medium-sized Ash-throated Flycatcher has a comparatively short bill, a medium brown crest, gives soft-voiced, burry *ka-brick* calls, and its cinnamon tail is tipped with dark corners. The weak sulphur color of its belly is softer and less noticeable than the pale yellow bellies of either Dusky-capped or Brown-crested Flycatchers. Distinctly larger, the kingbird-sized Brown-crested has a long, thick bill and narrow red inner webs on tail feathers extending to its tail tip; its loud, clear *whilp* and *whit-or-bew* notes ring out exclusively from the tall trees along Madera Creek.

Opposite the picnic ground is the paved road to the **Bog Springs Campground** (0.5 mile). Situated on an arid slope well above the canyon floor, the campground does not offer particularly good birding. Bog Springs itself can be reached from a small dirt road that takes off from the third campsite on the right (south) as you enter the camp. Walk this narrow, sandy road to the top of a little rise (0.7 mile). A steel sign on the left (east) indicates the well-used trail that climbs to Bog Springs (0.8 mile). A pair of truly stupendous Silverleaf Oaks among the tall Arizona Sycamores marks the site of the spring.

Breeding birds to look for here are Northern Pygmy-Owl, Elegant Trogon, Cordilleran Flycatcher, Sulphur-bellied Flycatcher, Plumbeous, Hutton's, and Warbling Vireos, House Wren, Hermit Thrush, Grace's Warbler, Painted Redstart, and both Hepatic and Western Tanagers. In the open woodland on the dry hillsides watch for Arizona Woodpecker, Ash-throated Flycatcher (summer), Bushtit, Black-throated Gray Warbler (summer), and Scott's Oriole (summer). A Flame-colored Tanager was discovered at Bog Springs in May 1994, and three of these tropical tanagers were using the area in May 1995. A probable hybrid male Flame-colored was present again in 1996. Remember that hybrid crosses with Western Tanagers are a common occurrence in Southeastern Arizona. Male Flame-colored Tanagers should never show either a solid black rear mantle or a bright yellow rump. More recently, in late May and early June 2001 a Crescent-chested Warbler was working in the lush vegetation at Bog Springs.

Santa Rita Lodge (0.15 mile), elevation 5,000 feet, is situated smack in the heart of this great birding area. The gift shop has a good selection of gifts, books, and bird checklists. Visitors are welcome to watch the lodge feeders from the parking lot on the right side of the road and from the benches in the viewing area. *Please respect the privacy of their guests. No snacks or public restrooms are provided. Picnicking is prohibited.* With advance reservations, visitors are also welcome to participate in a series of nature programs and bird walks offered year round. There is a small charge. Contact the lodge for the schedule of events. To stay at the Santa Rita Lodge during the prime spring and summer months, birders should make reservations well in advance (several months recommended). Call 520-625-8746 or write 1218 S. Madera Canyon Road, Madera Canyon, AZ 85614.

Some of the regularly-occurring birds at this point in Madera Canyon are Turkey Vulture, Zone-tailed Hawk (summer), Golden Eagle (rare), Montezuma Quail (rare), White-winged Dove (summer), Whip-poor-will (summer), White-throated Swift (summer), Northern "Red-shafted" Flicker, Acorn and Arizona Woodpeckers, Western Wood-Pewee (summer),

Dusky-capped, Brown-crested, and Sulphur-bellied Flycatchers (summer), Mexican Jay, Common Raven, Bridled Titmouse, Bushtit, White-breasted Nuthatch, Brown Creeper, Bewick's and Canyon Wrens, Eastern Bluebird (rare), Hermit Thrush, Plumbeous (summer) and Hutton's Vireos, Black-throated Gray Warbler (summer), Painted Redstart, Hepatic Tanager (summer), Black-headed Grosbeak (summer), Spotted Towhee, Yellow-eyed Junco, Bronzed and Brown-headed Cowbirds (summer), Scott's Oriole (summer), and House Finch. Migration brings Red-naped Sapsucker, Olive-sided Flycatcher (uncommon), Warbling Vireo, Townsend's and Hermit Warblers, and Western Tanager. In winter look for Ruby-crowned Kinglet, Townsend's Solitaire, American Robin, Dark-eyed Junco, and Cassin's Finch (irregular).

Every year brings a few surprises. Beginning in the past decade a Painted Redstart or two has overwintered at the Lodge and at private up-canyon residences, adding a new dimension to the annual Christmas Bird Count. Joining them at the sugar-water feeders are one or two Blue-throated and Magnificent Hummingbirds.

The Santa Rita Lodge is justifiably famous for its hummingbirds. In summer Broad-billed, Blue-throated, Magnificent, Black-chinned, Anna's, and Broad-tailed are the common species. Costa's is an uncommon wanderer upslope from Florida Wash. Rufous Hummingbirds, uncommon in spring, pass through in droves in late summer and fall, accompanied by an occasional Allen's. Only adult male Allen's is field separable. Calliope is rare in spring and uncommon in fall. The sought-after and seldom-seen Sierra Madrean specialties include White-eared, Berylline, Violet-crowned, and Lucifer Hummingbirds. In a feat that brings new insight into this unique family's powers of flight, a Berylline Hummingbird banded in Ramsey Canyon one July afternoon in 1987 appeared at the feeders at the Santa Rita Lodge the following morning. The straight-line distance between Ramsey and Madera Canyon is 40 miles. An immature Blue-throated Hummingbird navigated the same route overnight the following month.

Santa Rita Lodge is also renowned for two species of owls. At dusk every evening from April through June, guests and visitors alike gather to watch for the tiny visage of an Elf Owl framed in its utility pole nest hole. At last, with an audible gasp from the gallery, the one-ounce parent bird shoots out into the night to begin foraging for its offspring. Whiskered Screech-Owl is the other specialty species. Like Elf Owl, the Whiskered Screech has been known to use Acorn Woodpecker holes in powerline poles for nest cavities at the lodge. More frequently, one is sighted behind the lodge or below the Madera Picnic Area on a day roost in a sycamore cavity overlooking Madera Creek.

Birders will have to find these owls and the canyon's other species without using tapes—*the Forest Service has forbidden the use of all bird tapes in Madera Canyon*. With patience, it may be possible to view an owl calling from a fixed position.

Elf Owl with Black-headed Snake
Narca Moore-Craig

The Madera Amphitheater is located on the right (west) side of the road an easy walk above the lodge (0.25 mile). A nature trail with labeled plants along the first 200 yards begins at the Amphitheater. Beyond the stream the trail climbs the dry west hillside before it rejoins the road in the lowest parking area in the Hopkins Fork of Madera Canyon (1.7 miles). From there you can walk back down the road to your car. Or you can arrange a car shuttle. The birding is not particularly good along the trail, but there are repeated views of Madera Canyon backdropped by Mt. Wrightson 4,000 feet above.

For accommodations, the three cabins at the Madera Kubo (0.1 mile; 520-625-2908) offer a "gingerbread" décor alternative to the Santa Rita Lodge. The Kubo also features hummingbird and seed feeders, as well as a small gift shop. Situated at the shady confluence of the Wrightson Fork with

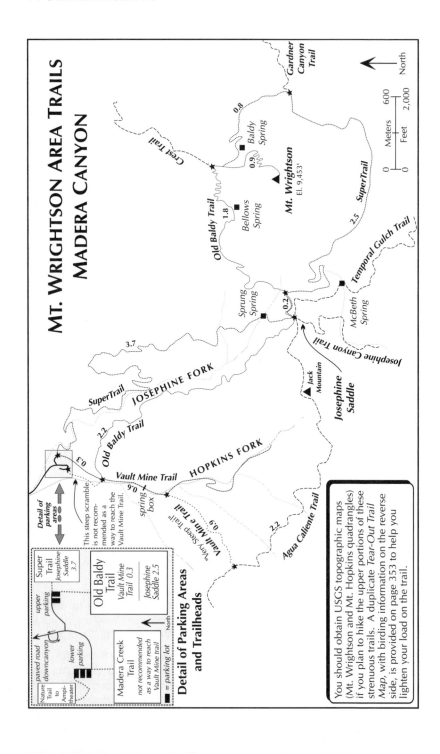

MT. WRIGHTSON AREA TRAILS
MADERA CANYON

Gardner Canyon Trail

Crest Trail

0.8

Baldy Spring

0.9

Mt. Wrightson
El. 9,453'

SuperTrail

2.5

Old Baldy Trail

1.8

Bellows Spring

Temporal Gulch Trail

Sprung Spring

0.2

McBeth Spring

3.7

Josephine Canyon Trail

SuperTrail

JOSEPHINE FORK

Jack Mountain

Josephine Saddle

2.2

Old Baldy Trail

HOPKINS FORK

Detail of parking areas

Vault Mine Trail

0.6

spring box

"Very Steep Trail"

Vault Mine Trail

0.9

Agua Caliente Trail

2.2

0.3

This steep scramble is not recommended as a way to reach the Vault Mine Trail.

Detail of Parking Areas and Trailheads

North

Nature Trail to Amphitheater

paved road downcanyon

upper parking

Super Trail | Josephine Saddle 3.7

Old Baldy Trail
Vault Mine Trail 0.3
———————
Josephine Saddle 2.5

lower parking

Madera Creek Trail
not recommended as a way to reach Vault Mine trail

North

= parking lot

You should obtain USGS topographic maps (Mt. Wrightson and Mt. Hopkins quadrangles) if you plan to hike the upper portions of these strenuous trails. A duplicate *Tear-Out Trail Map*, with birding information on the reverse side, is provided on page 353 to help you lighten your load on the trail.

Meters 600
Feet 2,000
0
North

the Main Fork of Madera, tall sycamores and conifers create excellent habitat for such species as Cooper's Hawk, Whiskered Screech- and Flammulated Owls, Blue-throated Hummingbird, Sulphur-bellied Flycatcher, House Wren, Painted Redstart, and Hepatic and Western Tanagers. A male Flame-colored Tanager summered here in 2003, apparently consorting with a female Western Tanager. In 2004 a pair of Flame-colored Tanagers returned to the tall trees across from the Madera Kubo and successfully fledged young.

Another lodging option, a small B&B called the Chuparosa Inn (0.6 mile above the Amphitheater; 0.85 mile above Santa Rita Lodge; 520-393-7370), just beyond two short, one-lane bridges, offers a third set of hummingbird feeders. Parking is limited to two or three vehicles here. *Do not park on the road.* Sometimes there are more hummingbirds here than at the Santa Rita Lodge. A female Lucifer was using the feeders at the Chuparosa in July and August 1990. A pair of Flame-colored Tanagers nested, albeit unsuccessfully, near Chuparosa in the summer of 1992.

Just beyond the Chuparosa Inn the road divides around an oval planted with introduced Arizona Cypress trees (0.1 mile). Both lanes rejoin in 50 yards at a T-junction. The left road leads to a two-tier parking area on the west side of the Josephine Fork of Madera Creek (0.1 mile). The right-hand road passes the Round-up Picnic Area and ends at a tri-level parking area on the east side of the Hopkins Fork of Madera Creek (0.1 mile). The lower lot in the Hopkins Fork is the well-signed upper end of the Madera Nature Trail. Both lots fill up with hikers on weekends and holidays.

The **Hopkins Fork** of Madera Canyon is both the best and the most popular destination for birders who care to hike. To reach the trailhead, it is recommended that you turn left just beyond the oval to reach the uppermost Josephine Fork parking area. A cable on the right, uphill end of the lot marks the easiest point of access for Hopkins Fork. An abandoned dirt road contours 0.3 mile across the ridge that divides Josephine Fork from the Hopkins Fork of upper Madera Canyon. It joins the Hopkins Fork at the beginning of the Old Baldy (an alternative, unofficial name for Mt. Wrightson) Trail in 0.3 mile. This very steep short-cut to Josephine Saddle is 2.2 miles long (instead of the 3.7-mile alternative "Super Trail"). Birders should ignore the Old Baldy Trail and take the route continuing straight up the bottom of Hopkins Fork.

The first bird you encounter here may be a House Wren. The upper branches of Madera have the largest concentration of House Wrens in Southeastern Arizona. A few minutes of quiet observation on a given spring morning should be enough to see one enter a nest cavity in a sycamore. Elegant Trogons have tried to nest just below the trail junction, but photographers invariably cause these nests to fail.

The most reliable area for Elegant Trogons in the Hopkins Fork has traditionally been in the basin one-quarter mile farther upcanyon. The trail follows the left side of the stream a couple hundred yards, then climbs a steep and rocky hill. Links of an old pipeline are frequent up to a concrete spring box on the right side of the path. This marks the lower end of the trogon nesting zone, although pairs patrol the whole length of Hopkins. Other summering species that share the big Silverleaf Oak and Alligator Juniper in the shady basin include Cooper's Hawk, Flammulated Owl, Magnificent Hummingbird, Greater Pewee, Cordilleran, Dusky-capped, and Sulphur-bellied Flycatchers, Plumbeous and Hutton's Vireos, Hermit Thrush, Grace's Warbler, Painted Redstart, and Hepatic Tanager. In migration Warbling Vireo, Swainson's Thrush, and Western Tanager are all usually common. One or two Red-faced Warblers are often here in April and May. Look for a nesting pair of Painted Redstarts near a permanent spring that cascades between a pair of slab-like boulders just 100 yards above the spring box. This little falls is trimmed with flowering Golden Columbine in May. Two Aztec Thrushes were discovered using the stretch of Hopkins Fork above the spring box in August 1994, and another was in this area in August of 2000. A Crescent-chested Warbler in late April 2003 was at the ford just up the trail.

The trail crosses the streambed in 0.25 mile and divides 200 yards beyond. The Vault Mine Trail to the Agua Caliente Trail is the "very steep trail" mentioned on the sign at the lower trail junction. (*It leads one-half mile to the abandoned Vault Mine, over 600 feet above. The Vault Mine Trail above this junction is not recommended.*) Birders who have still not seen the trogon should veer left another 200 yards up the bottom of Hopkins Fork to where the trail disappears into the rocks of the stream channel itself. The quarter-mile stretch above the stream crossing to where the trail ends in the streambed is just as good for trogons as the quarter-mile stretch below the stream crossing. If the trogons are nesting, you may have to wait all morning for a nest exchange before a bird passes by. *Under no circumstances should you disturb or knowingly approach an active nest tree.* From here back to the Josephine Fork parking area is 0.9 mile.

The eight-mile-long Super Trail to Mount Wrightson begins at the left end of the **Josephine Fork** parking lot. If you have plenty of stamina, this scenic path is great for birding. *Don't forget to carry plenty of water.* At first, you will be in the oak belt and the birds will be about the same as those which occupy the middle canyon near the Santa Rita Lodge. Elegant Trogons occasionally nest in sycamores along the stream approximately one mile up Josephine. A male Tropical Parula was using this area of Josephine from mid-July to mid-September 1984. A possible female Tropical Parula was seen with the male one day only in late July.

After one mile the trail makes a sharp switchback to the left and climbs a dry hillside. Hutton's Vireo, Black-throated Gray Warbler, and Scott's Oriole are the typical birds. Approximately three miles above the Josephine parking area, the trail enters a Ponderosa Pine forest, the home of Greater Pewee, Grace's Warbler, and Yellow-eyed Junco. Watch for Red-faced Warbler at Sprung Spring (3.8 miles above the parking area). This is about as low as the Red-faced Warbler is found in the nesting season. The first Eared Quetzal ever recorded in the Santa Rita Mountains was sighted here in July 1991. There were two more sightings from nearby areas the following month, but none subsequently. Josephine Saddle is only 0.2 mile beyond. Elevation change between the 5,400-foot-high parking area and elevation 7,100-foot Josephine Saddle is approximately 1,700 feet.

In forested glades along the remaining four miles on the Super Trail to the 9,453-foot-high summit of Mt. Wrightson, you should find a community of Transition and Canadian Life Zone birds which includes Broad-tailed Hummingbird, Hairy Woodpecker, Steller's Jay, Red-breasted and Pygmy Nuthatches, Brown Creeper, House Wren, Yellow-rumped, Grace's, Red-faced, and Olive Warblers, Hepatic and Western Tanagers, Yellow-eyed Junco, Red Crossbill (irregular), and Pine Siskin. The Baldy Saddle area (elevation 8,800 feet; 0.9 mile below Mt. Wrightson) is a particularly good location for most of these species. In May 1993 a Buff-breasted Flycatcher was also reported from the saddle. All of these birds also occur at road-accessible locations in the high Santa Catalina, Huachuca, or Chiricahua Mountains. But there is nothing quite like the satisfaction of seeing them in the 25,260-acre Mt. Wrightson Wilderness Area.

CAMPGROUNDS, RESTAURANTS, AND ACCOMMODATIONS

Bog Springs Campground, Madera Picnic Area, and Roundup Picnic Area in Madera Canyon have water, tables, fire pits, and toilets, but no showers. Overnight camping is permitted only at Bog Springs Campground. Fees apply at all areas. Continental Feedlot Café in downtown Continental serves hearty breakfasts after 7:00 a.m. Other restaurants are located at interstate exits in Green Valley.

The Santa Rita Lodge (1218 S. Madera Canyon Road, Madera Canyon, AZ 85614; 520-625-8746; www.santaritalodge.com) is a popular spot. Each room and cabin has a picture window that looks out on bird feeders. Make reservations for spring and summer visits well in advance (several months recommended). Cute and cozy are probably the best words to describe the gingerbread-style cabins at the Madera Kubo (1259 S. Madera Canyon Road, Madera Canyon, AZ 85614; 520-625-2908), just above the amphitheater in Madera Canyon. Another 0.5 mile upstream is the beautiful Chuparosa Inn B&B (1300 Madera Canyon Road, Madera Canyon, AZ 85614; 520-393-7370; www.chuparosainn.com). The Quality Inn (111 S. La Cañada, Green Valley 85614; 800-344-1441) and The Inn at San Ignacio (1861 Demetrie Loop, Green Valley, AZ 85614; 888-450-5444; www.InnAtSanIgnacio.com) also cater to birders.

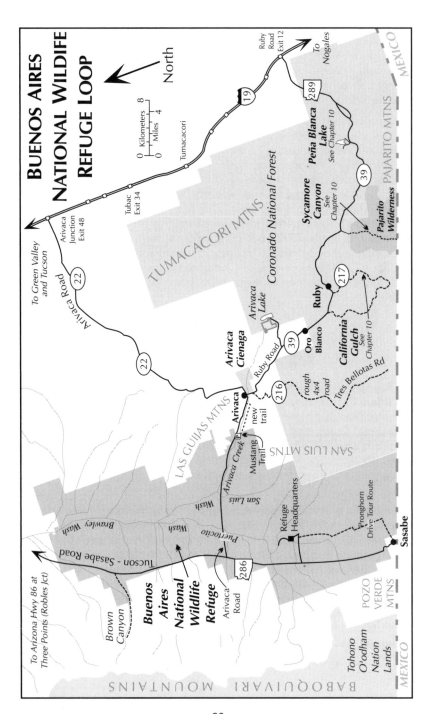

BUENOS AIRES NATIONAL WILDLIFE REFUGE LOOP

North

0 Kilometers 8
0 Miles 4

Ruby Road Exit 12

To Nogales

MEXICO

PAJARITO MTNS

Peña Blanca Lake
See Chapter 10

Sycamore Canyon
See Chapter 10

Pajarito Wilderness

289

39

217

Ruby

Oro Blanco

California Gulch
See Chapter 10

Tres Bellotas Rd

rough 4x4 road

Coronado National Forest

TUMACACORI MTNS

Tumacacori

19

Tubac Exit 34

Arivaca Junction Exit 48

To Green Valley and Tucson

Arivaca Road

22

22

Arivaca Lake

Arivaca Cienaga

Ruby Road

39

216

Arivaca

new trail

Arivaca Creek

LAS GUIJAS MTNS

Mustang Trail

SAN LUIS MTNS

San Luis Wash

Refuge Headquarters

Pronghorn Drive Tour Route

Sasabe

Puertocito Wash

Brawley Wash

Tucson - Sasabe Road

286

Arivaca Road

Buenos Aires National Wildlife Refuge

Brown Canyon

To Arizona Hwy 86 at Three Points (Robles Jct)

POZO VERDE MTNS

Tohono O'odham Nation Lands

MEXICO

BABOQUIVARI MOUNTAINS

MEXICO

CHAPTER 5

BUENOS AIRES NATIONAL WILDLIFE REFUGE AND ARIVACA CREEK LOOP

(154 miles/one or two days)

Purchased at a cost of nine million dollars in 1985, the 118,000-acre Buenos Aires National Wildlife Refuge boasts the largest ungrazed tract of grassland in the state of Arizona. Broad, grassy swales in the bottom of the Altar Valley provide the only habitat in the entire United States for the "Masked Bobwhite," a subspecies of the Northern Bobwhite. Arivaca Cienaga, a disjunct unit of the refuge acquired in 1990, preserves the headwaters of the only perennial stream in the Altar Valley. In 1995, the U.S. Fish and Wildlife Service added a four-mile-long stretch of Brown Canyon in the Baboquivari (*bob-oh-KEE-var-ee*) Mountains to the Refuge holdings. Set in Madrean pine-oak woodland, the beautiful sycamores of Brown Canyon lend a new dimension to both the Buenos Aires and our national refuge system. This loop tour visits all three of these rare and vanishing habitats.

Plan on a full day to visit Arivaca Cienaga and the Refuge Headquarters area in the upper Altar Valley. If you schedule a visit to Brown Canyon (by reservation for groups only; 520-823-4251), a second morning is advised. While Arivaca and the Refuge Headquarters offer exciting birding throughout the year, Brown Canyon is best in spring and summer.

The starting point is the junction of Interstate 10 and Interstate 19 in south-west Tucson. Take I-19 south to Exit 48 for Arivaca and Amado (33 miles). Turn right (west) away from the underpass (0.3 mile), then right again (0.1 mile) to find the beginning of Arivaca Road opposite the giant steer horns (0.1 mile). Turn left (west) on Arivaca Road.

Elevations from the beginning of Arivaca Road in the Santa Cruz Valley to the Buenos Aires Headquarters in the Altar Valley range between 3,000 and 4,000 feet, a belt formerly covered in a deep carpet of desert grassland. Wholesale changes in the savanna occurred in the late 1880s and early 1890s when ranchers stocked this corner of Arizona with 1.5 million cattle. A seven-year-drought began in 1885. By the time the rains returned in 1893 over half of the herd had starved to death, and the native grasses had been gnawed down to mineral ground. Without sod to check the heavy thunder-storms of summer, flash floods ensued. Most of the water funneled uselessly into newly cut erosion channels, pouring off the sun-baked soil as if off the clay tile roof of an old-style Spanish hacienda. Lacking a continuous stand of grass to carry fire, a shrub community dominated by mesquite replaced the grass-land. Even today mesquite remains the most conspicuous plant in this arid landscape. But from late February through April, vast swards of Mexican Gold Poppy transform the rolling hills into fields of gold. In spring there are more photographers than birders along the winding Arivaca Road.

Ash-throated Flycatchers are common from spring through late summer, and as common here in the cooler months as any location in the state. Other species that occur here, such as Gambel's Quail, Ladder-backed Woodpecker, Verdin, Cactus Wren, and Curve-billed Thrasher, are typical residents of the Sonoran Desert. This is also a good area for Desert Mule Deer. A large sign on the left (south) side of the pavement marks the Refuge parking area for **Arivaca Cienaga** (22.3 miles), just a short distance east of the small village of Arivaca (0.6 mile).

The Spanish root words for "cienaga," pronounced see-EN-ah-gah, literally translate to "100 waters," denoting a marsh. There are actually seven springs in this 1,000-acre unit of the refuge. The U.S. Fish and Wildlife Service has constructed a two-mile-long loop trail—in part a boardwalk—that keeps your shoes dry while you explore the far reaches of this unique Southwest habitat.

Vermilion Flycatcher is apt to be the first species you see upon arriving at Arivaca. In winter probably more Vermilion Flycatchers are concentrated in this boggy grassland than at any other location in Southeastern Arizona. Other resident species include Great Blue Heron, Green Heron, Killdeer, Common Ground-Dove, Gila Woodpecker, Northern "Red-shafted" Flicker, Black Phoebe, Bewick's Wren, Common Yellowthroat, Song Sparrow, East-ern Meadowlark, and Lesser Goldfinch. Joining these in summer are Gray Hawk, White-winged Dove, Yellow-billed Cuckoo, usually two pairs of Tropical Kingbirds, Barn Swallow, and Yellow Warbler. In winter watch for Green-winged Teal, Northern Pintail, Northern Shoveler, Gadwall, American Wigeon, Northern Harrier, Prairie Falcon (rare), Virginia Rail, Sora, Wilson's Snipe, Marsh Wren, Yellow-rumped Warbler, Savannah, Lincoln's, and Swamp Sparrows, and Western Meadowlark. A Streak-backed Oriole stole the show at the December 1991 Christmas Bird Count. A small flock of Ruddy Ground-Doves was using the refuge, as well as vacant lots in the town itself, in the winter of 1996–1997.

Probably the most sought-after bird at the Arivaca Cienaga is the Green Kingfisher (rare). The kingfisher—when seen—is usually at the largest impoundment, called Willow Pond. Look for it perched low over the water, and occasionally on the barbed-wire fence at the back side of the tank.

A list of recent sightings, a bird checklist, and general information about the Buenos Aires Refuge can be obtained at a small office next to the grocery store in downtown Arivaca (0.5 mile west of the refuge parking area). The office is located on the right (north) side of the road just before the main intersection. Staffed by volunteers from November through March, the refuge plans for year-round hours in the future. Bear right onto the Arivaca/Sasabe Road at the only major intersection in Arivaca (0.1 mile) to continue on to the main Buenos Aires National Wildlife Refuge Headquarters.

In 2003 a new acquisition to the refuge immediately west of the townsite of Arivaca opened up public access to upper **Arivaca Creek**. To find the planned visitor contact station and the adjacent trailhead, drive past the Baptist Church to a cinder-block wall with a large gate on the left (south) side of the road (0.3 mile west of the Sasabe Road intersection). This trail will follow Arivaca Creek for approximately 2.25 miles west to the Mustang Trail Parking Area (2.5 miles west of Arivaca via the Sasabe Road). Trimmed with big

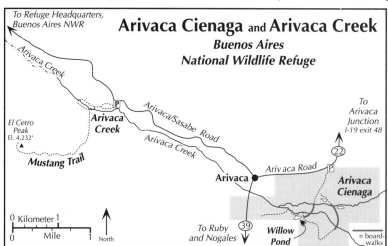

To Refuge Headquarters,
Buenos Aires NWR

Arivaca Cienaga and **Arivaca Creek**
Buenos Aires
National Wildlife Refuge

Arivaca Creek

El Cerro Peak
El. 4,232'

Arivaca Creek

Arivaca/Sasabe Road

Arivaca Creek

Mustang Trail

To Arivaca Junction
I-19 exit 48

22

Arivaca Road

Arivaca

Arivaca Cienaga

0 Kilometer 1
0 Mile 1
North

To Ruby and Nogales
39

Willow Pond

= board-walks

Masked Bobwhite
Narca Moore-Craig

Fremont Cottonwoods, this foothills stream is reminiscent of parts of Sonoita Creek near Patagonia—but without the crowds of birders. Many of the birds, too, are the same as those found at the Patagonia-Sonoita Creek Preserve. More ambitious birders can continue downstream another half-mile beyond the Mustang Trail, wade across, and return up the far bank. This longer route passes by the family homestead of author Eva Wilbur-Cruce, who wrote *A Beautiful, Cruel Country* about her experiences growing up and living here in the early 1900s. *This is private property—please respect No Trespassing signs.*

The summering birdlife along Arivaca Creek includes up to seven pairs of Gray Hawks, Broad-billed Hummingbird, Northern Beardless-Tyrannulet, Brown-crested Flycatcher, Thick-billed (rare) and Tropical Kingbirds, Yellow-billed Cuckoo, Bell's Vireo, Lucy's Warbler, Yellow-breasted Chat, Summer Tanager, and Hooded and Bullock's Orioles. All of these species depart before winter. Some of the cold-weather birds that replace them are Gray Flycatcher (uncommon), Ruby-crowned Kinglet, Hermit Thrush, Yellow-rumped Warbler, Green-tailed Towhee, Chipping, Savannah, Fox (rare), White-throated (uncommon), and White-crowned Sparrows. There are records of Buff-collared Nightjar here from 1991 and 1993. Up to four pairs of Rose-throated Becards nested here in the early 1980s. They have since disappeared but may return again—the habitat is excellent.

The hiking route with the best scenery and the fewest birds ascends 4,232-foot-high El Cerro Peak. Called the Mustang Trail, this path leaves the creek path at the ford one-quarter mile downstream, and gains 750 feet of elevation in 2.5 miles. Mustang Trail is very steep and rocky in sections. Watch for Rock Wrens, Rufous-crowned Sparrows, and Scott's Orioles (summer) in the oak grassland on El Cerro's slopes.

After birding Arivaca Creek, continue west into the Altar Valley on the Arivaca/Sasabe Road to Highway 286 (9.4 miles). Turn left (south) here. Turn left (east) again onto the Entry Road (4.4 miles), signed for Buenos Aires National Wildlife Refuge. Newly paved, the entry thoroughfare swings southeast across the floor of the Altar Valley to a T-intersection with Pronghorn Drive (2.0 miles). For much of the year Pronghorns are as common along the entrance road as they are farther south along the road that bears their name. Capable of achieveing speeds of 45 miles per hour, North America's fastest land mammals are not members of the Old World family of true antelopes. The herd of Pronghorn presently on the Buenos Aires, approximatley 40 adults in 2004, stems from a 1987 transplant of the Chihuahuan subspecies.

To reach the **Buenos Aires National Wildlife Refuge Headquarters** turn left (north) at the Pronghorn Drive junction (0.25 mile). The office is open daily 7:30 a.m. through 4:00 p.m., except holidays. Stop here for bird checklists and road condition information. There are picnic tables and restrooms at the office. Bird-seed feeders on the north side of the building occasionally attract the Masked Bobwhite subspecies of Northern Bobwhite for which the refuge was created. Prior to the refuge's establishment, the last wild Masked Bobwhite seen in Arizona was in 1897.

The Buenos Aires Ranch actually predates the 1884 discovery of the Masked Bobwhite, a race in which the male has a black throat and chestnut plumage. Pedro Aguirre founded a stage stop on the site in 1864. One hundred years later, Jim and Seymour Levy of Tucson discovered a remnant population of Masked Bobwhite near Benjamin Hill in Sonora, 100 miles due south of the Buenos Aires Ranch. Bobwhites collected at Benjamin Hill in the 1960s formed the nucleus of the breeding stock used by the U.S. Fish and Wildlife Service for their captive breeding efforts.

By 1974 Masked Bobwhites were being returned to their former range on the Buenos Aires Ranch. After good reproduction in 1979, a double whammy of drought and grazing had virtually exterminated the wild population again by 1982. It was obvious that the only hope for Masked Bobwhite lay in a cattle-free range. After several years of political bickering, the Buenos Aires National Wildlife Refuge came into existence in 1985. Using Northern Bobwhites from Texas as foster parents, sterilized to prevent genetic dilution, Buenos Aires boasted a population of approximately 100–200 Masked Bobwhites in 2004. Still perilously close to the brink of extinction as a wild subspecies, the goal at the Buenos Aires National Wildlife Refuge is a population of 500 breeding pairs of Masked Bobwhites.

The headquarters area is also good for a variety of other birds. Some of the resident and summering species here include Greater Roadrunner, Gambel's Quail, Costa's Hummingbird, Ladder-backed Woodpecker, Say's Phoebe, Western Kingbird, Chihuahuan Raven, Cactus Wren, Curve-billed Thrasher, Lucy's Warbler, Blue Grosbeak, Canyon Towhee, and both Hooded and Bullock's Orioles. Eastern Meadowlarks are common in the grasslands. During the winter months Western Meadowlarks join the Easterns. Western Meadowlarks have nested on the refuge, especially after winters with exceptional rainfall. Watch for an occasional Crested Caracara coasting by the headquarters in search of an easy meal.

From the headquarters area the road descends back into the bottom of the Altar Valley and continues north en route to Grebe Pond and Aguirre Lake (cheek-by-jowl at 1.2 miles). Originally constructed by Pedro Aguirre in the 1870s to irrigate alfalfa, Aguirre Lake varies in size from a dry mud puddle to a 100-acre reservoir. It is most apt to hold significant water after the summer rains. Perhaps the best bird ever seen here was Arizona's first record of a Garganey in April 1988. This was also the site of Southeastern Arizona's second record of Upland Sandpiper in May 1989. When at least some water is present during migration periods, species likely to be encountered include Eared Grebe, Great Blue Heron, White-faced Ibis, Willet, Solitary Sandpiper, Spotted, Western, and Least Sandpipers, Long-billed Dowitcher, and Wilson's Phalarope. Occasionally up to one thousand ducks use the lake—assuming it's wet! Bring a spotting scope just in case.

Pronghorn Drive begins a short distance south of the headquarters (0.25 mile). Part of a complex of approximately 200 miles of dirt tracks, the recently improved, partially paved Pronghorn Drive is now a self-guided auto loop that features interpretive signs. It is exactly 10 miles long. The rich Velvet Mesquite grassland on either side of the road hosts a world of sparrows. A sample of the species that occur here are Botteri's (summer), Cassin's (summer), Rufous-winged, Rufous-crowned, Chipping (winter), Brewer's (winter), Black-chinned (winter), Vesper (winter), Lark, Black-throated, Savannah (win-

Scaled Quail
Narca Moore-Craig

ter), Baird's (rare, winter), Grasshopper, Lincoln's (winter), White-throated (uncommon, winter), and White-crowned (winter) Sparrows. The refuge's major claim to fame, of course, is quail. With four species established at Buenos Aires, there are more here than at any other single location in the United States. Both Scaled and Gambel's Quail are common along this road; Montezuma Quail and Masked Bobwhite are uncommon. This loop drive is also excellent for the Pronghorns. *Birders should be aware that other refuge roads are impassable after heavy rains. Some roads should not be attempted without four-wheel-drive. Off-road travel is not permitted.*

From the Buenos Aires National Wildlife Refuge, the shortest way back to Tucson is north on Highway 286 to Three Points (also known as Robles Junction; 37.5 miles from the entrance). The Altar Valley is a hawk alley throughout the year, but especially during migration and winter. The most abundant species are Northern Harrier (winter), Cooper's (winter), Swainson's (summer), Red-tailed, and American Kestrel. Less common but possible are White-tailed Kite (some years four–six pairs use the refuge), Sharp-shinned Hawk (winter), Golden Eagle, Merlin (rare, winter), Prairie Falcon (winter), and Peregrine Falcon (winter). Altogether, 18 species of raptors have been recorded in the Altar Valley. On a good winter day it's possible to see 100 individual birds of prey between the refuge entrance and Three Points.

In 1995 the U.S. Fish and Wildlife Service completed negotiations to add 2,000 acres of **Brown Canyon** in the Baboquivari Mountains to the Buenos Aires National Wildlife Refuge. Access in 2004 was limited to groups with advance reservations; phone 520-823-4251. Brown Canyon drains all the way from the 7,730-foot-high summit of Baboquivari Peak. Interpretations vary, but the word Baboquivari is probably derived from Tohono O'odham roots meaning "Water-on-the-mountains." Canyons such as Brown hold year-round springs that make them magnets for wildlife. Looming some 3,000 feet above the canyon floor, it is easy to see how this stupendous granite dome came to be revered by the people of the Tohono O'odham Nation.

To reach Brown Canyon, look for the turnoff on the left (west) side of Highway 286 between mileposts 20 and 21 (13 miles north of the Buenos Aires entrance road; 25 miles south of Three Points). A good dirt road suitable for standard vehicles winds up the grassy apron at the outlet of the canyon to the gate at the lower end of the refuge area (4.0 miles). The Brown Canyon Visitor Center lies one-half mile upstream.

Sycamores dominate the canyon floor throughout the entire four-mile length managed by the refuge, and form an especially lush grove in the area above the visitor center. This is excellent Coues White-tailed Deer habitat. A pair of Mountain Lions has also been sighted here numerous times since the Fish and Wildlife Service assumed management responsibility for the area in 1995. Resident and summer birds using the sycamores and surrounding oak hillsides are Zone-tailed Hawk, Montezuma Quail, Acorn and Arizona Woodpeckers, Western Wood-Pewee, Sulphur-bellied and Dusky-capped Flycatchers, Mexican Jay, Bewick's Wren, Black-throated Gray Warbler, and Painted Redstart. Golden Eagles soaring overhead are a fairly common sight. Eight species of hummingbirds have been recorded in the canyon, and Elegant Trogons were sighted a few times in the past by the former homeowners. The dense hackberry and mesquite thickets in the foothill area harbor Buff-collared Nightjar and Varied Bunting. Up to two pairs of Black-capped Gnatcatchers were using the upper canyon in 1996 and 1997. In many respects the bird community in Brown Canyon resembles that found in the lower elevations of Madera Canyon to the east.

To conclude this loop return to Highway 286 (4.0 miles) and turn left (north). Continue up to Three Points (25 miles) and turn right (east) onto

*Baboquivari Peak (elevation 7,730 feet) dominates the western
horizon on the drive west from Arivaca toward Buenos Aires NWR.*
Cindy Lippincott

Highway 86 (Ajo Highway), which arrows its way almost without curves
straight into Tucson at Interstate 19 (19.2 miles). To find the starting point at
the junction of I-19 and I-10, turn left (1.0 mile).

CAMPGROUNDS, RESTAURANTS, AND ACCOMMODATIONS

There are 90 primitive campsites located throughout Buenos Aires National Wildlife Refuge (P.O. Box 109, Sasabe, AZ 85633; 520-823-4251).
Camping is permitted only at designated sites. Nearby is Casa Bella B&B
(16851 W. Hinkley, Arivaca, AZ 85601; 877-604-3385; www.casabella-bandb.
com). Rancho de la Osa (P.O. Box 1, Sasabe, AZ 85633; 520-823-4257;
www.ranchodelaosa.com; multi-night stays preferred) is a guest ranch located just six miles south of Buenos Aires National Wildlife Refuge.

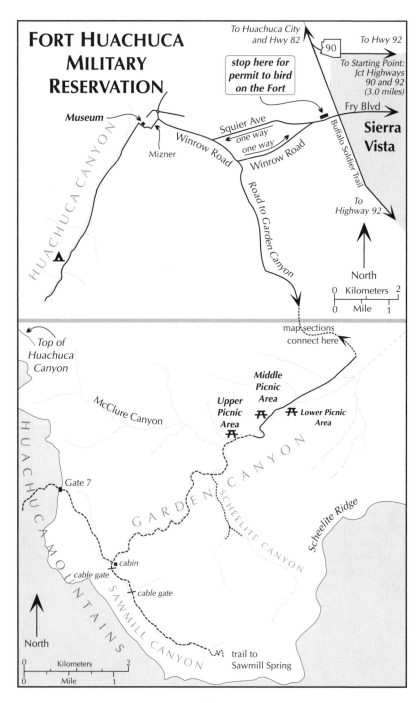

FORT HUACHUCA MILITARY RESERVATION

To Huachuca City and Hwy 82

To Hwy 92

90

To Starting Point: Jct Highways 90 and 92 (3.0 miles)

stop here for permit to bird on the Fort

Fry Blvd

Sierra Vista

Museum

Squier Ave
one way
one way

Winrow Road

Winrow Road

Mizner

Buffalo Soldier Trail

To Highway 92

Road to Garden Canyon

HUACHUCA CANYON

North

Kilometers

0   2

0   Mile   1

map sections connect here

Top of Huachuca Canyon

McClure Canyon

Middle Picnic Area

Upper Picnic Area

🏕 **Lower Picnic Area**

HUACHUCA MOUNTAINS

GARDEN CANYON

SCHEELITE CANYON

Scheelite Ridge

Gate 7

cabin

cable gate

cable gate

SAWMILL CANYON

trail to Sawmill Spring

North

Kilometers

0   2

0   Mile   1

108

CHAPTER 6

HUACHUCA
MOUNTAINS

The blue, alp-like peaks of the Huachuca Mountains actually straddle the international border at Coronado National Memorial and provide a home for a community of birds and wildlife with its roots in the Sierra Madre of Mexico. Viewed from Sierra Vista, four major summits dominate the 20-mile-long skyline of the Huachuca Mountains. Highest and easternmost is Miller Peak (El. 9,466 feet). Jutting up to the west in order of their appearance are Carr (El. 9,220 feet), Ramsey (El. 8,725 feet), and Huachuca (El. 8,410 feet) Peaks. The word "Huachuca," pronounced *wa-CHOO-ka*, comes from Apache cognates meaning "Thunder Mountain".

Two full days are required to bird the wet canyons, foothills, and forested highlands of the Huachuca front range. Most birders will also want to visit the adjacent San Pedro River to look for Gray Hawks and Green Kingfishers (see Chapter 7), adding a third or fourth day to their stay in the Sierra Vista area. With over 400 species of birds recorded within 15 miles of city limits, your time here will seem all too brief.

The starting point for this tour is the intersection of Highway 90 and Highway 92 in east Sierra Vista, 75 miles southeast of Tucson. From Tucson take Interstate 10 east 42 miles to the well-signed junction with Highway 90 at Exit 302. Turn right (south) onto Highway 90 and proceed south. (While on Highway 90, just before milepost 300, you will pass a signed gate on the right for **French Joe Canyon**. A few miles up this rough road, Rufous-capped Warblers have entertained many observers since the spring/summer of 1995. See Chapter 10 for birding directions.) At Huachuca City (23 miles) continue to the traffic signal at the Highway 90 Bypass on the north side of Sierra Vista (5.5 miles). Turn left (east) here. Follow the bypass for several miles until it turns south (right) again and intersects with Highway 92 at a traffic signal with an oversized gas station on the near right corner (4.7 miles).

For birders originating in Willcox—or points farther east—follow I-10 for 38 miles west of Willcox to Exit 302 for Highway 90. Then use the directions above to follow Highway 90 south to its intersection with Highway 92.

If you are birding east from Patagonia (Chapter 3), it makes sense to access the Huachuca Mountains via Highway 82. Drive north from Patagonia to Sonoita (12 miles), and continue directly east through town on Highway 82 across the grasslands to the intersection with Highway 90 (19 miles). Turn right (south) here. Follow Highway 90 south through Huachuca City (4.0 miles) to the bypass (5.5 miles), turn left, and continue on to its junction with Highway 92 (4.7 miles) as described above. The grasslands east of Sonoita are excellent for Grasshopper and Cassin's Sparrows on the fence-lines, Common Nighthawks early in the morning and at dusk, and a herd of Pronghorns that usually stays on the left (north) side of Highway 82. The Pronghorns, the fastest land mammal in North America, are often sighted in the grassy swales between the rolling hills in the first eight miles east of Sonoita. (See Chapter 3 for a more detailed discussion of the Sonoita Grasslands.)

From Douglas take U.S. Highway 80 west to Bisbee (23 miles), turn right at the traffic circle (on your left), pass the Lavender Pit, and continue through the Mule Mountain Tunnel to a well-signed turnoff to Sierra Vista and Highway 90 (9 miles). From here Highway 90 crosses the broad San Pedro River Valley before it reaches Sierra Vista and the junction with Highway 92 (20 miles). *Note:* When approaching Bisbee from Douglas, the signs for Sierra Vista are via Highway 92, not Highway 90. That road winds up in the same place as the intended route, but is ten miles longer.

SIERRA MADREAN CANYONS

GARDEN CANYON/RAMSEY CANYON TOUR

(49 miles/one day)

Unlike most other places in the southeast corner, Sierra Vista is relatively new. It was founded after Fort Huachuca was reactivated in 1954. In the past four decades the population has gone from approximately 100 to over 40,000. Until the U.S. government abolished it in 1876, these lands were part of the Chiricahua Indian Reservation. The post was established in the spring of 1877 to control marauding Apache warriors, who apparently resented being forcibly removed from their ancestral homelands, and it remained active until Geronimo surrendered for the fourth and final time in the fall of 1886. Today Fort Huachuca serves as a communications center and an electronics proving ground for the U.S. Army.

The Huachuca Mountains from the San Pedro Valley
Richard Cachor Taylor

Begin this tour early in the morning. The miles are not many, but the trail up Scheelite Canyon is steep, and you will want to move slowly there to maximize your chance of seeing the Spotted Owl, as well as the other species that share this beautiful wilderness defile. Don't forget to bring a water bottle.

To begin this tour drive west on Fry Boulevard from the starting point to the West Gate of Fort Huachuca (3.0 miles). The fort is normally open to the public during daylight hours (roughly 5:30 a.m. to 5:30 p.m. in the summer), but officials may close portions for reasons of national security, gunnery practice, or as a fire-prevention measure. Stop at the guard station on the right for a permit. You will be required to show your driver's license, proof of insurance, and vehicle registration if you are the car owner; rental car drivers must present a driver's license and a rental contract. Additionally, all passengers are required to show a photo ID at a checkpoint just beyond the guard station. Display your permit on your dashboard, get into the left lane, and proceed past the water tower on your right (1.8 miles), to a well-marked hard left (south) turn for Garden Canyon (0.3 mile). There is a sign for "Sportsman Club" and **Garden Canyon** straight ahead (0.4 mile) at the intersection at the bottom of the hill.

Resist the temptation to hurry to Garden Canyon. *Speed limits are strictly enforced on the post, and MPs are less inclined to leniency than civilian police.* Furthermore, every dry ravine crossing the road is lined with concrete. These constitute speed dips. Unless you slow down to *no more than 10 miles per hour* at each and every one, you can bend a car's chassis and sprain your neck. Seriously.

For the next several miles you will be traveling across a lush mesquite grassland populated by Botteri's, Cassin's, Rufous-crowned, and Grasshopper Sparrows. Botteri's and Cassin's are almost impossible to see unless they are singing. Your best chance of finding these birds is in July and August, after the summer rains have begun. *Remember to park completely off the pavement, and do not walk in the grass—you might stumble upon live ammunition.* Red-tailed Hawk and American Kestrel are both resident, but during migration in September multitudes of both species invade from the north, capping nearly every power pole with a raptor. It's an amazing spectacle. Other birds that share these grasslands include Northern Harrier (winter), Montezuma (rare) and Scaled Quail (uncommon), Greater Roadrunner, Black-chinned Hummingbird (summer), Rufous Hummingbird (on the flowering agaves, mid-summer), Western and Cassin's Kingbirds (summer), Cactus Wren, Loggerhead Shrike, Blue Grosbeak (summer), Canyon Towhee, Lark Sparrow, Eastern Meadowlark, and both Hooded and Scott's Orioles (on the flowering agaves, summer). Pronghorns are occasionally sighted early in the morning.

As the road approaches the canyon mouth, there are three picnic areas. Montezuma Quail are more likely along the edge of the road anywhere above the Lower Picnic Area (mile 4.0). Birders should continue on to the **Upper Picnic Area** (2.7 miles) without delay, especially on a weekend. After 9 a.m. on weekends it is likely that crowds of boom-box-toting soldiers and families will utterly demolish the acoustics. Remember, however, that it's their duty station.

Well-watered and with tall, shady trees, the Upper Picnic Area is a terrific place for Acorn and Arizona Woodpeckers, Buff-breasted Flycatcher (regular in summer since the spring of 1999), Sulphur-bellied Flycatcher (summer), Hutton's Vireo, Eastern Bluebird (irregular), Black-throated Gray Warbler (summer), Painted Redstart (summer), Lesser Goldfinch (especially summer), and many other species. From May through September, Elegant Trogons are almost always present in the groves of sycamores just upstream or immediately downstream from the picnic ground, and some winters in recent years a male has used the same area. Arizona's first record of a Crescent-chested Warbler came from this stretch of Garden Canyon in September 1983.

Option: You may want to bypass Scheelite Canyon now in order to bird first at Sawmill Canyon, which catches the morning sun earlier than Scheelite.

The pavement ends here, but Garden Canyon Road is reasonably broad and well-graded up to **Scheelite Canyon** (0.7 mile). Park at a wide pullout on the left side of the road. The trailhead is also on the left (south) side. Ordinarily a pair of Painted Redstarts are fluttering in and around the grove of Bigtooth Maples that shades the creek across the road from the parking area. The entrance to the trail is behind some enormous boulders meant to discourage off-road vehicles. A short distance beyond is a trail register which many birders use to describe the most recent location of the Spotted Owls.

SCHEELITE CANYON, FORT HUACHUCA

Duplicate Tear-Out Trail Map of Scheelite Canyon is provided on page 355.

● = Spotted Owl sighting locations since 1978

⋯⋯ = foot trail

Contour Interval: 100 feet

From data recorded by Robert T. Smith

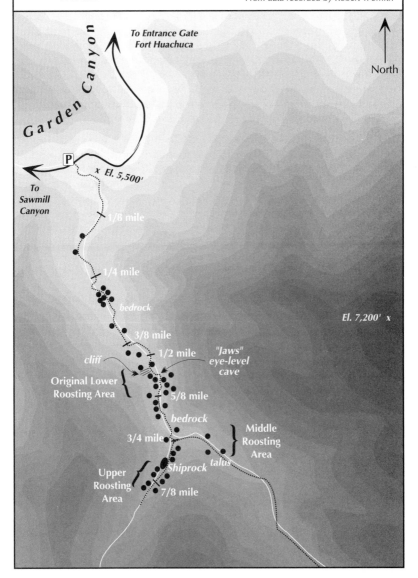

The trail up Scheelite Canyon is steep and mined with rolling rocks. There is no drinking water in the canyon. Nonetheless, owing to the work of a single man, Scheelite is one of the most visited areas in the entire Huachuca Mountains.

Robert T. Smith, "Smitty" to the 6,000-plus birders whom he led up the canyon from 1978 until his death in 1998, should be credited as the protector of the Spotted Owls of Scheelite. Even the trail to the owls is due in a large part to his planning, and accomplished with the labor and cooperation of Fort Huachuca staff. After showing birders what are undoubtedly the most-often-seen pair of Spotted Owls in the U.S., Smitty then made sure that his guests did not unwittingly disturb these precious birds. The birding community lost a good friend in the fall of 1998 when Robert T. Smith passed away. Continuing to protect and preserve the owls, and the unique environs in which they dwell, is perhaps the most appropriate tribute birders can pay to the dedicated man who so long served as the custodian of Scheelite Canyon.

Scheelite is most famous for its Spotted Owls, but it is also a good location for an impressive array of other pine-oak woodland birds. Watch for Bridled Titmouse, Virginia's Warbler (summer), and Rufous-crowned Sparrow in the lower canyon. This is also the best stretch for Montezuma Quail, Hammond's and Dusky Flycatchers (migration), Dusky-capped Flycatcher (summer), Western Scrub-Jay (screeching on the brushy slopes above), Hutton's Vireo, Black-throated Gray Warbler (summer), and Canyon Towhee. Some years a pair of Elegant Trogons nests in the dense riparian area midway between the canyon entrance and "Jaws." Baptized by Smitty, Jaws is a rock formation on the left side of the trail set amidst tall timber. Near Jaws listen for the distinctive vocalizations of Northern Pygmy-Owl, Whip-poor-will (occasionally even in the daytime during summer), Red-breasted Nuthatch, House Wren, and Hepatic Tanager (summer). After one-half mile (the indefatigable Smitty painted these useful mileage markers) the trail approaches an area with a towering cliff on the right side. This is the start of the "lower area" commonly used by the owls for roosting (although they can occur as low as the first one-quarter mile). Canyon Wrens generally sound the alarm as you approach. In summer Painted Redstarts are invariably here, and often a pair of Red-faced Warblers as well. Summering Cordilleran Flycatchers also nest in this cool, shady zone.

Ordinarily the Spotted Owls take perches under 20 feet in height, usually on a major limb in the lower half of a tree. In large oaks they may park well out on a bough, but look for them to sit near the trunk in small trees and conifers. The pair is often side by side, and almost always within 100 feet of one another if both are present. The code of self-restraint Smitty asked birders to exercise is simple:

Do not approach within 50 feet of the birds;

Do not talk loudly;

Spotted Owl
Gail Diane Yovanovich

Do not point at the birds or wave your arms;

Photographers should not use flash or make noise to get the birds' attention;

Do not use tape recordings or try to imitate the calls of Spotted Owls. (Spotted Owl calls are specifically prohibited on Fort Huachuca.)

Approximately 100 yards beyond the 5/8-mile marker, Scheelite narrows to a rocky chute with a small spring, except in extremely dry years. The platter-sized pools may attract up to three species of warblers bathing in a single puddle. The sight of Virginia's, Black-throated Gray, or Red-faced Warblers cavorting with a Painted Redstart or migrant species such as Nashville or Wilson's Warblers will strike a chord in any birder. White-throated Swifts (summer) zoom overhead and an occasional Golden Eagle floats across the narrow slit of sky. Check here for Greater Pewee (summer) and Plumbeous Vireo (summer). Mexican Jays occur throughout Scheelite, but above the chute Steller's Jays are also common. At mile marker 3/4, approximately 150 paces beyond the seep, Scheelite splits into two major canyons. Elevation here is 6,350, 600 feet above the parking area.

The main trail continues up the left fork another 2.8 miles, climbing steeply 2,000 more feet before it joins the Crest Trail. The Spotted Owls sometimes roost near the junction—and infrequently in the first 200 yards up the left fork, but usually—when not in the lower area—the birds are up the unmaintained track ascending the right fork. Look for them in dense stands of maple or oak, especially 200 yards above the junction to about 3/8 mile up the canyon. The trail peters out 200 or so yards beyond "Shiprock," a prow-shaped boulder in the center of the dry creek bed. Smitty, who was born in 1918 and climbed the Scheelite Trail several times a week until his death in 1998, called this stretch the "Upper Area." If you go this far to find the owls, I'm sure you'll agree the name is well chosen.

Beyond the Scheelite parking area, the Garden Canyon Road narrows and requires either high clearance or skill and determination to negotiate the steep, concrete-lined stream crossings. An abundance of purple Rothrock's Star Thistle and magenta Wheeler Thistle, which trim the road after the summer rains, transform upper Garden Canyon into a butterfly-lovers' paradise. Over 130 species have been recorded to date. The huge, black-and-yellow beauty is a Two-tailed Swallowtail, a show-stopper in anyone's book.

For a five-minute cultural detour, park by a bridge on the right side of the road (1.5 miles). From here a 100-foot-long path leads through a grove of Bigtooth Maple trees to a cliff with petroglyphs that probably date back to at least A.D. 1200. Depicted among the two dozen or so figures are plainly discernible raptors. This artwork should remind birders to scan the skies. Red-tailed Hawks, Zone-tailed Hawks, and Golden Eagles are all regular in Garden Canyon.

Continue up the canyon bottom to an old log cabin at the entrance to Sawmill Canyon (0.6 mile). A seldom-used campground for military personnel lies 200 yards beyond a cable gate on the left. Buff-breasted Fly-catchers (summer) are likely anywhere from the cable gate near the log cabin to the far end of the campground. A loose colony of perhaps as many as six to eight pairs nest in this open stand of Chihuahua and Apache Pines. These particular Buff-breasteds are easily the most sought-after—and seen—birds of their species in the entire United States.

Also using the area are Cooper's Hawk, Northern Pygmy-Owl, Hairy Woodpecker, Pygmy Nuthatch, Brown Creeper, Greater Pewee (summer), Western Wood-Pewee (summer), Dusky-capped Flycatcher (summer), Cassin's Kingbird (summer), Steller's Jay, Eastern Bluebird (irregular), Grace's (summer) and Olive Warblers, Hepatic Tanager (summer), and Yellow-eyed Junco. Occasionally Sawmill hosts Northern Goshawk, Elegant Trogons (summer), Cassin's Finches (irregular, winter), and Evening Grosbeaks. Red-faced Warblers (summer) can usually be found a half-mile or so upcanyon from the picnic area. Williamson's and Red-naped Sapsuckers are winter visitors, and in the winter of 1996–1997 Clark's Nutcrackers were also present.

It will be hard to leave Garden Canyon and its tributaries, but unless you've had exceptional luck, the day is half gone and bird activity has practically dried up. The sensible way to pass the slow hours of afternoon is drowsing in the shade at the Ramsey Canyon Preserve, Beattys' Guest Ranch in Miller Canyon, or Mary Jo Ballator's B & B in Ash Canyon, watching the eye candy at the hummingbird feeders with your eyelids at half-mast. Miller and Ash Canyons will be treated later in this chapter.

To find Ramsey Canyon return to the East (Main) Gate and leave the fort. Continue straight ahead (east) on Fry Boulevard through Sierra Vista to the starting point at Highway 92 (3.0 miles). Turn right (south). The road into Ramsey Canyon turns right (west) off Highway 92 after exactly 6.0 miles. An alternative route is to turn right onto Buffalo Soldier Trail as you leave the fort. This road joins Highway 92 south of town, bypassing busy Fry Boulevard.

Along Ramsey Canyon Road, look for Swainson's (summer) and Red-tailed Hawks perched on the utility poles, and Scaled Quail pecking in the yards along the right (north) side of the pavement over the first stretch of mesquite savanna (2.2 miles). The desert grassland leading into the canyon entrance is also prime habitat for Greater Roadrunner, Ladder-backed Woodpecker, Ash-throated Flycatcher (summer), Cassin's and Western Kingbirds (summer), Cactus Wren, Curve-billed Thrasher, Pyrrhuloxia, Blue Grosbeak (summer), and Lark Sparrow. Parking is prohibited along the shoulder of Ramsey Canyon Road after it enters the oak woodland and the canyon proper. Approximately 100 yards after the Ramsey Creek crossing (1.3 miles; 3.5 miles from Highway 92), the road passes the right-hand turnoff and parking area (guests only) for the Ramsey Canyon Inn. Not surprisingly, the same hummingbirds use the feeders at the inn as at the preserve just 50 yards beyond. The kitchen window feeder on the east (downcanyon) side of their main building is sometimes the best stake-out in the whole canyon for White-eared Hummingbird. *Non-guests of Ramsey Canyon Inn are asked to birdwatch from the Ramsey Canyon Road.*

With 30,000 visitors annually, The Nature Conservancy's 300-acre **Ramsey Canyon Preserve** is indisputably the most popular natural-history site in the Huachuca Mountains. Advance parking reservations are no longer required since the parking lot was expanded. A fee of $5/person ($3 for Cochise County residents and Nature Conservancy members) for a seven-day pass is collected at the visitor center/book store/office. Please do not attempt to bring a vehicle or RV over 20 feet long up this steep, narrow, winding mountain road. The preserve is open daily from 8:00 a.m. to 5:00 p.m. March–October, 9:00 a.m. to 5:00 p.m., November–February, except for Thanksgiving, Christmas, and New Year's Day (520/378-2785). Guided walks are offered at 9:00 a.m. Tuesday, Thursday, and Saturday, March–October. *Pets, smoking, and picnicking are not allowed. The use of tape recorders is forbidden at the Ramsey Canyon Preserve.*

Much of Ramsey's reputation comes from the variety of hummingbirds that patronize the preserve's sugar-water feeders. While greater numbers and similar diversity are found in Miller and Ash Canyons to the south, nonetheless up to 12 species have been recorded at the Ramsey Canyon Preserve on a single August day, although six to ten is more typical. The regular species

Blue-throated Hummingbird
Georges Dremeaux

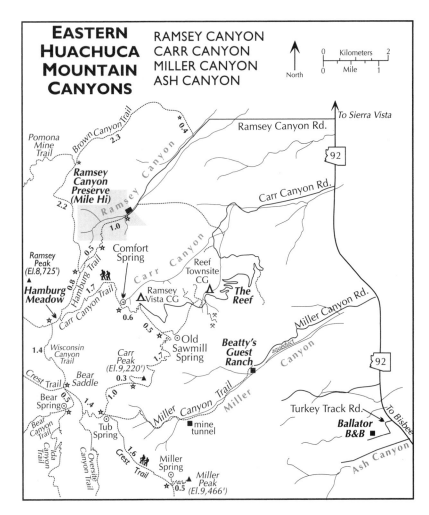

EASTERN HUACHUCA MOUNTAIN CANYONS

RAMSEY CANYON
CARR CANYON
MILLER CANYON
ASH CANYON

North

0 — Kilometers — 2
0 — Mile — 1

To Sierra Vista

Ramsey Canyon Rd.

92

Pomona Mine Trail

Brown Canyon Trail

0.4
2.3

Ramsey Canyon

Carr Canyon Rd.

Ramsey Canyon Preserve (Mile Hi)
2.2

1.0

Ramsey Peak (El.8,725')

0.5

Comfort Spring

Carr Canyon

Reef Townsite CG

The Reef

Hamburg Trail

0.8
1.7

Hamburg Meadow

Carr Canyon Trail

Ramsey Vista CG

Miller Canyon Rd.

92

0.6

0.5

1.4 Wisconsin Canyon Trail

Carr Peak (El.9,220')

1.7

Old Sawmill Spring

Beatty's Guest Ranch

aqueduct

Miller Canyon

Crest Trail

Bear Saddle

0.3

0.5

Bear Spring

1.4

1.0

Miller Canyon Trail

Miller

Turkey Track Rd.

To Bishee

Bear Canyon Trail

Tub Spring

mine tunnel

Ballator B&B

Ida Canyon Trail

Oversite Canyon Trail

Crest Trail

1.6

Miller Spring

Ash Canyon

0.5

Miller Peak (El.9,466')

from April through August are Broad-billed, Blue-throated, Magnificent, Black-chinned, Anna's, and Broad-tailed. Most summers, Ramsey is also one of the best locations in Arizona for White-eared and Berylline Hummingbirds.

An afternoon watching the feeders usually produces at least a few bonus hummers. During fall migration—July through September for this family—the core group of species is joined by Calliope, Rufous, and Allen's (uncommon and—except for extremely scarce adult males—basically not identifiable in the field). Additionally, the Sierra Madrean species which breed after the rainy season are most apt to appear in late summer. These include such sought-after living jewels as White-eared, Berylline, Violet-crowned, and Lucifer Hummingbirds.

Although records of Costa's Hummingbird span the warmer months, spring is the season it is most likely to visit Ramsey. To date, Plain-capped Starthroat has yet to put in an appearance at the Ramsey Preserve, although there are hearsay accounts, and the starthroat has been recorded in nearby Ash and Miller Canyons. Ramsey Canyon has the distinction of being the only place in the U.S. in which Bumblebee Hummingbird has possibly occurred. Two females were collected in July 1896. There has never been a subsequent observation, and many have speculated that the locality for the specimens was mislabeled. Even without the Bumblebee, 14 species of hummingbirds occur virtually annually at the Ramsey Canyon Preserve.

The combination Ramsey Canyon visitor center/bookstore/gift shop is set at an elevation of 5,550 feet among cool sycamore, maple, oak, and conifer trees next to the nearly perennial waters of Ramsey Creek. Because all wildlife is protected, birdlife of all kinds is common. Some of the many species that occur here include Wild Turkey, Mexican Jay, Bridled Titmouse, White-breasted Nuthatch, Bewick's Wren, Plumbeous Vireo (summer), Black-throated Gray Warbler (summer), Hepatic Tanager (summer), Black-headed Grosbeak (summer), Yellow-eyed Junco, and Scott's Oriole (summer). Occasionally a Whiskered Screech-Owl chooses a day roost visible from the parking area, or Golden Eagles occupy a ledge directly above the bookstore, but these are never guaranteed. Most summers a lone Coati, a tropical relative of the Raccoon, can be seen foraging for insects and lizards somewhere within the preserve.

After watching the feeders for hummingbirds, the best way to see most other birds in Ramsey is from the half-mile-long nature trail. The same birds occur here as in the lower canyon. Also watch for Zone-tailed Hawk (summer), Montezuma Quail, Acorn and Arizona Woodpeckers, Greater Pewee (just beyond the "frog pond," summer), Western Wood-Pewee (summer), Hammond's Flycatcher (migration), Dusky-capped and Sulphur-bellied Flycatchers (summer), Hutton's Vireo, Grace's Warbler (summer), Painted Redstart (mainly summer, although one occasionally overwinters), and Western Tanager (summer). In 1994 Elegant Trogons nested successfully in the preserve for the first time since it was established in 1974. Recent years have seen additional nests, and at least one trogon is ordinarily in the canyon throughout the summer. Both Aztec Thrush and Flame-colored Tanager may have also colonized Ramsey Canyon in the 1990s. While your chances of sighting either the thrush or the tanager are remote, this is one of the places where sightings of these rarities occur every few years.

The steep, rocky, switchbacking trail that leads to **Hamburg Meadow** has seen a substantial increase in birder traffic since 1991, the year that Eared Quetzals were discovered nesting in upper Ramsey Canyon. Although months or years may elapse between sightings, even the remote chance of seeing one of these 13-inch-long birds flashing brilliant red, green, and white colors as it launches across a wilderness canyon is enough to quicken nearly anyone's pulse.

But a warning is in order: this is emphatically *not* a walk for the faint-hearted or for those who are out of shape. It is especially difficult for people coming from sea level. Allow at least four hours to complete the 4.6-mile-long round trip to Hamburg Meadow, and remember the preserve itself closes at 5:00 p.m. If the purpose of your hike is truly birding, I personally advise spending the whole day and packing a lunch. *Remember there is no picnicking at Ramsey Canyon Preserve, so you must be off the property for lunch. Be sure to carry water.*

The Hamburg Trail begins as the nature trail/service road that follows the south side of the canyon bottom to the staff residence (0.4 mile). One hundred yards beyond, the road swings left and begins to climb through a Madrean pine-oak woodland. A pair of Crescent-chested Warblers appeared and sang near here in April and May 1984, but failed to nest. This is also the area of the canyon used by a nesting pair of Flame-colored Tanagers from April to July 1993. In winter watch for Red-naped Sapsucker and Hammond's Flycatcher (very rare) in the vicinity of the staff residence.

The trail switchbacks up 700 feet to an elevation of 6,390 feet at Ramsey Vista (0.6 mile). Downstream lies a wide expanse of the grassy San Pedro River Valley; upcanyon Ramsey is heavily forested. Common summer birds at the viewpoint are White-throated Swift, Violet-green Swallow, Canyon Wren, and Spotted Towhee. Listen for the distinctive *squeal-chuck!* calls of the magnificent Eared Quetzal. This is the lower end of the zone in Ramsey the birds most often used in the 1990s, and the acoustics at the viewpoint are superb.

After a gradual descent to the stream (0.3 mile), the trail crosses the water and continues to a junction with Brown Canyon Trail (0.2 mile), 1.5 miles from the preserve bookstore. In no other place in the entire Huachucas Mountains are Red-faced Warblers (summer) more common.

Other birds to watch for in this moist area of Bigtooth Maple and White Fir include Cooper's Hawk, Northern Goshawk (rare), Band-tailed Pigeon, Spotted Owl (rare), Hairy Woodpecker, Greater Pewee (summer), Cordilleran Flycatcher (summer), Steller's Jay, Common Raven, White-breasted and Red-breasted Nuthatches, Brown Creeper, American Robin, Hermit Thrush, Warbling Vireo (summer), Yellow-rumped and Grace's Warblers (summer), Western Tanager (summer), and Yellow-eyed Junco. After the Brown Canyon junction the trail climbs steadily, but generally stays on the bottom of Ramsey, winding through tall conifers broken by glades of maple until it connects with the Carr Canyon Trail (0.8 mile; elevation of 6,850 feet), just 50 yards below Hamburg Meadow. Carr Canyon Trail is described in the next tour. The return from Hamburg Meadow back to the Ramsey Canyon Preserve parking area is 2.3 miles and a total of 1,300 feet elevation change.

From the Ramsey Canyon Preserve parking area back to the starting point at the Intersection of Highways 90 and 92 is 9.5 miles. To reach the starting point turn left (north) at the Ramsey Canyon Road junction with Highway 92.

For the ambitious who have planned ahead and have a spouse, relative, or friend waiting in a car, it is possible to continue up the Carr Canyon Trail to Ramsey Vista Campground (2.3 miles; about 600 feet elevation change). Access to Carr Canyon Trail is described in the next tour. The trail from the Ramsey Canyon Preserve up to Ramsey Vista Campground (4.6 miles total; 1,850 feet elevation change) is one of the most rewarding hikes for high-elevation birds in the entire Huachuca Mountains.

EASTERN HUACHUCA MOUNTAIN CANYONS

CARR CANYON–MILLER CANYON– ASH CANYON TOUR
(45 miles/one day)

Carr, Miller, and Ash Canyons provide birders with a good alternative to the heavily visited Ramsey Canyon Preserve, especially on weekends and holidays. Upper Carr Canyon Road offers the only vehicular access to the Ponderosa Pine of the high Huachuca Mountains. Besides the famous hummingbird show at Beattys' Guest Ranch, upper Miller Canyon plumbs the highest peaks of the range, and offers foot access to a cool, streamside forest of Douglas-fir and White Fir. Ash Canyon is the best site for foothill hummingbirds in the entire Huachuca Mountains.

To find **Carr Canyon** from the starting point at the intersection of Highways 90 and 92, follow Highway 92 due south exactly one mile past the Ramsey turnoff to the well-marked junction (7.0 miles). A housing development in the lower drainage precludes serious birding until after the pavement ends (1.1 miles; the last house is actually at mile 1.4). National Forest property above here presents the birder with an opportunity to see most of the species found in Ramsey Canyon without the crowds. There are several pullouts with unimproved picnicking and camping sites in this short stretch.

Birds in lower Carr are representative of the Madrean pine-oak woodlands: Cooper's Hawk, Montezuma Quail, Western and Whiskered Screech-Owls (night), Blue-throated, Magnificent, and Black-chinned Hummingbirds (summer), Acorn and Arizona Woodpeckers, Northern "Red-shafted" Flicker, Western Wood-Pewee (summer), Dusky-capped, Ash-throated, and Brown-crested Flycatchers (summer), Cassin's Kingbird (summer), Mexican Jay, Bridled Titmouse, Bushtit, White-breasted Nuthatch, Bewick's Wren, Plumbeous Vireo (primarily summer), Virginia's and Black-throated Gray Warblers (summer), Painted Redstart (summer), Black-headed Grosbeak (summer), Canyon and Spotted Towhees, and Rufous-crowned Sparrow. In the summer of 1994 a pair of Buff-breasted Flycatchers was using the area near the stream crossing (0.8 mile).

This is the same part of the canyon where Jim Lane lived in the early 1960s. Jim launched the "Lane Guides" in 1965 with the first edition of this tour book for Southeastern Arizona. If you bird in Carr at daybreak, and witness the red rocks of the high Huachucas catching the first butterscotch light of dawn, the source of Jim's inspiration will be obvious.

The next section of the road climbs 1,750 feet up the stupendous band of Cambrian cliffs known as The Reef (3.9 miles). Vehicles over 20 feet long and trailers over 12 feet long are not permitted on the hair-pin turns above. If you are bothered by driving on the edge of cliffs, I strongly suggest you do not attempt this road.

The one-lane track zigzags nine times up the towering east wall of Carr Canyon to a vista that sweeps all the way from the Santa Catalina Mountains north of Tucson to the Sierra Madre Mountains in northern Mexico. Sierra Vista and the Upper San Pedro River Valley lie directly below. Beyond the viewpoint on top **The Reef**, the road passes Reef Townsite Campground (0.4 mile), and then wanders through an open stand of primarily Ponderosa Pine before it ends at the Ramsey Vista Campground (1.25 mile; elevation 7,400 feet). The U.S. Forest Service charges $10 fees at both campgrounds. Drinking water was not available at either area in 2003.

Most of the high-elevation species of the border ranges can be found by birding along this beautiful stretch of forest. Watch the dead treetops for Band-tailed Pigeon and Greater Pewee, and scan the living pines for Grace's and Olive Warblers. A human-caused fire in June 1977 consumed 10,000 acres before the advent of the summer rainy season extinguished the blaze. Time has healed the worst scars and several species—notably Buff-breasted Flycatcher—have actually benefited from the burn. Other highland birds underscore the strong Rocky Mountain influence on the avifauna in the upper elevations of the Huachucas. Some of these are Whip-poor-will (after dusk, summer), Broad-tailed Hummingbird (summer), Hairy Woodpecker, Cordilleran Flycatcher (summer), Steller's Jay, Pygmy Nuthatch, House Wren, Yellow-rumped Warbler (summer), and Western Tanager (summer). In migration watch for Olive-sided Flycatcher in dead treetops, and mixed flocks containing dozens of Townsend's and Hermit Warblers.

The well-marked trail to **Comfort Spring** begins off the west end of the Ramsey Vista Campground, drops 200 feet in elevation, and loops through the burn around the headwater ravines of Carr Canyon. There are Red-faced Warblers in the Gambel Oak in the first draw just a quarter-mile below the trailhead, and the past two decades have seen records of Berylline Hummingbird (1986), Eared Quetzal (1990), and Aztec Thrush (1991–1992), all between the parking area and Comfort Spring (0.6 mile). Comfort Spring is a permanent seep that always harbors a pair of Buff-breasted Flycatchers. They share this open area with Eastern Bluebirds, which also enjoy the lush undergrowth amid the skeleton forest left behind by the fire.

If you have the time, energy, and can make arrangements, continue beyond the spring to Hamburg Meadow (1.7 miles) in upper Ramsey Canyon, then down Ramsey to the preserve visitor center (2.3 miles; see description of this trail in the previous Garden-Ramsey Canyon Tour) to a friend waiting with a vehicle. *Before you begin this 4.6-mile-long hike, please note that Ramsey Canyon Preserve closes at 5:00 p.m.*

Assuming you do not have a ride waiting for you in Ramsey, a rewarding plan is to relax among the whispering pines at the end of the Carr Canyon Road. Probably any species you missed in the morning will come wafting by on an updraft generated by The Reef itself. During summer there is no cooler place reached by road for a picnic lunch anywhere in the Huachucas.

To continue this tour, however, you must return to Highway 92 (7.7 miles). Turn right (south) on Highway 92, A large sign marks the entrance to **Miller Canyon** (2.0 miles/9.0 miles south of the junction of Highways 90 and 92). Of all the canyons in the front range, Miller has the highest headwaters. Draining the 9,466-foot-high summit of Miller Peak itself, nearly all of the habitats and nearly all of the birds of the border ranges can be found somewhere in or along the tall riparian forest that follows Miller Creek down the mountain to the 5,000-foot-elevation canyon outlet. The two major reasons that birders visit Miller, however, are the array of hummingbird feeders at Tom and Edith Beatty's apple orchard, and rarities such as Eared Quetzal, Aztec Thrush, and Flame-colored Tanager along the trail in the upper canyon. Miller Road begins in a housing area set in a grassland punctuated with Soaptree Yucca, Honey Mesquite, and an occasional Arizona Sycamore. The large white flowers of the Arizona Prickle Poppy and the purple flowers of the Wheeler Thistle add color to the roadside in summer. This is the home of Greater Roadrunner, Acorn and Ladder-backed Woodpeckers, Say's Phoebe, Mexican Jay, Chihuahuan Raven, Verdin, Cactus Wren, Northern Mockingbird, Curve-billed Thrasher, and Pyrrhuloxia. In summer Western Kingbirds sit on the fencelines, utility wires, and other conspicuous perches. After the rains start in early July, listen for the songs of both Botteri's and Cassin's Sparrows. The desert grassland and the housing both end with the pavement (0.85 mile).

A short distance beyond the end of the pavement there is a U.S. Forest Service restroom on the left side of the road. This is the only public facility in the canyon, and there are no developed camping or picnic sites.

As the graded road enters the mountain, the birds are approximately the same as those found in nearby Garden, Ramsey, and Carr Canyons. At night (primarily in the spring and summer), listen for the calls of Flammulated Owl,

Eared Quetzal
Narca Moore-Craig

Western and Whiskered Screech-Owls, Great Horned Owl, and both Common Poorwill and Whip-poor-will. During the day look for Cooper's, Zone-tailed, and Red-tailed Hawks, Acorn and Arizona Woodpeckers, Northern "Red-shafted" Flicker, Hutton's Vireo, Mexican Jay, Bushtit, White-breasted Nuthatch, Bewick's Wren, Blue-gray Gnatcatcher, Spotted and Canyon Towhees, and Lark and Rufous-crowned Sparrows. In summer expect Ash-throated, Dusky-capped, and Brown-crested Flycatchers, Western Wood-Pewee, Plumbeous Vireo, Black-throated Gray Warbler, and Black-headed Grosbeak. Montezuma Quail is most common at the canyon mouth, particularly in grassy woodland. Extensive tree-thinning by the U.S. Forest Service along the Miller Road in 2003 should improve the habitat for both quail and Wild Turkey in forthcoming years.

Miller Canyon Road terminates at an oval parking lot cut into a dense grove of oaks at an elevation of 5,750 feet (1.7 miles/2.5 miles from Highway

92). Arizona Woodpecker, White-breasted Nuthatch, Plumbeous Vireo, Painted Redstart, and Hepatic Tanager enliven the area at the road end.

Just 50 yards beyond the parking area lies **Beattys' Guest Ranch**. Birders are welcome to check the feeders located along the downcanyon fenceline for, perhaps, the largest concentration of hummingbirds in the Huachuca Mountains. Aside from sheer numbers, Beatty's is also the best place to see the high-elevation Huachuca Mountain species: Blue-throated, Magnificent, Calliope (migration), and Broad-tailed. Most years Miller Canyon is the best area in Arizona for White-eared Hummingbird. Berylline is also occasional here. Use caution when identifying Berylline Hummingbird, however, since an apparent hybrid with a Magnificent Hummingbird has been present in Miller Canyon since the summer of 1999. This gorgeous bird has a white dot behind the eye, a solid black bill, and a lustrous blue chest. In early June 2003 thirteen species of hummingbirds were recorded at Beatty's on a single day, the one-site record for hummingbirds in one day in the entire U.S.

Owners Tom and Edith Beatty have even provided a public viewing area with a picnic table to enhance birders' comfort. Aside from six rental housekeeping units, the Beattys operate a small store featuring their homegrown honey and apples when in season, as well as snacks, postcards, and a few books. Reservations are suggested to use either their "controlled access" or "hawk watch" sites, where the Beattys have located two other viewing stations. The fee to visit these two sites was $5/person or $20 for groups over four in 2004.

Ambitious, well-conditioned hikers may elect to continue up the canyon in search of some of the most prized birds in the entire Huachucas. To do this area and yourself full justice, I suggest arriving at daybreak. *Do not forget to bring a water bottle.* The best birding is along the abandoned road in and near the canyon bed between mile 0.5 and 2.2.

The first half-mile of the **Miller Canyon Trail**, marked by a Forest Service sign across from the parking lot, circles north around the Beatty orchard through a stand of manzanita, oak, and juniper. Then it rejoins the old road to the city of Tombstone's water supply in a moist, steep-walled section of the canyon. Ignore Hunter Canyon Trail at the junction and stay right (0.1 mile). A road branching left toward the stream a short distance beyond leads 100 yards to the fenced intake of the spring. Colorful birds summering among the large sycamores include Sulphur-bellied Flycatcher, Painted Redstart, Hepatic Tanager, Scott's Oriole, and—sometimes—an Elegant Trogon. In the winter check for Red-naped and Williamson's (uncommon) Sapsuckers, and listen for the halting carols of Townsend's Solitaires on still, sunny mornings.

The main trail continues straight ahead as the canyon walls loom progressively higher. After 0.5 mile (1.5 miles above the parking area) it crosses the stream and climbs through a coniferous forest on the shady, north-facing side of the canyon. The immediate area around the abandoned mine tunnel on the left (south) side of the trail (0.6 mile; 2.1 miles above the parking area) was the most reliable area for the Flame-colored Tanager in 2002 and again in 2003. Watch closely for Spotted Owls on a day roost in the short section up to the next stream crossing (0.1 mile). The Miller Peak tributary cascades down to the main canyon just above here, and creates an especially propitious situation for highland birds.

Among the host of tropical rarities that have been found in Upper Miller Canyon were a pair of Short-tailed Hawks in the summer of 1999 and 2004, and—after a five-year hiatus—an Eared Quetzal in the fall of 1999. A flock of no fewer than nine Aztec Thrushes were using the canyon in August and September of 1996. Arizona's second record of a Tropical Parula was roaming this zone of Miller in the summer of 2001, and here, too, Slate-throated Redstart was recorded for the first time in Arizona in mid-April 1980. More recently, a particularly orange male Flame-colored Tanager showed up in the summer of 2002, and presumably the same individual returned again in 2003. This male is known to have mated with a female Western Tanager and successfully fledged young. Obviously, beware of hybrid tanagers in Miller Canyon.

Other regular occupants of the upper canyon include Northern Pygmy-Owl, Broad-tailed Hummingbird (summer), Hairy Woodpecker, Greater Pewee (summer), Cordilleran Flycatcher (summer), Buff-breasted Flycatcher (summer), Plumbeous, Hutton's, and Warbling Vireos (all in summer), Steller's, Western Scrub- and Mexican Jays, Common Raven, Red-breasted Nuthatch, Brown Creeper, House Wren, Hermit Thrush, Grace's and Red-faced Warblers (both summer), Western Tanager (summer), Chipping Sparrow, and Yellow-eyed Junco. Birds in upper Miller reflect the Huachuca Mountain's position midway between the Rockies to the north and the Sierra Madre of Mexico.

Do not attempt to follow Miller Canyon into the 20,190-acre Miller Peak Wilderness unless you have budgeted a full day for the outing, have plenty of food and water, and have made appropriate transportation arrangements. Do not forget to bring a map showing the hiking trails of the Huachuca Mountains. There are no regularly-occurring birds in the wilderness area that warrant this expenditure of time and energy. There are, however, breathtaking panoramas that encompass vast tracts of southern Arizona and northern Mexico.

Over the next 1.3 miles the Miller Canyon Trail climbs 1,700 feet up to the Crest Trail at Bathtub Spring, elevation 8,540 feet. Most of the route lies within the blackened, picket-post remains of the 1977 Carr Fire. To the southeast, the Crest Trail continues another 2.1 miles to the aspen-clad summit of 9,466-foot-high Miller Peak, and then descends to Montezuma Pass, elevation 6,575 feet, in Coronado National Memorial (5.0 miles). To the west, the Crest Trail joins feeder routes leading to the end of the Carr Canyon

Road (3.2 miles) and Ramsey Canyon Preserve (5.2 miles). The vegetation along much of the Crest Trail is Ponderosa Pine and Gambel Oak. Aside from Quaking Aspen, the north face of Miller Peak is a verdant admixture of White Pine, Douglas-fir, and a few Rocky Mountain Maples. The birds are the same as those listed for upper Miller Canyon. Northern Goshawk, Red-tailed and Zone-tailed Hawks, American Kestrel, and Golden Eagle are often seen soaring over the mountain-tops.

A sh Canyon rose to prominence as an important stop on the Arizona hummingbird trail in August of 2002 when Mary Jo Ballator realized that birders desperately wanted to see the Plain-capped Starthroat visiting her B&B. Following in the tradition of the Spoffords in Portal, the Patons in Patagonia, and the Beattys in nearby Miller Canyon, Mary Jo opened her yard. Other stars in Ash Canyon in 2003, aside from a returning starthroat, were reliable Lucifer and sporadic Berylline Hummingbirds among a throng of a dozen species. One of the Beryllines was an apparent cross with a Broad-billed Hummingbird; caution is always recommended when identifying Berylline Hummingbird in Arizona.

Positioned where mesquite gives way to oak, and significantly drier than either Miller or Ramsey, Ash Canyon is better situated to attract foothill species. Broad-bills, for example, are common at Mary Jo's feeders, and Costa's are regular in the summer. Other yard birds include both Ladder-backed and Arizona Woodpeckers, Mexican Jays, Bridled Titmice, Verdins, Curve-billed Thrashers, and Canyon Towhees. A sleeve of riparian vegetation west of the house also provides habitat for a pair of Cooper's Hawks and a family of Sulphur-bellied Flycatchers. To find the Ballator home, turn right on Highway 92 from Miller Canyon, and drive south to milepost 332 and continue 0.7 mile past it to Turkey Track Road (2.6 miles from Miller Canyon Road; 0.3 mile *before* Ash Canyon Road). Turn right (west) onto Turkey Track Road, and follow the narrow track through two right-angle turns (it becomes Spring Road after the second bend) to its end opposite a partially-stuccoed, straw-bale wall (0.5 mile). As you enter through the wrought-iron gate, the feeders are located both in front and on the south and west sides of the house. Comfortable lawn furniture and attractive native plantings enhance the setting, and make long vigils for rare hummers possible. There is also a rental cottage on the lot.

To return to the starting point from Ash Canyon B&B, follow the road back to Highway 92, and turn left (north). The total distance from the Ballator home in Ash Canyon to the starting point at the junction of Highways 90 and 92 is 12.0 miles.

CAMPGROUNDS, RESTAURANTS, AND ACCOMMODATIONS

Reef Townsite and Ramsey Vista at the end of the Carr Canyon Road are the only improved campgrounds (vehicles over 20 feet not permitted; no trailers over 12 feet long). *Drinking water is not available at either campground.*

The Tombstone RV Park & Resort (formerly KOA) (Route 80, P,O, Box 99, Tombstone, AZ 85638; 800-348-3829 or 520-457-3829) and the Tombstone Territories RV Resort (2111 E. Highway 82, Huachuca City, AZ 85616; 877-316-6714 or 520-457-2584) are recommended for RV users and trailer campers.

The Ramsey Canyon Inn B&B (29 Ramsey Canyon Road, Hereford, AZ 85615; 520/378-3010; lodging@ramseycanyoninn.com), just 50 yards down canyon from the preserve, is tastefully done and has the same hummingbirds as the neighboring preserve. Beattys' Guest Ranch (2173 E. Miller Canyon Road, Hereford, AZ 85615; 520-378-2728; BeattysGuestRanch@earthlink.net) offers six housekeeping cabins with a view. The views vary but all offer panoramas of the highest canyon in the Huachuca Mountains. To acquire information about Mary Jo Ballator's guest house, write Ash Canyon B&B, 5255 E. Spring Road, Hereford, AZ 85615; 520-378-0773; 2mjb@ mindspring. com.

There are numerous restaurants and motels in Sierra Vista. Owing to their proximity to Ramsey, Carr, Miller, and Ash Canyons, many birders gravitate to either the Quality Inn (1631 S. Highway 92, Sierra Vista, AZ 85635; 800-458-0982 or 520-458-7900; qualityinnsv@aol.com), or the Windemere (2047 S. Highway 92, Sierra Vista, AZ 85635; 800-825-4656 or 520-459-5900; reservations@windemerehotel.com), which includes breakfast in its room rate.

Two B&Bs located along the San Pedro River also cater to birders: Casa de San Pedro B&B (8933 S. Yell Lane, Hereford, AZ 85615; 888-257-2050 or 520-366-1300; www.bedandbirds.com) and San Pedro River Inn (8326 S. Hereford Road, Hereford, AZ 85615; 520-366-5532; www.sanpedroriverinn.com). Both sites are described in the following chapter.

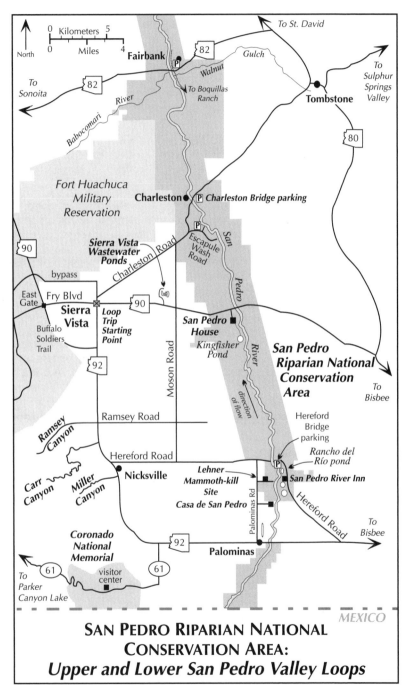

North

0 Kilometers 5
0 Miles 4

To St. David

Fairbank 82 Walnut Gulch

To Sonoita 82 River

To Boquillas Ranch

To Sulphur Springs Valley

Tombstone

80

Babocomari

Fort Huachuca Military Reservation

Charleston Charleston Bridge parking

Sierra Vista Wastewater Ponds

Escapule Wash Road

San Pedro River

90

bypass

East Gate

Fry Blvd

Sierra Vista

Loop Trip Starting Point

90

San Pedro House

Kingfisher Pond

San Pedro Riparian National Conservation Area

To Bisbee

Charleston Road

Buffalo Soldiers Trail

92

Moson Road

direction of flow

Ramsey Canyon

Ramsey Road

Hereford Bridge parking

Hereford Road

Rancho del Río pond

Nicksville

Lehner Mammoth-kill Site

San Pedro River Inn

Carr Canyon

Miller Canyon

Casa de San Pedro

To Bisbee

Palominas Rd

Hereford Road

Coronado National Memorial

92

Palominas

To Parker Canyon Lake

61

61

visitor center

MEXICO

SAN PEDRO RIPARIAN NATIONAL
CONSERVATION AREA:
Upper and Lower San Pedro Valley Loops

CHAPTER 7

SAN PEDRO VALLEY LOOPS

D raining all the way from Sonora, the long, shady pools of the upper San Pedro River constitute the most important valley riparian system in all Southeastern Arizona. More Gray Hawks live here than anywhere else in the United States. The San Pedro also hosts the largest concentration of Yellow-billed Cuckoos in the U.S., as well as Arizona's largest population of Green Kingfishers. This continuous, 40-mile-long grove of cottonwood and willow trees provides migratory birds with a conduit of food and cover unmatched elsewhere in the American Southwest.

The Bureau of Land Management acquired this mile-wide, 50,000-acre tract of river bottom only in 1986. After designating the upper San Pedro a National Conservation Area the following year, all grazing and farming was officially eliminated. The ensuing surge of new plant growth in the riverine forest has astonished even seasoned ecologists. And bird populations simply exploded. Song Sparrows, for example, have increased fifty-fold. All told, at least 350 species of birds have been recorded along the San Pedro River in just the past decade. Today the San Pedro River National Conservation Area probably represents the most miraculous conservation achievement in the recent history of Arizona.

That does not mean the future of the river is secure. With continuous population growth and groundwater pumping, the San Pedro may vanish just like the Santa Cruz River in Tucson, and for just the same reasons.

The starting point for both loops in this chapter is the intersection of Highways 90 and 92 on the east side of Sierra Vista. (Access to this junction is described in detail in Chapter 6 for the Huachuca Mountains.) In summer it is important to bird the gallery forest along the river early, since most bird activity subsides by 10 a.m.

UPPER SAN PEDRO
VALLEY LOOP

(56 miles/one day)

This loop begins with a sunrise trip to the river, overshooting the Sierra Vista Wastewater ponds (3.0 miles), where the waterfowl and shorebirds tend to be present throughout the day.

Take Highway 90 due east from the starting point. The pavement descends gradually through a parched Chihuahuan Desert landscape characterized by thorny shrubs, until abruptly the lush green ribbon of the San Pedro appears directly ahead. Turn right (south) at the base of the terrace at the well-signed entrance drive to the **San Pedro House** (4.0 miles). A combination bookstore/gift shop/information center, the San Pedro House (0.25 mile) is run entirely by a non-profit conservation group called Friends of the San Pedro River. The house is open from 9:30 a.m. to 4:30 p.m. daily, except Thanksgiving and Christmas.

Nearly every bird known from the San Pedro has occurred in the general neighborhood of the San Pedro House and the nearby Highway 90 bridge. A typical summer list of species seen along the entrance drive and the edge of the parking area will include Swainson's Hawk, American Kestrel, Gambel's Quail, Common Ground-Dove, Black-chinned Hummingbird, Gila Woodpecker, Gilded Flicker, Vermilion Flycatcher, Say's Phoebe, Cassin's and Western Kingbirds, Cactus Wren, Lucy's Warbler, Summer Tanager, Blue Grosbeak, Canyon and Abert's Towhees, Eastern Meadowlark, and Bullock's Oriole. In late July and August listen for the characteristic songs of Botteri's and Cassin's Sparrows on the perimeter of the parking area. In winter watch for Northern Harrier, Northern "Red-shafted" Flicker, Mountain Bluebird, Green-tailed Towhee, Brewer's Sparrow, and Western Meadowlark.

A one-mile loop trail leads to **Kingfisher Pond**, an abandoned gravel quarry that has filled with groundwater, on the south end of the circuit. The trail begins off the left rear (southeast) corner of the San Pedro House. A note of caution: if there has been a significant rain within 24 hours, deep mud can render the trail almost impassable and the banks of the river treacherous. If you decide to venture down to the pond anyway, there's a hose in front of the house. As one who's trudged back from the river on two-inch-thick mud suction cups weighing at least 10 pounds each, you have my solemn word you'll be ridiculously grateful to wash off the adobe gunk caked to the soles of your boots.

Since rainfall averages only 12 inches per year, heat is usually the most serious problem. Open-country birds—doves, kingbirds (summer), shrikes, and meadowlarks—are the common species as the route crosses an abandoned alfalfa field to a line of cottonwood trees (0.3 mile). Turning right (south), the

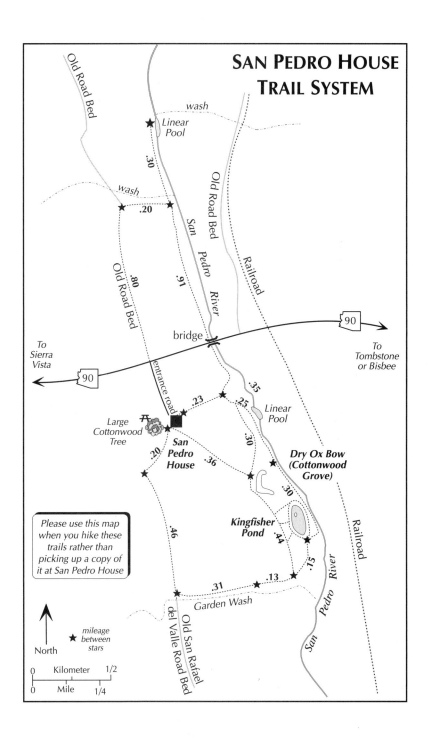

SAN PEDRO HOUSE TRAIL SYSTEM

Old Road Bed

wash

Linear Pool

.30

wash

.20

Old Road Bed

San Pedro River

Old Road Bed

Railroad

.80

.91

bridge

90

To Sierra Vista

To Tombstone or Bisbee

90

entrance road

.23

.35

.25

Linear Pool

Large Cottonwood Tree

San Pedro House

.30

Dry Ox Bow (Cottonwood Grove)

.20

.36

.30

Kingfisher Pond

.46

.44

.15

Railroad

San Pedro River

.31

.13

Garden Wash

Old San Rafael del Valle Road Bed

Please use this map when you hike these trails rather than picking up a copy of it at San Pedro House

North

mileage between stars

Kilometer   1/2
0

Mile   1/4
0

trail continues along the edge of an old river terrace through tall Sacaton Grass and mesquite to the west edge of the one-acre pond (0.3 mile). Look for Vermilion Flycatcher (primarily summer), Summer Tanager (April–September), and Abert's Towhee along the way. Abert's Towhee are as common here as any other area in Arizona or the U.S.

Gaps in the shoreline cottonwoods and willows allow glimpses of the far bank. Take time to check low branches overhanging the water for Green Kingfisher. A pair of Tropical Kingbirds (summer) has nested at Kingfisher Pond since 1993, and early in the morning watch also for possible Snowy Egret (uncommon, late summer) or Black-crowned Night-Heron. Other birds present include Green Heron, Common Moorhen, Lesser Nighthawk (skimming the surface of the water on summer mornings), Cliff Swallow (summer), Common Yellowthroat, and Red-winged Blackbird.

Probably the two most abundant species along the San Pedro in the summer are Yellow Warbler and Common Yellowthroat, but Yellow-breasted Chat and Summer Tanager are also commonplace. To find the river, circle the far (south) end of Kingfisher Pond about halfway, then veer right (east) on the trail-of-use for about 50 yards to the bank of the stream. Turn left (north) downstream to continue the loop. Unless there have been heavy recent rains, the San Pedro River is a series of long, quiet pools linked by a stream 10 to 20 feet wide. These pools are inhabited by the subspecies of Mallard formerly known as the Mexican Duck. Drakes have yellow-olive bills, but otherwise look like dark-plumaged hen Mallards. Also watch for Great Blue Heron, Gray Hawk, Yellow-billed Cuckoo, Great Horned Owl, Belted Kingfisher (primarily migration periods), Black Phoebe, Brown-crested Flycatcher (summer), White-breasted Nuthatch, Bewick's Wren, and Song Sparrow.

The path that parallels the river is narrow but generally well-defined. During migration Lazuli Buntings dodge in and out of the rank growth along the water. Possible passage Empidonax flycatchers (Willow, Hammond's, Dusky, Gray, and Pacific-slope) sprinkled among the young of both Western Wood-Pewees and Vermilion Flycatchers, create enough identification challenges for even the most masochistic of birders. The trail leaves the cottonwoods almost due east of the parking lot (0.4 mile). Check the river in both directions for Green Kingfisher before hiking the last leg. Since first confirmed as an Arizona nesting species in 1988, the kingfisher's San Pedro population has fluctuated. A census found 15 kingfishers using the upper river in 1993. Although numbers have declined since the mid-1990s, Green Kingfishers still turn up throughout the year.

It is approximately 300 yards across an open field to the comfortable chairs on the front porch of the San Pedro House. Picnickers will find a couple of tables under one of the most enormous cottonwoods in the entire Southwest. Don't forget to record your observations at the visitor center, and re-

Green Kingfisher
Narca Moore-Craig

member, any profits from the books, T-shirts, and sodas sold here go to support the conservation efforts of the Friends of the San Pedro.

To visit the **Sierra Vista Wastewater Ponds** turn left (west) onto Highway 90 and retrace your route back toward the city. Watch for the large green fields on the right (north) that signal your approach to the entrance into the facility (4.0 miles; open daily during daylight hours). Follow the pavement straight ahead, then through a long curve around a field to a new raised viewing area and shade ramada created by the city of Sierra Vista in 2001.

There is not much of a view. The single narrow lead of open water not choked by reeds may harbor White-faced Ibis, Mallards, Northern Pintails, or Northern Shovelers, but other ducks, rails, and shorebirds usually stay out of view in ponds off-limits to the public. Probably this wetland hosts as many different birds as it did previously; a special tour of the facility in October 2003 found a Prothonotary Warbler. Scan the fields as you return to Highway 90. Among the plethora of species you may see are Northern Harrier (winter), Red-tailed and Swainson's Hawks (summer, especially on the central-pivot irrigation system), Peregrine and Prairie Falcons (primarily winter), Scaled Quail, Greater Roadrunner, Lesser Nighthawk (at dawn and dusk in summer), Say's Phoebe, Western and Cassin's Kingbirds (summer), Horned Lark (primarily winter), Chihuahuan Raven, American Pipit (winter), Lark, Vesper, and other Sparrows (primarily winter), Lark Bunting (fall through spring), Eastern Meadowlark, Western Meadowlark (winter), Yellow-headed Blackbird (especially winter), Brewer's Blackbird (winter), Great-tailed Grackle, and Brown-headed Cowbird.

Depending on your luck with the birds, chances are the sun is high. If your lunch plans involve an air-conditioned restaurant, now is the time to return to Sierra Vista (3.0 miles to the starting point). If it's a particularly warm day, I suggest an afternoon in the shady confines of nearby Garden, Ramsey, Carr, or Miller Canyons in the cool Huachucas (see Chapter 6). But during migration periods and winter, a visit to the upper San Pedro River Valley warrants the effort.

To continue with the loop turn left (east) onto Highway 90. At the far end of the Sierra Vista Wastewater fields, angle right (south) at the sign for Moson Road (0.9 mile; 3.9 miles east of the starting point). Throughout its length, Moson cuts through Chihuahuan desertscrub dominated by mesquite and acacia. Watch the power poles, utility wires, and fencelines for an occasional Scaled Quail, Golden Eagle, Prairie Falcon (winter), Great Horned Owl (night), Ladder-backed Woodpecker, Ash-throated Flycatcher (summer), Western Kingbird (summer), Chihuahuan Raven, Cactus Wren, Northern Mockingbird, Curve-billed Thrasher, Loggerhead Shrike, and Pyrrhuloxia. Turn left (east) where Moson dead-ends at a T-intersection with Hereford Road (7.9 miles).

Hereford Road drops like a plumb bob through mesquite grassland that hosts Scaled Quail, Swainson's Hawk (summer) and Ferruginous Hawk (uncommon, winter), Greater Roadrunner, Verdin, Bendire's Thrasher, and Black-throated Sparrow. Botteri's and Cassin's Sparrows sing in tracts of tall grasses during the summer monsoon months. A Scissor-tailed Flycatcher added interest to the drive to the river in August of both 1992 and 1993. The one lane **Hereford Bridge** (5.1 miles) provides another access point to the San Pedro. *Please note: Hereford Bridge was closed for repairs in the summer of 2003, and it was not scheduled to re-open until December 2004. If the bridge is closed at the time of your visit, it is possible to run the upper San Pedro route in reverse by turning right (south) on Palominas Road (4.0 miles from the T-intersection with Moson Road), as described later in this chapter.* Birders should continue east to the BLM parking area on the right (south) side of the road (0.2 mile). *It is unsafe to stop on the bridge.* From here it is possible to hike along unmaintained trails on the east side of the river, both north and south of the Hereford Bridge.

Today the Upper San Pedro averages 10–20 feet in width, but in former times, it had numerous marshes and Beaver ponds. John Spring, who served at Fort Huachuca in the late 1800s, wrote that it was necessary to detour well into Mexico to cross the river during the rainy season. He also recalled seeing huge flocks of ducks and geese, which were shot for the fort's mess hall. By his estimate, fur trappers took over a million Beaver from this area at the turn of the twentieth century.

While the strand of cottonwoods is narrow along this stretch of the San Pedro, an impressive list of regional rarities have been observed here. These include Little Blue Heron, Black Swift (still hypothetical in Arizona), Elegant Trogon, Thick-billed Kingbird, Gray Catbird, Rufous-backed Robin, Brown Thrasher, Prothonotary Warbler, and Orchard Oriole. Wild Turkeys are suspected of breeding somewhere between the San Pedro House and the Hereford Bridge. More expected near the Hereford Bridge parking area are Gambel's Quail, Common Ground-Dove, Great Horned Owl, Gila and Ladder-backed Woodpeckers, Gilded Flicker, Verdin, Curve-billed and Crissal Thrashers, Phainopepla, Northern Cardinal, Pyrrhuloxia, and Abert's Towhee. In summer watch for White-winged Dove, Yellow-billed Cuckoo, Lesser Nighthawk, Black-chinned Hummingbird, Ash-throated Flycatcher, Bell's Vireo, Yellow-breasted Chat, Summer Tanager, Blue Grosbeak, and Bullock's Oriole. In winter, Western and Mountain Bluebirds, Green-tailed Towhee, and White-crowned Sparrow are typically common. Rare or uncommon sparrows of interest that have appeared here include Baird's, Black-chinned, Fox, and Sage.

Turn right (east) from the BLM Hereford Bridge parking area to continue the tour. The Hereford Road soon swings south to the Rancho del Río Pond (1.0 mile), a pretty little cottonwood-lined pond which has proven a good spot year round for Black Phoebe and Vermilion Flycatcher. Occasionally Black-bellied Whistling-Ducks settle here, and, in summer, Tropical Kingbirds are possible. Visitors are asked to view the pond from the edge of the highway without disturbing the owners.

After Rancho del Río, two more ponds are visible from Hereford Road, but the best way to see them is by parking at the **San Pedro River Inn** (turn right at the drive at 0.9 mile). Hours for non-guests are from 8:00 a.m. to dusk. To visit before 8:00 a.m. or for group visits, please call in advance (520-366-5532). San Pedro River Inn also offers guided bird walks for their guests; others may join the birding walks (nominal fee) with advance registration. Yellow-headed Blackbirds use the huge fields beyond the ponds throughout the year, and on late winter afternoons the cottonwood trees near these ponds may fill up with thousands of Yellowheads in a spectacle not soon forgotten. After acquiring the property in 1995, Walter and May Kolbe created an oasis for birds. Now run by birders Donna Knox and Michael Marsden, the inn boasts a yard list of over 240 species. Among those species are resident Barn and Great Horned Owls, and a breeding pair of Tropical Kingbirds.

A Rufous-backed Robin was feasting on Pyracantha berries outside the inn's cottages over the winter of 1998–1999. At the same time, Arizona's first record of an over-wintering Rufous-capped Warbler was discovered using thickets along the San Pedro River on the west edge of the property. To access the river—*no vehicles permitted*—walk south on the service road between the main house/office and the pond, and follow the road as it curves west and makes a beeline to the strand of tall cottonwood trees that mark the course of the San Pedro. So many birders chased the Rufous-capped Warbler during the winter of 1998–1999 that it was probably inevitable that some other rarity would be discovered. Sure enough, a Field Sparrow stationed itself near the far end of the river access road from December 1998–February 1999, establishing a first record for Southeastern Arizona. Please record your discoveries on the sightings board before leaving. Return to Hereford Road and turn right to continue the loop.

After passing the last pond, Hereford Road swerves away from the river and enters an area of limestone soil with low, thorny brush. Vegetation is Chihuahuan desertscrub and the dominant plants are Littleleaf Sumac, Tarbush, Sandpaper Bush, Creosote Bush, and White-thorn Acacia. This is good habitat for Cactus Wren, Crissal Thrasher, and Black-throated Sparrow. Turn right (west) onto Highway 92 (3.6 miles).

Before you lies a panorama of the San Pedro Valley that spans two nations and embraces a history of more than four and one-half centuries. This is the valley through which Francisco Vásquez de Coronado first rode into the present day United States in 1540, accompanied by 225 other bold explorers, four priests, and nearly a thousand Native Americans for support. They passed through the San Pedro Valley in search of the fabulous Seven Cities of Cíbola. Although no golden cities were ever discovered, the Coronado Expedition opened the American Southwest to European colonization.

Coronado National Memorial on the east end of the Huachuca Mountains interprets the history of early Spanish exploration. The visitor center features exhibits and a bookstore. To take this side trip, drive due west to the well-signed junction (9.1 miles), and turn left (south). The visitor center is situated in an oak woodland at the mouth of Montezuma Canyon (4.8 miles). Be sure to check the wildlife watering pool outside the rear windows. Plain-capped Starthroat has been sighted out these windows on several occasions, most recently in May 1994. Beyond the center, the road narrows and zigzags up the steep canyon walls to Montezuma Pass (3.5 miles). A vast expanse of Sonora and Southeastern Arizona is visible from the summit (6,575 feet elevation). Hikers can connect to the Huachuca Crest Trail from the west side of Montezuma Pass (see the trail description under Miller Canyon in Chapter 6). To re-join the main loop tour, return to Highway 92, turn right (east) to Palominas Road (5.6 miles).

To continue the main tour without a visit to the Coronado Memorial, follow Highway 92 west from its junction with Hereford Road to the San Pedro River at the small community of Palominas (3.0 miles). The river here is only five miles north of the border with Sonora. After crossing the San Pedro River, turn right (north) just beyond and across from the post office on Palominas Road (0.5 mile).

Watch for **Palominas Pond**, a quarter-mile-long farm pond immediately north of the community of Palominas (0.3 mile), about 300 yards east of the road (scope recommended). Green Heron, American Coot, Vermilion Flycatcher, and Yellow-headed Blackbird are regular here, and occasionally Cattle Egret and Black-bellied Whistling-Duck put in an appearance. Possible rarities in winter include Greater White-fronted Goose, Bald Eagle, and Sandhill Crane. In late August 1988 a Tricolored Heron stayed at Palominas Pond for a full week. *Motorists are reminded to pull completely off the pavement.*

The most extensive grasslands in the upper San Pedro Valley are on the west side of Palominas Road. Birds using these grasslands include Scaled Quail, White-tailed Kite, Northern Harrier (winter), Greater Roadrunner, Lesser Nighthawk (summer evenings), Western Kingbird (summer), Scissor-tailed Flycatcher (sporadic in summer), Chihuahuan Raven, and Loggerhead Shrike. Winter birding is especially rewarding. Both Ferruginous and Rough-legged Hawks (rare) are possible, as are Short-eared Owl (January 1986) and Northern Shrike (winter 1988–1989). This is also excellent winter habitat for Sprague's Pipit (rare), Mountain Bluebird (numbers fluctuate), and both McCown's (casual) and Chestnut-collared Longspurs.

To reach Casa de San Pedro turn right (east) on Waters Road (2.0 miles) and drive to the road-end (1.0 mile). The Casa is a beautiful, territorial-style bed and breakfast built around a courtyard with a fountain. It features numerous bird feeders and lies adjacent to both the San Pedro River and the San Pedro National Conservation Area. (Call 888/257-2050 for information, or visit their website at www.bedandbirds.com.)

Continue north up Palominas Road to the signed junction with Lehner Road on the right (east) side (2.4 miles). The dirt road drops due east down toward the San Pedro. A pullout on the left (north) with a National Historic Landmark plaque (0.5 mile) commemorates the site where the late Ed Lehner discovered an enormous bone in 1952. Excavations conducted by the Arizona State Museum in 1955–1956 and 1974–1975 revealed the fossil remains of 12 immature Woolly Mammoths, as well other members of the Pleistocene megafauna, including tapir, bison, camel, and horse. Clovis Culture projectile points, stone tools, fire hearths, and other artifacts dated through both radiocarbon and stratigraphy place these prehistoric hunters here 11,000–13,000 years before the present. The Lehners have generously donated this important site to the Bureau of Land Management.

To complete this loop, continue north on Palominas Road to the T-intersection with Hereford Road (1.3 mile). Turn left (west) here and follow the Hereford Road up to its junction with Highway 92 (7.4 miles). Turn right (north) on Highway 92 to return to the starting point at Sierra Vista (8.25 miles).

LOWER SAN PEDRO VALLEY LOOP

(50 miles/one day)

History buffs will appreciate that this tour actually connects three dots on the map made famous as outlaw hideouts. Charleston and Fairbank are ghost towns today, but Tombstone is a thriving community with a population of 2,000 people. For birders the Lower River Loop offers three more access points to the San Pedro, downstream from the popular San Pedro House and the Highway 90 bridge. While the birds are much the same as those found up-river, some of the more wary species such as Gray Hawk and Varied Bunting may be easier to see at these less-visited areas.

The first birding site is **Escapule** (*es-cah-POOL*) **Wash**. It behooves birders to start early, as activity on the river usually dies after 10 a.m. From the starting point, drive north on Highway 90 to the next traffic signal, which marks the beginning of Charleston Road (0.25 mile). Turn right (east) at the T-intersection here. The right-hand (south) turnoff on Escapule Wash Road (6.0 miles) is well away from Sierra Vista, halfway through the first major curve on Charleston Road. A short link of gravel, secondary road leads to a BLM pullout on the left (east) side (0.3 mile), where a stile through a fence marks the start of a trail that parallels the wash.

Escapule Wash proper cuts across the road beyond the pullout (0.1 mile). Birders are advised to park their vehicles at the designated pullout, and then hike down the wash bed itself. Scattered cottonwood trees shade the wide, sandy wash as it gradually descends approximately 0.5 mile to the San Pedro River. Halfway down, a three-foot-high stone ledge forces a permanent spring to the surface. Some of the best birding is near this short stretch of permanent water.

A pair of Gray Hawks (summer) nest annually along Escapule, and this tendril of tall cottonwoods is an excellent migrant trap for passerines. Among the possible birds of passage are Willow, Hammond's, Dusky, Gray, and Pacific-slope Flycatchers, as well as Orange-crowned, Nashville, Chestnut-sided (casual), Townsend's (rare), Black-and-white (rare), American Redstart (rare), Northern Waterthrush (rare), MacGillivray's, Hooded (rare), and Wilson's Warblers. Summer breeders include Northern Beardless-Tyrannulet (locally rare along the upper San Pedro), Bell's Vireo, Yellow-breasted Chat, Summer Tanager, and Abert's Towhee.

Once down at the river, it is possible to turn left (north) downstream and bushwhack all the way to the Charleston Bridge (about 1.5 miles). Birders contemplating this hike should be aware that no trail exists and that knee-deep pockets of quicksand create tough slogging. The old railroad line on the east—opposite—side of the San Pedro offers reasonably easy going for the final mile or so, *but hikers need to watch and listen for trains.* Originally laid in the early 1880s, these tracks are still in use today.

R eturn to Charleston Road and turn right to continue the loop. Although the highway is winding, **Charleston Bridge** is almost due north of the junction with Escapule Wash Road (1.5 miles). The BLM has built a parking area off the southeast corner of the bridge (0.1 mile).

Lacking adequate water in Tombstone, a stamp mill for the silver mines was located on the San Pedro just north of here in 1879. The mill site was given the prosaic name of Millville, and the village where the workers and merchants lived across the river was called Charleston. According to legend, banditos like Curley Bill Brocius used Charleston as a bedroom community for commuting to work in nearby Tombstone. But in spite of its low reputation in the East, no shipment of bullion nor moneys for payroll were ever lost to outlaws in the one short decade the town thrived. The end was in sight after the mines flooded in 1886 and the water pumps were shut down by striking miners.

The best birding is from an abandoned bridge adjacent to the parking area. Lazuli, Indigo, and even Varied and Painted Buntings are all possible from the old Charleston Bridge in August and September. Also watch for Gray Hawk (summer) and Green Kingfisher. Varied Bunting and Black-throated and Rufous-crowned Sparrows are all more likely in the arid mesquite thickets along the railroad tracks which serve as a *de facto* trail north and south of the Charleston Road. *Please note, however, that the railroad line is still in operation: birders must use caution if they walk the railroad right-of-way.*

Charleston Road climbs through Chihuahuan desertscrub and slices through a group of low hills before arriving in Tombstone (8.8 miles). The roads that lead to Highway 80 a couple of hundred yards east are fairly obvious. Charleston Road changes into Sumner Street; at the stop sign, turn right (south) onto Allen Street. Go one block— actually only about 50 yards— then turn left (east) onto the continuation of Sumner Street. Highway 80 is straight ahead. To continue the tour without even a backward glance at history, turn left (north) onto Highway 80.

There are few birds in the immediate precincts of Tombstone, although the nearby Tombstone Hills have historically served at winter quarters for a roost of Long-eared Owls. Today souvenir and antique shops line the business district. But the lineaments of "the town too tough to die" are still visible on a stroll up Allen Street.

Founded on top a fabulous silver lode discovered by prospector Ed Schieffelin in 1878, only a few years later Tombstone boasted a population of 20,000, and was the largest city between St. Louis and San Francisco. The wealthy citizenry supported the arts, and the Bird Cage Theatre hosted some of the most famous performers of the age. But today Tombstone is probably best remembered for the gunfight at the OK Corral. In 1881 Wyatt Earp, his brothers Virgil and Morgan, and their friend Doc Holliday faced six cowboy gunslingers led by Ike Clanton. When the smoke cleared, three gunslingers had run and the other three lay dead.

But their feud was not over. Virgil and Morgan were both ambushed in the next few months, crippling Virgil for life and killing Morgan. Morgan's assailants were identified by eyewitnesses, but Sheriff Johnny Behan, bitter over losing the affections of a woman named Josephine Marcus to Wyatt, decided all four men had credible alibis, and released them. Wyatt executed his own revenge. Within a week he had gunned down three of the perpetrators, including the notorious Curley Bill Brocius. Then he left town with Josephine Marcus. She was still with him when he died peacefully in California in 1929.

In 1886 the mines under Tombstone flooded, and the town never recovered. The Tombstone County Courthouse Building, the Bird Cage Theatre, and other buildings remain, dating back to the first turbulent decade of the town's existence, and a sandwich hour spent on Allen Street can't help but evoke a sense of this chapter of America's past.

D rive north on Highway 80 to continue the tour. Boothill Graveyard (0.2 mile from the intersection of Sumner Street) on the right (east) side marks the outskirts of old Tombstone. A few minutes later turn left (west) onto Highway 82 (2.6 miles). The highway follows the north edge of Walnut Gulch almost down to the river bank at **Fairbank**, established in 1883 (5.9 miles). The entrance on the right (north) side of the highway is easy to overshoot—get ready to turn right when you see red corrals on the left.

Fairbank is a natural vagrant trap situated at the axis of Walnut Gulch from the east and the Babocomari River from the west. Aside from the summer green of cottonwoods along the San Pedro, the site supports a large mesquite *bosque,* or woodland. Today all that remains of the town of Fairbank is the historic Adobe Commercial Building. Several modern house trailers, one staffed by a BLM host, are nearby. A pair of easily seen Vermilion Flycatchers haunts the grassy park between these structures. Until 1994 the Bureau of Land Management administered the entire San Pedro National Conservation Area from Fairbank. As a consequence the list of vagrants recorded at Fairbank is long. Included are species from the high Huachucas, such as Red-breasted Nuthatch, and from Mexico, such as a Yellow Grosbeak recorded in May 1992.

The scene here was not always so peaceful. Three-finger Jack Dunlap and his gang attacked the train at Fairbank early in 1900. By chance ex-Texas Ranger Jeff Milton was guarding the Wells Fargo express car. When the smoke cleared Three-finger Jack and another outlaw were dead, and Jeff Milton lay unconscious in a pool of blood from a gunshot wound in his arm. Before he fainted he tossed the keys to the strongbox into a corner. The remaining bandits boarded the bullet-riddled car but failed to find the keys in the gloom. Milton ultimately recovered from his wound, and lived to be 85 years old before he finished his life as a lawman in Tucson.

B irders have a choice of two trails at Fairbank. A narrow path wanders from the parking area to a railroad overpass (300 yards), then tunnels through shady mesquites to the San Pedro River (400 yards). In summer this woodland is alive with the voices of Gambel's Quail, Gila Woodpecker, Northern Beardless-Tyrannulet, Ash-throated Flycatcher, Bewick's Wren, Bell's Vireo, Summer Tanager, and Abert's Towhee. Watch for a Gray Hawk fly-by as you approach the river. Gray Flycatcher and Green-tailed Towhee occupy the same bosque in winter. The Highway 82 Bridge is only 100 yards south, just below the confluence of the Babocomari River with the San Pedro. Although the Babocomari is no more than a small stream, it nonetheless represents the single largest tributary entering the entire upper San Pedro River north of Mexico and south of Interstate 10.

Continuing south upstream another 300 yards, it is possible to make a loop by turning left and hiking east up the dry bed of Walnut Gulch. Bell's Vireo, Yellow-breasted Chat, and Varied Bunting are common in the brush in the lower wash during summer. From the confluence of Walnut Creek with the San Pedro to the Boquillas Ranch Road is only 300 more yards. Fairbank is approximately 100 yards north across Highway 82. The round-trip hike is one mile long.

The other trail begins straight across Highway 82 from the parking area at Fairbank. This is the dirt road that leads south to Boquillas Ranch (2.0 miles), currently used to house research staff for the BLM. Private vehicles are not permitted on the road at present, but walking it in summer should produce Ladder-backed Woodpecker, Ash-throated Flycatcher, Cactus Wren, Curve-billed Thrasher, and Varied Bunting. Chances of seeing these and other desert species are improved with an early start. There is no reason this loop, which features a possible hike either at Fairbank or Escapule Wash, cannot be run beginning with Fairbank.

To return to the starting point in Sierra Vista, turn right (east) and cross the San Pedro River (0.3 mile). Continue east to the intersection of Highways 82 and 90 (9.6 miles). Turn left (south) to follow Highway 90 south to its intersection with Highway 92 (13.5 miles).

CAMPGROUNDS, RESTAURANTS, AND ACCOMMODATIONS

Facilities for the San Pedro Valley are identical to those for the Huachuca Mountains described in the preceding chapter.

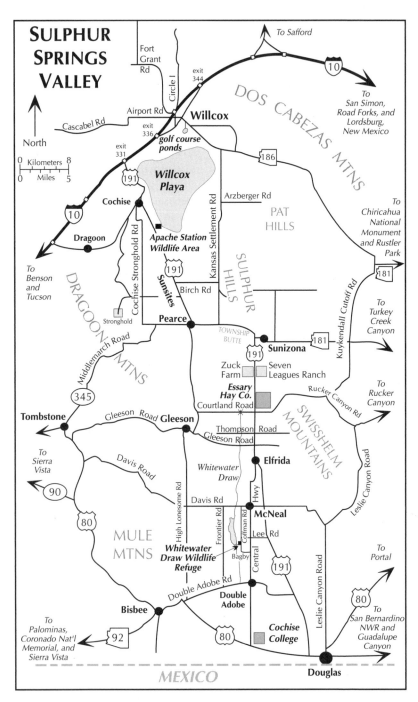

SULPHUR SPRINGS VALLEY

To Safford

Fort Grant Rd

exit 344

Circle I

10

DOS CABEZAS MTNS

To San Simon, Road Forks, and Lordsburg, New Mexico

Airport Rd

Cascabel Rd

exit 336

Willcox

North

exit 331

0   Kilometers   8

0   Miles   5

191

golf course ponds

186

Cochise

Willcox Playa

Arzberger Rd

PAT HILLS

To Chiricahua National Monument and Rustler Park

10

Dragoon

Kansas Settlement Rd

Cochise Stronghold Rd

■ *Apache Station Wildlife Area*

191

SULPHUR HILLS

181

To Benson and Tucson

DRAGOON MTNS

Sunsites

Birch Rd

Stronghold

□

Pearce

TOWNSHIP BUTTE

191

181

Sunizona

Kuykendall Cutoff Rd

To Turkey Creek Canyon

Middlemarch Road

345

Zuck Farm

Seven Leagues Ranch

Essary Hay Co.

Courtland Road

Rucker Canyon Rd

To Rucker Canyon

Tombstone

Gleeson Road **Gleeson**

Thompson Road

Gleeson Road

SWISSHELM MOUNTAINS

To Sierra Vista

Davis Road

Whitewater Draw

● **Elfrida**

90

High Lonesome Rd

Davis Rd

Hwy

Leslie Canyon Road

80

MULE MTNS

Frontier Rd

Coffman Rd

McNeal

Lee Rd

191

To Portal

Whitewater Draw Wildlife Refuge

Bagby

Central

Bisbee

Double Adobe Rd

Double Adobe

80

To Palominas, Coronado Nat'l Memorial, and Sierra Vista

92

80

Cochise College

■

Leslie Canyon Road

To San Bernardino NWR and Guadalupe Canyon

Douglas

MEXICO

CHAPTER 8

SULPHUR SPRINGS VALLEY TOUR

(88 miles to Douglas/one day)
(129 miles to Sierra Vista/one day)
(160 miles round-trip from Willcox/one day)

Stretching 100 miles on a north-south axis and ranging from 15 to 25 miles in width, the 4,000-foot-high Sulphur Springs Valley has earned a reputation as the best winter raptor location in Southeastern Arizona. Up to 14 species of birds of prey find a cold-season niche in the broad grasslands and extensive farms in what has come to be known as Arizona's "hawk alley." Additionally, approximately 20,000–25,000 Sandhill Cranes make these fields their winter headquarters. With shorebird passage ending in June and beginning again in July, this important migratory bird corridor is actually a prime destination throughout the year.

The starting point for this tour is the town of Willcox. Willcox is located on Interstate 10 approximately 80 miles east of Tucson. Take the first exit, #336, and follow Haskell Street directly into downtown Willcox to the traffic signal (mile 4.0) at the beginning of Highway 186. If you are connecting to this tour from Portal, drive north on the San Simon Road to I-10 (23 miles), and then follow the interstate west to the northernmost Willcox Exit, #344 (38 miles). The distance from the exit overpass down Haskell Street to the stoplight at Highway 186 is 4.2 miles. Coming from Chiricahua National Monument (see Chapter 9), take Highway 181 to a T-intersection with Highway 186 (3.0 miles from the entry station), then follow Highway 186 northwest to Willcox (28 miles). Zero your odometer at the intersection of Haskell and Highway 186 to follow this tour. Willcox hosts one of the largest concentrations of Chihuahuan Ravens in Southeastern Arizona. Harris's Hawks,

Golden Eagles, Scaled Quail, and Burrowing Owls are occasionally spotted on any approach to Willcox.

Birders starting from Douglas or Sierra Vista may well choose to run this tour in reverse sequence, and then deadhead back to their point of origin, or continue on from Willcox to another loop. There is no major birding advantage to beginning this tour either from the north end at Willcox or from the south end near Douglas. Bendire's and Crissal Thrashers, however, are more common in the southern half of the valley, and easiest to see early in the morning.

The most famous single location in the entire Sulphur Springs Valley is the large wastewater pond on the eastern side of Willcox that the chamber of commerce has dubbed **Lake Cochise**. (This birding area is often also referred to as Willcox Lake, Twin Lakes, or Willcox Playa. Technically speaking, the playa itself is the large dry lakebed, mostly inaccessible to birders.) Adjacent to a perennially-green municipal golf course with its own small ponds, Lake Cochise constitutes an important oasis in the otherwise arid and barren northern valley. To find these ponds turn east on Highway 186 toward Chiricahua National Monument at the Willcox stoplight (a right turn off Haskell if you are coming from Tucson; a left if coming from Portal). One block east of the stoplight the road crosses the railroad tracks that gave rise to this western town. Founded in 1882, Willcox was an important cattle shipping point on the Southern Pacific line. The livestock industry remains an integral part of the town's economy, but today agriculture is the biggest employer for the 4,000 people who call Willcox home. Corn, sorghum, lettuce, and cotton are the most important crops, followed by watermelons, chiles, apples, and pecans.

Continue east to Rex Allen Jr. Drive, the only paved road on the right side of the highway at a sign for Twin Lakes golf course (0.5 mile). Turn south here. Birds along the road to the clubhouse (1.1 miles) are typical of the grasslands the entire length of the Sulphur Springs Valley. Watch for Red-tailed Hawk, Greater Roadrunner, Burrowing Owl (uncommon), Cactus Wren, Northern Mockingbird, Bendire's (uncommon) and Curve-billed Thrashers, Loggerhead Shrike, Eastern Meadowlark, and House Finch. In summer there are almost always Swainson's Hawks and Western Kingbirds present. In winter Northern Harriers, American Kestrels, Prairie Falcons, and Lark Buntings are common.

Look for Scaled Quail from the cattleguard that marks the beginning of the golf course on the right (west) side of the road. The golf course and the area adjacent to the ponds is probably one of the best locations in Arizona for "Cottontop Quail," as the locals call them. A particularly good spot to check is the work yard on the right, just south of the clubhouse.

The road divides 100 feet beyond the work yard; both forks lead 100 yards to ponds, and each pond is apt to have different species. Straight ahead across the cattleguard is the earthen embankment of the principal sewage lagoon, Lake Cochise. On either side are seasonal puddles that may harbor a migrating Solitary Sandpiper. A third, practically permanent puddle across the old entrance road has a solid bottom, but after heavy rains the rim of the big pond may be a muddy quagmire. Do not attempt to drive up on it after a recent storm. The road follows the rim around the entire pond.

In 2003, owing to a drought-induced, greater-than-normal demand for treated water on the golf course, municipal authorities allowed the water level in Lake Cochise to fall to an unprecedented depth. This change probably improved shorebird habitat, but it definitely hurt its potential for waterfowl. Water levels were high again in 2004, but you should expect a fluctuating shoreline at Lake Cochise.

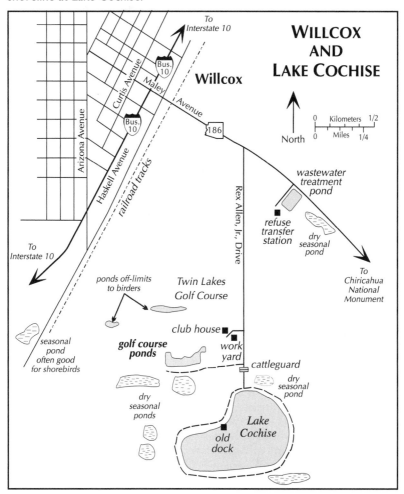

Prairie Falcon
Narca Moore-Craig

Usually the ducks are concentrated on the back end of the quarter-mile-long reservoir. The raised elbow halfway along the western edge offers the best vantage point for scanning. A scope is highly recommended. The sandy spit directly in front of the remnants of an old pier and the comparatively barren near shoreline usually harbor the most shorebirds. Although irregular, Willcox represents the only breeding location for Snowy Plover in southern Arizona. Eared Grebes, and—seasonally—cormorants, White-faced Ibis, Greater White-fronted Goose (rare), Black-necked Stilt (uncommon), American Avocet (summer), Long-billed Curlew, and other long-legged waders seem to favor the western arm of the big sewage lagoon. Depending on water levels, tussocks of grass and tall weeds may conceal them. Other birds to watch for in, around, and over the water include Western and Clark's Grebes (fall, winter, and spring), Great Blue Heron, Horned Lark, American Pipit (winter), and Savannah Sparrow (winter), as well as up to six species of swallows in migration.

Lake Cochise is often blanketed with birds early in the morning. In winter and in migration these may include ten or more species of ducks: Green-winged Teal, Mallard (usually the Mexican Duck subspecies is the predominant form), Northern Pintail, Blue-winged and Cinnamon Teal, Northern Shoveler, Gadwall, American Wigeon, Canvasback, Redhead, Ring-necked Duck, Lesser Scaup, Bufflehead, Common Merganser, and Ruddy Duck. Hundreds of Wilson's and small numbers of Red-necked Phalaropes cut gyroscopes on the surface, and dozens of Long-billed Dowitchers jab in the shallows like miniature oil rigs. Check the early arriving fall dowitchers for Short-bills. The red-breasted immatures are the easiest targets, since their Long-billed counterparts are ordinarily pale-breasted by September. Remember, however, voice is always the best clue when identifying dowitchers. Other migratory shorebirds occurring regularly at Lake Cochise include Greater and Lesser Yellowlegs, Long-billed Curlew, and Spotted, Western, Least, and Baird's Sandpipers. Less common but annual are Willet, Marbled Godwit, Semipalmated Sandpiper, Pectoral Sandpiper, Dunlin, and Stilt Sandpiper. Ring-billed Gull is the typical larid, sometimes absent, but occasionally in flocks of over 50. A sprinkling of Franklin's, Bonaparte's, and California Gulls also drop in, primarily during migration periods. Black Terns pass through from May to September, Forster's Tern is recorded a few times annually, and Least Terns have shown up for at least one day every May for the past decade.

Lake Cochise has recorded too many rarities to recount in any complete way. A sampling would include Eurasian Wigeon, Surf Scoter, Long-tailed Duck, Common Loon, Horned Grebe, American Golden-Plover, White-rumped Sandpiper, Red Phalarope, Sabine's Gull, and Black Skimmer. Most of these are one-day wonders.

After working Lake Cochise return to the junction near the cattleguard and turn left (west) for the smaller, cattail-ringed golf course pond (100 yards). There is a convenient parking area on the east or near side of the water. Early in the morning during winter watch for Wilson's Snipes to wander across the nearby greens, for all the world as blasé as a group of starlings. It is always worthwhile to scan the golf course and its trees for American Wigeon, Scaled Quail, Lark Bunting (winter), Chestnut-collared Longspur (winter), and Brewer's Blackbird (winter), as well as for raptors, Say's Phoebe and other fly-catchers, thrashers, Loggerhead Shrike, and migrant warblers. In the fall of 2003 both Dickcissel and Bobolink were recorded. The golf course adjacent to the pond was one of the first places Eurasian Collared-Dove was discov-

Sandhill Cranes at Apache Station Wildlife Area
William S. Bickel

ered in Arizona in 2000, and a pair has been sighted sporadically here ever since. Once again, a scope will be useful.

Approach the pond quietly. The eastern end is rimmed with a narrow mudflat that may harbor shorebirds nearly any month of the year. Resident are Ruddy Duck, American Coot, Killdeer, Black Phoebe, Common Yellowthroat, and Red-winged and Yellow-headed (uncommon) Blackbirds. During winter these are joined by other ducks and occasionally a Snow Goose (with a Ross's Goose for comparison the winter of 1992–1993), Marsh Wren, and both Song and Swamp Sparrows. Dozens of Lazuli Buntings pass through during a typical August in migration, along with a few Willow Flycatchers. While Bank Swallows may also use Lake Cochise during migration, they seem to prefer the golf course pond.

A short, abandoned road parallels the left (south) edge of the golf course pond. This may yield some additional species, especially if there is water in the weedy swale on the left side of the dead-end track. A handful of Hudsonian Godwits has used this patch of water sporadically during May in the past decade. During winter the weeds along the road are usually good for a few extra sparrows.

An earthen bank on the right side at the west end of the road offers a good vantage point—with the serious disadvantage of tricky footing—overlooking the far (west) end of the golf course pond. If you haven't yet spotted your Scaled Quail, scan the surrounding area carefully, especially the golf course.

APACHE STATION WILDLIFE AREA

(80 miles/one-half day)

From Tucson, the closest—and perhaps the surest—Sandhill Crane roost is located at the Apache Station Wildlife Area. Cooling effluent from the electric plant has created a wetland that the Apache Electric Power Cooperative manages in a stewardship agreement with the Arizona Game and Fish Department. Aside from cranes, this area has proven opportune for Snow Geese (with an occasional Ross's Goose to add sweetening to the flock) and Bald Eagles.

To find Apache Station take Interstate 10 east of Tucson to Exit 331 and Highway 191 (70 miles from the junction of I-10 with I-19; 9 miles west of Willcox at Exit 340). Turn right (south) and continue to the well-signed entrance to the wildlife area on the left (east) side of the highway (8.6 miles), approximately one-half mile before (north of) the imposing towers of the electric generating plant. The well-graveled, all-weather road leads to a parking area (0.9 mile) a short walk from a raised, concrete viewing platform. The cranes, 5,000 or more on the average, are most apt to be present at daybreak, noon, and just before sundown. Since the wetland is approximately one-half mile away from the viewing platform, a scope will prove invaluable. The wildlife area is open to the general public from 5:00 a.m. to 6:00 p.m. daily from November 1–March 15, and on Saturdays and Sundays only from March 16–October 31. (Call 520-586-5137 for a recorded message.)

This end of the golf course pond is also a favorite hangout for a Vermilion Flycatcher.

Allow at least one hour—preferably two—to do a proper job of birding Lake Cochise and the golf course pond. Then return to Highway 186 and turn right. The road traverses an area of dunes that date back at least 8,000 years to when the whole Willcox Playa was a 50-square-mile lake. Fossil evidence discovered on the shores of ancient lake-bed discloses that thousands of years earlier Native Americans were killing the young of Woolly Mammoths with a uniquely fluted spearhead known as the Clovis point. Scientists today speculate that the people of the Clovis culture, using this primitive technology to specialize on immature animals, hunted mammoths to extinction throughout North America in just 500 years. Fossil pollen analysis from Willcox Playa shows that no abrupt climatic changes occurred that would otherwise account for the sudden extinction of these grand elephants.

Watch for White-tailed Kite as you approach the Y-junction with **Kansas Settlement Road** (7.0 miles from the traffic stoplight at Haskell). Turn right (south) here. The first fields of this agricultural development begin about three miles down the road. Farming gets the credit for attracting the Sandhill Cranes that use the area today. Midwesterners migrated to the east side of Willcox Playa during the dust bowl era of the 1930s, and over the next few decades converted over 26,000 acres of desert grassland to irrigated cropland. Cranes were first noted using the fields in the 1960s, and in 1970 the first Arizona Game and Fish Department census tallied approximately 850 Sandhills. Recent winter surveys in the 2000s show that the present Sulphur Springs Valley population fluctuates between 20,000 and 25,000 birds, approximately twice the number as at the well-known Bosque del Apache National Wildlife Refuge in New Mexico.

The daily regimen of valley Sandhills includes several shuttles between roosts and feeding areas that may be up to 10 miles apart. Cranes prefer open corn fields where the stalks have been cultivated, disked under, or trampled by cattle. Look for cranes in any patch of corn stubble from mile 3 to mile 15 along the Kansas Settlement Road. If you do not locate any birds, wait and watch the skies to see where the flocks are settling down. Lateral farm lanes provide access to outlying fields.

Cranes are not the only attraction along the Kansas Settlement Road. Ferruginous Hawks are fairly common in winter, and roadside corrals may also harbor huge flocks of Yellow-headed Blackbirds. Golden Eagles are especially possible near the crane flocks, but are resident year round. Although large groups of Long-billed Curlews—often in flocks up to a hundred—exploit freshly-tilled fields, they are tough to spot in the furrows.

Follow Kansas Settlement Road south to its terminus at Highway 191 (21 miles). Turn left (east) at the T-intersection. Watch for Golden Eagles where the highway swings across the north side of a rocky foothill known as Township Butte. A pair has nested near here for many years. Wintering Ferruginous Hawks perched on utility poles become fairly common south of Sunizona (5.0 miles). Bare fields at Seven Leagues Ranch on the left (east) side of the highway (4.8 miles) literally swarm with wintering Horned Larks. With a good scope and enough patience, it is usually possible to finesse one or more McCown's Longspurs out of the flock. Up until early February, both sexes resemble female House Sparrows with pinkish bills. Horned Larks are also in the lush, green alfalfa fields across Highway 191 at the Zuck Farm (formerly called Rainbow Ranch). During winter check these flocks for Chestnut-collared Longspurs.

Several prominent grain silos on the left (east) side of the road mark the headquarters of the **Essary Hay Company** (formerly Spitler Land and Cattle; 3.0 miles). *Stop at the office to obtain permission to drive along the farm lanes that divide their half-mile-wide fields. Please be considerate when birding this*

Mountain Plover
David A. Sibley

area: do not enter fields, stay away from cattle and livestock, do not blocks lanes or access to equipment. If pressed for time, another strategy is to simply continue down Highway 191 to the left (east side) junction with the well-graded Rucker Canyon Road (0.5 mile). Most of the best birds can usually be found by scoping from the edges of this public thoroughfare. Essary Hay Company is a raptor-lover's paradise throughout the year, but it is especially wonderful in winter. Among the wintering species one could tally in a couple of hours are Bald Eagle, Northern Harrier, Sharp-shinned Hawk, Cooper's Hawk, Red-tailed Hawk, Ferruginous Hawk, Golden Eagle, American Kestrel, Merlin, Peregrine Falcon, and Prairie Falcon. Check any conspicuous perch; aside from fence posts, powerline poles, and a few scattered cottonwoods, all of the eagles, hawks, and falcons are fond of the expensive central-pivot irrigation rigs used to water the fields. Two of these hunters are even comfortable sitting complacently in the grass. Female Northern Harriers are hard to spot on the ground, but the white chest of a Ferruginous Hawk will probably attract your attention in a flash.

One of the recent raptor identification guides will come in handy at Essary Hay Company, both for birds in flight and for variant plumages. Aside from immatures, Essary is famous for its red-morph and dark-morph Redtails, as well as dark-morph Ferruginous Hawks.

If you can tear yourself away from this feast of raptors, there is a nice assortment of other birds that also winter at Essary Hay. These include Killdeer, Barn Owl in the outbuildings, White-throated Swift, Say's Phoebe, Horned Lark, Chihuahuan Raven, Mountain Bluebird (irregular but present most winters), Bendire's Thrasher in mesquite hedgerows, American Pipit, Loggerhead Shrike, Brewer's, Vesper, Lark, and White-crowned Sparrows, Lark Bunting, McCown's (rare) and Chestnut-collared Longspurs, Red-winged Blackbird, Eastern and Western Meadowlarks, and Brewer's Blackbird. Mountain Plovers prefer shortgrass fields, particularly those that have been recently cut, and, occasionally, recently plowed fields. The mid-winter flock of Mountain Plovers may number from a handful to better than a hundred.

Summer at Essary Hay offers its own rewards to the birder. Half a dozen or more Swainson's Hawks may come together to perform graceful aerial ballets in the wake of the mowing machines, feeding on the insects and mice left without cover. Like Ferruginous Hawks, they perch on the ground between forays. During August the alfalfa fields load up with Mallards, Blue Grosbeaks, Lazuli Buntings, Red-winged Blackbirds, and Eastern Meadowlarks. And don't forget to scan the skies for Golden Eagles, which are year-round guests at the Essary Hay Company.

During winter, raptor enthusiasts will enjoy a side trip on Courtland Road, which leads west from the Highway 191/Rucker Canyon Road intersection. Follow the pavement to a large field on the right (north) side of the road (1.7 miles). Perhaps owing to its strategic location at the head of Whitewater Draw, this single field ordinarily hosts several Ferruginous Hawks throughout the winter. Frequently there are more, and concentrations of up to a dozen are occasionally recorded. Many years one of these birds is a dark-morph Ferruginous. This one field is probably the best single location for Ferruginous in Southeastern Arizona.

Return to Highway 191 and turn right (south). Watch for a small group of Harris's Hawks in the desert on the left (east) side of the highway for the next few miles. You may even find them sharing a cottonwood roost with a Great Horned Owl. The Elfrida landfill site off Thompson Road (3.0 miles) on the left (east) side of Highweay 191 is good for Crissal Thrasher, which is also regular in mesquite thickets north of Elfrida.

Another excellent location for Ferruginous Hawks in winter is Gleeson Road (1.0 mile). Turn right and continue to a farm driveway on the right (north) side of the road. The best place to observe the hawks is from the driveway entrance on the far (west) corner of the field. *Remember, however, not to block the farmer's driveway or to trespass on private property.*

During wet winters Sandhill Cranes also use this area. Track their loud, trumpeting calls to locate the birds if they are not conspicuous in the field itself. Areas of shallow standing water both north and south of the small Whitewater Draw Bridge are frequent day roosts. Once again, wherever there are cranes watch for eagles. And don't be surprised if you also see Coyotes. These handsome canines are probably the chief predator on cranes in the Sulphur Springs Valley.

Elfrida, Arizona, population approximately 500, begins at the junction with Gleeson Road. The town features a church, a gas station, a post office, and a small cafe called A Family Restaurant, whose food is recommended. There is a major Y-junction on the south end of Elfrida (1.6 miles). Highway 191 veers left and dead-ends at U.S. 80 just west of Douglas (23 miles). To continue the tour, however, drive straight south on what is now Central Highway to a major four-point intersection with Davis Road at McNeal (6.3 miles).

Corn-stubble fields here are another excellent area for viewing Sandhill Cranes. There are two major flocks wintering in the Sulphur Springs Valley, and the Whitewater Draw area represents the southern roost. To find their usual mid-day resting place, turn right onto Davis Road. Go west on Davis to a signed intersection with a dirt road called Coffman (1.0 mile). Unless there have been unusually heavy winter rains, turn left (south) onto Coffman. Ruts left behind by farm machinery and trucks will tell you whether or not Coffman is passable. En route to the cranes, don't ignore the barren desert or newly plowed fields on the left (east) side of the road. Both Mountain Plover and McCown's Longspur are possible, and Horned Lark is probable in these seemingly sterile areas. Watch for Scaled Quail, Greater Roadrunner, Cactus Wren, and Bendire's, Curve-billed, and Crissal Thrashers in the roadside thickets, as well as Pyrrhuloxia and a host of sparrows.

The centerpiece of the **Whitewater Draw Wildlife Refuge** (formerly Hyannis Cattle Company) is a shallow pond on the right (west) side of the road that may extend over two miles in length during wet periods. In dry years the same pond shrinks to little more than a mud puddle. The Sulphur Springs Valley is so level that it may be difficult to determine whether the water level is high or low, but—if present—the cranes should be eminently visible and audible about a quarter-mile off Coffman. Mid-winter Arizona Game and Fish Department surveys have recorded up to 14,500 Sandhills at this single location. A scope is suggested. *Bird only from the road.*

One to three Bald Eagles—always a rarity in Southeastern Arizona—routinely winter at Whitewater Draw, and Golden Eagles are apt to soar over several times each day, every day of the year. Some winters a Rough-legged Hawk frequents the same area. And just for sweetener, White-tailed Kites have nested in the scrawny little cypress trees at the lone house on the right (2.6 miles) that the Arizona Game and Fish Department uses as its administrative site. For the record, however, in some summers the kites are absent altogether from the lower Sulphur Springs Valley. The entrance to the refuge is a short distance beyond the building (0.1 mile) on the right (west) side of Coffman Road. A quarter-mile-long drive leads to a parking oval and a restroom, and a short trail continues down to the low earthen dam that bottles up the pond in Whitewater Draw.

The dam and its viewing platforms constitute a discrete birding venue. Some of the species to watch for include Sora, Common Ground-Dove,

Black and Say's Phoebes, Vermilion Flycatcher (year round), Rock and Marsh Wrens (winter), Crissal Thrasher (winter), Yellow Warbler (summer), Common Yellowthroat, Yellow-breasted Chat (summer), a host of wintering sparrows, Blue Grosbeak (summer), and Lazuli (migration), Indigo (migration), and Painted (late summer–early fall) Buntings. Both Barn and Great Horned Owls occasionally roost in the willows on the dam. It's always worth checking the large willow grove on the south side of the smaller south pond for either of these two species on a day perch. Obviously, the dam also provides the closest vantage point for most of the waterfowl and shorebirds. Raised viewing platforms on both the south and the east berms facilitate scanning.

Whitewater Draw was purchased by the state of Arizona in 1997 to protect not just the Sandhill Crane roost, but as a refuge for an astonishing diversity of waterbirds. A short sampling includes Black-bellied Whistling-Duck, Greater White-fronted, Snow, Ross's, and Canada Geese, Tundra Swan, Common Loon, Western and Clark's Grebes, American White and Brown Pelicans, Neotropic and Double-crested Cormorants, Great, Snowy, and Cattle Egrets, Black-crowned Night-Herons, and virtually every other heron, duck, rail, shorebird, gull, and tern known to have ever occurred in the southeastern corner. A Little Blue Heron was here in May 2001 and an Elegant Tern put in an appearance in July of the same year. When the reservoir at Whitewater Draw is high, overwintering waterfowl will number in excess of 10,000 birds.

Upon returning to Coffman, turn right (south) and scan the fields on both sides as you round the broad curve where the road turns east and becomes Bagby Road (0.4 mile). Long-billed Curlews have been sighted along Bagby nearly every month of the year, and they are actually fairly common during spring and fall migration periods. During the winter of 1998–1999 a Short-eared Owl was using this zone of the Sulphur Springs Valley for its crepuscular hunting forays. Bagby rejoins the pavement at Central Highway (1.0 mile). Lee Road (left or north 1.0 mile) is a good detour for Sage Sparrow most winters.

To continue the tour turn right (south) onto Central Highway. The remaining distance to Double Adobe Road (6.0 miles) passes through a major chile-growing region. Once again the hedgerows are excellent habitat for Bendire's Thrasher.

One of the great unsolved avian mysteries of the Sulphur Springs Valley involves the disappearance of the Harris's Hawks of Double Adobe. Readily seen throughout the 1980s, this communally nesting species abruptly abandoned the area in July 1991. Single Harris's Hawks are reported annually, but at this writing in 2004, they still had not re-pioneered Double Adobe. Any dark raptor in the vicinity deserves a second look. Platform nests in every Soaptree within a half-mile radius of the Double Adobe/Central Highway intersection are all that remain of the breeding colony today.

Continuing straight ahead, Central Highway turns into a well-graded gravel road. Chihuahuan desertscrub characterizes the terrain on both sides. Appropriately, Chihuahuan Ravens are probably the most conspicuous bird along this stretch. Where the grass has been overgrazed, there are patches of mesquite. You will notice that nearly every shrub has a mound under it. Sometimes erroneously attributed to prairie dogs, they are actually the work of Banner-tailed and Merriam's Kangaroo Rats.

The last prairie dogs in Southeastern Arizona were poison-baited into oblivion by the Federal government in 1938 in a misguided effort to improve the range for livestock use. Without the millions of Black-tailed Prairie Dogs burrows to capture rainwater, sheet flooding and erosion ensued, and aquifers were no longer recharged. Grasses have disappeared, the range sustains fewer cows than ever, and Coyotes have learned to augment their diet with occasional entrees of veal. The demise of the grasslands in the southern Sulphur Springs Valley probably accounts for the absence of Aplomado Falcons. The last individual in the lower valley was recorded in this vicinity in November 1939.

The desertscrub is still good for Crissal Thrashers and Sage Sparrows (winter). During summer, Swainson's Hawks are common on the telephone pole yardarms. Golden Eagles tend to sit on top the pole itself. Early in the morning it is sometimes possible to count a half-dozen of these magnificent birds of prey between Double Adobe and U.S. 80 (6.2 miles). A huge pasture on the right (west) side of Central Highway just before it meets Highway 80 offers birds another habitat. Lark Buntings and Red-winged, Yellow-headed, and Brewer's Blackbirds are the standard winter birds. In mid-winter 2002–2003 they were joined by a small flock of Mountain Plovers.

Unless time is short, a good way to conclude the Sulphur Springs Valley tour is with a quick visit to the main campus of **Cochise College**. To find the school, turn left (east) on Highway 80. Turn left again (north) at the well-signed entrance (0.6 mile). Like Lake Cochise, Kansas Settlement, Essary Hay Company, and the Whitewater Draw Wildlife Refuge, Cochise College is an oasis surrounded by desert, affording birds both greenery and water. The entrance road divides just 100 yards inside the gate and describes a one-mile-long loop around this attractive and modern campus.

In winter, unless there's a car right behind you, I suggest a pause to peruse the evergreen lawn in front of the first tier of buildings. From November through March American Pipits strut around the well-groomed grass like so many chickens. The mammal sharing the turf is the Spotted Ground Squirrel, otherwise uncommon in Southeastern Arizona. Turn right to park in the Visitor's Lot (100 yards). Flycatchers gravitate to the basketball and tennis court area just east of the parking area. Say's Phoebe is resident, and Ash-throated Flycatcher passes the summer here. The half-dozen Arizona Cypress trees rimming the basketball courts are occasionally the day roost for either Barn or Great Horned Owls.

Return to your car and continue on to the next parking lot on the right (0.2 mile). Due east lies the track, enclosing another oval of well-irrigated green. Horned Larks and Killdeer are habitués of the grass here throughout the winter. The baseball diamond is obvious to the southeast. In early spring a Bendire's Thrasher occasionally uses the backstop for an elevated song perch. Watch for Mountain Bluebirds catching flies in the outfield.

A 100-yard-long line of Tamarisk trees runs due east from the baseball field to the Cochise College Sewage Lagoon, otherwise known as Lake Irma (for one of the college's first receptionists). *This pond was posted as a "Restricted Area" in 2003, but it may re-open again. Please obey any signs.* Check the trees and the patch of nearby desert for either Scaled or Gambel's Quail, Verdin, Cactus Wren, House Wren (winter), Ruby-crowned Kinglet (winter), Northern Mockingbird, Curve-billed Thrasher, Loggerhead Shrike, Orange-crowned and Yellow-rumped Warblers (winter), Western Tanager (migration), Northern Cardinal, Blue Grosbeak (summer), White-crowned Sparrow (winter), and Bullock's Oriole (summer).

Assuming access is permitted, a scope is helpful, since Lake Irma is about 300 yards long. Resident birds include Great Blue Heron, the olive-billed "Mexican Duck" form of the Mallard, Killdeer, Black Phoebe, and Red-winged Blackbird. Migration periods bring the most interesting birds. A Sabine's Gull arrived here in mid-September 1986, and an early Yellow-billed Cuckoo showed up in late May 1988. White-tailed Kites (summer) are fairly regular off the far (east) end of the pond.

During summer, the buildings on campus provide a perfect nest substrate for hundreds of Cliff and Barn Swallows. Eastern and Western (winter; rare) Meadowlarks and Great-tailed Grackles use the expansive green between the dorms and the classroom areas. Ornamental plantings attract significant numbers of female and immature Calliope Hummingbirds every fall. During summer the trees pull in both Cassin's and Western Kingbirds. Nearby tracts of desert grassland are used by Scaled Quail, Burrowing Owl, Ladder-backed Woodpecker, and Pyrrhuloxia. Finally, at night the well-lit parking areas are a magnet for Lesser Nighthawks from May through September.

To reach Douglas turn left (east) on U.S. 80 (8 miles). Turn right (west) to find Bisbee (16 miles) and Sierra Vista (49 miles).

Campgrounds, Restaurants, and Accommodations

There are basic campgrounds available at Chiricahua National Monument (33 miles east of Willcox), Cochise Stronghold (15 miles west of the junction of Kansas Settlement Road with Highway 191), and Rucker Canyon

(21 miles east of Essary Hay Company). Willcox has a modern KOA with full hook-ups and amenities (520-586-3977) off Interstate 10 just west of Exit 340.

A number of fast-food chains are represented in both Willcox and Douglas on either end of the tour. A Family Restaurant in Elfrida (open 6:00 a.m.–9:00 p.m. daily; 520-642-3348) is probably the best place to eat along the route. The historic Gadsden Hotel restaurant in Douglas (open at 5:30 a.m.; 520-364-4481) has a wide selection of entrees, including Mexican food that I can personally endorse.

In Willcox are a Motel 6 (520-384-2201; www.motel6.com), a Super 8 (620-384-0888 or 800-800-8000), and a Best Western (520-384-3556). The Best Western Plaza Inn has a good restaurant which opens at 6:00 a.m. In Douglas, the Gadsden Hotel (520-364-4481; robin@gadsden) has an authentic, turn-of-the-century flavor with refurbished rooms at reasonable rates. Also in Douglas is the comparably priced and strictly institutional Motel 6 (520-364-2457; www.motel6.com). If you are heading west after completing this tour, nearby Bisbee, only 16 miles west of Cochise College, has many fine restaurants and the historic Copper Queen Hotel (520-432-2216).

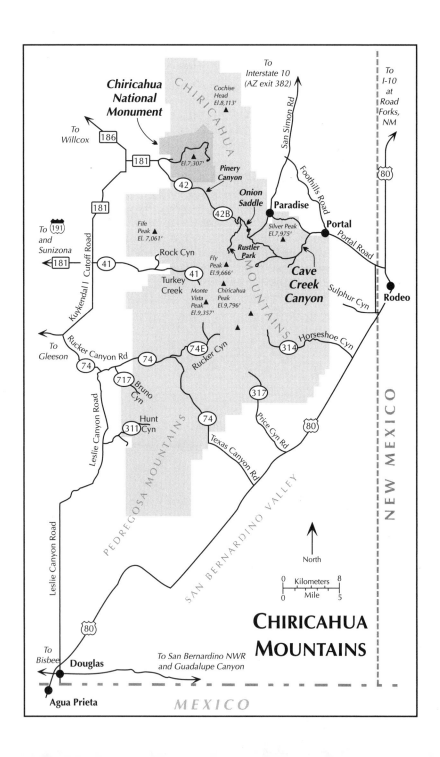

Chiricahua
National
Monument

CHIRICAHUA

Cochise
Head
El.8,113'

To
Interstate 10
(AZ exit 382)

To
I-10
at
Road
Forks,
NM

To
Willcox

186

181

San Simon Rd

Foothills Road

80

El.7,307'

42

Pinery
Canyon

Onion
Saddle

Paradise

181

42B

Silver Peak
El.7,975'

Portal

Portal Road

To 191
and
Sunizona

Fife
Peak
El. 7,061'

Rock Cyn

Rustler
Park

181

41

Fly
Peak
El.9,666'

Cave
Creek
Canyon

Rodeo

Kuykendall Cutoff Road

Turkey
Creek

41

Monte
Vista
Peak
El.9,357'

Chiricahua
Peak
El.9,796'

Sulphur Cyn

CHIRICAHUA MOUNTAINS

To
Gleeson

Rucker Canyon Rd

74

74

74E

Rucker Cyn

Horseshoe Cyn

314

Leslie Canyon Road

717

Bruno
Cyn

317

80

Hunt
Cyn

311

74

Price Cyn Rd

Texas Canyon Rd

PEDREGOSA MOUNTAINS

SAN BERNARDINO VALLEY

NEW MEXICO

North

0   Kilometers   8

0   Mile   5

CHIRICAHUA
MOUNTAINS

Leslie Canyon Road

To
Bisbee

80

Douglas

To San Bernardino NWR
and Guadalupe Canyon

Agua Prieta

MEXICO

CHAPTER 9

CHIRICAHUA
MOUNTAINS

Even in scenic Arizona, the Chiricahua Mountains are spectacular. Homeland of the Chiricahua Apaches, these mountains boast airy panoramas, a unique geology, and the single most diversified land-bounded plant and animal community in the entire United States. Many birders consider the Chiricahuas the premier birding location in all of North America.

The name "Chiricahua," according to Native Americans, comes from Opata words meaning "Big Mountain." Stretching over 40 miles in length and measuring 25 miles in width, the Chiricahuas encompass an area of approximately 1,000 square miles. Rising from Chihuahuan desertscrub at an elevation of about 3,800 feet in the San Simon Valley to Hudsonian spruce forest on the 9,796-foot-high summit, the Chiricahuas are the single largest mountain mass south of the Gila River in Arizona. In order to do the Chiricahua region justice, you should plan on birding here no fewer than two full days—excluding travel days—and three or more are preferable.

The starting point is the hamlet of Portal at the outlet of Cave Creek Canyon on the eastern flank of the range. There are no less than four possible approaches to Portal, and depending on recent weather events, your departure point, and your time limitations, each has its own advantages.

From Tucson the fastest way to reach Portal is to follow I-10 east to Willcox (about 80 miles; the last inexpensive gas and groceries) to Exit 382, San Simon/Portal Road (42 miles), on the east side of San Simon. Follow the frontage road east past the truck weigh station to the signed turnoff on the right (south) side (1.1 miles) for Portal. The first 7.4 miles are paved, but the remaining 17.8 to the pavement again at Portal Road are a well-graded gravel route—unless there have been heavy rains. Turn right toward the mountain to find Portal (0.7 mile). After recent storms this route is *not* recommended because of flash flood danger. Instead of exiting at San Simon, continue east on I-10 to Road Forks, New Mexico (15.0 miles) and turn south onto U.S. 80.

Road Forks (17 miles west of Lordsburg, the last cheap gas) is also the best exit if you are approaching Arizona on I-10 from the east. It is 28 miles south on U.S. 80 to the well-signed, right-hand (west) turnoff to Portal. A commercial building on the southwest corner—starkly evident in the sparsely vegetated desert—marks the beginning of the 7.0-mile drive to the village. While this route adds an additional 27 miles to the total distance from Tucson, it has the advantage of being entirely paved and is open in any weather.

From May through October during most years, and if time is not a major consideration, the scenic route to Portal is via the **Trans-mountain Road** over Onion Saddle, elevation 7,600 feet. To reach the Trans-mountain Road follow signs along State Highway 186 from Willcox to Chiricahua National Monument (31 miles), and turn right (south) on the unpaved road into Pinery Canyon just 100 yards before the entry station into the monument. It is 26 miles over Onion Saddle (described later in this chapter) to Portal. Snow frequently closes this pass between November and April. It is not recommended for vehicles over 20 feet in length or for anyone towing a long trailer.

If you are approaching **from the lower Sulphur Springs Valley or the Sierra Vista area**, take U.S. 80 northeast from Douglas. Watch for Golden Eagles, Scaled Quail, Burrowing Owls, and Grasshopper Sparrows in the mile-high grasslands between milepost 390 (mile 22.0) and milepost 400 at the Price Canyon turnoff (mile 32.0). Pronghorns are also frequently sighted east of the highway in this area. The Rodeo Store (last gas) is on the right side of the highway, 2 miles into New Mexico (mile 47.0). A former lumberyard, the only building in the barren desert, marks the turnoff to Portal 2.5 miles beyond Rodeo (49.5 miles from Douglas). From the junction with Highway 80 turn left (west) for Portal (7.0 miles).

There are three ecologically different birding areas within easy reach of Portal: desert valley, canyons, and mountain highlands. Ideally each deserves an early morning visit for the most productive birding, but realistically it is possible to combine any two in a single day, using Portal as a base.

DESERT VALLEY LOOP

(32 miles/one morning)

This route should be birded in the morning. Not only are desert birds far more apt to sing and be active early in the day, but from May through September temperatures in the valley can easily reach 90 degrees by 10 a.m. Once the heat comes up, it frequently becomes windy in the San Simon Valley.

Confluence of South Fork and
Cave Creek Canyons, Chiricahua Mountains
Richard Cachor Taylor

Downtown **Portal** is comprised of about a dozen homes, a library, post office, and a combination store, café, and lodge (highly recommended). Many of the residents are birders, and it fully warrants a walk up the only paved street, Rock House Road, for a taste of their yard birds. If you arrive before daylight in the spring listen for Western Screech-Owl, Great Horned Owl, and Elf Owl. All three species nest in the sycamores that line the 0.2-mile length of pavement.

The complete list of birds that joins the Portal dawn chorus from April through September contains about 60 species. Some of the more noteworthy are Gambel's Quail, Cooper's Hawk, White-winged Dove, Acorn and Ladder-backed Woodpeckers, Northern Beardless-Tyrannulet (erratic), Western Wood-Pewee, Black Phoebe, Dusky-capped, Ash-throated, and Brown-crested Flycatchers, Cassin's and Western Kingbirds, Bell's and Plumbeous Vireos, Western Scrub-Jay, Mexican Jay, Violet-green Swallow, Bridled and Juniper (uncommon) Titmice, Verdin, White-breasted Nuthatch, Cactus, Canyon, and Bewick's Wrens, American Robin, Northern Mockingbird, Curve-billed and Crissal Thrashers, Lucy's and Black-throated Gray Warblers, Summer and Western (migrant) Tanagers, Northern Cardinal, Black-headed and Blue Grosbeaks, Lazuli, Indigo, and Painted Buntings (migration only), Canyon Towhee (frequently under your car if you park by the store), Bronzed Cowbird (vastly outnumbered by Brown-headeds), Hooded, Bullock's, and Scott's Orioles, House Finch, and Lesser Goldfinch. You may even be fortunate enough to catch the Thick-billed Kingbird that generally shows up in metro-

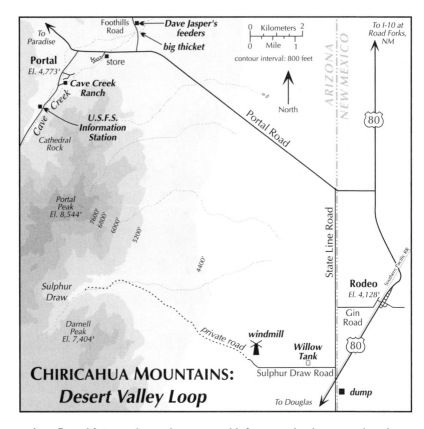

CHIRICAHUA MOUNTAINS:
Desert Valley Loop

politan Portal for one day each summer. Unfortunately, there are also plenty of European Starlings and House Sparrows.

Winter birding in Portal is nearly as exciting. Usually a few Blue-throated and one or two Magnificent Hummingbirds spend the coldest months alternating bouts of amazing aerial gnat-catching proficiency with visits to feeders. These are the two largest members of their family in the United States, and their large body sizes enable them to withstand snow and temperatures down to zero. Typically, a black, white, and crimson Painted Redstart vies with the hummingbirds for attention all winter long. Some years Cassin's Finches and Evening Grosbeaks lead the onslaught of House Finches, Pine Siskins, and Lesser and American Goldfinches at homeowners' seed trays, while Acorn Woodpeckers, Bridled Titmice, and White-breasted Nuthatches patronize the suet sticks. The first winter record of an Aztec Thrush in January 1991 and the second U.S. record of a Blue Mockingbird from January through mid-April 1995 both came from upcanyon on the grounds of the Cave Creek Ranch. (*Note:* Cave Creek Ranch's grounds are for paying guests only. Individuals or small groups *may* be allowed to bird here with advance permission; 520-558-2334.)

The greater Portal area is probably the best place to see Calliope Hummingbirds in Southeastern Arizona during fall migration from late July through September. Most of the other hummers for which the Chiricahuas are famous visit the feeders in downtown, and a Plain-capped Starthroat put in an appearance at a feeder hung across the street from the post office for much of August 1992. A Violet-crowned Hummingbird has nested in the 100 yards between the "Rock House"—the first home upcanyon from the Portal Store— and the post office every year since 1995. The owners of the Rock House, Chuck and Joan Jensen, generously permit birders to watch the hummingbird and seed feeders in their yard and their upcanyon lot. In recent years their home has been the most reliable site for Lucifer Hummingbird in the Chiricahua Mountains. *Watch the feeders from outside their stone fence; please respect their privacy.* If you are a newcomer to Arizona birds, or even if you just enjoy seeing lots of birds, you'll certainly enjoy early morning in this sleepy little village!

Tear yourself away. The Portal Road parallels Cave Creek for the first 0.7 mile east of Portal to a T-junction with the Foothills/San Simon Road immediately beyond a cattleguard. After the summer monsoons arrive in July it is worth the time to stop at this intersection to listen for Cassin's Sparrow in the grasses opposite the intersection. During winter the mesquite scrub here is good habitat for Sage Thrasher.

Turn left (north) onto the Foothills/San Simon Road and proceed 0.5 mile to the big thicket that flanks lower Cave Creek on both sides of the road. *This is private property, but it is permissible to bird from the road edges.* The specialty bird of the **Big Thicket** is Crissal Thrasher. Listen for its distinctive *cheery-cheery toweet! toweet!* calls on calm sunny mornings from February through October, and watch for it to sing from exposed perches in the low desert vegetation. Aside from its call, the dull eye, scimitar-curved bill, and unspotted chest will distinguish Crissal from Curve-billed Thrasher, which also sings from exposed perches in the Big Thicket at the same time of year.

Most of the desert birds mentioned for Portal are more common here, including Gambel's Quail, Ladder-backed Woodpecker, Bell's Vireo, Western Scrub-Jay, Cactus Wren, Verdin, Lucy's Warbler, Green-tailed (winter), Spotted, and Canyon Towhees, Black-throated and White-crowned (winter) Sparrows, and Pyrrhuloxia. Gila Woodpecker, usually restricted to the cottonwood groves and Saguaro Cactus forests farther west, is occasional here, as are Scaled Quail and Black-tailed Gnatcatcher. Aggregations of Lesser Nighthawks at dusk, especially near the concrete ford where Cave Creek crosses the road, may number up to a hundred or more during the summer. Just after dark and an hour or two before first light, this is a favored area to hear Common Poorwills giving their poignant, two-note calls. While rare,

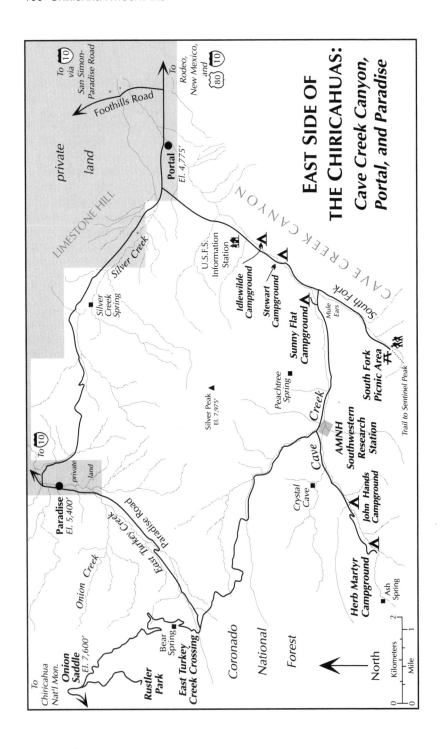

EAST SIDE OF
THE CHIRICAHUAS:
*Cave Creek Canyon,
Portal, and Paradise*

both Abert's Towhee and Varied Bunting, both quite local in the Chiricahua region, have also been reported.

In 1995 Dave Jasper opened his feeders in the Big Thicket to birders (7:30 a.m.–7:30 p.m.). All of the birds mentioned above occur on his property, and his are the only feeders open to the public where Crissal Thrashers actually slip out of the brush to consume seed in plain view. To find Dave Jasper's property, continue north past the concrete ford across Cave Creek about 75 more yards to a pullout on the right (east) side of Foothills Road. This is "Crissal Lane." There is room for up to three vehicles to park on either side of the gate. Walk in through the gate, follow the driveway until it curves right at the house, and then continue on the broad trail approximately 75 yards past an outbuilding to a group of chairs in the shade of a sycamore tree.

Naturally all the bird activity in the Big Thicket attracts raptors. Sharp-shinned (winter) and Cooper's Hawks, and even an occasional Northern Goshawk, well below its breeding habitat high in the mountains, take advantage of this banquet in the desert, as do Red-tailed Hawks and Golden Eagles. During summer there is a daily sunrise exodus of several hundred Turkey Vultures pouring out of the mouth of Cave Creek Canyon into the broad San Simon Valley.

Usually a half-hour to one hour is enough time to finesse the Big Thicket. Return south to the paved Portal Road and turn left (east) to descend to the floor of the San Simon Valley. Burrowing Owls formerly occupied the Chihuahuan desertscrub along Portal Road, but they disappeared mysteriously in the early 1980s; sightings have been rare in recent years, primarily near Rodeo. Scaled Quail, Swainson's Hawk, Golden Eagle, Greater Roadrunner, Western Kingbird, Loggerhead Shrike, Black-throated Sparrow, and Scott's Oriole still remain. At the cattleguard that delineates the boundary between Arizona and New Mexico (5.6 miles), turn right (south) onto Stateline Road—unless there have been recent heavy rains.

Dust is usually a worse problem than mud on Stateline Road, but give the road at least 24 hours to dry out before attempting it if you see fresh ruts left by farm trucks. Stateline Road is surveyor straight and 4.0 miles long. The agricultural area beyond Gin Road, the back road into Rodeo, New Mexico (2.5), offers the most intriguing birding. Bendire's Thrasher occurs along the entire route, but is most apt to be seen at thickets, especially near the derelict buildings south of Gin Road. In August and September scores of Blue Grosbeaks gather in the hedgerows along the irrigated fields of cotton and chiles, mixed with flocks of Lazuli Buntings and early-arriving Lark Buntings.

When present, but still not found every year, White-tailed Kites hunt the same fields. From mid-October through February a small flock of Sandhill Cranes is usually on the far side of the fields in the stubble.

Turn right (west) onto Sulphur Draw Road (3.8 miles) just before Stateline Road intersects with U.S. 80. It is only 0.6 mile to **Willow Tank**, arguably the most important pond on the entire eastern flank of the Chiricahuas—when it contains water. In the summer of 2004 Willow Tank was completely dry, but in the fall of 2004 the Arizona Game and Fish Department entered into an agreement with the landowner to subsidize the costs of pumping water into the pond. A single weeping willow on the raised bank near the road gives its name to this one-acre, rectangular impoundment. During winter this tree is frequently the perch of a Merlin or some other raptor; be sure to check it closely before leaving your car. *There is no parking area, so please pull as far off the road as possible; be careful, however, not to mire your car in deep mud if the road is wet.* In 1999 local residents created a gated entry in the barbed-wire fence about 25 yards before the pond to facilitate access to the water. Try to approach quietly: there is very little cover for any birds present, and they flush easily.

While birds are usually not abundant here, the quality of birds is high. One group surprised a Tricolored Heron in August 1994, and perhaps Arizona's first documented Trumpeter Swan was found at Willow Tank during the Christmas Bird Count of the same year. Several winters Tundra Swans have also been recorded. Migration periods offer the best chances for rarities: a Least Tern was present in May 2003 and a Dickcissel was at Willow Tank the same October. Southeastern Arizona's second record of Field Sparrow put in an appearance in March 2000. Northern Waterthrushes pass through every spring, and probably Painted Buntings are present in late summer and early fall every year. The Mexican Duck form of the Mallard is a year-round visitor, as are Great Blue Heron, American Coot, a variety of shorebirds, Common Yellowthroat, and Red-winged Blackbird, all otherwise scarce in this waterless valley. During winter Willow Tank hosts Sora, Marsh Wren, Song Sparrow, Swamp Sparrow, Chestnut-collared Longspur (in the swale behind the pond), and an occasional Yellow-headed Blackbird.

Continue up Sulphur Draw until the road bends right around a house, crosses a wash, and arrives at a puddle-sized waterhole by an old corral on the right (north) side of the road (1.4 mile). Stop here for the only reliable pair of Vermilion Flycatchers in the whole Portal area (summer is better than winter, however). The small cottonwoods across the road from the corrals harbor Gila Woodpeckers (more typical of the Sonoran than the Chihuahuan Desert), and the brushy swale is a good location for Crissal Thrasher, Varied Bunting, and Abert's Towhee. A family of Harris's Hawks can often be found in the scattered cottonwoods or perched on utility poles. *Land on both sides of the road is private property. Although there are no fences, birders are not permitted off the road.*

The upper Sulphur Draw Road is ordinarily not particularly productive for birds, so the best plan is to return to Stateline Road (2.0 miles) and turn right to access U.S. 80. (0.2 mile). If you still haven't seen a Bendire's Thrasher, there are several locations on the return route in New Mexico that are worth checking. The first is directly across the Stateline Road at the Rodeo Town Dump. Turn left into the dump after 0.15 mile. The raised dumping ramp offers an ideal viewing platform from which to check for the bird in piles of debris.

Return to U.S. 80 and follow it north for 2.0 miles to the Rodeo Store on the right (east) side of the highway. (Gas is expensive here, but nonexistent in Portal.) The vacant lots surrounding the church just a block behind (east of) the store is another good site for Bendire's and, occasionally, Crissal Thrashers. While in Rodeo watch for Scaled Quail, Inca Dove, Gila Woodpecker, and Great-tailed Grackle.

To return to Portal take Gin Road, the dirt road opposite the Rodeo Store, back to Stateline Road (1.1 miles). Initially this farm lane parallels the highway before swinging due west in front of a house (0.2 mile). Bendire's Thrasher is frequently in the mesquite and soaptrees on the west side of the house. A short distance beyond, a locked cotton gin on the right (0.3 mile) usually harbors Barn Owls. Sometimes they can be seen through holes and slots in the galvanized walls as they snooze away the daylight hours on steel beam perches. The field on the right (north) side of the road after the cotton gin is good for Cassin's Sparrows (primarily in July and August).

At the T-junction with Stateline Road turn right (north). It is 2.5 miles back to the pavement at Portal Road. Turn left (west) here and continue back to Portal (6.3 miles). By now bird activity has subsided in the lowlands, and the best way to cap off the morning is with a visit to either the big canyons or the scenic highlands of the Chiricahuas.

Please note that with Sally Spofford's death in October 2002, all birders lost a good friend. She and her husband Walter, who passed away in November 1995, were the first people in Arizona to share their private yard with visiting birders from throughout the U.S. and abroad. Some 15,000 birders availed themselves of their hospitality every year. Although the Spofford property is now closed, their legacy of goodwill toward birders lives on in Chuck and Joan Jensen, Dave Jasper, Mary Jo Ballator, Tom and Edith Beatty, Jackie and Winston Lewis, Marion and the late Walter Paton, and others who have since selflessly opened their yards to the birding public.

CANYONS LOOP
(25 miles/one day)

This loop begins at Portal and circles 7,975-foot elevation Silver Peak, exploring five ecologically different canyon areas. The view up Cave Creek from Portal is one of the most spectacular vistas in all of the American Southwest.

Elegant Trogon
David A. Sibley

A half-mile west of Portal a dirt road on the right at a conspicuous Y-intersection leads up Silver Creek to the old mining town of Paradise. This road will be treated later as the last link in the Canyons Loop; continue up the canyon on the pavement. You are traversing an alluvial flat covered by shrubby mesquite, which harbors a surprising variety of birds. Early in the morning you may find Montezuma Quail on the road edges, and during summer you'll pass several male Blue Grosbeaks singing from mesquite tops. In July and August watch the flowering agave stalks for hummingbirds (Rufous is the most common) as well as all three species of the breeding orioles, Hooded, Bullock's, and Scott's. In winter it's usually possible to high-grade a few Black-chinned and Rufous-crowned Sparrows out of the big flocks of White-crowns and Chippers. The Dark-eyed Juncos traveling with them are an assortment of "Oregon," "Pink-sided," and "Gray-headed," with a few Yellow-eyed Juncos mixed in for good measure. Adding a touch of winter cheer, almost every flock contains Northern Cardinals and Pyrrhuloxias.

The road soon passes between twin rock pylons at a cattleguard marking the boundary of the Coronado National Forest, and then drops through a long curve to the parking area in a large field on the right for the U.S. Forest Service Portal Information Station (1.3 miles). This is a good place to get a status report on road conditions in winter or after summer rains, and the small bookstore offers a nice selection of natural-history materials. Feeders on the porch attract an occasional rarity, such as a White-eared Hummingbird in May 1994. The large grassy field adjacent to the parking area north of the station is a good spot to see and hear Common Poorwill on summer evenings.

Beyond the Information Station the road tunnels through a beautiful gallery forest of broadleaf trees dominated by graceful, white-barked Arizona Sycamore. The multi-tiered, strawberry-colored rhyolite walls of Cave Creek stair-step over 3,000 feet above. You have entered the premier habitat for Elegant Trogon in the U.S. With it comes a community of birds commonly associated with the pine-oak woodlands of the Sierra Madre of Western Mexico. Some of the resident and summer birds to watch for as you drive—or better, walk—up Cave Creek include Montezuma Quail, Band-tailed Pigeon, White-throated Swift, Blue-throated and Magnificent Hummingbirds, Acorn and Arizona Woodpeckers, Western Wood-Pewee, Dusky-capped, Brown-crested, and Sulphur-bellied Flycatchers, Plumbeous and Hutton's Vireos, Mexican Jay, Bridled Titmouse, White-breasted Nuthatch, Brown Creeper, Canyon and Bewick's Wrens, Virginia's, Black-throated Gray, and Grace's Warblers, Painted Redstart, Hepatic Tanager, Black-headed Grosbeak, Spotted Towhee, Rufous-crowned Sparrow, and Lesser Goldfinch.

Diurnal raptors that hunt Cave Creek are Cooper's, Zone-tailed, and Red-tailed Hawks, with an occasional sweep through by a Peregrine Falcon. On the night shift, Cave Creek is famous for its owls. Flammulated Owls and Whiskered Screech-Owls replace the Western Screech-Owls found lower down in the canyon, joined by Northern Pygmy-Owls and Spotted Owls. Elf Owls, while concentrated near Portal, span Cave Creek up to the Southwestern Research Station.

A gentle, three-quarter-mile trail hugs the base of Silver Peak between the bridge just before Stewart Campground (park in Stewart, 0.7 mile, and cross the bridge on foot back to the trailhead) and Sunnyflat Campground (1.8 miles), threading through a magnificent stand of streamside sycamores. For most birders, however, the walk up **South Fork Cave Creek** is the single most desirable hike in the Chiricahua Mountains. To find South Fork Road drive upcanyon beyond the entrance to Stewart Campground an additional 0.9 mile (2.9 miles above the Portal Store). The pavement veers right at the junction; South Fork Road continues straight ahead as a dirt road. Many knowledgeable birders with previous experience in South Fork elect to hike the entire length of South Fork Road (1.3 miles). In April 2004 a Rufous-capped Warbler was discovered just below the South Fork ford. Lower South Fork is wider, and viewing opportunities are enhanced. The first Elegant Trogons to arrive in April are often found in this scenic, lower stretch of the canyon. *To protect the trogons, the use of tape recorders for any birds, including owls, is prohibited in South Fork Cave Creek.*

Since the 27,500-acre Rattlesnake Fire in 1994, the South Fork ford (mile 0.9) has become treacherous when flooded. *Do not attempt to drive across the stream with your car if the Forest Service has set up barriers.* Improvements to make the ford passable year round were scheduled for late 2004. The South Fork Road ends at a turn-around oval and a picnic area 0.4 mile beyond.

There is a Forest User Fee for the Douglas Ranger District, payable at the self-service pay station on the lower end of the oval (fee $5/day; Golden Age, Golden Access, and Golden Eagle Pass accepted.) Permits purchased for Madera Canyon or Mount Lemmon and the Santa Catalina Mountains are also good here.

D o not rush hastily up the trail. Elegant Trogons patrol through the picnic area several times a day throughout the summer, and there is generally an Arizona Woodpecker present until the advent of the summer monsoons in July. Other regulars in the picnic area include Blue-throated Hummingbird, Sulphur-bellied Flycatcher, Hutton's Vireo, Mexican Jay, Bridled Titmouse, Brown Creeper, Black-throated Gray and Grace's Warblers, Painted Redstart, and Hepatic Tanager. Some years Yellow-eyed Juncos hop tamely under the picnic tables, but in other years they are absent.

Much of South Fork's reputation is owing to the spectacular scenery. Towering rose-colored cliffs, pocked with grottoes and stained lime green or citrus orange on protected facades, shelter the ribbon of forest that follows the sparkling clear little stream. Moreover, up to 10 pairs of Elegant Trogons nest in South Fork Cave Creek. It was here in October 1977 that the first Eared Quetzal known to enter the U.S. was discovered, and the first Flame-colored Tanager recorded north of the international boundary arrived in South Fork in April 1985. Even without its spectacular scenery, South Fork would be important in the annals of North American ornithology.

The trail up South Fork continues for 7.25 miles to the Chiricahua Crest Trail. The best birding, however, occurs in the first 2.25 miles below The Nose, a gargantuan rock formation on the right (west) side of the canyon as you ascend. Both Peregrine and Prairie Falcons have maintained eyries on this imposing monolith in recent years, although never both species in the same year. Groves of Bigtooth Maple along the stream at the base of The Nose also harbor the lowest breeding Mexican Chickadees and Red-faced Warblers in the canyon; post-breeding-season wandering may bring both species all the way down to the picnic area in August. After the maples change in early November, Winter Wren and American Dipper are occasional in upper South Fork.

South Fork Trail leaves the canyon bed after 2.5 miles and grows progressively steeper as the canyon becomes narrower. At mile 4.0 it deserts the main canyon and continues up the dry Sentinel Fork tributary, switchbacking over 2,500 feet up the remaining several miles to the Crest Trail. Since the big fire in 1994, there are places in the uppermost portion where the trail is no longer discernable.

To rejoin the Canyons Loop return down the South Fork Road to the paved Cave Creek Road and turn left (west).

The main canyon of Cave Creek is peppered with numerous caverns along the base of the cliffs, formed when vast quantities of volcanic ash were expelled from a nearby caldera in a series of violent eruptions approximately 15–25 million years ago. Gas pockets trapped in the falling ash created the plethora of pot-holes and small caves that visitors see as they drive up the canyon today. These caverns formerly sheltered prehistoric people who were part of the Mogollon cultural tradition. Artifacts, bits of broken pottery, and corn cobs, some dating back 1,000 or more years, have been discovered in grottoes within the main canyon near its confluence with South Fork. *Remember, it is unlawful to remove any relic of our prehistoric past from public lands.*

In the late 1500s a new wave of emigrants entered the area from the northeast—the Chiricahua Apaches. The Chiricahuas apparently used caverns like these for concealed burial chambers, interring their deceased behind a wall constructed of native rock and adobe. Their natural mausoleums are so well-camouflaged that only three such traditional Apache burial sites have ever been discovered in the Southwest, and just one from the Chiricahua Mountains.

The artificial clearing on the right side of the road dates back to a homestead founded in approximately 1900; astonishingly, a few apple trees still survived in 2004. It was across the road from the old Maloney Orchard where Arizona's first recorded Rufous-capped Warbler attempted to nest in July 1977, and then reappeared in April 1978. Zone-tailed Hawk and Elegant Trogon are frequently observed above and below the Maloney Orchard during summer. *The Maloney Orchard is private property; birders must stay on the road.*

Turn left (west) onto Herb Martyr Road (mile 1.8 above South Fork Road), cross the creek, and go another 50 yards to reach the entrance to the **Southwestern Research Station**. The American Museum of Natural History maintains the facility as a field station and laboratory for scientists. From June through August researchers are given preference and no advance reservations are accepted from birders. Cabins with meals are available to birders and naturalists from September through May (meals not available November–February). Most of the projects at the Southwestern Research Station focus on biological and ecological questions, and more dissertations in the natural sciences have been based on research conducted in the Chiricahua Mountain region than any other area in the United States.

Please remember that this is a study area, not a public museum. While the staff is friendly, they do not have time to give you a guided tour. A small gift shop in the office is open to everyone. Next door, the log cabin incorporated into the director's residence was built in 1879 by pioneer Stephen B. Reed, the first settler on the east side of the Chiricahuas. Birders are welcome to watch the hummingbird feeders in the central clearing.

Situated in a shady grove of cottonwoods at the confluence of the main branch of Cave Creek with North Fork Cave Creek, a number of rarities have been discovered at the Research Station. Records include a Pine Warbler in March 1991 and a Yellow Grosbeak in June 1974. Buff-breasted Flycatchers often spend all of May on the grounds, and are possibly breeding nearby. Some of the pine-oak birds that occur on a regular basis are Montezuma Quail (in the grasses just across the Herb Martyr Road from the entrance), Zone-tailed Hawk, Flammulated Owl (especially in dense junipers), Whiskered Screech-Owl, both Common Poorwill and Whip-poor-will, Magnificent Hummingbird, Elegant Trogon, Arizona Woodpecker, Sulphur-bellied Flycatcher, Painted Redstart, and Yellow-eyed Junco. Black Phoebes hang out by the swimming pool, and Say's Phoebes nest under the porch roof of the cabins. Protected here from hunters, the Coues form of the White-tailed Deer is a regular evening visitor to the central meadow between the office and the dining hall.

Exiting the Southwestern Research Station, turn left (west) onto the dirt road to **Herb Martyr Campground**. The first half of the road to John Hands Picnic Area parallels the Main Fork of Cave Creek (1.1 miles). Wild Turkey (rare), Hepatic and Western (summer) Tanagers, and Red Crossbill (erratic) use this wet stretch of the main canyon. Above John Hands the road climbs up into arid pine-oak woodland frequented by Montezuma Quail, Arizona Woodpecker, Hutton's Vireo, Mexican Jay, Bridled Titmouse, Bushtit, Bewick's Wren, Black-throated Gray and Virginia's Warblers (summer), Spotted Towhee, and Scott's Oriole (summer). There is an almost continuous view of 396-feet-high Winn Falls almost straight ahead all the way to the parking area at Herb Martyr Campground (1.1 mile).

Tall dead snags near the parking lot provide perches for Greater Pewee, whose melodic *José Maria* calls are one of the characteristic calls of the dawn chorus in spring. At the crack of daylight, a dozen or more species may be working the perimeter of the parking area, including Grace's Warbler and Painted Redstart. If the birds seem to be concentrating on one tree alone, check it carefully for a possible Northern Pygmy-Owl.

A short but potentially rewarding trail from Herb Martyr leads to Ash Spring and the Cima Creek Cienaga. Birds here include Steller's Jay, Mexican

Arizona Woodpecker
Narca Moore-Craig

Chickadee, Red-breasted Nuthatch, Warbling Vireo, and Western Tanager. Take the trail that begins off the southwest corner of the parking lot, cross Cima Creek, and continue to a trail junction 150 yards beyond. Turn right (north) here and take the Basin Trail 0.7 mile to a stream crossing in a grove of very tall Douglas-fir and White Fir, interwoven with the white limbs of exceptionally tall Arizona Sycamores. A series of small springs emerges in the cool shade of the conifers below the trail, creating an isolated pocket of habitat similar to that found along the Chiricahua crest, 3,000 feet above. This area is excellent for Flammulated Owl. Ash Spring is only 200 yards beyond the stream crossing. Red-faced Warbler occasionally nests in the wet ravine below the spring. A steep, rocky, abandoned road drops from Ash Spring 0.7 mile down to the Herb Martyr parking area. There are superb views of Winn Falls en route. The whole loop is only 1.5 miles long, and the elevation change is from 5,750 feet at Herb Martyr to 6,200 feet at Ash Spring.

Return to the Cave Creek Road (2.2 miles), and turn left (north). The pavement ends 100 yards beyond the Southwestern Research Station, but the gravel road which continues is suitable for standard passenger vehicles—except after heavy winter storms. The road follows the canyon bottom of North Fork Cave Creek at the base of Silver Peak through a grassy area of scattered sycamores, walnuts, and junipers. Eastern Bluebirds formerly nested in these open glades, but sometime in the early 1990s they disappeared as a breeding resident; North Fork still hosts Eastern Bluebirds in the winter. Ordinarily one or two pairs of Elegant Trogons (summer) occupy this stretch of North Fork, too. After the upper stream crossing (mile 1.7), the road enters the same short-stature Sierra Madrean pine-oak woodland as along the upper Herb Martyr Road, and the birds are identical. Once the summer rains commence, this is a good area for Montezuma Quail and Arizona Woodpecker.

The next birding stop is at the Paradise Road junction (2.3 miles). The grove of Douglas-fir and Gambel Oak on the shady slope above East Turkey Creek usually contains the lowest road-accessible Mexican Chickadees on the east side of the Chiricahuas. Other breeding birds here include Northern Goshawk (occasionally soaring over), Hutton's Vireo, Steller's Jay, Red-breasted Nuthatch, Brown Creeper, Virginia, Grace's, and Red-faced Warblers, Western Tanager, and Yellow-eyed Junco. All of the these birds are more common in the high Chiricahuas, but if time is at a premium, the East Turkey Creek crossing is a good place to try for them.

Make a sharp right (east) turn onto the Paradise Road to continue the Canyons Loop. The road crosses East Turkey Creek three times in the next few miles as it drops out of the pines into the oaks and junipers at Paradise (2.6 miles). Founded in 1901 and once boasting a population of 1,500, Paradise was a classic boom-and-bust silver mining camp. By 1910 the population had dwindled to fewer than 50, and in 1970 there were only three families in the settlement. But the past decade has seen a resurgence of new residents, here to take advantage of the cool summer temperatures that the early miners likened to Paradise itself. A few of the old buildings still remain, including the home of the town's first settlers, George and Lula Walker. Refurbished in 1993, the George Walker House opened as a guest house the following year. A Berylline Hummingbird was among their first visitors in June 1994, and a family of Juniper Titmice are year-round habitués at the seed trays. In the summer of 2003 Montezuma Quail became somewhat regular in the yard, and oddities found in 2004 included an Orchard Oriole in spring and an extremely early Williamson's Sapsucker in mid-August. Owners Jackie and Winston Lewis welcome birders to watch their feeders. To find the George Walker House, look for the small sign on the left (west) side of the road in mid-town Paradise (0.4 mile).

To continue the loop, follow the road north to a T-junction (0.3 mile), and turn right (east) across the concrete bridge over East Turkey Creek. A pair of Western Screech-Owls ordinarily holds a territory centering on the bridge. Across the stream, the road winds through an open, grassy juniper woodland that attracts wintering Western and Mountain (irregular) Bluebirds, Townsend's Solitaires, and Cedar Waxwings. The habitat changes abruptly at Silver Creek Pass (mile 1.5).

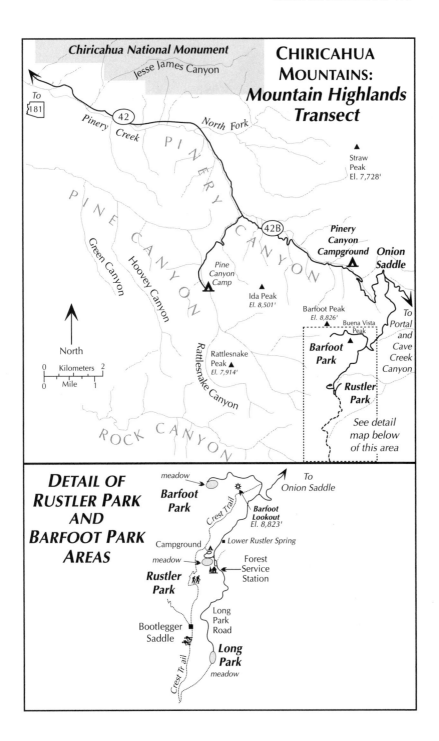

Chiricahua National Monument

Jesse James Canyon

CHIRICAHUA MOUNTAINS: *Mountain Highlands Transect*

To 181

42

Pinery Creek

North Fork

PINERY

PINE CANYON

CANYON

Green Canyon

Hoovey Canyon

42B

▲ Straw Peak El. 7,728'

Pinery Canyon Campground ▲

Onion Saddle

Pine Canyon Camp ⌂

Ida Peak ▲ El. 8,501'

Barfoot Peak ▲ El. 8,826'

Buena Vista Peak ▲

Barfoot Park

To Portal and Cave Creek Canyon

North

0 Kilometers 2
0 Mile 1

Rattlesnake Peak ▲ El. 7,914'

Rattlesnake Canyon

Rustler Park

ROCK CANYON

See detail map below of this area

DETAIL OF RUSTLER PARK AND BARFOOT PARK AREAS

meadow

Barfoot Park

Crest Trail

To Onion Saddle

Barfoot Lookout El. 8,823'

Campground

meadow

Rustler Park

Lower Rustler Spring ■

Forest Service Station

Long Park Road

Bootlegger Saddle ■

Crest Trail

Long Park

meadow

Olive Warbler
Narca Moore-Craig

Silver Creek's pinyon-juniper woodlands and interior chaparral are a consequence of the drainage's geographic position in the rain shadow of Silver Peak and the crest of the Chiricahuas to the south and west. This arid habitat attracts a triplet of species more typical of Central Arizona: Western Scrub-Jay, Juniper Titmouse, and Black-chinned Sparrow. Cactus, Acacia, and Ocotillo on the hot, south-facing slopes support an enclave of desert birds that include Greater Roadrunner, Ash-throated Flycatcher (summer), Rock Wren, Crissal Thrasher, Canyon Towhee, and Scott's Oriole (summer). Sporadically present as migrants in April–May and August–September are Gray Flycatcher and Gray Vireo (very rare). In July and August watch the flowering agave stalks for hummingbirds. Rufous is the most abundant species, but Calliopes are not uncommon, and a Plain-capped Starthroat was here in August 1987. The best place to try for these birds is between Silver Creek Spring and the right-hand roadside pullout over the next 0.7 mile. Walking the road from the spring to the pullouts is recommended.

To find Silver Creek Spring watch for an abrupt right lane that leads a few yards to an oval parking area with one big oak (mile 1.3). Here, a 200-yard-long path follows the stream down to a collapsed corral and water trough under some huge, old sycamores. If Cave Creek is running too strongly in Portal to hear the Elf Owls and Western Screech-Owls, this sycamore grove is a handy nearby location with flood-proof acoustics.

Exercise caution as you continue down Silver Creek Road; the road is narrow and has several blind curves. An inconspicuous lane on the right side near the lower end of the canyon (mile 2.0) leads to a small parking area near a stock tank. The area near the pond can be dynamite—or dead. Both Indigo and Varied Buntings (summer) have attempted to colonize this area, but some years neither is present. White-throated Swifts and Violet-green Swallows both drink from the small pool behind the earthworks. And both Curve-billed and Crissal Thrashers nest in the nearby ravines. Black-throated Sparrow is regular here throughout the year, and Black-chinned Sparrow is fairly common by the pond in winter.

It is one more mile down the Silver Creek Road to the paved Cave Creek Road. Portal is 0.5 mile down canyon to the left (east).

Mountain Highlands Transect

(28 miles/one-half day to Rustler Park)
(80 miles/one day to Chiricahua National Monument)

The first 8.7 miles of this trip—from Portal to the Paradise Road junction at East Turkey Creek—are described above in the Canyons Loop section. Assuming that you do not detour on either the South Fork or Herb Martyr Road en route to East Turkey Creek, it will take approximately 30 minutes of travel time to reach East Turkey Creek from Portal.

The Trans-mountain Road above the crossing is a narrow, steep, and winding mountain route. *It is important that drivers keep right on blind curves; we strongly recommend sounding the horn before entering them.* This road is not safe for vehicles over 20 feet in length or for vehicles pulling trailers. During winter and after major summer thunderstorms, the road may be closed. Nonetheless a visit to Rustler Park and, time permitting, Chiricahua National Monument is one of the highlights of any birder's pilgrimage to Southeastern Arizona.

Among birders who maintain a North American list, Mexican Chickadee is perhaps the bird most-wished for on a visit to the Chiricahua Mountains. Unlike Elegant Trogon or even Eared Quetzal, Mexican Chickadees simply do not occur elsewhere on public lands north of Mexico. In fact, the small population on the privately-owned Gray Ranch in the adjacent New Mexico panhandle cannot be reached without a strenuous hike. Fortunately, Mexican Chickadee is common in the upper Chiricahuas. This does not mean the chickadees are always easy to find. While they are attending nests in April and

May, it is often easier to see them at the East Turkey Creek crossing on the Trans-mountain Road, or in the forested ravines en route to Onion Saddle (3.3 miles), than at the end of the road in Rustler Park. Depending on the year, dead pine snags along this stretch may also be the best place to search for Northern Pygmy-Owl during spring.

At Onion Saddle, elevation 7,600 feet, turn left (south) toward Rustler Park. For the next two miles the route follows the crest of the Chiricahuas, threading in and out of Ponderosa Pine stands, alternating with dense thickets of oak. These dry, brushy hillsides are good for Virginia's Warbler.

The vista at the oak grove between mile 1.3 to 1.6 is especially magnificent. Cave Creek Canyon—7,975-foot Silver Peak on the left and 8,544-foot Portal Peak on the right—cuts a 3,000-foot-deep chasm in the foreground, and the rugged peaks of southwestern New Mexico unfurl for a hundred miles to the horizon. Do not forget to watch for birds. Aside from chickadees, the pines along the lower Rustler Road are also good for Hairy Woodpecker, Olive Warbler, Western Tanager (summer), Chipping Sparrow, Yellow-eyed Junco, and Red Crossbill (irregular).

After a big switchback, the road levels out and then "T's" at **Barfoot Junction** (2.0 miles). The left spur continues to Rustler Park (1.0 mile), and the right fork goes to Barfoot Park (1.0 mile). Bird here. *Vale la pena,* as they say in Mexico—it's definitely worth the trouble. Some of the birds present throughout the summer at Barfoot Junction include Hairy Woodpecker, Greater Pewee, Violet- green Swallow, Steller's Jay, Common Raven, Mexican Chickadee, Pygmy Nuthatch, Brown Creeper, House Wren (about half are the "Brown-throated" subspecies of the Sierra Madre), Western Bluebird, "Audubon's" Yellow-rumped, Grace's, and Olive Warblers, Hepatic Tanager, Black-headed Grosbeak, and Yellow-eyed Junco. Other birds to watch for among the Ponderosa Pines are Northern Goshawk, Band-tailed Pigeon, and Northern Pygmy-Owl. Northern Saw-whet Owls have nested near the parking area on the right (north) side of Barfoot Junction. A little spring arises from the bed of Rocky Mountain Iris on the left (south) side of the road at the intersection. If bird activity seems light, a hundred-yard walk down to the spring is sometimes worth the effort. Hammond's and Dusky Flycatchers are often fairly common in this swale during spring and fall migration.

Barfoot Park, elevation 8,200 feet (1.0 mile), is a small, grassy meadow with a trickling spring, set directly beneath the talus-strewn slope of 8,823-foot-high Barfoot Lookout. The last half of the road to Barfoot Park can be rough for cars with low clearance. You may want to walk after reaching the pass. Lacking improved campsites, Barfoot is ordinarily less crowded than Rustler Park. It is also one of the most reliable sites for Zone-tailed Hawk in the Chiricahuas. Watch for them to waft up over the half-dome of rhyolite on the south side of the meadow. Since 2001 a pair of Short-tailed Hawks (summer) uses the same location, occasionally even harassing the Zone-tail or a wandering Red-tail. The first Arizona record of this rare visitor from Mexico came from nearby Onion Saddle in 1985, but it was not until 1999 that they were reported again from the Chiricahuas, and 2003 marked the first year they are known to have fledged young. Thus far all Chiricahua birds have been light-morph hawks with dark helmets, white throats, white wing linings, and a mostly pale tail with a dark subterminal band. Almost invariably they are seen soaring. The best vantage point is the meadow itself.

Meanwhile Broad-tailed Hummingbirds will be working the flowers by the spring near the pump house. Be careful not to confuse the common Northern "Red-shafted" Flicker with female Williamson's Sapsuckers, which migrate through in May and September. Barfoot is also excellent for Greater Pewee (summer), Red-breasted and Pygmy Nuthatches, Western Bluebird, and both Red-faced and Olive Warblers (summer). The Red-faces prefer the aspen grove where the road drops into the meadow. Olives can be anywhere, but seem particularly fond of the pines near the foundations of an old Boy Scout camp on the west side of the clearing.

Retrace your route back to Barfoot Junction (1.0 mile) and continue straight ahead to reach Rustler Park (1.0 mile).

As you follow the road through open stands of Ponderosa Pine to **Rustler Park**, keep an eye out for Wild Turkeys (uncommon, reintroduced in 2003 and 2004), particularly on the downhill side. The fingers of burnt timber are part of the enormous 1994 Rattlesnake Fire. Check the woodpeckers using the burn; Hairy is common, but Southeastern Arizona is overdue for its first record of Three-toed. A pullout and restroom on the left marks the entrance to the Rustler Park Recreation Site, where there is a Forest User Fee, payable at the self-service pay station on lower end of the campground. (The same $5.00 day-use fee and passes apply as described for South Fork Cave Creek in the Canyons Loop section of this chapter.) Just beyond the pullout on the left there is a small spring enclosed by a rail fence. The short-needled, deep green conifer inside is an Engelmann Spruce, a timberline species present north to British Columbia. The Chiricahuas have the southernmost Engelmann Spruce stands in North America.

Summer birds likely to be present in the immediate precincts of the spring include Band-tailed Pigeon, Northern Pygmy-Owl, Steller's Jay, Mexican Chickadee, Red-breasted and Pygmy Nuthatches, House Wren, Western Bluebird, Hermit Thrush, American Robin, Yellow-rumped, Grace's and Olive Warblers, Hepatic and Western Tanagers, Black-headed Grosbeak, Chipping Sparrow, Yellow-eyed Junco, Pine Siskin, and Evening Grosbeak (irregular). Beyond the spring, the road forks. The left branch goes to the ranger station (0.15 mile), while the right fork leads to campsites along the north edge of the meadow.

Rustler Park is an enchanting spot. In June, when it turns blue with Rocky Mountain Iris, the shrill trill emitted by the wings of airborne male Broad-tailed Hummingbirds competes for your ear with the flute-like notes of Hermit Thrushes. In August and early September hundreds of migrating Rufous

Hummingbirds join the Broadtails in pitched battle over feeding rights to blossoming Bluebells and Delphiniums throughout the Chiricahua meadows, as well as to patches of Lemmon's Salvia on the rocky, south-facing slopes. The largest concentration of migrating hummingbirds occurs up the old Long Park logging road, south of the Rustler ranger station. Watch for them after the road levels off and makes an abrupt right turn (0.4 mile), and again in 9,000-foot-elevation Long Park itself (1.5 miles). This steep road is badly eroded and is better walked than driven.

Before hiking up the old logging road that leads from the ranger station to Long Park, spend a few moments birding around the small log cabins used by seasonal firefighters. Every summer Cordilleran Flycatcher nests at the Forest Service horse corral and barn. Here, too, are the most accessible breeding Golden-crowned Kinglets in Southeastern Arizona. If you are still searching for Red-faced Warbler, try the short fire-break trail behind the cabins that circles back to upper Rustler Park. Buff-breasted Flycatcher is occasionally found in the grassy burn 200 yards east of the Rustler cabins, and every few years small flocks of Clark's Nutcrackers or Cassin's Finches are found around the perimeter of the meadow.

On the west end of the upper campground loop, an access trail climbs straight up the slope for 250 feet and then divides. The left branch leads through the Chiricahua Wilderness to the top of 9,795-foot-elevation Chiricahua Peak (5.25 miles), the highest point in the mountains. This is an all-day hike, but rewarding. Along the way the trail passes through a series of small meadows, swings across openings with vistas that encompass the entirety of Southeastern Arizona, and tunnels through beautiful stands of Engelmann Spruce. Since the 1994 Rattlesnake Fire, there are also long stretches of trail that cross blistered landscapes where not a single tree survived the destruction. Birds in the wilderness area are the same as those found at Rustler and Barfoot Parks.

The right fork of the trail above the campground follows the crest 1.25 miles north to Barfoot Lookout on top 8,823-foot-high Buena Vista Peak. The first mile of the trail stays just under the east side of the ridge. During the summer this portion of the Crest Trail affords birders a great opportunity to see Yellow-rumped and Grace's Warblers and Western and Hepatic Tanagers right at eye level. When you pause to rest, watch for a small brown lizard darting after insects amid the shocks of Muhly Grass. This is the Bunch Grass Lizard, a Sierra Madrean species confined in the U.S. to the archipelago of high mountains along the Mexican border.

Bird diversity is usually low the final few hundred yards below the summit, but Pygmy Nuthatches and Brown Creepers are often present, and a Red-faced Warbler usually pops up where the trail zigzags through a grove of Gambel Oaks just under the top. Yellow-eyed Juncos hop around on the rocky crown itself. The view from Barfoot Lookout is superb as you overlook the billiard-green bowl of Barfoot Park, the Sulphur Springs Valley (see Chap-

Northern Pygmy Owl spies a Katydid
Narca Moore-Craig

ter 8) unrolls to the west, the Chiricahua Wilderness Area rises to south, a vast tract of New Mexico stretches to the east, and to the north lies the jagged stone garden of Chiricahua National Monument with Cochise Head as a backdrop. White-throated Swifts zoom by almost continuously on a typical summer day at Barfoot Lookout. An hour-long vigil may be rewarded with eye-level views of a Short-tailed Hawk.

When you can finally bring yourself to leave the Rustler Park area, return to Onion Saddle (3.0 miles). It is probably best to turn sharply right (southeast) and return to Portal (11.7 miles) now if you have only budgeted half a day for your visit to the high country. If you have a full day to explore, or if you intend to continue on to Willcox, Douglas, or Tucson, bear left (northwest) to descend the west side of the mountain.

Heading west for the first mile or so, the road is narrow, winding, and a bit of a cliff-hanger, but it soon improves. **Pinery Canyon Campground** (2.0 miles below the saddle) is a good place to find Cordilleran Flycatcher (summer), Hutton's Vireo, Mexican Chickadee, the "Brown-throated" form of the House Wren, and both Olive and Red-faced Warblers. Continue past the main campground entrance, and stop at a right-hand pullout 100 yards beyond, next to the skeleton of a huge Gambel Oak. The clearing opposite this tremendous dead oak is often productive. Pinery Canyon Campground has earned a reputation for great owling. If Flammulated Owls are not calling in Cave Creek Canyon, they usually are in Pinery. Watch for Flammies to sit close to the trunk of a fairly dense conifer or juniper. Whiskered Screech-Owl is also common in Pinery, and Northern Saw-whet Owl is occasional.

From here on down the birds are about the same as those observed on the Cave Creek side, but as a rule they are not as abundant. Dead snags the first few miles below Pinery Campground are often used for perches by migrating Olive-sided Flycatchers. After the Trans-mountain Road crosses Pinery Creek (3.0 miles), check the road edges carefully for Montezuma Quail. American Kestrels, Horned Larks, Lark Sparrows, and Eastern Meadowlarks are typical of the final two miles of valley grassland leading to the pavement at the junction of State Highway 181 (9.0 miles; 14.0 miles from Onion Saddle). Turn right (east) to enter **Chiricahua National Monument.**

Approximately 27 million years ago volcanic eruptions nine miles south in West Turkey Creek buried this area under a 2,000-foot-deep mantle of white-hot ash, which solidified into a fine-grained rock called rhyolite. As the stone cooled, it cracked into hexagonal columns, some hundreds of feet high. Eons of wind, rain, and frost widened the cracks, leaving the columns freestanding. One spire known as the Totem Pole is over 300 feet tall and only three feet wide at the base. Big Balanced Rock has an estimated weight of over 1,000 tons, yet sits on a pedestal only a few feet thick. Other columns have eroded into grotesque stone caricatures of people or animals. As you drive up the Monument Road through this "wonderland of rock," as it is popularly known, with thousands of monoliths poised overhead, you will be impressed by the magnitude of the geological cataclysms that wrought the surrounding stone forest.

Stop at the monument visitor center (mile 2.0) to pay fees and for a bird checklist and information about trails, campgrounds, and history of this unique area. The bookstore here has a broad selection of books, maps, cards, and videos. An easy way to learn the trees is to take the short nature trail up Rhyolite Canyon from the parking lot. Birds along this level, quarter-mile route are typical of the Sierra Madrean pine-oak woodlands. If the National Monument marks your entry into the Chiricahuas, this is an excellent place to watch for your life bird Arizona Woodpecker, Dusky-capped Flycatcher (summer), Mexican Jay, Bridled Titmouse, Painted Redstart (summer), and Scott's Oriole (summer). Also look for Apache Squirrels, endemic to this range alone in the entire United States.

As you drive into Bonita Canyon, check the Organ Pipe Formation (1.0 mile) for Prairie Falcons. A pair has nested in these towering rock columns in recent years. Also scrutinize every Turkey Vulture—Zone-tailed Hawks frequent the same rhyolite spires as the falcons. A Berylline Hummingbird fledged two young near the Natural Bridge Trail pullout in mid-September

1984, the second known successful nesting in the U.S. Watch for Anna's Hummingbird in the roadside thistle patches here.

At the end of the road to Massai Point (6.0 miles), there is another nature trail and a spectacular overlook of the Monument. Every year a pair of Mexican Chickadees flits through the stunted Douglas-fir, Arizona Cypress, Pinyon Pine, and small oaks that crowd the 6,870-foot summit. Other summer birds at Massai include Red-tailed Hawk, White-throated Swift, Violet-green Swallow, Common Raven, Bridled Titmouse, Canyon Wren, Black-throated Gray Warbler, Painted Redstart, Spotted Towhee, and Black-headed Grosbeak. The best way to find these birds is take the half-mile-long interpretive trail that circles the western side of Massai Point.

As you begin the drive down, a mile-long stone profile of a man's face known as Cochise Head dominates the northern horizon and commemorates the great leader of the Chiricahua Apaches who strove so hard to protect his homeland. This is a fitting end to any visit to the Chiricahua Mountains.

From Chiricahua National Monument entry station it is 25.7 miles east on the Trans-mountain Road over Onion Saddle to Portal. Willcox and Interstate 10 are 31 miles to the west on State Highways 181 and 186.

CAMPGROUNDS, RESTAURANTS, AND ACCOMMODATIONS

There are basic campgrounds in Cave Creek Canyon, Rustler Park, and in Chiricahua National Monument.

Good cooking and large portions can be had at the Portal Store Café adjacent to the Portal Peak Lodge (P.O. Box 16282, Portal, AZ 85632; 520-558-2223; www.portalpeaklodge.com). Established in 1994, the lodge is modern and comfortable. Remodeled in 1998, Cave Creek Ranch has comfortable housekeeping cabins and very birdy grounds. The office features a cozy meeting room and a small gift shop (P.O. Box 16554, Portal, AZ 85632; 520-558-2334; www.cavecreek.com). The Southwestern Research Station has dormitory-style rooms available to birders from September through May (family-style meals available, except November–February) (P.O. Box 16553, Portal, AZ 85632; 520-558-2396). Just downstream from Portal, the Myrtle Kraft Cottage has private feeders on a 40-acre tract of property at the mouth of Cave Creek (P.O. Box 16384, Portal, AZ 85632; 520-558-2443; www. myrtlekraftcottage.com). The George Walker House in Paradise has feeders open to birders and is an historic home that has been renovated for guests (2225 W. George Walker Lane, Portal, AZ 85632; 520-558-2287; www. thegeorgewalkerhouse.com). Also located in Paradise is the Paradise Springs B & B (520-558-1118; foh@vtc.net).

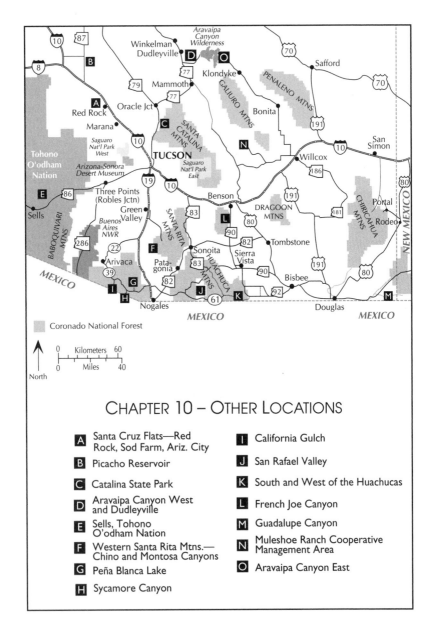

CHAPTER 10 – OTHER LOCATIONS

CHAPTER 10
OTHER LOCATIONS

A. SANTA CRUZ FLATS—
RED ROCK, SOD FARM,
AND ARIZONA CITY

(147 miles round-trip north of Tucson/one-half day)

West of Picacho (*pea-CAH-cho*, Spanish for "peak") Peak the Santa Cruz River unbraids into a great alkali basin called the Santa Cruz Flats. The Hohokam formerly practiced ditch irrigation in this region, but a prolonged drought in the late 1200s forced these ancient peoples to abandon their fields, leaving only the nearby ruins at Casa Grande as testimony to a bygone civilization. Today, with the help of deep wells, the Santa Cruz Flats are once again being converted to agriculture. Three areas are of particular interest to birders.

Ruddy Ground-Doves were discovered at a cattle feedlot near the small town of **Red Rock** just southeast of Picacho Peak in the winter of 2002–2003. Unlike virtually all other Ruddy Ground-Doves recorded in Arizona since their arrival in the state in October 1981, at least a few birds summered at the Red Rock feedlot. In the winter of 2003–2004 that number had grown to about a dozen—to date, one of the largest known concentrations of this species in the United States. For anyone interested in also adding Eurasian Collared-Dove to their Arizona list, Red Rock provides a sure-fire site.

To reach Red Rock take Interstate 10 (northwest) toward Phoenix to Exit 226 (35 miles north of Tucson from the junction of Interstates 10 and 19). Cross Interstate 10 and turn right (north) on the frontage road. Proceed 0.2 mile to the T-intersection with Sasco Road and turn left (southwest). Bendire's Thrasher occurs in the mesquite thickets that line both sides of the pavement most of the way to a Y-junction (2.3 miles). Crested Caracara sightings have been sporadic in the same area.

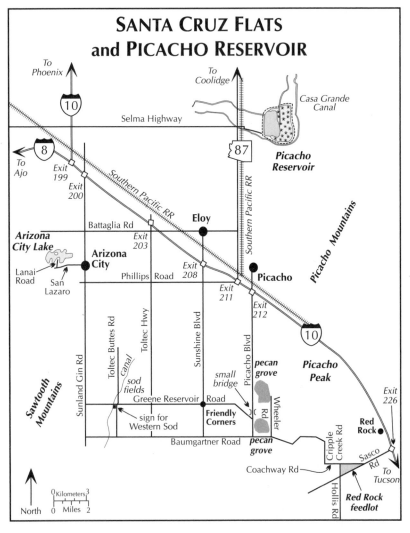

SANTA CRUZ FLATS
and PICACHO RESERVOIR

The cattle corrals lie within the nearly mile-long pie-wedge between Sasco and Coachway Roads. Hollis is the 0.3-mile-long paved street that connects Coachway with Sasco at the west end of the feedlot. The Ruddy Ground-Doves could occur along the entire triangular perimeter of the feedlot, but frequently are within the fence by a cylindrical water tank near the northwest corner of Coachway and Hollis, or in the large deciduous trees about halfway down Sasco.

Astute birders will doubtlessly notice a number of employee homes within the feedlot area, especially near the deciduous trees, and that a large private residence also occupies the northwest corner of Coachway and Sasco. *Do not trespass onto any private property. Under no circumstances should birders train their binoculars or telescopes on the homes or the people who live and work at the feedlot. Under no circumstances should birders park in such a way as to obstruct local traffic or block access to driveways or gates. Do not enter the corrals. Obviously, don't spook the cattle.* The use of common sense is essential if birders are to retain the privilege of visiting this unique site.

Aside from Ruddy Ground-Dove and Eurasian Collared-Dove, the Red Rock feedlot operation attracts a smorgasbord of Columbids, including Rock Pigeon, White-winged Dove (even overwintering), Mourning Dove, and Inca Dove. In winter blackbirds are also well-represented. Watch for Red-winged, Yellow-headed, and Brewer's Blackbirds, as well as Western Meadowlark and Brown-headed Cowbird. American Crow, a vagrant in the region, was recorded in February 2004. Fields due south of the feedlot and 0.6 mile west on Sasco Road occasionally host White-tailed Kite, as well as wintering Ferruginous and Rough-legged Hawks. In winter the Santa Cruz River may flow all the way to Sasco Road, 1.6 miles west of Hollis Road, furnishing habitat for a different community of birds.

In August 1998 Arizona's first Pacific Golden-Plover was recorded at **Western Sod**. Mountain Plovers occasionally use the same area. To find the large expanses of well-manicured lawn at the Western Sod turf farm, there are two options, depending on weather and the amount of time you can budget.

In inclement weather or if time is tight, the best course from Red Rock is to follow Interstate 10 north toward Phoenix to Exit 212 (14 miles northwest of the Red Rock Exit; 49 miles north of Tucson from the junctions of Interstates 10 and 19). Turn left (south) onto Picacho Boulevard and watch for a conspicuous grove of pecan trees on the left (east) side of the road (7.0 miles). Just beyond the pecan grove, Picacho Boulevard crosses a small bridge over a tendril of the Santa Cruz River (0.3 mile). An abrupt acute-angle turn to the right (northwest) on the south side of the river (50 yards) marks the beginning of Greene Reservoir Road (7.3 miles altogether from Interstate 10), a well-graded gravel thoroughfare. In winter the barren saltbush and creosote desert on either side of this stretch is good for Sage and Bendire's Thrashers, as well as Brewer's and Sage Sparrows. After the Greene Reservoir Road turns due west (1.2 miles), it beelines through continuous fields past a four-way stop at Friendly Corners (2.0 miles) to the first fields of Western Sod (4.5 miles).

However, if time allows, a series of back roads and farm lanes—most unpaved—with potentially interesting birds also connect the Red Rock Feedlot to Greene Reservoir Road and Western Sod. If you elect to use this route begin at the northwest corner of Coachway and Hollis (0.0). Pavement ends on Coachway Road at this point, and the route described may be temporarily impassible after heavy rains. Assuming it hasn't rained recently, proceed 1.0 mile west on Coachway until it ends at an abrupt right (north) turn onto Cripple Creek Road (unsigned). Follow Cripple Creek for 1.6 miles until it angles left (northwest) across a canal (2.6 miles). After 0.5 mile it joins Baumgartner Road (unsigned; 3.1 mile). Turn left (west) onto Baumgartner. There will be an abrupt jog to the left (south) after three miles (6.1 miles) and then right again (northwest) at a large metal water tank in 0.3 mile (6.4 miles) as Baumgartner skirts a large field. After 0.7 mile Baumgartner swerves right (north) and soon makes a right-angle turn to the left (west; 7.2 miles). The road to the right (north) is Wheeler. Rows of olive trees and homes on the northwest side of the corner mark this intersection. Turn left (west) onto Baumgartner, which is paved.

Baumgartner crosses the Santa Cruz River 100 yards west of the intersection of Baumgartner and Wheeler. A weedy thicket surrounded by a pecan grove lies on the north side of the road here. During winter this is a good site for Ruddy Ground-Dove and Lewis's Woodpecker. Both species should be visible from the road shoulder. *Do not park on Baumgartner Road. Do not trespass onto private property or enter the pecan grove.* Most of the birds recorded less than 10 miles away—as the crow flies—at the Marana Pecan Grove are also possible at the Baumgartner Pecan Grove.

To access Greene Reservoir Road continue west 2.0 miles to Picacho Highway (9.2 miles) and turn right (north), following the pavement. Unpaved Greene Reservoir Road angles left (northwest) off Picacho Boulevard after 1.3 miles (10.5 miles from the intersection of Coachway and Hollis at the Red Rock Feedlot). From the junction of Greene Reservoir Road to Western Sod is 7.7 miles.

The Western Sod turf farm is on both sides of Greene Reservoir Road for the next one-half mile. Pull completely off the dirt road to scan the fields for Mountain Plovers, Long-billed Curlews, or Mountain Bluebirds. A scope will be useful. Other migratory species here as early as late July include Solitary, Least, and Western Sandpipers, Wilson's Snipe, American Pipit, and Lark Bunting. Horned Larks are abundant in winter and Killdeer are present throughout the year. Turn right (north) opposite the sign for Western Sod (0.5 mile), staying on the right side of the canal to continue scanning, but *be sure to park clear of farm traffic.* Fields of grass continue on the right (east) side for one mile.

The lake at **Arizona City** provides habitat for yet another set of species that uses the Santa Cruz Flats. Return to Greene Reservoir Road and turn right (west). Early in the morning and late in the afternoon Burrowing Owls perch on top of the row of broken concrete slabs that parallel the road on the right (north) side for the next quarter-mile. Continue west on Greene Reservoir Road until it ends at a T-intersection with Sunland Gin Road (2.0 miles from the sign for Western Sod) at the foot of the Sawtooth Mountains. Turn right (north) on paved Sunland Gin Road. Watch for Golden Eagles and other raptors along the way to the small retirement community at Arizona City (8.0 miles). A scattering of tall palms in the housing development on the left (west) identifies the lake. Turn left (west) onto San Lazaro (0.1 mile), then right (north) onto Lanai Road (0.35 mile) to access the water. The list of waterbirds and waterfowl that have occurred at Arizona City's lake includes Western and Clark's Grebes, Neotropic Cormorant, White-faced Ibis, Snow Goose, and Long-billed Curlew. More common are Pied-billed Grebe, Mallard, Cinnamon Teal, and American Coot. The rock island on the west end of the 20-acre impoundment serves as a roost for Great Blue Herons—and a few hundred Rock Pigeons. Osprey is occasional here in migration, and the lake area is also a good site for Lesser Nighthawk (summer) and Bendire's Thrasher.

To return to Tucson via Interstate 10, return to Sunland Gin Road and turn left (north); proceed all the way through Arizona City to Battaglia Drive (1.8 miles). Turn right (east) and follow Battaglia to the intersection with Toltec Highway (3.0 miles). Turn left (north) onto Toltec Highway. The on-ramp for Interstate 10 south to Tucson is on the near side of the freeway overpass (0.85 mile). Tucson is about 57 miles. Alternatively, Picacho Reservoir on the northeast corner of the Santa Cruz Flats is seductively close. Battaglia Road travels underneath Interstate 10 (no access to I-10) and ends at Highway 87 (9.0 miles). Turn left (north) onto Highway 87 and continue to Selma Highway (6.0 miles). Turn right (east). From here follow directions to Picacho Reservoir in the next account.

B. PICACHO RESERVOIR

(61 miles north of Tucson/one-half day)

Picacho Reservoir is the best location in Southeastern Arizona for Least Bittern. Located at an elevation of just 1,500 feet in a desert basin near the confluence of the Santa Cruz and Gila Rivers, Picacho marks the usual eastern range limits for a phalanx of species more common on the Lower Colorado River. Some of these include American White and Brown Pelicans, Double-crested Cormorant, American Bittern, and Clapper Rail. Picacho is also a magnet for lost birds. Some of the vagrants recorded recently are Least Grebe in January 1995, Yellow-crowned Night-Heron in late May 1992, White Ibis late June through mid-September 1986, Roseate Spoonbill, June through October 1973, and Purple Gallinule, August 1993.

To find Picacho Reservoir, take Interstate 10 north of Tucson to Exit 211, just north of Picacho (50 miles north of Tucson at the junction of Interstates 10 and 19). Turn right (north) onto Highway 87 toward Coolidge (see previous map). Follow this road to the intersection with Selma Highway (9.3 miles) on the right (east) side. In spite of the fancy name, this is only a dirt road and easy to miss. Watch for a big, water-filled canal, which passes under Highway

87 at this point. After turning right onto the Selma Highway, you soon cross the canal (0.1 mile) and then also cross railroad tracks (0.2 mile). Turn right (south) onto a dirt road (0.1 mile) along the tracks, and then turn left (east) onto the road on the top of the canal levee (0.1 mile). This will lead you to the embankment around Picacho Reservoir (0.8 mile). Turn left onto a small dirt road along the base of the earthen dam, and follow it until you can drive up onto the top of the dam. From here you can scope the water.

The cattails, drowned trees, and open water at Picacho Reservoir attract regularly-occurring ducks and shorebirds, as well as Great Blue and Green Herons, Great and Snowy Egrets, White-faced Ibis, and other waders. The south end of the reservoir is generally best for birding. Check the mesquite trees near the irrigation canal off the southeast corner of the dam for passerines. The water level varies greatly, depending on seasonal differences and rainfall. *In dry years it may be nearly empty during summer. The temperatures from late spring through early fall are simply torrid. Carry water!* Picacho Reservoir is open to hunters.

C. CATALINA STATE PARK

(16 miles north of Tucson/one-half day)

This 5,500-acre tract set aside by Arizona in 1983 preserves a beautiful parcel of Saguaro-studded Sonoran Desert just a handful of miles north of Tucson. Three intermittent streams, Cañada del Oro, Sutherland Wash, and Romero Canyon, connect in a lush mesquite bosque at the foot of the Santa Catalina Mountains. A loop Nature Trail (0.7 mile-long) and the Canyon Loop Trail (2.3-miles-long) provide access to the full spectrum of Catalina State

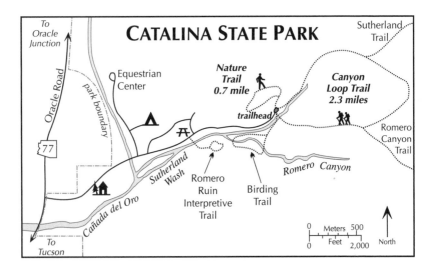

Park habitats. *After heavy rains in the Santa Catalina Mountains, it is necessary to wade the streams to walk the Canyons Loop Trail. Especially since the 2003 Aspen Fire, do NOT attempt to cross if the streams are flash-flooding.* The common birds at the park include Gambel's Quail, Cooper's Hawk, White-winged Dove (summer), Costa's Hummingbird (primarily spring), Gila Woodpecker, Black Phoebe, Vermilion Flycatcher, Verdin, Cactus Wren, Western Bluebird (winter), and Northern Cardinal. Northern Beardless-Tyrannulet occurs throughout the year in the mesquites along Cañada del Oro, although it is rare in winter.

Night birding is a real treat at Catalina. Arrive early to watch the butterscotch-colored light fade on the west slope of the mountains, which loom over 6,000 feet above. As dusk deepens in the valley, listen for the distinctive calls of Western Screech-Owl, Great Horned Owl, and Elf Owl (summer). The voice of Common Poorwill is also part of the summer evening chorus. May 1978 saw the first report of Buff-collared Nightjar in Sutherland Wash. This rarity has been reported near the road end at Catalina at widely-spaced intervals ever since. A Long-eared Owl roosted in the tamarisks behind the group site during winter in the mid-1980s.

To reach Catalina State Park drive north on Interstate 10 from the junction of Interstates 10 and 19 to Exit 256, Grant Road (3.75 miles), and turn right (east). Continue to Oracle Road, Highway 77. Turn left (north) onto Oracle Road (0.75 miles) and stay on this highway as it crosses northwest Tucson and enters the foothills of the Santa Catalina Mountains. The well-signed entrance to Catalina State Park lies on the right (east) side of Highway 89 (12.0 miles). The entry station is staffed from 7:00 a.m. to 5:00 p.m., and a map and bird checklist are included in the entry fee ($6 per vehicle for day use, primitive campsites $12/night, and full hook-ups for trailers $19/night in 2004.). Self-pay instructions are posted for those arriving after 5:00 p.m. (correct change required). For more information contact Catalina State Park, P.O. Box 36986, Tucson, AZ 85740; 520-628-5798.

D. ARAVAIPA CANYON WEST AND DUDLEYVILLE

(68 miles north of Tucson to Aravaipa/one day)
(60 miles north of Tucson to Dudleyville/one day)
(84 miles north to Aravaipa & Dudleyville/one day)

This trip is primarily to see three species of raptors. The only road-accessible Common Black-Hawks in Southeastern Arizona occur in Aravaipa Canyon. Since their discovery in Arizona in 1970, Mississippi Kites have nested in the cottonwoods along a 40-mile-long stretch of the San Pedro

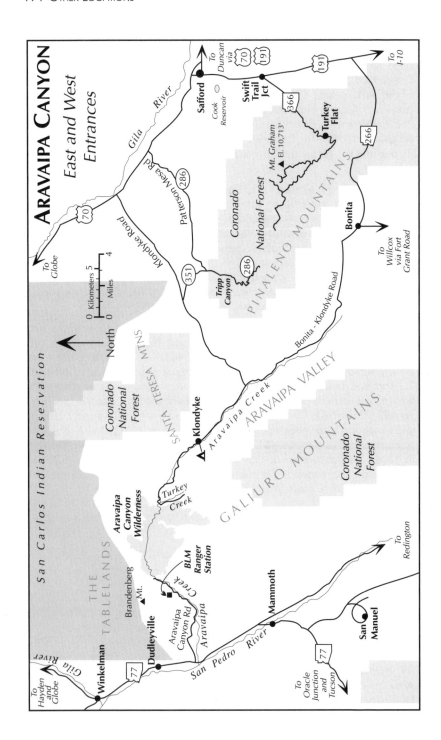

Immature Common Black-Hawk
Narca Moore-Craig

River centering on Dudleyville. They share the cottonwood gallery here with a healthy population of Gray Hawks. Typically, both the Common Black-Hawks and Gray Hawks arrive in mid-March and depart in October.

To reach the west entrance of **Aravaipa Canyon**, drive north on Interstate 10 from the junction of Interstates 10 and 19 to Exit 256, Grant Road (3.8 miles), and turn right (east). Continue east to Oracle Road and turn left (north). Follow Oracle Road, which becomes Highway 77, through the town of Oro Valley to Oracle Junction (21.0 miles). Continue right (east) onto Highway 77. After 10 miles the highway skirts the community of Oracle and drops down a long, steep hill before reaching Mammoth on the San Pedro River. The Mammoth Sewage Ponds are located on the left (west) side of the road, immediately before you cross the bridge over the San Pedro River (22.5 miles). Occasionally a Greater Scaup or some other interesting waterbird joins the changing flocks that settle here during migration. *Viewing is from the edge of the highway only, so be sure that both you and your vehicle are well off the pavement.* Just beyond the milepost 124 marker turn right (east) onto Aravaipa Canyon Road (7.9 miles). The first 4.5 miles of the Aravaipa Canyon Road are paved. Upper Aravaipa Road becomes a well-graded gravel route that continues to the Bureau of Land Management Ranger Station (4.8 miles), set under the imposing cliffs of Brandenburg Mountain. Watch for Golden Eagles and Peregrine Falcons cruising the updrafts generated by the mountain's volcanic facades. The road ends at a parking area and entry station for the Wilderness

Area (3.2 miles/12.5 miles from Highway 77). Buff-collared Nightjar was seen under the floodlight outside the former ranger residence here in the summer of 1980, and has reappeared in this area sporadically.

Fortunately for raptor enthusiasts, Gray Hawks, Common Black-Hawks, and Zone-tailed Hawks all occur along the length of Aravaipa Canyon Road *before* it reaches the Wilderness Area, especially in areas with tall trees along the creek. *Please conduct all birding from the roadway, and be very careful not to obstruct the road with your vehicle, especially on blind curves. The land on both sides of the road is privately owned.*

Intrepid birders with permits may wish to explore the Aravaipa Canyon Wilderness Area. Aside from the calls of Canyon Wrens spiraling down from the thousand-foot-high walls that flank the stream, and an occasional Peregrine Falcon dodging between the cliffs, Desert Bighorn Sheep are frequently sighted. Arizona Game and Fish biologists estimated there were 125 wild sheep roaming Aravaipa in 2004. With seven species of native fishes, Aravaipa Canyon supports the most diversified sample of endemic piscifauna in all of Arizona. Two species, the Spikedace and Loach Minnow, are on the federal list of threatened wildlife.

Only 50 people per day are permitted in the 11-mile-long Aravaipa Canyon Wilderness Area. To obtain a permit contact the Bureau of Land Management, Safford District Office, 711 14th Avenue, Safford, AZ 85546; 520-348-4400; www.safford.az.blm.gov. Because of limited availability, the BLM strongly recommends making reservations by phone or online 13 weeks in advance. A map, fee info, and reservations calendar are all available online on the website. There is a charge of $5.00 per person per day. Plan on wearing stout, high-top shoes or boots to wade the stream: you will have to cross it dozens of times. High-top footgear will eliminate some of the gravel sluicing into your socks.

The way to **Dudleyville** is the same as the way to Aravaipa Canyon Road. Instead of turning off at the canyon, however, continue north past the first signed turnoff to Dudleyville. Turn left (west) off of Highway 77 just beyond the Milepost 129 marker (4.9 miles). Within moments you enter "downtown" Dudleyville. At the stop sign, turn right (north) onto Dudleyville Road, then left (west) onto the first paved side street, San Pedro Road. The pavement plays out just before the river (0.5 mile). Proceed to the river crossing, where a sign welcomes visitors and lists conditions for using this private property. Park here, on either side of the river crossing, being careful to leave plenty of room for large trucks to cross the river. *Do not attempt to cross the river if the San Pedro is high.*

Watch for Mississippi Kites and Gray Hawks all the way in from Highway 77. Scan the cottonwoods along the river for perched birds. Trails-of-use lead both upstream and downstream, but remember that the property on both sides of the river is privately owned. Other species recorded here in-

Mississippi Kite
Gail Diane Yovanovich

clude Tropical and Thick-billed Kingbirds. Streak-backed Orioles have nested at Dudleyville since the summer of 1993, and as many as two pairs have been recorded.

If you fail to intercept Mississippi Kite at the Dudleyville site, it may be worth driving north on Highway 77 toward Winkelman (5.7 miles). Sometimes the kites are visible from the highway, and occasionally they can be seen in the city park at the confluence of the Gila River with the San Pedro. To find the park, stay on Highway 77 (bear right) at its junction with Highway 177 on the north side of the bridge across the Gila River, and then turn right (east) at the sign for Winkelman Flats Park (0.2 mile). Aside from potential summering raptors, the park has a suite of colorful Sonoran Desert birds that includes Vermilion Flycatcher, Summer Tanager, and Northern Cardinal.

E. SELLS, TOHONO O'ODHAM NATION

(54 miles west of Tucson/one-half day)

The only somewhat reliable Crested Caracaras in Southeastern Arizona occur west of the Baboquivari Mountains on the vast, 2,800,000-acre

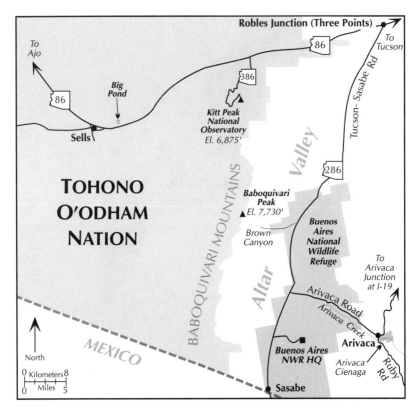

Tohono O'odham Nation (formerly known as the Papago Indian Reservation). Approximately the size of Connecticut, this is the second-largest area owned by Native Americans in the United States. Some 8,000 Tohono O'odham (Piman words for "Desert People") call it home. Because most of this sprawling, Saguaro-spiked area lies in the Sonoran Desert at an elevation of 2,500 feet or lower, the best time to visit is in winter. The caracaras can usually be spotted along Highway 86 between the turnoff to Kitt Peak and the tribal capital at Sells.

To look for the Crested Caracaras, start at the junction of Interstates 10 and 19, and follow I-19 south to the first freeway interchange, Exit 99, Ajo Way (1.0 mile). Turn right (west) onto Ajo Way. Continue west on Ajo Way, which becomes Highway 86, past Three Points (21.5 miles) onto Tohono O'odham Nation lands.

The well-signed road to Kitt Peak Observatory, operated by the National Science Foundation since its inception in 1958, is located on the left (south) side of Highway 86 (16.0 miles). This 13-mile-long paved road climbs over 3,500 feet to the 6,875-foot summit of Kitt Peak, site of some 21 telescopes, including several that are among the world's largest. A picnic area at mile 11.5

offers the best birding spot. The common birds here include Acorn Woodpecker, Mexican Jay, Common Raven, Bewick's Wren, and Spotted Towhee.
Return to Highway 86 and continue west.

Early morning is best for the Crested Caracaras. Watch for them to perch
inside and below the tops of the mesquite and Palo Verde trees that line the
Ajo Highway. Occasionally the birds can be seen soaring low over the desert.
The pullout for Big Pond, a quarter-mile-diameter stock tank, is located on the
right (north) side of the highway just beyond the Milepost 116 marker (15.5
miles). Walk the little road that goes 150 yards north to a corral. *Close the
gate behind you.* Veer left around the corral and walk quietly the last 100 yards
through the mesquites to the impoundment. During winter and migration
there are frequently herons, ducks, and shorebirds on Big Pond. A Solitary
Sandpiper was found here on the late date of December 29 in 1993. A scope
will be useful. Black and Say's Phoebes, Vermilion Flycatcher, Verdin, and
Black-tailed Gnatcatcher are the winter passerines. Occasionally a Crested
Caracara is perched in the mesquites on the west edge. Watch for both Black
and Turkey Vultures, fairly common here, but rare elsewhere in Southeastern
Arizona during the winter.

Gambel's Quail, Gilded Flicker, Curve-billed and Crissal Thrashers,
Northern Cardinal, and Rufous-winged Sparrow are the common birds along
the road back to your car. There are no facilities for tourists west of Big Pond
in Sells (1.2 miles). *A permit is required to travel in other areas belonging to the
Tohono O'odham off Highway 86. Please restrict your birding to Big Pond and from
pullouts along Highway 86.*

F. WESTERN SANTA RITA MOUNTAINS—
CHINO AND MONTOSA CANYONS

(about 40 miles south of Tucson/one-half day)

In the 1980s Black-capped Gnatcatchers and Five-striped Sparrows were
found nesting in Chino Canyon on the west slope of the Santa Rita Mountains. While the Five-stripes haven't been seen since the early 1980s,
Black-capped Gnatcatchers have been recorded in most recent years. In 2003
Black-capped Gnatcatchers were also found in Montosa Canyon a few miles
south of Chino Canyon, and this pair was present through the summer of
2004. Birders with time and curiosity should consider visiting one or both of
these locations, especially during spring and summer, for other interesting
birds of sub-tropical thornscrub, such as Buff-collared Nightjar (rare), Northern Beardless-Tyrannulet, Bell's Vireo, Lucy's Warbler, Varied Bunting, and
Rufous-crowned Sparrow. Go early in the morning and bring plenty of water.
The last few miles of the road to Chino Canyon are very primitive and suitable only for

vehicles with high clearance, preferably with four-wheel-drive. The road into Montosa Canyon is paved for most of its length.

To access either canyon, take the Canoa exit (Exit 56) off Interstate 19, 27.7 miles south of the junction of I-10 and I-19 in Tucson. Go under I-19 to the frontage road on the east side. Turn right (south) to Elephant Head Road (3.1 miles). Follow Elephant Head across the Santa Cruz River (0.5 mile), across the railroad tracks, to Mt. Hopkins Road (0.8). From this point you can drive to either Chino Canyon or Montosa Canyon. To find Montosa Canyon, turn right (south) onto Mt. Hopkins Road and follow the directions later in this section. To continue on to **Chino Canyon**, proceed to a big curve where the pavement sweeps left (north) and the road name changes to S. Canoa Drive (0.2 mile). Immediately after crossing a cattleguard (0.4 mile), take the left fork, Canoa Road. Traveling northward, the fourth road you encounter will be Hawk Way (1.8 miles) where you turn right (east). Stay on Hawk Way to the end of the pavement (2.0 miles). The road soon turns right (south). You are now traveling across State Trust Land. *No stopping, picnicking, or camping is permitted without a special permit.* Ignore the junction to the left (0.8 mile) and continue south along a fenceline to a gate (0.7 mile). Just beyond (0.4 mile), the road divides and turns south across Madera Wash. *Here it may be best to leave your vehicle, and walk the additional 1.4 miles into the canyon.* There will be two gates (0.2 mile and 0.9 mile) before you arrive at the traditional parking spot (0.3 mile) under an oak tree at the base of Elephant Head. The mountain-bike trail up the valley provides a convenient foot path to the high end of the basin.

When present, the Black-capped Gnatcatchers usually occur in and near hackberry trees close to the rock slope on the south side of Elephant Head, the enormous granite formation that looms overhead. (Be aware that two other species of gnatcatcher are regularly seen here: Black-tailed and Blue-gray.) The Five-striped Sparrows were usually found on higher and drier slopes. There have also been other avian surprises at Chino Canyon, including Buff-collared Nightjar and Lucifer Hummingbird. *Please do not use tapes in this tiny pocket of habitat for these sensitive species.*

Lacking four-wheel-drive, birders can find virtually the same habitat and the same species of birds in **Montosa Canyon** by simply following the paved Mt. Hopkins Road 6.6 miles from its junction with Elephant Head Road to the Whipple Observatory Visitor Center. The pavement ends here, but it resumes at the first ford across Montosa Creek (0.6 mile). The ford is located between the jaws of two cliff-sided foothills that tower nearly one thousand feet above on either side of the usually dry streambed. Frequently the Black-capped Gnatcatchers are in the dense thornscrub here or just upstream at the outlet of Montosa Basin. A parking area is located about 100 yards up the rocky little side road that turns off to the right (south) immediately beyond the ford. *Please do not block either this side road or the Mt. Hopkins Road itself.*

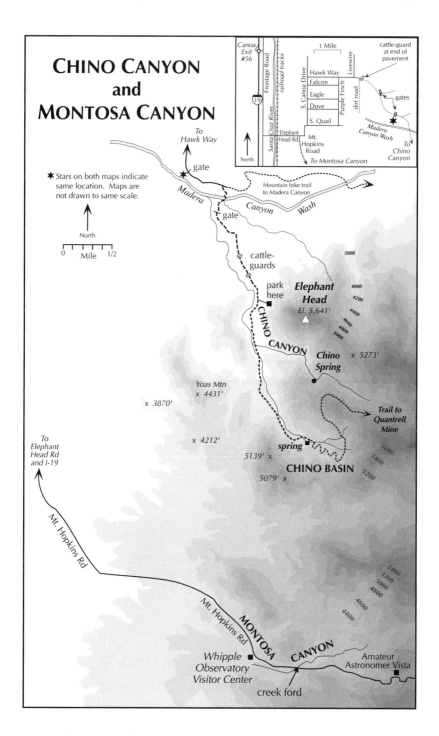

CHINO CANYON
and
MONTOSA CANYON

Canoa
Exit
#56

Frontage Road

railroad tracks

19

Santa Cruz River

S. Canoa Drive

1 Mile

Hawk Way
Falcon
Eagle
Dove
S. Quail

Purple Finch

Livewire

cattle-guard
at end of
pavement

dirt road

gates

Madera
Canyon Wash

To
Chino
Canyon

Elephant
Head Rd.

Mt.
Hopkins
Road

To Montosa Canyon

North

To
Hawk Way

gate

✳ Stars on both maps indicate
same location. Maps are
not drawn to same scale.

North

0   Mile   1/2

Madera

Canyon   Wash

Mountain bike trail
to Madera Canyon

gate

cattle-
guards

park
here

*Elephant
Head*
El. 5,641'

3800

4000
4200
4400
4600
4800
5000

CHINO CANYON

*Chino
Spring*

x 5273'

Yoas Mtn
x 4431'

x 3870'

x 4212'

spring

5139' x

5079' x

CHINO BASIN

*Trail to
Quantrell
Mine*

5600
5400
5200

To
Elephant
Head Rd
and I-19

Mt. Hopkins Rd

Mt. Hopkins Rd

MONTOSA

CANYON

Whipple
Observatory
Visitor Center

Amateur
Astronomer Vista

creek ford

5400
5200
5000
4800
4600
4400

A few small sycamores and some large oaks trace the route of Montosa Creek on the right side of the Mt. Hopkins Road for the next mile to Amateur Astronomer Vista. The vista point is a small parking lot on the left (north) side of the road a short distance from a nearby knoll, situated at an elevation of 5,000 feet. This is the end of the pavement. Crissal Thrashers are fairly common residents here and throughout the Montosa Basin. An Elegant Trogon and Rufous-winged Sparrows—rare at this elevation—were also roaming the basin in February 2004.

G. PEÑA BLANCA LAKE

(65 miles from Tucson/1 day)

This trip is more for exploration than birding. There are no birds to be regularly found in this area that cannot be seen more easily elsewhere, with the possible exception of Montezuma Quail. What makes this trip so enticing is its proximity to the border. Who knows what may wander up from Mexico?

The starting point is off Interstate 19, 55.5 miles south of the junction of I-10 and I-19 in Tucson, or 7.2 miles north of Nogales, at Exit 12, Ruby Road (Highway 289). Going west on Ruby Road, you will pass through rolling grasslands interspersed with mesquite and live oaks. This is prime habitat for the Montezuma Quail. They can often be seen feeding right along the road, particularly early in the morning.

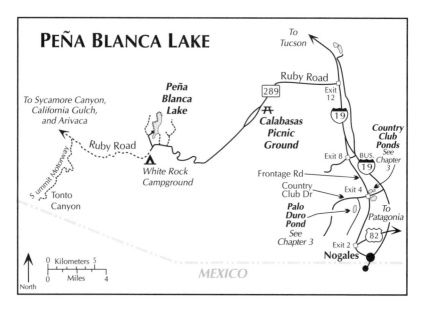

At the Calabasas (Spanish for "squashes") Picnic Grounds, elevation 4,000 feet (6.4 miles), look for Ash-throated Flycatcher, Mexican Jay, Bridled Titmouse, Bushtit, and Black-throated Gray Warbler in the Emory Oaks, and for Canyon Towhee and Rufous-crowned Sparrow in the brush.

The best birding on this trip is usually around Peña Blanca Lake Recreation Area (2.8 miles). The name is pronounced *PAIN-yah BLAHN-cah* and means "White Rock" in Spanish. In winter there are normally a few Eared Grebes and ducks, as well as Marsh Wren and Swamp Sparrow in the cattails. Great Blue Heron and American Coot are resident. Both Double-crested (uncommon) and Neotropic Cormorants (rare) also frequent Peña Blanca. Numerous landbirds are attracted to the cover along the edge of this cerulean blue, 50-acre impoundment. By hiking at least part-way around the lake on a fisherman's path that originates at the small store, you may see Black and Say's Phoebes, Vermilion Flycatcher, Bewick's and Rock Wrens, Phainopepla, Northern Cardinal, Pyrrhuloxia, House Finch, and Lesser Goldfinch. In summer watch for White-winged Dove, Ash-throated Flycatcher, Cassin's and Western Kingbirds, Bell's Vireo, Black-headed and Blue Grosbeaks, and Scott's Oriole. Look for Anna's Hummingbird, Red-naped Sapsucker, Hermit Thrush, Orange-crowned and Yellow-rumped Warblers, and Green-tailed Towhee in winter. Varied Thrush and Fox Sparrow have both put in appearances in recent years, and a Yellow-bellied Sapsucker was present in October 2004.

There are two primitive campgrounds with tables, water, and pit toilets open year round at Peña Blanca Lake.

H. SYCAMORE CANYON

(75 miles south of Tucson/one day)
(26 miles west of Nogales/one day)

The turnoff for Sycamore Canyon is on the left (south) side of Ruby Road, a one-half to one-hour drive (9.4 miles) beyond the end of the pavement at Peña Blanca Lake (see access information for Peña Blanca Lake above; 74.1 miles from Tucson). Ruby Road is narrow, rocky, winding, and washboarded. Watch for oncoming traffic on blind curves. Park at the Hank and Yank Spring parking area south of the Ruby Road (0.5 mile). If you can hike over broken terrain, the drive in is worth it.

Sycamore is a rock-walled canyon set between elevations of 4,000 feet at the Forest Service parking area and 3,500 feet seven miles downstream at the barbed-wire fence that marks the international boundary. The hillsides flanking the defile support the lowest pine-oak woodland in Arizona. Velvet Ash and Arizona Sycamore line a permanent but intermittent stream. Its waters empty into a tributary of the Río de la Concepción in Mexico, providing a natural gateway for tropical species from the south. Such novelties as the Tarahumara Frog (probably extinct since 1980) and a fish called the Sonoran Chub occur(red) nowhere else in the United States.

Sycamore's reputation for harboring southern rarities began in 1974 when Rose-throated Becards were first recorded in the canyon. The following year saw the arrival of Elegant Trogons. In 1977 Five-striped Sparrows appeared. Today there are more Five-striped Sparrows in Sycamore Canyon than any other location in Arizona. The most recent visitors include a Fan-tailed Warbler in June and early July 1987 and a Rufous-capped Warbler from mid-March through June 1994, again in December 1998, and once again in July 2004.

N o one should attempt to hike down Sycamore Canyon without water. From April through October, plan on hauling three or four quarts per person. Unless you depart in the spooky gray light well before sunrise — which is recommended — carry lunch, too. Because there is no trail for most of the way, a spill is entirely probable, so add a first aid kit to your knapsack. This is not a well-traveled area, and help may not come for several days. If at all possible, bird Sycamore with a companion who could go for assistance in the event of a severe sprain or broken leg. If you are prepared to accept the risks, however, a day birding in Sycamore is one of the most enjoyable experiences in Southeastern Arizona.

The route begins at the melting adobe ruins of Hank and Yank Bartlett's 1870s homestead. After wet winters, huge patches of Parry Penstemon along a trail-of-use that leads to the stream are frequented by Costa's Hummingbird in April and May. Broad-billed and Black-chinned Hummingbirds (summer) are the common species after the trail drops into the streambed. Ferruginous Pygmy-Owls used an area just above Montana Canyon in the spring and summers of 1979, 1981, and 1986. The big ash trees at the confluence of Montana Canyon (0.5 mile) on the right (west) side of Sycamore ordinarily mark the upper limits patrolled by Elegant Trogons.

Slightly over one mile downstream from the Hank and Yank parking area, the canyon twists around a small waterfall—best negotiated by climbing over a small spur on the left (east) side—and the first scrawny sycamores appear. A pair of Sulphur-bellied Flycatchers nests here. The waterfall signals the beginning of the Upper Box area of Sycamore. For the next 0.25 mile the water threads its way through a tortuous stone vise. At the bottom end of the Upper Box the stream plunges across polished granite through a gap only 10 feet wide. Unless you are *very sure* of your footing, plan on getting wet. Acrobatic birders may be able to pass this pool by spidering along the right (west) wall of the stream.

A series of plunge pools carved out of solid rock, locally called *tinajas,* on the right (west) side immediately below the Upper Box indicate the confluence of Arch Canyon. A short distance beyond a little brook trimmed with

SYCAMORE CANYON

The darker the shading, the higher the elevation.
The darkest areas have elevations above 4,800 feet.
The lightest areas have elevations between 3,400
and 3,600 feet. Contour interval is 200 feet.

*Duplicate Tear-Out
Trail Map is provided
on page 357.*

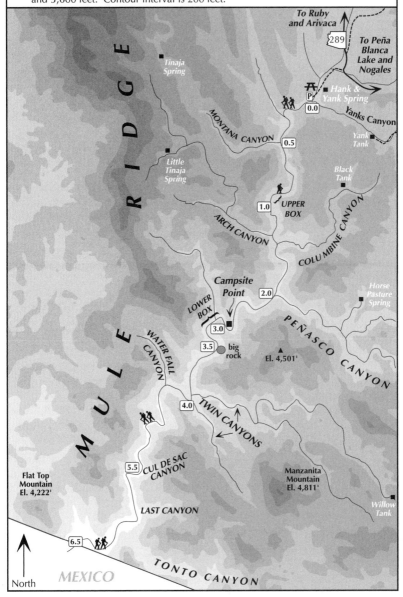

Sycamore Canyon
Richard Cachor Taylor

Golden Columbine trickles into Sycamore from the left (east) side. This is Columbine Canyon. Stay on the right side of Sycamore Canyon to negotiate the next few canyon bends and boulder fields. The canyon will suddenly widen and sycamore trees will spread their delicious shade across the canyon floor the remaining 0.25 mile down to the Peñasco Canyon tributary, which joins Sycamore from the left (east) side. Peñasco (*PAIN-yahs-coh*) means a large rock or crag in Spanish. By now you will be wondering why all the feeder canyons aren't named Peñasco.

It's worth the time to pause here to bird. All of the Madrean pine-oak woodland species of the border ranges occur in this area of Sycamore, many a full thousand feet below their usual altitudinal limits in the Chiricahua, Huachuca, and Santa Rita Mountains. Some of the summering species to watch for at the Peñasco confluence include Montezuma Quail, Zone-tailed Hawk, Band-tailed Pigeon, Elegant Trogon, Arizona Woodpecker, Northern "Red-shafted" Flicker, Western Wood-Pewee, Dusky-capped, Brown-crested, and Sulphur-bellied Flycatchers, Cassin's Kingbird, Violet-green Swallow, Mexican Jay, Bridled Titmouse, Bushtit, White-breasted Nuthatch, Bewick's Wren, Hermit Thrush, Plumbeous Vireo, Painted Redstart, Hepatic and Summer Tanagers, Black-headed Grosbeak, Spotted and Canyon Towhees, Rufous-crowned Sparrow, Hooded, Bullock's, and Scott's Orioles, House Finch, and Lesser Goldfinch. In migration these are joined by Warbling Vireos and Western Tanagers, and in winter by Red-naped Sapsuckers and Yellow-rumped Warblers (predominantly "Audubon's," but mixed with the "Myrtle" form as well). Watch for Louisiana Waterthrush (very rare) from mid-July through mid-March.

A trail-of-use generally hugs the base of the left (east) wall of Sycamore Canyon all the way down to Campsite Point, a spur with a natural flat top about 15 feet above the stream level that projects into the canyon from the right (west) side at about mile 3.0. I spent a sleepless night here on a trogon survey in the early 1980s, listening to the hoots, yips, and wails of a pair of Spotted Owls that may have been courting—or having a nasty domestic spat. Just beyond Campsite Point, the canyon takes a sudden jog to the north, then the west, as it negotiates the Lower Box. Once again, depending on the to-pography of the streambed in the wake of the most recent flash floods, wading may be unavoidable.

Tillandsia recurvata, or Ball Moss, is most common in the stretch of canyon below the Lower Box. Resembling nothing more so much as a sea urchin, this air plant is a tropical relative of the bromeliad family. One-seed Juniper seems to be the preferred substrate for this Medusa-headed, pale gray epiphyte. It underscores the subtropical character of the lower half of Sycamore Canyon. Just behind "Big Rock," a huge boulder on the left (east) side of the canyon at mile 3.5, a Fan-tailed Warbler set up housekeeping in June and July 1987. The mile or so of Sycamore below Big Rock is probably as apt to shelter an

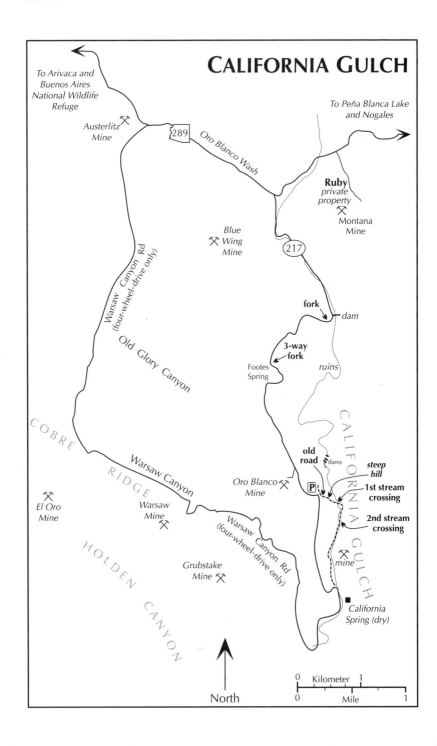

CALIFORNIA GULCH

To Arivaca and
Buenos Aires
National Wildlife
Refuge

To Peña Blanca Lake
and Nogales

Austerlitz
Mine

289

Oro Blanco Wash

Ruby
private
property

Montana
Mine

Blue
Wing
Mine

217

Warsaw Canyon Rd
(four-wheel-drive only)

fork ——dam

Old Glory Canyon

3-way
fork

Footes
Spring

ruins

COBRE

old
road   dams

steep
hill

RIDGE

Warsaw Canyon

Oro Blanco
Mine

P

1st stream
crossing

2nd stream
crossing

El Oro
Mine

Warsaw
Mine

Warsaw Canyon Rd
(four-wheel-drive only)

mine

HOLDEN

Grubstake
Mine

CALIFORNIA GULCH

CANYON

California
Spring (dry)

North

0   Kilometer   1

0   Mile   1

overwintering trogon (or two) as any area in Arizona. During summer Varied Bunting is common below Big Rock.

Two canyon outlets only a few yards apart coming in from the left (east) side of Sycamore at approximately mile 4.0, identify the upper end of the Rose-throated Becard, Thick-billed Kingbird, and Five-striped Sparrow zone of Sycamore. Researchers call this double confluence "Twin Canyons." One or two football-shaped becard nests typically overhang the creek in the next 200 yards below a sharp elbow in the stream—when they are in residency. Some summers no Rose-throated Becards are detected in Sycamore Canyon.

The Five-stripes, however, are probably present every year. While the population fluctuates, in an average summer there are about 50 adults. Listen for their songs on the steep hillsides above the stream from mid-April through August. The slopes of lower Sycamore used by the sparrows are those matted with impenetrable thickets of thornscrub. The males usually sing from exposed perches.

Unless you are conducting a census, ordinarily there is no reason to continue down the canyon beyond the "Cul de Sac Canyon" at mile 5.5 below Hank and Yank parking area. Saguaros now dominate both walls of Sycamore, and the birds are similar to those on the outskirts of Tucson. The trip back to your car will take at least as long as the hike down, even without birding. Watch your footing!

1. CALIFORNIA GULCH

(84 miles south of Tucson/one day)

California Gulch has the only Five-striped Sparrows presently adjacent to a "road" in the United States. More recently, Buff-collared Nightjar has been regular along the route at Oro Blanco Mine since the summer of 2002. A high-clearance vehicle is strongly recommended, especially during the summer monsoon season in July and August. *Be sure you have enough water for 24 hours, in case of a breakdown, and be absolutely certain you have a lug wrench, jack, and spare tire with good tread.* The sparrows are best found when they are singing between mid-April and late August.

To find the steep, rocky, frequently washed-out track that leads into California Gulch continue west on the Ruby Road several turns beyond the old Ruby townsite (0.7 mile; 5.6 miles west of the turnoff to Hank and Yank Spring; see directions to Peña Blanca Lake and Sycamore Canyon in the two preceding sections). Watch for the downhill turnoff for Forest Road 217 on the left (south) side of the Ruby Road. If you are approaching from Tucson, take I-19 south to Exit 48 at Amado (33 miles south of the junction of I-10 with

Five-striped Sparrow
Narca Moore-Craig

I-19). Drive past the parking area for Arivaca Cienaga (22.5 miles) to the Ruby Road Junction (1.6 miles). Turn left (south) onto Ruby Road. Continue past the turnoff to Arivaca Lake (4.9 miles) and the end of the pavement (0.4 mile) to the junction with Forest Road 217 at California Gulch (5.5 miles; 11.0 miles from Arivaca). Turn right (south) into California Gulch.

After an initial steep drop-off into a grassy canyon, you should be able to reach a dam (1.3 miles) on the left (east) side without much problem. Be aware, however, that stream crossings in late summer may be 12–18 inches deep. This is the best area for Montezuma Quail. Bear right at the fork (0.1

mile) past the dam, turn left at the 3-way junction (0.8 mile), and then right soon thereafter (0.1 mile), and stay on the obvious main road. Avoid the private roads on the left. *Although this is mostly Coronado National Forest land, be aware that there are private inholdings.* Immediately after crossing the yellow cattleguard, watch for the conspicuous mining site at Oro Blanco Mine on the right (west; 1.2 miles). The Buff-collared Nightjar uses the whole basin surrounding the mine. To continue to the Five-striped Sparrow site, bear left uphill to the ridge top (0.4 mile). Turn sharply left (north) and park in the small, flat area used by other vehicles.

To look for the Five-striped Sparrows hike down a steep grade on the "old road" for about 0.3 mile to the bottom of California Gulch (elevation change approximately 200 feet). This abandoned track crosses the streambed twice in a 0.25-mile-long stretch. Usually there are two pairs of Five-striped Sparrows between these two stream crossings. Listen and look for males singing from exposed perches above the subtropical thornscrub high on the steep slopes. Some of the other birds that regularly occur here in summer, when the Five-stripes are singing, include Gray, Zone-tailed, and Red-tailed Hawks, White-throated Swift, Broad-billed, Black-chinned, and Costa's Hummingbirds, Northern Beardless-Tyrannulet, Bell's Vireo, Cactus, Canyon, and Bewick's Wrens, Black-tailed Gnatcatcher, Lucy's Warbler, Summer Tanager, and Lazuli and Varied Buntings. Rare but recorded species include Buff-collared Nightjar, Thick-billed Kingbird, and Black-capped Gnatcatcher.

J. SAN RAFAEL VALLEY

(33 miles round-trip from Patagonia/one-half day)

The best grasslands in Southeastern Arizona—and one of the premier grasslands in the United States—lie east of the Patagonia and west of the Huachuca Mountains. Cradled in gentle, rolling hills at an elevation of approximately 5,000 feet, the headwaters of the Santa Cruz River rise on a Mexican land grant dating back to 1825. Most of the San Rafael Valley is still in private ownership today. Visitors are asked to either bird from the public roads or to walk to their destination. *Off-road vehicular travel is prohibited.*

During summer all of the birds of prey and sparrows found in the San Rafael are easy to see at other more accessible locations. In winter, however, the San Rafael Grasslands offer some of the best birding in Southeastern Arizona. To find this area start in Patagonia and take the street parallel to and one block east of Highway 82. Go north past the post office on the left (west) side for a short distance to a broad curve that sweeps to the right (east). This is Harshaw Road.

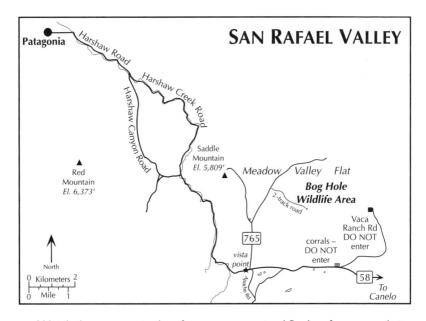

Watch the pavement edges for enormous mixed flocks of sparrows (winter) as the road traverses the broad, flat agricultural area where Harshaw Creek meets upper Sonoita Creek. Soon after entering the foothills of the Patagonia Mountains, a well-graded road sheers off to the left at a Y-intersection (3.1 miles from the Post Office). This is the Harshaw *Creek* Road, a fine alternate route that ties back into the main Harshaw *Canyon* Road if time is not an important consideration.

In recent years **Harshaw Creek** has developed a reputation as an important vagrant trap. In August 2000 a Yellow-green Vireo patrolled an area approximately one mile above the junction with the main Harshaw Canyon Road. The same neighborhood was patronized by a Least Flycatcher the same fall. During spring and summer Harshaw Creek hosts several Gray Hawk families, a pair of Zone-tailed Hawks, and a suite of other breeding species which includes Montezuma Quail, Yellow-billed Cuckoo, Northern Beardless-Tyrannulet, Sulphur-bellied Flycatcher, Thick-billed Kingbird, both Rock and Canyon Wrens, and Summer Tanager. The avifauna is an interesting mixture of both valley and canyon riparian species. Harshaw Creek Road rejoins the Harshaw Canyon Road at a major confluence of two canyons (2.4 miles). Watch for Eastern Bluebird here.

The easiest access to the San Rafael Valley is to stay right (south) on the paved **Harshaw Canyon Road**. Golden Eagles and Montezuma Quail are relatively common the entire length of Harshaw. A Spotted Owl has occasionally been found in the rocky grottoes high up the slope on the right directly above where the pavement ends (0.7 mile). This is a tough scramble up approximately 500 feet on a treacherous slope without any certainty that the owl will be waiting. It is not recommended for non-fanatics. *(See page 114 for Spotted Owl etiquette.)*

There are two more major roads between the end of the pavement and the San Rafael Grasslands. Ignore both the right fork (2.3 miles) and the left turn onto Harshaw Creek Road (0.5 mile; this route, however, offers a nice change of scenery upon your return). Stay on the widest, most well-used thoroughfare. Quite suddenly, just as the Harshaw Canyon Road tops out on a low ridge, a breath-taking panorama of golden savanna unrolls across the valley to a blue horizon created by the Canelo Hills and the Huachuca Mountains (3.9 miles). This sweeping vista of the San Rafael Grasslands is one of the most satisfying visual experiences available to birders in all Southeastern Arizona.

There is a four-way intersection at the *de facto* vista point. The left (north) road follows the edge of the grasslands into Meadow Valley Flat. Turn right at a little track (2.0 miles) to find **Bog Hole Wildlife Area** (0.5 mile). Most years the concrete dam here backs up a few acres of water, and an equal amount of cattail marsh. In winter the regular ducks are Green-winged Teal, Mallard (including the Mexican Duck race), Northern Pintail, Blue-winged and Cinnamon Teal, Northern Shoveler, Gadwall, and American Wigeon. American Coot is common, and both Marsh Wren and Swamp Sparrow lurk in the reeds. The dry uplands along the Meadow Valley Road are good for Sprague's Pipit and Chestnut-collared Longspur, and White-tailed Kite is often present. Meadow Valley Flat is one of the few areas where Ferruginous Hawk occurs away from agricultural fields in the Southeast corner. Also noteworthy is a herd of Pronghorn that tends to browse on the gentle, grassy hills downstream from Bog Hole.

Continue straight east into the **San Rafael Valley** from the vista point at the junction with the Meadow Valley Road. During winter watch for Short-eared Owls. Early morning before sunrise is best. One or two are typical in most years, but on pre-dawn visits in the winter of 1999–2000 some birders found up to six owls. Baird's Sparrows also occasionally use the fencelines paralleling the road as convenient perches. Be careful not to confuse the Savannah with the Baird's Sparrow. They are superficially similar, but Baird's has a buff median stripe in the crown and an overall rich buff face and nape. In a quick glimpse the Baird's shows bolder contrast on the back stripes. Savannah is more apt to occur in roadside swales.

Large flocks of Horned Larks prefer short grass or bare ground, especially near water. Mixed in with the Horned Larks may be a few McCown's Longspurs. Until the end of January both sexes of the McCown's resemble nothing so much as female House Sparrows with pinkish bills. It is not until February that the males develop the black cap, bill, moustache, and breast band that easily distinguish them from all other finches and sparrows. During the spring of 2000 a male Lapland Longspur was frequently seen in the company of the Horned Larks and McCown's Longspurs. *The Vaca Ranch corrals on the left (north) side of the road (2.4 miles) are now off-limits. Here, as elsewhere in cattle country, please take care not to spook livestock, block any gates or access roads, or interfere with ranch operations in any manner.*

Continue east to the junction with the Canelo Road (1.1 mile) where the main San Rafael Valley Road turns right (south). This is bottom of the grassy basin where the Santa Cruz River is born. The actual streambed lies straight ahead a couple of hundred yards farther east toward Canelo. Most winters—unless there have been recent rains—the river is dry.

Other birds that frequent the area are American Kestrel, Say's Phoebe, Savannah Sparrow, and Eastern Meadowlark. Check for Bald and Golden Eagles perched in the big cottonwoods. Prairie Falcons are also fond of this section of the San Rafael Grasslands.

Farther east a confusing complex of roads connects the San Rafael Grasslands to Sonoita, Fort Huachuca, and Coronado National Memorial. These roads are dusty and badly wash-boarded in dry weather, and apt to mire you in deep clay during rains or snow storms. The fastest and most straightforward way to access these locations is to return the way you came from Patagonia (14 miles to the Post Office; add 0.4 mile if you detour down Harshaw Creek).

K. SOUTH AND WEST OF THE HUACHUCAS

(72 miles round-trip from Sierra Vista/one day)

This trip begins at an elevation of 6,575 feet in Montezuma Pass, the highest point reached by road in Coronado National Memorial. To find Montezuma Pass from the intersection of Highways 90 and 92 in Sierra Vista, follow Highway 92 south for approximately 10 miles through a huge curve east to the well-signed, right-hand turnoff for Coronado National Memorial (13.6 miles). Take the Monument Road to the Visitor Center (4.8 miles). (A brief history of Coronado's passage up the San Pedro River Valley is contained in the "Upper Valley Loop" in Chapter 7.) The road up to Montezuma Pass turns into dirt (1.25 mile) at a stream crossing, but the final miles up to the top are well-graded and suitable for most passenger cars (2.1 miles; 21.75 miles from Sierra Vista). Montezuma Pass marks the southern end of the Crest Trail, which climbs nearly 3,000 feet in 5.5 miles to the 9,463-foot summit of Miller Peak.

Beyond Montezuma Pass Forest Road 61 becomes a steep, rocky, dusty wash-boarded route that is definitely *not* suitable for sight-seeing. However, it does offer access to some scenic destinations with interesting birds. The first

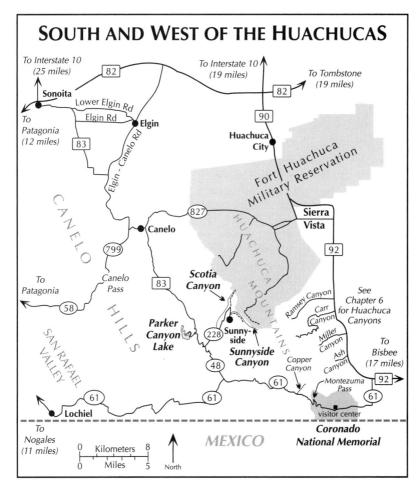

SOUTH AND WEST OF THE HUACHUCAS

To Interstate 10
(25 miles)

82

Sonoita

To
Patagonia
(12 miles)

Lower Elgin Rd

Elgin Rd

Elgin

83

Elgin - Canelo Rd

CANELO

To Interstate 10
(19 miles)

82

To Tombstone
(19 miles)

90

Huachuca
City

Fort Huachuca
Military Reservation

827

Canelo

799

To
Patagonia

58

Canelo
Pass

83

Scotia
Canyon

Sierra
Vista

92

HUACHUCA

Ramsey Canyon

Carr
Canyon

See
Chapter 6
for Huachuca
Canyons

HILLS

Parker
Canyon
Lake

228

Sunny-
side

48

Sunnyside
Canyon

MOUNTAINS

Miller
Canyon

Copper
Canyon

Ash
Canyon

To
Bisbee
(17 miles)

SAN RAFAEL VALLEY

61

61

61

Montezuma
Pass

92

61

Lochiel

visitor center

To
Nogales
(11 miles)

0   Kilometers   8

0   Miles   5

North

MEXICO

Coronado
National Memorial

canyon on the right side is Copper Canyon (0.9 mile). Canyon Wrens nest just inside the rocky gates that flank the little stream. Occasionally an Elegant Trogon uses the basin by a small spring a few hundred yards inside Copper Canyon, and Lucifer Hummingbirds have been observed in the same area. The next drainage to the west, Cave Canyon (2.7 miles), also usually hosts Elegant Trogons. A Canada Warbler was discovered here in early September 1993. Soon after the road swings right (north), FR 61 divides at a major junction (5.4 miles). Birders should continue straight ahead on FR 48, signed for Parker Canyon Lake, ignoring the abrupt left turn for FR 61.

One of the least birded and most deserving sites in Southeastern Arizona is the **Sunnyside/Scotia complex** (3.1 miles). Located on the southwest corner of the Huachuca Mountains, both canyons can have Elegant Trogons and Buff-breasted Flycatcher. The road that follows the grassy ridge most of the way to the junction between the drainages (2.6 miles) is one of the best places in Southeastern Arizona to watch for Common Nighthawk (dawn and dusk, summer). Owling here is simply terrific. Flammulated Owl (uncommon) and Whiskered Screech-Owl are the two species most often heard, but Great Horned Owl and Northern Pygmy-Owl are also present. As many as five Whiskered Screech-Owls have been known to be attracted to an imitation of the owl's toot here.

The division between Scotia and Sunnyside lies in a basin inside Sunnyside Canyon just below the first real curve on the road. Go left to find a flat place to park on the brink of Scotia Canyon (0.25 mile). Both Elegant Trogons and Buff-breasted Flycatchers usually occur in the Chihuahua Pines in the first half mile upstream. Turn right, down canyon at the T-junction to enter Sunnyside. It is possible to drive slightly farther into Sunnyside (0.75 mile), but many of the best birds occur in this stretch of lower Sunnyside. Some of the other species to watch for include Montezuma Quail, Northern Goshawk, Zone-tailed Hawk, Band-tailed Pigeon, Arizona Woodpecker, Greater Pewee, Sulphur-bellied Flycatcher, Eastern Bluebird, Hutton's Vireo, Grace's Warbler, Painted Redstart, and Hepatic Tanager. In surveys conducted in the early 1980s, I always found more Elegant Trogons in the Sunnyside/Scotia complex than any other area of the Huachuca Mountains. Altogether there were usually six to eight pairs using the two canyons, occasionally interacting across the low-lying intervening ridge.

Return to Forest Road 48, continue for 2.3 miles, and join Highway 83 (paved at the junction for access to the lake and the campground). **Parker Canyon Lake**, one mile to the left, is mobbed by fishermen on summer weekends and holidays. In winter, however, this is probably the best location in Southeastern Arizona for a visiting Common Loon. Eared Grebes, and a variety of ducks including Common Goldeneye, Bufflehead, and Common Merganser, also use this 130-acre trout fishery. Bald Eagles have stayed at the lake until early summer. Eastern Bluebird is typically common near the junction.

From Parker Canyon Lake, it is almost exactly equidistant to return to Sierra Vista via Fort Huachuca (17.0 miles; 35.7 miles to the junction of Highways 90 and 92) or to retrace your route back to Montezuma Pass (14.4 miles; 36.2 miles to the junction of Highways 90 and 92). To completely circle the Huachuca Mountains, however, continue northeast on Highway 83.

The Canelo townsite junction (11.5 miles) is the only major intersection between the lake and the West Gate at Fort Huachuca. Highway 83 turns left (west) here and wanders through low hills with scattered oaks and spreading grasslands all the way to Sonoita (17.0 miles). To continue this tour, stay right on Forest Road 827. Watch for Montezuma Quail, Golden Eagle, and Prairie Falcon.

Be prepared to show your driver's license and either your registration or rental agreement to enter the West Gate of Fort Huachuca (5.5 miles). Passengers may have to produce photo ID as well.

The Apaches called Southeastern Arizona the land of two springs. Nowhere is the reason for this more apparent than here on the south side of the Huachuca Mountains. For most of the year, a sea of coarse, dry grasses covers the crooked, yellow horizon. Neither the cold rains of winter, nor the infrequent sprinkles of spring, are sufficient to stir new growth. But soon after the summer rains begin in July, new shoots transform the southern facade of the Huachucas into a verdant green carpet dotted with blue and red wildflowers. Old-timers and birders heave a sigh of contentment. Once again, it's springtime in July!

L. FRENCH JOE CANYON

(10 miles south of Benson/one-half day)

The spring of 1995 saw the discovery of at least two Rufous-capped Warblers in French Joe Canyon in the Whetstone Mountains. Before a full year had elapsed, this small canyon located about midway between Tucson and Sierra Vista, had produced a handful of select rarities, including Plain-capped Starthroat, Lucifer Hummingbird, Aztec Thrush, and Kentucky, Hooded, and Fan-tailed Warblers. The Rufous-caps returned to the same location in 1996, and they have been present ever since. Other Arizona specialties such as Montezuma Quail, Costa's Hummingbird, and both Rufous-crowned and Black-chinned Sparrows all potentially add panache to a morning bird walk in French Joe. Birders who elect to visit this canyon, however, should come prepared for a very rugged, rock-studded, rutted dirt road that requires a high-clearance vehicle. Summer temperatures soar soon after sunrise; plan on carrying at least a half-gallon of water per person on any trip to this seldom-visited site.

To reach French Joe Canyon from Tucson, take Interstate 10 east to the Highway 90 turnoff (42 miles) at Exit 302. Follow Highway 90 south parallel to the Whetstone Mountains on your right (west) past Kartchner Caverns State Park to the signed gate for French Joe Canyon just before milepost 300 (10 miles). Set your trip odometer to zero here. Turn right onto the dirt road and drive 0.8 mile to the first of several forks. Turn left at this junction. A half-mile later you'll cross a cattleguard just before another junction (odometer 1.4 miles). Bear right here and continue toward the canyon mouth looming up in front of you. The road divides at mile 2.6. Either branch leads into French Joe Canyon, and they unite again in another few hundred yards (mile 2.9). There is a good parking location just beyond on the left side. Walk upcanyon another quarter-mile to an unimproved campsite near a concrete

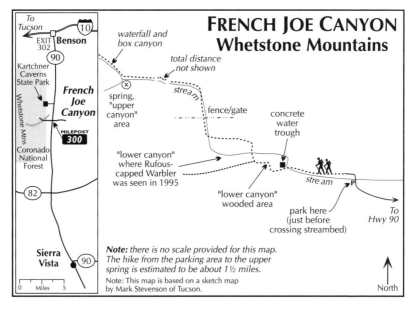

FRENCH JOE CANYON
Whetstone Mountains

To Tucson
EXIT 302 Benson
Kartchner Caverns State Park
French Joe Canyon
MILEPOST 300
Coronado National Forest
Sierra Vista

waterfall and box canyon
total distance not shown
spring, "upper canyon" area
stream
fence/gate
concrete water trough
"lower canyon" where Rufous-capped Warbler was seen in 1995
"lower canyon" wooded area
park here (just before crossing streambed)
stream
To Hwy 90

Note: there is no scale provided for this map. The hike from the parking area to the upper spring is estimated to be about 1½ miles.

Note: This map is based on a sketch map by Mark Stevenson of Tucson.

North

0 Miles 5

water trough—this stretch of the canyon offers some of the best birding in French Joe. When the agaves are in blossom—from late May through early August—watch the hillside on the right (north) for six or more species of hummingbirds, Scott's Oriole, and possibly a Coati.

The Rufous-capped Warblers have been found anywhere from the spring in the grove of tall Velvet Ash where the road ends to the upper end of French Joe at another spring near the terminus of the foot trail at a rock wall ornamented with Golden Columbine. Both the Hooded and Fan-tailed Warblers were within one-quarter mile of the road end. The Kentucky Warbler was bathing in a rain puddle at the beginning of the trail.

The trail begins on the left (south) side of the streambed, winding around the base of the hill for approximately 200 yards before it crosses the creek again just above a small waterfall (which may be dry). A natural amphitheater at the confluence of two canyons just ahead marks the setting where a Rufous-capped Warbler was often found during 1995. To continue up the trail to the upper Rufous-capped Warbler site, bear right into the north canyon. Although the going is comparatively rocky, following the streambed in many places, the trail is obvious for the remaining mile until it ends at a jumble of boulders at the upper spring. In recent years, Rufous-capped Warblers have been most often found in this moist pocket of lush vegetation by the cliff face with the flowering Columbine. This is also the area where the Rufous-caps have successfully nested since 2000. Listen for their song, which begins with a few loud chips, then accelerates into atonal trills and warbles. An Aztec Thrush put in a characteristically brief appearance here in August 1996.

M. GUADALUPE CANYON

(31 miles east of Douglas/one-half day)

This trip follows the Mexican border east from Douglas to Guadalupe Canyon, one of the most fascinating birding spots in the country. The canyon is located in the Peloncillo Mountains in the extreme southeastern corner of Arizona on the headwaters of the Río Yaqui, which in turn serves as a natural conduit for Mexican species entering the U.S. Buff-collared Nightjar in 1960 and Thick-billed Kingbird in 1958 were both first records for the United States. The first Fan-tailed Warbler in the U.S. came from a tributary drainage, Baker Canyon, in 1961. Another Fan-tailed Warbler was photographed in Guadalupe in September 1990.

Guadalupe Canyon is privately owned. Birders are allowed to enter Guadalupe only on foot. Groups of over four persons are not permitted. Overnight camping is prohibited. The road leading to the canyon is dusty and sometimes rough, particularly during the rainy season. After heavy storms the road may be impassable because of mud. The canyon is about 4,000 feet in elevation and summers are hot. It is wise to arrive as early as possible in the morning. *Do not forget to carry plenty of water.*

The gate at the entrance to Guadalupe Canyon
Cindy Lippincott

The starting point is the intersection of Highway 80 (A Avenue) and 15th Street. Go east on 15th Street toward the big "D" on the mountain. You are now on the Geronimo Trail. The pavement plays out a few miles east of Douglas near the summit of a range of low hills. All the way to the Guadalupe Canyon turnoff, the road passes through a section of the Chihuahuan Desert characterized by Creosote, Ocotillo, and Whitethorn Acacia growing on limestone soil. Birds using this spare habitat are Scaled Quail, Golden Eagle, Swainson's Hawk (summer), Greater Roadrunner, Pyrrhuloxia, and Black-throated Sparrow.

The major Y-junction for the **San Bernardino Ranch** is the first significant side road (17.0 miles). Turn right (south) if you wish to visit the historic ranch and adjacent ponds (fee, open 10:00 a.m. to 3:00 p.m., Wednesday-Sunday, 520-558-2474). The ranch was once owned by Texas John Slaughter, the famous sheriff who cleaned up Tombstone after Wyatt Earp departed for California. Some of the birds that have nested here include Gray Hawk, Virginia Rail, and Tropical Kingbird.

On the right just past the ranch turnoff and mile marker 16 is the parking area (marked Hunter's Access) for the San Bernardino National Wildlife Center. The refuge is open for walk-in visitors daily during daylight hours. It is a short hike to the ponds from the parking area.

Continue east on the Geronimo Trail to find the turnoff to Guadalupe Canyon on the right (south) side (5.2 miles). Watch for Burrowing Owls, Lesser Nighthawks, and Bendire's Thrashers along the first several miles of the road. A stock tank on the right (south) side of the road (4.0 miles) usually holds a few "Mexican Duck" Mallards. A short distance beyond, a swale filled with a deep stand of Sacaton grass is excellent for Botteri's Sparrows after the summer rains have begun. From the Geronimo Trail to the canyon proper is 9.0 miles.

Guadalupe Canyon comes as a welcome relief from the dry, dusty desert. The view overlooking the bright green ribbon of trees winding between hills covered with low-growing, subtropical thornscrub will gladden any true birder's heart. Large Arizona Sycamores and Fremont Cottonwoods grow along the valley floor, interspersed with patches of willow following an intermittent stream. A gate with parking spaces for two cars just as the road reaches the canyon floor marks the end of the drive. *Use designated parking sites only; do not park on the road.* A white monument and a barbed-wire fence approximately 200 yards down the canyon to the right (south) indicate the Mexican border. *The entirety of Guadalupe Canyon is private property and may be closed at some future date. Please behave in a manner to ensure that birders will always be welcome.*

Arrive early. Many birds quit singing by 10 a.m. After mid-May the first bird you encounter at the gate may well be a purple-and-blue male Varied Bunting. Savor its colors until the querulous calls of Bell's Vireo or the brilliant

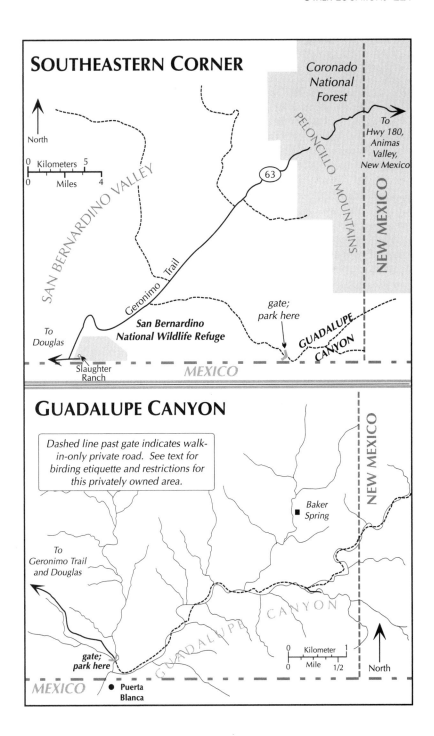

SOUTHEASTERN CORNER

Coronado
National
Forest

PELONCILLO MOUNTAINS

To
Hwy 180,
Animas
Valley,
New Mexico

North

NEW MEXICO

0   Kilometers   5
0   Miles   4

SAN BERNARDINO VALLEY

63

Geronimo Trail

gate;
park here

GUADALUPE
CANYON

To
Douglas

San Bernardino
National Wildlife Refuge

Slaughter
Ranch

MEXICO

GUADALUPE CANYON

Dashed line past gate indicates walk-
in-only private road. See text for
birding etiquette and restrictions for
this privately owned area.

NEW MEXICO

Baker
■ Spring

To
Geronimo Trail
and Douglas

GUADALUPE CANYON

gate;
park here

0   Kilometer   1
0   Mile   1/2

North

MEXICO   ● Puerta
Blanca

hues of Northern Cardinal draw your attention elsewhere. Some of the other summer birds that share the lower end of Guadalupe are Montezuma and Gambel's Quail, Cooper's and Zone-tailed Hawks, White-winged Dove and Common Ground-Dove, Western Screech-, Great Horned, and Elf Owls, Common Poorwill, Black-chinned, Broad-billed, and Violet-crowned Hummingbirds, Northern "Red-shafted" Flicker, Acorn, Gila, and Ladder-backed Woodpeckers, Northern Beardless-Tyrannulet, Western Wood-Pewee, Black and Say's Phoebes, Vermilion, Dusky-capped, Ash-throated, and Brown-crested Flycatchers, Cassin's and Thick-billed Kingbirds, Western Scrub- and Mexican Jays, Bridled Titmouse, Verdin, Bushtit, Cactus, Rock, Canyon, and Bewick's Wrens, Black-tailed Gnatcatcher, Curve-billed and Crissal Thrashers, Phainopepla, Bell's Vireo, Lucy's Warbler, Summer Tanager, Black-headed and Blue Grosbeaks, Spotted and Canyon Towhees, Rufous-crowned Sparrow, Bronzed Cowbird, Hooded and Bullock's Orioles, House Finch, and Lesser Goldfinch. In July 1998 a Yellow-green Vireo was present for two days.

All of these birds can be seen in the first mile of Guadalupe Canyon. Only Sonoita Creek at Patagonia can match the density of Violet-crowned Hummingbirds found in Guadalupe. It remains on a par with Patagonia for Thick-billed Kingbirds, and it is still probably the best place in the U.S. for Buff-collared Nightjar. The nearest motels are in Douglas and at Portal.

N. MULESHOE RANCH COOPERATIVE MANAGEMENT AREA

(110 miles east of Tucson/one or two days)

With five permanently flowing streams and five species of native fishes, the Muleshoe Ranch was a natural for acquisition by The Nature Conservancy. Together with the Bureau of Land Management and the U.S. Forest Service, a Cooperative Management Area encompassing 48,200 acres has been set aside since 1982 to protect Arizona's single most precious resource: water. The Nature Conservancy estimates that over 80 percent of all the species of flora and fauna in the CMA are dependent on these year-round streams.

That is certainly true of at least two of its trio of Southwest specialty raptors. The Muleshoe is famous for its summering Common Black-, Gray, and Zone-tailed Hawks. Redfield Canyon is the best area in the CMA for Common Black-Hawk, but in 1995 both Hot Springs and Bass Canyons hosted one pair each in the shady cottonwood groves near the ranch headquarters. Here they may consort with two or three pairs of the ranch's resident Gray Hawks. Zone-tailed Hawks occur throughout. The best way to find these birds of

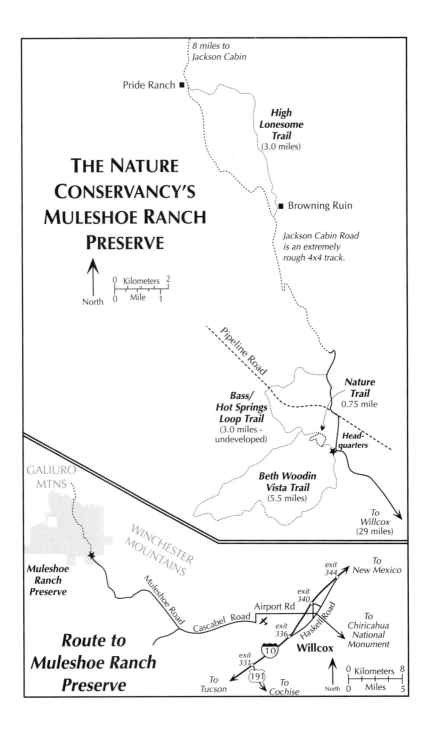

8 miles to
Jackson Cabin

Pride Ranch ■

**High
Lonesome
Trail**
(3.0 miles)

**THE NATURE
CONSERVANCY'S
MULESHOE RANCH
PRESERVE**

■ Browning Ruin

*Jackson Cabin Road
is an extremely
rough 4x4 track.*

0 Kilometers 2

North 0 Mile 1

Pipeline Road

**Bass/
Hot Springs
Loop Trail**
(3.0 miles -
undeveloped)

**Nature
Trail**
0.75 mile

**Head-
quarters**

GALIURO
MTNS

**Beth Woodin
Vista Trail**
(5.5 miles)

*To
Willcox
(29 miles)*

WINCHESTER
MOUNTAINS

**Muleshoe
Ranch
Preserve**

Muleshoe Road

Cascabel Road

Airport Rd

exit
344

*To
New Mexico*

exit
340

exit
336

Haskell Road

*To
Chiricahua
National
Monument*

**Route to
Muleshoe Ranch
Preserve**

exit
331

10

Willcox

191

*To
Tucson*

*To
Cochise*

0 Kilometers 8

North 0 Miles 5

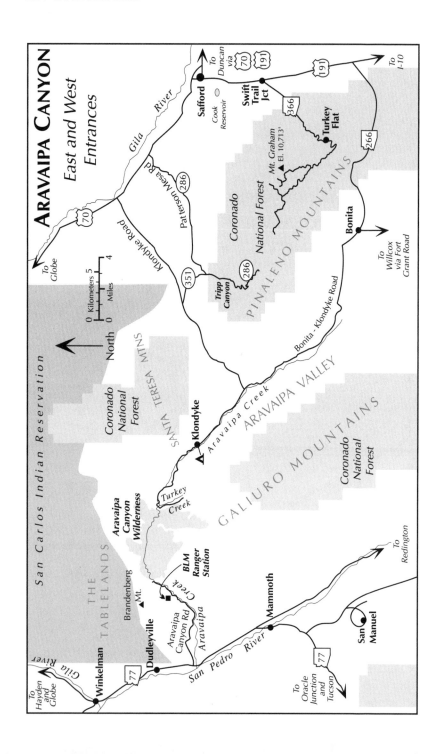

ARAVAIPA CANYON

East and West Entrances

prey, as well as other wildlife, is to hike any one or combination of the three trails that originate at the headquarters/visitor center/guest cabin area. Only 0.75-mile-long, the Nature Trail is the shortest option. The Bass-Hot Springs Canyon Loop Trail is 3 miles long. The 5.5-mile-long Beth Woodin Trail forms another loop in the hills southwest of the Headquarters.

To reach Muleshoe Ranch, take Interstate 10 east to the second exit for Willcox, #340, Rex Allen Drive. Turn right (east) and go one block to Bisbee Avenue, the street between the shopping center and the truck stop (0.15 mile). Turn right (south) here and continue past the high school (0.8 mile). Turn right (west) onto Airport Road and go over the interstate. After mile 3.1 the pavement ends and Airport Road turns into a well-graded county road. Follow it west to a Y-intersection with Muleshoe Road at a group of mailboxes (12.3 miles). Bear right (north) here. There are no other major junctions before the road drops into the headquarters area at Hooker's Hot Springs (14 miles). *Be aware, however, that heavy rains can render the last, long hill above the ranch impassable without four-wheel-drive.* This is especially true after the summer monsoons have started, and again after winter storms. Call in advance for current road conditions.

Hooker's Hot Springs were originally developed as a health spa just before the turn of the 20th century by Colonel Henry Clay Hooker, whose Sierra Bonita Ranch once covered over 800 square miles, the largest ranch in Arizona in its day. The Nature Conservancy has renovated three buildings with five housekeeping units available for rent to the public. Overnight lodging guests are welcome to use the hot springs for a soak. Set at an elevation of 4,000 feet under big trees, this is a wonderful place both to relax and to bird throughout the year. For further information contact the Muleshoe Ranch Headquarters, 6502 N. Muleshoe Ranch Road, Willcox, AZ 85643; 520-507-5229; www.nature.org/arizona.

O. ARAVAIPA CANYON EAST

(152 miles east of Tucson/one or two days)

The east end of the Aravaipa Canyon Wilderness Area is generally regarded as the pretty entrance. The last few miles of road wander through a pastoral setting of big cottonwoods, small orchards, and brilliant green fields, all butted up against the pocked and pitted adobe-brown walls of the canyon, as if for contrast. One or more Common Black-Hawks ordinarily soar by before you ever reach the designated parking area at Turkey Creek Canyon. Homesteaded over a century ago, the Salazar Family Church makes a photogenic foreground for a herd of Desert Bighorn Sheep that often browse poetically on the slopes above. Meanwhile every field has a resident

Aravaipa Canyon
Richard Cachor Taylor

male Vermilion Flycatcher, snapping up aerial minutiae like a voracious spark, and providing an unending distraction for "serious" birders.

Unfortunately, four-wheel-drive vehicles with high clearance are frequently necessary to negotiate the crossings on Aravaipa Creek for the final 3.5 miles of the road. Call the Bureau of Land Management (928-348-4400) for recent road condition information.

To reach the east entrance of Aravaipa Canyon drive east on Interstate 10 to Willcox, and take Exit 340 (80 miles). The last inexpensive gas and picnic supplies are available at this exit in Willcox, and neither may be available at any price farther on. Take Rex Allen Drive left (west) across Interstate 10, and stay on the pavement until it ends (14.0 miles). The remainder of the road to Bonita (17.0 miles) is well-graded and suitable for passenger cars—except after extremely heavy rains. Both Scaled Quail and Sandhill Crane (winter) are often sighted from the road between Willcox and Bonita. Turn left at Bonita on the Klondyke Road. The next 10 miles pass through an undeveloped grassland where White-tailed Kite nests in Soaptree Yuccas. In winter watch for Ferruginous Hawk. According to the 2004 Arizona Game and Fish census, the herd of Pronghorn that occupies this area numbers approximately 125 animals.

Almost without warning, the Klondyke Road abruptly drops into the mesquite thickets at the headwaters of Aravaipa Canyon. Mesquite dominates the terrain on both sides of the road for the remaining 20-odd miles all the way to Klondyke (31 miles from Bonita). There is a trailer staffed by the Bureau of

Land Management ranger in the center of Klondyke's business district (across the street from the only other structure). If you intend to hike or backpack into the Aravaipa Canyon Wilderness Area you must stop here for a permit. The same regulations apply on the "East End" as at the "West End." (See also Section D of this chapter.) To wit: only 50 people per day are permitted in the 11-mile-long Aravaipa Canyon Wilderness Area. To obtain a permit contact the Bureau of Land Management, Safford District Office, 711 14th Avenue, Safford, AZ 85546; 520-348-4400; safford.az.blm.gov. Because of limited availability, the BLM strongly recommends making reservations by phone or online 13 weeks in advance. A map, fee info, and reservations calendar are all available on the website. There is a charge of $5.00 per person per day. Plan on wearing stout, high-top shoes or boots to wade the stream: you will have to cross it dozens of times. High-top footgear will eliminate some of the gravel sluicing into your socks.

Non-backpackers may wish to use the developed facilities southeast of Klondyke. Fourmile Campground, a BLM fee site, is located one mile up the road across from the ranger trailer.

Beyond Klondyke the road continues on to the first stream crossing (3.7 miles), and the beginning of a riparian avian community that includes Yellow Warbler and Yellow-breasted Chat. The property on both sides of the road is owned by the Arizona Chapter of The Nature Conservancy for the remainder of the way to the Turkey Creek Parking Area. Birding is not permitted off the Aravaipa Road without pre-arrangement or permission from the manager. The manager's house is located just before the second stream crossing (2.7 miles). The only commercial lodging in Aravaipa Canyon is a guest house maintained by The Nature Conservancy. For more information contact the Aravaipa Canyon Preserve at 41099 W. Aravaipa Canyon Road, Willcox, AZ 85643; 928-828-3443; www.nature.org/arizona.

Unless the stream is exceptionally low, birders are *not* advised to plunge into Aravaipa Creek in a low-slung automobile, especially if it's of recent vintage. If the creek is high, this may be the end of the road without four-wheel-drive. *Turn back if in doubt—or if it looks like it may rain while you're in the canyon.* A short aside here: flash floods in October 1983 literally swallowed a small pickup truck. Its owner was first incredulous, then suspicious, and finally just plain depressed after learning from the BLM that it had vanished. Flash floods over 10 feet deep occur every decade.

Bear Canyon (2.0 miles) is a dry tributary that feeds into Aravaipa immediately before the third ford. Bear Canyon is renowned among local birders as the most reliable site for Gray Vireo in Southeastern Arizona. The BLM has constructed a small parking area at the entrance for use when Aravaipa's lower crossings are impassable. Up the wash the road varies with the season, but it is usually passable with standard transportation if the driver stays out of soft sand. Park at the foot of the obvious switchback (1.1 mile). The vireos stay low in Bear Canyon's dense juniper and mesquite thickets. Other birds here include several species more typical of interior chaparral in Central Arizona. These include Western Scrub-Jay, Juniper Titmouse, and Black-chinned Sparrow.

Common Black-Hawks are usually easy to see between mid-March and mid-October the remaining distance to the end of the road at the Turkey Creek Parking Area (1.5 miles). Long-term research, conducted since the early 1970s by Jay Schnell, a resident of Aravaipa Canyon, shows that between 10 and 16 pairs of Common Black-Hawks breed annually over a 17-mile-long stretch of the canyon. The stability of this population is probably owing to Aravaipa's protected status.

As the road ends, a Vermilion Flycatcher is ordinarily the first bird you notice. A male will probably be zooming around the parking lot. Zone-tailed Hawk, however, is the specialty at the Turkey Creek confluence. Up to three pairs nest in this lush feeder drainage. A four-wheel-drive road on the left leads up Turkey Creek to primitive campsites approved for overnight use by the BLM.

Birders can see almost all of the same species on the Aravaipa Road as hikers observe along Aravaipa Creek in the 19,410-acre Wilderness Area. American Dipper (winter) is probably the only species that is restricted to the confines of the inner canyon. But if time allows, a backpack into the heart of Aravaipa Canyon will reshape your image of both the Sonoran Desert and the beauty of its birdlife. Once experienced, it is easy to understand why this area was chosen in 1984 as the very first Bureau of Land Management Wilderness in the entire United States.

SPECIALTIES OF
SOUTHEASTERN
ARIZONA

Listed below are the avian specialties found in Southeastern Arizona that are of particular interest to out-of-area birders, as well as species—often locally rare—of special interest to birdwatchers who live within the area. In some instances closely related birds are also included to underscore the relative status and habitat preferences of the specialty birds.

Abundance, seasonal status, habitat, and specific locations are given for each species listed. An effort has been made to list at least three known sites for every bird. Since most visitors and residents alike begin their birding at Tucson, locations are arranged with those closest to Tucson first, followed by sites that are progressively farther away. All of the suggested areas were selected because they represent good places with reasonable access to observe the birds.

Ducks and Geese—In winter and migration up to 15 species can be found on a single visit to such places as Avra Valley Sewage Ponds west of Tucson, Picacho Reservoir, Peña Blanca Lake, Nogales Sewage Ponds, Patagonia Lake, Sierra Vista Wastewater Ponds, Parker Canyon Lake, and Lake Cochise at Willcox. Except for the two species of whistling-duck, the "Mexican Duck" subspecies of Mallard, and Cinnamon Teal, all of the ducks and geese in Southeastern Arizona are widespread in the U.S. They are treated under the bar graphs in Section III.

Black-bellied Whistling-Duck—Uncommon resident whose numbers fluctuate with the year. Prefers tree-lined ponds such as Kino Springs, Palo Duro Pond, and Patagonia Lake, but it occasionally uses locations lacking any shoreline cover, such as the Avra Valley Sewage Ponds, the Nogales Sewage Ponds, and the Cochise College Sewage Pond west of Douglas. Also found in flooded fields, such as at Río Rico east of the Santa Cruz River bridge, and wooded streams such as Sonoita Creek at the Patagonia Roadside Rest.

Fulvous Whistling-Duck—Strictly a vagrant, although it was fairly common 50 years ago along the lower Colorado River at Yuma. The most recent record in Southeastern Arizona is one seen at Kino Springs from late April to mid-May 1990. Other records in the 1990s have come from the Phoenix area.

"Mexican Duck" —This subspecies of Mallard, in which the drake is "female-plumaged," is a fairly common—if local—permanent resident. Hybrid males typically exhibit the olive-yellow bill of pure strains, but have curly black tail feathers and/or black tail coverts. At present, easiest to find at Lake Cochise at Willcox, Sierra Vista Wastewater Ponds, and in pools along the San Pedro River, where it is the breeding type. Less frequently it also occurs at Sweetwater Wetlands, Buenos Aires NWR, San Bernardino NWR, and on ponds near Rodeo.

Cinnamon Teal—Fairly common winter visitor and uncommon summer resident in valley lakes and ponds. Check for Cinnamon Teal throughout the year at Sweetwater Wetlands and Lake Cochise. Other locations include any pond along the Santa Cruz River, Avra Valley Sewage Ponds, and Whitewater Draw Wildlife Refuge.

Wild Turkey—Reintroduced into all of the higher mountains. Now an uncommon permanent resident of Madrean pine-oak woodlands and grassy openings in coniferous forest in the Santa Rita, Huachuca, and Chiricahua Mountains. Recent observations along the San Pedro River and Guadalupe Canyon seem to be of individuals of the Mexican subspecies, *mexicana*, apparently the result of a natural range expansion from Sonora. Wild Turkeys in Ramsey Canyon are the best habituated to people.

Montezuma Quail—Fairly common permanent resident of open, grassy oak woodlands and glades in coniferous forest in all mountain ranges. The first one can be exasperatingly difficult to find. Often seen at the edge of a road, particularly early in the morning and late in the afternoon. Instead of flying when a car approaches, a Montezuma usually squats. Areas to check include just above Proctor Road in Madera Canyon, along Ruby Road between Interstate 19 and California Gulch, along Harshaw Road near Patagonia, in French Joe Canyon in the Whetstones, at the outlets of Garden, Ramsey, and Miller Canyons in the Huachucas, and both along the road in Cave Creek Canyon and at George Walker House in Paradise in the Chiricahua Mountains.

Northern Bobwhite—The "Masked Bobwhite" is the native subspecies extirpated in 1897. Reintroduction efforts began at the present-day Buenos Aires Wildlife Refuge in 1974. The verdict is still out, but recent transplants have had limited success. The 2004 census showed approximately 100–200 birds at Buenos Aires. The population in Sonora, Mexico, is estimated at fewer than 1,000 birds. Apparently eliminated by overgrazing and the subsequent invasion of mesquite and Lehmann Lovegrass, this species is an obligate of grassy swales in wide valley bottomlands. Male Masked Bobwhites have black throats and chestnut breasts and bellies, but females resemble the typical Northern Bobwhite hens of the eastern U.S.

Scaled Quail—Common permanent resident of valley grasslands and the Chihuahuan Desert, primarily east of the Santa Cruz River. Lake Cochise at Willcox is a good location, but it can also be found in the housing development north of the lower Ramsey Canyon Road, throughout the Sulphur Springs Valley, east of Douglas on Highway 80, and at Willow Tank near Rodeo. Populations fluctuate with the year.

Gambel's Quail—Common to abundant permanent resident of both Sonoran and Chihuahuan desertscrub, particularly in areas of mesquite. Easy to find at the Shannon-Broadway Desert in Tucson, at the San Pedro House on the San Pedro River, and in the residential area of Portal.

Least Grebe—Very rare straggler to ponds near the Mexican border from Nogales west to the Colorado River, with about 20 records altogether for Arizona. After a hiatus of 17 years, a Least Grebe put in an appearance at Picacho Reservoir from December 1994 through mid-February 1995. There have been five subsequent observations, beginning with an August record from a pond in West Turkey Creek in the Chiricahuas and a November bird at Lake Cochise near Willcox, both in 1998. More recently, a lone Least Grebe has been present at Sweetwater Wetlands in Tucson, at least intermittently, since June 2000, and another was found at Sam Lena Park in Tucson in April 2003. In July 2004 another lone Least Grebe appeared at Kino Springs. Periodic erroneous reports frequently pertain to Eared Grebes with dull yellow eyes. Least Grebe is substantially smaller than Eared, with a proportionately shorter neck, and *bright* yellow eyes. It seems to be more buoyant than other members of the family, and rides high on the water, almost like a "toy grebe."

Western Grebe—In recent winters an uncommon visitor, primarily to lakes and larger ponds below 5,000 feet. Probably most common at Patagonia Lake, but occurs annually at Lake Cochise, and most winters a bird or two is somewhere around Tucson or in Avra Valley. When water levels are high, Whitewater Draw Wildlife Refuge frequently hosts this species. Often consorts with Clark's Grebe.

Clark's Grebe—Found at the same places and same time of year as Western Grebe, and usually found with Western Grebe. During winter both *Aechmorphorus* grebes may have pale lores and an incomplete eyebrow, so bill color is the best distinction. Clark's bill is orange and Western Grebe's bill is greenish-yellow. Similarity in appearance creates confusion, but in Southeastern Arizona it appears that Westerns outnumber Clark's Grebes at least 2:1.

Neotropic Cormorant—Uncommon but regular visitor to valley ponds and lakes, primarily in the Nogales area at Patagonia Lake, and less commonly at Kino Springs and Peña Blanca Lake. Care should be used in separating Neotropic from Double-crested Cormorant, which is also uncommon at the same locations. Note that the bare gular patch tapers to a point in

Neotropics and is rounded in Double-crested. Immature Double-cresteds are variably whitish below, while immature Neotropics are Arizona's brownest cormorants. In flight note the kinked neck of Double-crested and the noticeably long tail of Neotropic—as long as the head and neck combined.

Black Vulture—An uncommon permanent resident of the upper Santa Cruz Valley near Nogales and Patagonia, and near Sells on Tohono O'Odham lands. In the past decade it has been seen regularly at the Marana Pecan Grove. Since the winter of 1993–1994, two or three Black Vultures have often roosted on the grounds of the Arizona-Sonora Desert Museum. Two nests are known from Arizona, both from Organ Pipe Cactus National Monument west of our area.

White-tailed Kite—Uncommon in summer, rare in winter in valley grassland and desert agricultural areas throughout the southeast corner. Some summers they seem to turn up in all appropriate habitats, but during years when they are scarce the most reliable areas have been fields south of the Marana Pecan Grove, Buenos Aires National Wildlife Refuge, the San Rafael Valley, fields along the upper San Pedro River near Palominas, and fields near Cochise College west of Douglas. The first record of White-tailed Kite in Arizona was 1972.

Mississippi Kite—Uncommon local summer resident of valley riparian woodlands, primarily along a 25-mile-long stretch of the lower San Pedro River between Mammoth and Winkelman. The most famous location for this species is near the community of Dudleyville. In 2000 a new colony appeared in the vicinity of the Highway 80 bridge across the San Pedro River just west of Saint David. The first record of Mississippi Kite in Arizona was 1970.

Bald Eagle—Uncommon winter visitor at Patagonia Lake, in the San Rafael Grasslands, at Parker Canyon Lake, and in agricultural areas of the Sulphur Springs Valley. Casual but possible in valleys throughout the region. Defying all conventional wisdom, in southern Arizona it is generally easier to find a Bald Eagle feasting on a deer or cow carcass than devouring a fish. Then again, in most of Southeastern Arizona fish are less common than eagles.

Northern Goshawk—Rare permanent resident of the mountains, more widespread in winter. While unusual, lone goshawks may be observed hunting at the mouths of canyons in savanna and desert any time of the year. Has nested in the Santa Rita, Huachuca, and Chiricahua Mountains. Watch for it in Madera, Garden, and Cave Creek Canyons. Most often seen soaring over the forests. Occasionally a birder off the beaten track discovers a goshawk nest when a parent bird makes a surprise, hurricane pass at the back of her or his head. Unless you've experienced it, it's hard to convey just how terrifying this feels. Researchers have been seriously maimed by goshawks protecting their young. The blackish-backed "Apache Goshawk" of Mexico is a race which occasionally occurs in the border rangers and averages 10 percent larger than the northern subspecies.

Gray Hawk—Fairly common summer resident of valley riparian cotton-woods, primarily along the upper Santa Cruz River, Arivaca Creek, Sonoita Creek, and the San Pedro River, which has the largest concentration of these birds in the United States. Typically there are two pairs at Kino Springs (one pair at each pond) and three pairs nesting on the Patagonia-Sonoita Creek Preserve, where they are present from mid-March to early October. Very rare in winter, usually in the Santa Cruz River Valley.

Common Black-Hawk—Uncommon summer resident in Aravaipa Canyon, where perhaps a dozen pairs nest, along the San Pedro River near Winkelman (five miles north of Dudleyville), and in Redfield Canyon in the Galiuro Mountains. In 2004 a pair set up a territory near Summerhaven in the upper Santa Catalina Mountains. The last nest at Patagonia was in 1976. A pair of Common Black-Hawks attempted to nest in Rucker Canyon of the Chiricahua Mountains in 1996, and there are annual reports of migrants from Cave Creek Canyon in spring and fall. A lone bird is sighted sporadically along the upper San Pedro River. Common Black-Hawks remain fairly common in Central Arizona.

Harris's Hawk—Fairly common permanent resident of Sonoran Desert Saguaro thornscrub northwest of Tucson, and uncommon in Chihuahuan Desert thornscrub farther east. Widely scattered populations exist on the Tohono O'Odham Nation lands, in the Sulphur Springs Valley, and in the San Simon Valley. Can ordinarily be found at Roger Road Ponds or adjacent Sweetwater Wetlands in Tucson, and along Highway 77/79 somewhere between Tucson city limits and Florence. Look for it just north of Willcox, off Davis Road, and near Elfrida in the Sulphur Springs Valley. Small numbers also occur near San Simon and along Sulphur Draw Road in the Chiricahua Mountains.

Short-tailed Hawk—Rare during the summer in upper mountain canyons and soaring along rimrock. Two early records by experienced observers, one at Barfoot Junction in the Chiricahua Mountains in August 1985 and another from Sawmill Canyon in the Huachuca Mountains in July 1988, presaged the arrival of a pair in upper Miller Canyon in the summer of 1999. Since 2001 a pair has summered every year at Barfoot Park in the Chiricahua Mountains, and this pair successfully fledged young in 2003. Expanding their range into yet another area, in 2004 a pair frequented the area near Summerhaven in the Santa Catalina Mountains. Most Arizona birds are light-morph individuals, but one bird in Miller Canyon in 1999 was a dark morph. Watch for Short-tailed Hawks riding updrafts on the cliffs overlooking Barfoot Park.

Swainson's Hawk—Common summer resident of the valley mesquite grasslands. Just a few of the localities where Swainson's occur include Highway 82 east of Sonoita, Highway 90 both north and east of Sierra Vista, Highway 92 west of Bisbee, anywhere around Willcox, and Highway 80 both west and east of Douglas—not to mention Interstate 10 from Tucson east to the New Mexico border. In September large numbers of Swainson's Hawks stage in the Sulphur Springs Valley prior to migration.

Zone-tailed Hawk—Fairly common summer resident, rare in winter. Typically nests in the tallest trees in foothill or mountain canyons, but may be observed from the desert in and around Tucson to the summit of Chiricahua Peak. Frequently sighted in Aravaipa Canyon, in Madera Canyon, in the Patagonia-Sonoita Creek Preserve, in Harshaw Canyon, over the Ramsey Canyon Preserve, in the main fork of Cave Creek Canyon between Sunnyflat Campground and the Southwestern Research Station, and in Guadalupe Canyon. To see this bird, double-check every Turkey Vulture. In winter Zone-tailed Hawk is sporadically sighted in Tucson, especially in Reid Park.

Ferruginous Hawk—Fairly common winter visitor in the Sulphur Springs Valley and uncommon in winter elsewhere in valley grasslands and deserts. While Ferruginous is widely distributed throughout the Sulphur Springs Valley, the best place to see them is the agricultural areas off Highway 191 between Elfrida and Sunizona. Ticking a half-dozen of these beautiful raptors is typical if you stick to the highway, but it is not unusual to see 20 or more if you cruise the farm roads in this vicinity. Watch for them perched on the ground in the fields, as well as on irrigation units and power poles. Most are the light morph. Perhaps one in twenty is a dark-morph hawk. Other locations include the San Rafael Grasslands, Marana Pecan Grove, and Red Rock.

Rough-legged Hawk—Rare winter visitor to valley deserts and grasslands. Rough-legs can occasionally be found in the fields east of San Xavier Mission near Tucson, south of the Marana Pecan Grove at the Trico Road-Santa Cruz River crossing, or among the Ferruginous Hawks in the Sulphur Springs Valley.

Golden Eagle—Uncommon permanent resident of valleys and mountains. In years when it is active, there is a an eyrie visible on the cliffs above the Ramsey Canyon Preserve. Other areas to check in summer include the Box Canyon Road on the north end of the Santa Rita Mountains, Garden Canyon in the Huachucas, and Foothills Road on the east side of the Chiricahuas. In winter back roads in the San Rafael Grasslands are frequently productive. Whitewater Draw Wildlife Refuge and Essary Hay are good areas to check year round in the Sulphur Springs Valley.

Crested Caracara—Uncommon permanent resident of the Sonoran Desert, particularly on the Tohono O'odham Nation lands. Watch for them along Highway 86 from the Kitt Peak Junction to Sells. Nearly every winter one turns up in Avra Valley west of Tucson, often roaming the area near the Marana Pecan Grove. Caracaras are also recorded some winters at the Green Valley Sewage Ponds, at Picacho Reservoir, or at the Buenos Aires Wildlife Refuge. Farther east, there are rare reports from the southern Sulphur Springs Valley and the San Bernardino Ranch east of Douglas.

Aplomado Falcon—Locally extirpated. In 1887 H. C. Benson found five nests on Ft. Huachuca, but in three seasons of field work there beginning in 1896 ornithologist Harry S. Swarth never encountered a single Aplomado Falcon. The last state record accepted by the Arizona Bird Committee was of a bird near St. David in the San Pedro Valley in 1940. Misidentified Prairie Falcons and juvenile Swainson's Hawks are thought to account for all subsequent reports of Aplomado Falcon in Arizona. (There are, however, valid recent reports from the Animas Valley in New Mexico.)

Peregrine Falcon—Rare in summer near mountain cliffs and locally uncommon in winter near Tucson and in valley grasslands. Watch for Peregrines soaring above Lemmon Rock Lookout in the Santa Catalina Mountains, over the cliffs in Cave Creek Canyon in the Chiricahuas, or hunting the Sierra Vista Wastewater Ponds during migration in August and September. A pair of Peregrines nested in downtown Tucson in 1995. Because of possible collection by falconers, other known breeding sites are not listed.

Prairie Falcon—Rare in summer near mountain cliffs and uncommon in valleys during winter. Has nested for years in the Organ Formation at Chiricahua National Monument. Because of falconers, other known breeding sites are not listed. During winter watch power poles, dead trees, and other conspicuous perches along the Santa Cruz River near Tucson, in the San Rafael Grasslands, along the San Pedro River, and in the Sulphur Springs Valley.

Sandhill Crane—Common winter visitor to the Sulphur Springs Valley, where approximately 25,000 birds occur in three major groups. The northern population feeds in the stubble fields north and east of Willcox Playa in the area of Kansas Settlement and roosts at Apache Station Wildlife Area and at the Arizona Game and Fish pond north of Kansas Settlement. The southern group frequents the fields southwest of Elfrida between Central Highway and Frontier Road and its primary roost is at Whitewater Draw Wildlife Refuge. A smaller third group is found in fields northwest of Willcox towards Bonita. Both "Lesser" and "Greater" Sandhills are present, but Lessers are by far the most abundant subspecies.

Whooping Crane—Found as a consequence of reintroduction attempts using ultralight aircraft and the Sandhill Crane foster-parent program at Grays Lake, Idaho. These wayward (and "non-countable") Whoopers are seen rarely during winter in the Sulphur Springs Valley. They accompany Sandhill Cranes from the Grays Lake, Idaho, flock. Not detected every year, the first Arizona sighting was in late December 1980, and the most recent was of another that over-wintered in 1998–1999. Probably they will be even less likely in the future, since the foster-parent program using Sandhills to rear Whoopers has been discontinued by the U.S. Fish and Wildlife Service.

Shorebirds—A protracted migration period that begins in July and ends in June means that at least some shorebirds are present every month of the year. The only species which actually breed annually are Killdeer and the summering population of American Avocets at Lake Cochise in Willcox. Snowy Plovers and Black-necked Stilts also nest on occasion. Except for Snowy and Mountain Plovers, all of Southeastern Arizona's regularly-occurring shorebirds are widespread and range to both coasts of the United States. They are treated under the bar graphs in Section III. Shorebirds are found at sewage ponds in Tucson, Nogales, Sierra Vista, and Willcox; irrigated fields in the Santa Cruz and Sulphur Springs Valleys; and around lakes, such as Peña Blanca, Patagonia, and Parker Canyon.

Snowy Plover—Rare and irregular summer and fall resident at Lake Cochise in Willcox, where it has bred. Rare migrant at other valley sewage ponds, such as those near Tucson and Sierra Vista, in late April and May and again in August and September.

Mountain Plover—Most years an uncommon but very local winter visitor to barren valley fields and open desert. Some years there are 100 birds or more during January in a large flock along Rucker Canyon Road at Essary Hay in the Sulphur Springs Valley. A smaller group can occasionally be found a few miles away in the fields off Central Highway south and west of McNeal. Most winters Mountain Plovers are also recorded near the Marana Pecan Grove and at the Arizona Sod Farm in the Santa Cruz Flats. In rare years Mountain Plover goes almost entirely unreported in Southeastern Arizona.

Band-tailed Pigeon—Fairly common summer resident of oak, pine-oak, and coniferous forests in the mountains. Rare and irregular in winter. The nesting and feeding habits of Band-tails are erratic, so it is difficult to predict just where and when these birds will be found. The loud clapping of their wings upon take-off is usually the first clue of their presence in areas like Barfoot Park, South Fork Cave Creek, or at the Southwestern Research Station in the Chiricahuas. Also watch for them in tall, dead snags along the Reef Road in the Huachucas, or along the Catalina Highway above Bear Canyon in the Santa Catalina Mountains. Most summers a few are also present just upstream from the Patons' home in Patagonia, or at the Patagonia-Sonoita Creek Preserve. There are a few recent reports from Tucson.

Eurasian Collared-Dove—First recorded at Marana Pecan Grove in 2000, and now apparently established as a year-round resident in agricultural valleys. The largest colony in Southeastern Arizona at this writing is about 30 miles northwest of Tucson at Red Rock, where there are more than 50 birds at the feedlot alone. Another group is located in residential Benson, and for the past several years a pair has attempted to nest at the Willcox golf course adjacent to Lake Cochise. Records now exist for most other agricultural areas throughout the region.

White-winged Dove—Common summer resident of the Lower Sonoran Life Zone and the lower oak woodlands. A few winter near Tucson, Red Rock, Green Valley, Nogales, Patagonia, and Douglas. Common from April through September in such areas as the Arizona-Sonora Desert Museum, Saguaro National Park, lower Madera Canyon, Patagonia-Sonoita Creek Preserve, along the San Pedro River, and Portal.

Inca Dove—Common permanent resident in cities and towns at lower elevations. Avoids unpopulated areas. Look for it in city parks in Tucson, at the Arizona-Sonora Desert Museum, at the Patons' home in Patagonia, and at the 10th Street Park in Douglas. Numbers fluctuate, probably in response to long-term weather patterns.

Common Ground-Dove—Fairly common permanent resident of better-watered valleys at lower elevations. Avoids town areas but frequents weedy farm fields. Can be found in Avra Valley, along the Santa Cruz River, Sonoita Creek, and the San Pedro River. A few specific locations are Avra Valley Sewage Ponds, Kino Springs, Patagonia-Sonoita Creek Preserve, and the San Pedro House. Approximately once a year one turns up at Portal or Willow Tank on the east side of the Chiricahua Mountains.

Ruddy Ground-Dove—Rare but regular in recent winters in the same river valleys as Common Ground-Doves. Recently, very rare in summer at Red Rock. Ironically, Ruddies often ignore the little flocks of closely related Commons, and choose to associate with Inca Doves. Distinguishing between female Ruddy and Common Ground-Doves can be difficult. Ruddies have dark gray bills (never reddish), lack scaling on the neck and breast, have black (not violet or chestnut) markings on the wing coverts and scapulars, and a longer tail which is warm brown (not gray). The Marana Pecan Grove, Arivaca, and Patagonia all have a good track record for attracting this Mexican stray, but in 2003 and 2004 the best location was 30 miles up Interstate 10 northwest of Tucson at the cattle feedlot in Red Rock. Ruddy Ground-Dove was first recorded in Arizona in October 1981.

Thick-billed Parrot—Formerly irruptive to the mountains of southeastern Arizona. The last wild flock was reported from Chiricahua National Monument in 1938. Twenty-six birds were released in the Chiricahua Mountains in 1986, but unfortunately none of these apparently survived for more than a few years. The re-introduced (and "non-countable") flock tended to leave the Chiricahuas in summer. Thick-bills attempted to nest several times near Payson in central Arizona, but no nests are known to have succeeded. After breeding season, the parrots returned to the Chiricahuas in late summer or fall. Unless more releases occur in the future, Thick-bills may have vanished from Arizona for the last time.

Yellow-billed Cuckoo—Fairly common summer resident of valley riparian woodlands. Although a few individuals show up in May, the bulk of the population does not arrive until the second week of June. The largest concentration of Yellow-billed Cuckoos in the U.S. breed along the San Pedro River, and they are also relatively common at the Patagonia-Sonoita Creek Preserve, Kino Springs, and Arivaca Creek. Every summer a stray bird shows up in Portal or Garden Canyon in mountain canyon groves, generally for one day only.

Greater Roadrunner—Common permanent resident of open deserts and valley grasslands, occasionally entering lower mountain canyons. Occurs in and around Tucson at places like Sweetwater Wetlands and Agua Caliente Park. Farther afield, try the back roads in Avra Valley, the Marana Pecan

Grove, lower Ramsey Canyon Road, Coffman Road near Whitewater Draw in the Sulphur Springs Valley, and the road between San Simon and Portal.

Groove-billed Ani—A sporadic visitant across the Mexican border, primarily in summer and fall, to wet valley areas with rank vegetation. Approximately 20 records since 1980. Some of the locations where anis have been found include Marana Pecan Grove, Arivaca Creek, Sierra Vista Sewage Ponds, and near the confluence of Escapule Wash with the San Pedro River. If present, it will be on the Tucson Audubon Society hotline and the AZ/NM BirdChat Listserve.

Barn Owl—Fairly common permanent resident of old buildings, abandoned mine shafts and wells, highway bridge abutments, and dense groves of trees in valleys and foothills. Inquiring minds can usually find this owl during the daytime if they check enough potential roosts—or ask the local owlers. Some of the best areas to search are in Avra Valley west of Tucson, the Marana Pecan Grove, and the Sulphur Springs Valley north of Douglas. *Ask permission before trespassing on private property or snooping around someone's barn!*

Flammulated Owl—Fairly common but rarely seen summer resident of mountain pine-oak woodland and Ponderosa Pine forest, often along streams where the trees are large. Locations include one-half-mile up the trail in the Hopkins Fork of Madera Canyon (*use of tapes not permitted*) in the Santa Rita Mountains, one mile up Miller Canyon Trail in the Huachuca Mountains, South Fork Cave Creek (*no tapes permitted*), and either Pinery Canyon Campground or Rustler Park in the Chiricahua Mountains. Some years present between Idlewilde and Sunnyflat Campgrounds in Cave Creek Canyon of the Chiricahuas, but other years there are none in that area. When feeding at dawn or dusk, it is usually silent. During the remainder of the night when it is less active, it will often sit on the same perch and softly hoot for hours. However, its call, consisting of a single low toot given at regular intervals as much as five seconds or more apart, is easily missed. Although Flammulated will readily answer an imitation of its call, it seldom shows itself. Look for it close to the trunk of a large, dense tree, especially a Douglas-fir or an Alligator Juniper. Flammulated Owl is almost entirely silent after July.

Western Screech-Owl—Fairly common permanent resident of Saguaros, valley cottonwoods, and open, lower canyon woodlands. It seems to avoid the dense Madrean pine-oak woodlands occupied by the Whiskered Screech-Owl. Responds well to either an imitation or a tape-recording of its call. Proven locations include Catalina State Park north of Tucson, the Patagonia-Sonoita Creek Preserve (*no tapes permitted*), the Hereford Bridge on the San Pedro River, and Portal and Paradise in the Chiricahua Mountains.

Whiskered Screech-Owl—Common permanent resident of Madrean pine-oak woodlands in all the major ranges. Its characteristic "Morse Code" call may be heard from April to June in the Santa Catalina Mountains at Bear Canyon Campground, in Madera Canyon in the Santa Rita Mountains anywhere from the lower picnic area to the upper end of the road (*tapes not permitted*), at the end of the road in Miller Canyon in the Huachuca Mountains, and either in Cave Creek Canyon above the Visitor Information Station, or at Pinery Canyon Campground in the Chiricahua Mountains. Occasionally during nesting season, a male may be found snoozing on a daytime roost at the entrance to its hole.

Northern Pygmy-Owl—Uncommon permanent resident throughout the mountains, especially in pine-oak woodlands with big Alligator Juniper trees, but also in Ponderosa Pine. Although this owl responds well to imitations of its call both day and night, and almost at any season, it has a very large territory up to a mile in length. Your chances of hearing it are best at dawn. Walk a mountain trail at daybreak and stop every half-mile to try its call. Bog Springs in Madera Canyon, upper Garden Canyon in the Huachuca Mountains, and Cave Creek Canyon anywhere above Sunnyflat Campground in the Chiricahuas are all good locations. "Mountain Pygmy-Owl," the subspecies found in the border ranges, uses a fast, double-noted toot. In Southeastern Arizona the slower, single-tooting *pinicola* form of the Northern Pygmy-Owl is probably limited to the upper elevations of the Santa Catalina Mountains.

Ferruginous Pygmy-Owl—Rare and local resident in the Lower Sonoran Life Zone from Tucson west. Seen once at the Patagonia Roadside Rest Area and found several times in upper Sycamore Canyon west of Nogales, not far from Hank and Yank Spring. Most records are for the spring or summer. The subspecies found in our area is called the "Cactus Ferruginous Pygmy-Owl," and it was still federally listed as endangered in 2004, although efforts were underway by the Arizona homebuilding industry to de-list it. Some recent sightings have been in northwest Tucson, off the north end of the Tucson Mountains, at Dudleyville, at Buenos Aires National Wildlife Refuge, and at Organ Pipe Cactus National Monument, west of our area. In June this owl toots monotonously throughout much of the day, especially at dawn.

Elf Owl—Common summer resident of desert Saguaros, valley and foothill cottonwood groves, and sycamore canyons in the mountains. Best located between March and mid-July by their weird, laughing calls at Catalina State Park, Madera Canyon, or Cave Creek Canyon. For years, Elf Owls have nested in telephone poles at the Santa Rita Lodge, and standing vigil to see them emerge at dusk has become a springtime ritual for both local and out-of-area birders.

Burrowing Owl—Uncommon and declining summer resident of open deserts and valley grassland. Rare in winter in the same locations. Has been found along the Santa Cruz River near San Xavier Mission, the Marana Pecan Grove, Western Sod Farm in the Santa Cruz Flats, in the desert east of Cochise College near Douglas, and along Stateline Road near Portal. Populations of Burrowing Owls collapsed throughout Southeastern Arizona in the 1980s.

Spotted Owl—Uncommon permanent resident of dense coniferous forest and cool, shady canyons. "Mexican Spotted Owl," the race that occurs in Southeastern Arizona, nests almost exclusively in pot holes in cliffs. Roosts, however, are usually in thick groves of trees, 15 feet or less above the ground. Each pair has a large territory of several square miles. Except in the narrow confines of Scheelite Canyon in the Huachucas, this is a difficult species to see. Some locations where it has been heard are above the end of the road in Madera Canyon in the Santa Rita Mountains, in Harshaw Canyon east of Patagonia, French Joe Canyon in the Whetstone Mountains, upper Miller Canyon in the Huachuca Mountains, and along the South Fork Road in the Chiricahua Mountains. Spotted Owl has also wintered at low elevation in Sabino Canyon in the front range of the Santa Catalina Mountains, and in February and March of 2003 in the town of Oro Valley just northwest of Tucson.

Northern Saw-whet Owl—Rare permanent resident in mountain pine-oak woodland and coniferous forest. Most winters at least one bird is found roosting in dense shrubbery at a valley oasis such as the Arizona-Sonora Desert Museum. Almost all other sightings occur between mid-March and mid-June when the birds are calling. Most records are from the Chiricahuas, either from near Barfoot Junction or Pinery Canyon Campground, but there are also recent reports from Rose Canyon Lake and Willow Canyon in the Santa Catalina Mountains. To see this bashful owl, check the Tucson Audubon Society hotline or the AZ/NM BirdChat Listserve.

Lesser Nighthawk—Common summer resident in deserts and valley grasslands. At dawn and dusk, aggregations of a dozen to over a hundred assemble over stock tanks and sewage ponds, around street lights and parking lots in shopping malls, and along dirt roads and arroyos in the desert. The Avra Valley Sewage Ponds on Snyder Hill Road, the intersection of Speedway and Anklam Road west of Tucson, lower Madera Canyon, the Sierra Vista Wastewater Ponds, Kingfisher Pond near the San Pedro House, Cochise College west of Douglas, and the ford over Cave Creek on the San Simon Road east of Portal are all dependable localities.

Common Nighthawk—Uncommon and local summer resident of the high grasslands near Sonoita, south of the Huachucas, and west of the Chiricahua Mountains. Lesser Nighthawks outnumber Commons by at least 1000 to 1 at all other locations in the Southeast corner, and cannot safely be separated simply by how high above the ground they forage. Look for the pointed wing-tip of Common Nighthawk; Lesser's have a rounded wing-tip.

Common Poorwill—Common summer resident of deserts and foothills on dry, warm slopes. A few are active in winter. This is the only bird known to hibernate. The poorwill is usually found at lower elevations than the Whip-poor-will, although infrequently both species may be heard calling from the same canyon clearing in pine-oak woodland. One way to find this bird is to drive back roads through the desert at night and watch for its bright orange eyeshine. Some good roads to try are the Box Canyon Road which turns off halfway up the Madera Canyon Road, Escapule Road along the San Pedro River, and dirt roads near Portal, such as the San Simon Road or the Silver Creek Road to Paradise. On warmer, moonlit nights near Portal a sleepy Poorwill may sound off even in mid-winter.

Buff-collared Nightjar—Rare summer resident of foothill thornscrub canyons with rocky hillsides. Buff-collared Nightjar was first discovered in the United States in Guadalupe Canyon in 1960. Since then it has been detected in virtually every appropriate subtropical habitat in Southeastern Arizona. Its accelerating, ascending, piano-like song sounds like *Presta-me-tu-cuchillo*—or "Lend-me-your-knife" to the people in Mexico, and that is its Spanish name. This inconfusable call is the best way to identify the Buff-collar, since the color of its neck band is difficult to see after dark, even with powerful lights. Primary locations include the west end parking area at Aravaipa Canyon, Sutherland Wash in Catalina State Park, McCleary Wash just east of the Madera Canyon Road, and Guadalupe Canyon east of Douglas. In the summers of 2002, 2003, and 2004 the only reliable Buff-collared Nightjar in Southeastern Arizona was using the Oro Blanco Mine area, a short distance from the Five-striped Sparrow site in California Gulch.

Whip-poor-will—Common summer resident in Madrean pine-oak woodland and coniferous forest in the mountains. Easy to hear in major canyons of the border ranges, such as Madera, Miller, or Cave Creek. Also common in campgrounds at high elevations in the Santa Catalina, Huachuca, and Chiricahua Mountains. It feeds low among trees, as well as in clearings, and it often lands on a low limb, rather than on the ground. The loud, repetitive songs of Whip-poor-wills in the higher mountains during May and June have caused more insomnia than any actual or imagined incidents involving Black Bears and Mountains Lions combined. Southwestern Whip-poor-wills sing a low-pitched, burry song—*purple-whip!*—that may lead to full species rank for this race in the future.

Black Swift—Very rare and irregular migrant and summer resident in upper Cave Creek Canyon above Herb Martyr Recreation Area in the Chiricahua Mountains, with sight reports separated by intervals of several years. Most records fall between May and August. Once observed in the Upper San Pedro Valley at Hereford in late September 1988. In the absence of photographic documentation, this species is considered only hypothetical in Arizona.

Vaux's Swift—Rare spring and uncommon fall migrant through valleys and along mountain crests. Vaux's are reported every year from Tucson, Nogales, and Patagonia. It is most common in the western sector of Southeastern Arizona, although there are a few reports annually from the upper San Pedro River and the Chiricahua Mountains.

White-throated Swift—Common summer resident and uncommon in winter around cliffs at all elevations. Less active in cold weather. Its twittering call signals its presence throughout the summer at Sabino Canyon, Gates Pass in the Tucson Mountains, Madera Canyon, the Patagonia Roadside Area, the Reef in upper Carr Canyon, Montezuma Pass in Coronado National Monument, Chiricahua National Monument, and Cave Creek Canyon. Lookouts stationed on Mt. Bigelow in the Santa Catalina Mountains and on Barfoot in the Chiricahua Mountains observe White-throated Swifts exhibiting their aerial skills throughout the summer. In winter also watch for it in valley areas well removed from the mountains, such as at the Marana Pecan Grove, Río Rico, Kino Springs, and Essary Hay in the Sulphur Springs Valley.

Broad-billed Hummingbird—Common summer resident in mesquite, cottonwood, and sycamore riparian woodlands of foothills and the lower parts of the mountains. A few are resident in the upper desert housing areas around the northern and western perimeter of Tucson. Most easily found from April through August in Sycamore Canyon west of Nogales, the lower half of Madera Canyon, the Patagonia-Sonoita Creek Preserve, and Guadalupe Canyon, particularly at feeders. In recent years this species has become established in the eastern canyons of the Chiricahua Mountains, especially at Portal, but it is still uncommon there.

White-eared Hummingbird—Rare summer visitor to the mountains. Wintered at Ramsey Canyon in 1993, where one to six birds have been present either at the Preserve or at the Ramsey Canyon Inn Bed & Breakfast just downcanyon every year since 1989. Recently more birds have been reported from Miller Canyon than from any other location in Southeastern Arizona. Although most observations come from feeders in Madera, Ramsey, Miller, and Cave Creek Canyons, this is a bird of pine-oak forests in the Sierra Madre. Look for it high in the mountains where penstemons are still blooming in late summer, such as at Comfort Spring in the upper Huachuca Mountains and feeders at the Iron Door Ski Lodge in the Santa Catalina Mountains.

Berylline Hummingbird—Very rare but virtually annual visitor to Sierra Madrean pine-oak woodland in the border ranges in summer. Recorded from feeders in Madera, Ramsey, Miller, Ash, and Cave Creek Canyons. It has also been recorded in the Transition Life Zone at Comfort Spring in the Huachuca Mountains. First nested successfully in the Ramsey Canyon Preserve in 1978, and at the head of the Natural Bridge Trail in Chiricahua National Monument in 1984. Since then has nested multiple times in Ramsey Canyon, most recently in 2004. Hybrids with both Magnificent and Broad-billed Hummingbirds are probably more common than pure Beryllines in Southeastern Arizona. Look for clues of mixed ancestry such as a blue chest, brown wings, solid black bill, or a white dot behind the eye to determine whether a bird is a hybrid or a true Berylline.

Cinnamon Hummingbird—Vagrant to Patons' feeders in Patagonia in July 1992. This dry-tropic species ranges from northwest Costa Rica to northwest Mexico, so it was not entirely unexpected. Birders should be alert for stray Cinnamons in the same subtropical thornscrub situations used by

Buff-collared Nightjar, Black-capped Gnatcatcher, and Five-striped Sparrow. Look for a fairly large hummer with entirely cinnamon underparts, a rufous tail, and an almost all-red bill.

Violet-crowned Hummingbird—Locally uncommon summer resident and rare in winter in the riparian woodlands of the foothills and lower mountains. Your best chance of seeing one is at Patons' feeders at Patagonia, which have had as many as four present at once. They are also regular at the Patagonia Roadside Rest Area, at the Southeastern Arizona Bird Observatory's feeders in Banning Creek, in Guadalupe Canyon, and at the Jensons' feeders in downtown Portal. After that, they are most apt to be found at feeders in Madera, Ramsey, Miller, Ash, and Cave Creek Canyons. The nest is in a sycamore tree on a twig with a large overhanging leaf for a roof. In winter Violet-crowned Hummingbird is most often seen at private residence feeders in Tucson, Green Valley, Patagonia, Bisbee, and Douglas. The first overwintering Violet-crowned Hummingbird in Portal was recorded in 1998–1999, and they are now also regular there.

Blue-throated Hummingbird—Fairly common summer resident of sycamore canyons in the border mountains; rare there in winter. Invariably present at feeders in Madera, Ramsey, Miller, and Cave Creek Canyons, where a few ordinarily overwinter every year. Has also wintered at feeders in Tucson. It usually announces its arrival with loud, piercing *seep* notes. This is the largest hummingbird in the United States, and it is dominant over all other species.

Magnificent Hummingbird—Common summer resident of sycamore canyons and open glades in coniferous forest up to 9,000 feet in all the mountains of the southeast corner. Rare in sycamore canyons in winter. Common at feeders at Ski Valley in the Santa Catalina Mountains, and in Madera, Ramsey, and Cave Creek Canyons, where a few ordinarily overwinter every year. As the second-largest U.S. hummingbird, Magnificents are subordinate only to Blue-throats at feeding stations.

Plain-capped Starthroat—Very rare summer visitor to arid, lower mountain canyons with agaves, almost annual since 1985. Records since then have come from Sabino Canyon, McCleary Wash, Atascosa Mountains, Patagonia, French Joe Canyon in the Whetstone Mountains, Stump Canyon and Coronado National Memorial in the Huachucas, and the east side of the Chiricahuas in Portal, Silver Creek, and Whitetail Canyon. In the summer of 2002 a Plain-capped Starthroat banded in Miller Canyon moved to nearby Ash Canyon, and the same individual returned to Ash Canyon again in 2003. Altogether there have been about 20 records of starthroat since 1985.

Lucifer Hummingbird—Rare summer resident in arid, lower mountain canyons with agaves. Most apt to be seen at canyon feeders in April and May and again in August and September, before and after the peak agave blossoming period. Some recent records are from northeast Tucson, the Santa

Rita Lodge in Madera Canyon, Sonoita, Patagonia, Ramsey Canyon Preserve, Miller Canyon, Coronado National Memorial, reliably at Mary Jo Ballator's feeders in Ash Canyon of the Huachuca Mountains, and also annually at the Southeastern Arizona Bird Observatory's field office feeders in Banning Creek in the Mule Mountains. Formerly fairly common in and around Portal, Lucifers largely disappeared from the eastern flank of the Chiricahuas in 2001, but they are likely to return in the future.

Black-chinned Hummingbird—Common summer resident of the desert, foothills, and lower mountain canyons. From April through September Black-chins are the most abundant and widespread hummingbird in this area. Invariably at feeders in Tucson and Patagonia and in Madera, Ramsey, Miller, Ash, and Cave Creek Canyons.

Anna's Hummingbird—Common winter resident and uncommon summer visitor primarily in the western deserts and western foothills. Some birds reach 7,000 feet in Ponderosa Pine forest in the Santa Catalina Mountains. In late summer and early fall squadrons of Anna's invade the lower canyons of the Huachuca and Chiricahua Mountains. In fact, since the early 1980s this has become one of the most abundant hummingbirds from August through mid-October in Ramsey, Miller, and Ash Canyons in the Huachuca Mountains and at Portal in the Chiricahua Mountains. During winter Anna's is common at flowers and feeders in Tucson and at the Marana Pecan Grove, and progressively less common to the east. From spring through mid-summer only a few birds are apt to be seen at the Patons' feeders in Patagonia, the Beattys' feeders in Miller Canyon, Mary Jo Ballator's feeders in Ash Canyon, and private feeders in Portal.

Costa's Hummingbird—Fairly common in winter and spring on the low deserts around Tucson, where it nests; uncommon in summer and very rare in fall in foothill and valley riparian thickets. After nesting it begins to disperse in May, and most are gone by July. In winter and spring, it can usually be found at Tucson feeders, the Arizona-Sonora Desert Museum, and Florida Canyon where it intersects the Madera Canyon Road. In summer look for this species at the head of Sycamore Canyon west of Nogales, Kino Springs, the Patons' home in Patagonia, the Ballator home in Ash Canyon, and feeders at Portal. Document any Costa's sighting anywhere away from the Arizona-Sonora Desert Museum in September and October.

Calliope Hummingbird—Rare spring and uncommon fall migrant in the mountain canyons and meadows. From September through October females also exploit gardens and ornamental plantings in the valleys. Feeders at the Ski Valley area in the Santa Catalina Mountains, Miller Canyon, and at the Portal Store, and the agave stand at Silver Creek Spring four miles northwest of Portal have proven reliable locations for males of the smallest avian species in the U.S. In fall apricot-bellied little females are fairly common on flowers at Cochise College west of Douglas, as well as at the sites mentioned above.

Bumblebee Hummingbird—Two females were collected in July 1896 and labeled from Ramsey Canyon in the Huachuca Mountains, although now there is some doubt about this actually being the locale. Since then there have been no other accepted records. The nearest Mexican population is 300 miles southeast in the Sierra Madre of Chihuahua, where the birds prefer low brambles in pine-oak woodland. Females resemble female Calliopes, but they average one-half inch shorter, have short wings that do not project beyond the tail, have bright cinnamon sides that contrast with a white collar, and have extensively rufous-based tails that usually feature buffy outer tail-feather tips. Tiny male Bumblebees have elongate purple-red gorgets and extensive rufous-cinnamon at the base of tail.

Broad-tailed Hummingbird—Common summer resident of the coniferous forests of the higher mountains. Less common along streams in the Sierra-Madrean pine-oak woodlands. During spring and fall Broad-tails can also be found at flower patches anywhere from desert oases to the summits of all major ranges. The high-pitched trill generated by the wings of the male is heard more frequently than the bird is seen. While it occurs throughout the mountains of Southeastern Arizona, in mid-summer it is most common at feeders in the high Santa Catalina Mountains, at Ramsey and Miller Canyons in the Huachucas, and from Portal and Paradise. When the Rocky Mountain Iris blossoms in June, the shrill wing trills of fighting males are a serious threat to the serenity of meadows such as Rustler Park in the Chiricahuas.

Rufous Hummingbird—Uncommon spring migrant in the Sonoran Desert near Tucson, and almost rare in lower mountain canyons; common fall migrant in the mountains at all elevations, and at desert oases such as Tucson. From late July until October, it may be seen at feeders at Ski Valley and Summerhaven in the Santa Catalinas, Madera Canyon in the Santa Ritas, the Patons' feeders at Patagonia, Ramsey, Miller, and Ash Canyon in the Huachucas, and Portal and Paradise in the Chiricahuas. Agave stands like the one at Silver Creek Spring in the Chiricahuas are heavily patronized by returning Rufous. When the delphinium and salvia are in bloom from late July till mid-September, the mountain meadows may swarm with these golden fighters.

Allen's Hummingbird—Recent banding studies have shown that female and immature Allen's are uncommon migrants in the mountain canyons in July and August. Adult males are rare migrants in the same areas, primarily in July, although a few turn up at feeding stations as late as mid-August. Most records are from the Huachuca Mountains westward. Since female and immature Allen's and Rufous are virtually impossible to separate under field conditions, only adult males of this species can be safely identified. Watch for full adult male Allen's at feeders in Ski Valley and Summerhaven, at Sonoita and Patagonia, and at Madera, Ramsey, and Ash Canyons.

Elegant Trogon—Fairly common summer resident of deep sycamore canyons within Sierra Madrean pine-oak woodland in the border ranges. In spring and early summer trogons are frequently heard (emitting a series of croaking *co-ah* calls) before being seen, as males patrol up and down riparian corridors, advertising for mates or maintaining territorial boundaries. After the young fledge in July or August, however, adult trogons are largely silent. Territories average one-half-mile long in prime habitat such as Sycamore Canyon in the Atascosas, Madera and Josephine Canyons in the Santa Ritas, Sunnyside and Garden Canyons in the Huachucas, and Cave Creek and South Fork Canyons in the Chiricahua Mountains. Trogons in Madera, Garden, and Cave Creek Canyons are ordinarily the most accessible. But in 1994 a pair successfully fledged two young in the Ramsey Canyon Preserve, and the family was often observed on the edge of the visitor center parking lot. Probably one to five trogons overwinter in Arizona every year. Sonoita Creek above Patagonia Lake has been a reliable location for the past decade. Other areas with recent wintering trogons are lower Madera Canyon and Florida Canyon in the Santa Rita Mountains, Sycamore Canyon in the Atascosas, Garden Canyon in the Huachucas, and lower Cave Creek Canyon near Portal in the Chiricahua Mountains.

Eared Quetzal—Probably a very rare resident of upper pine-oak woodland and coniferous forest in the Huachuca and Chiricahua Mountains, most often descending into sycamore canyons during fall. Also recorded in the Josephine and Hopkins Forks of Madera Canyon in the Santa Rita Mountains in July and August of 1991. Since its first appearance October 1977 in the South Fork of Cave Creek Canyon, Eared Quetzal has been observed most of the intervening years, usually between August and November. In October 1991 a nest found high in Ramsey Canyon subsequently failed when an early freeze apparently killed the nestlings. Eared Quetzals have also been seen in Scheelite, Carr, and Miller Canyons in the Huachucas, and the North Fork, Snowshed Fork, and Main Fork of Cave Creek in the Chiricahuas. Listen for its *squee-chuck* call.

Green Kingfisher—Rare resident of valley tree-lined ponds and sluggish waters along Arivaca and Sonoita Creeks, and the Santa Cruz and San Pedro Rivers. The first known successful nesting of Green Kingfisher in Arizona was in the San Pedro National Conservation Area in 1989. In 1993 BLM biologists noted at least 15 kingfishers using the NCA, but numbers have fallen in recent years. The most reliable place to look for this species is at the appropriately named Kingfisher Pond, one-half-mile south of the San Pedro House, and along the river trail that runs north from the pond almost to the Highway 90 Bridge. Other proven sites are Kino Springs east of Nogales and the north railroad bridge abutment in the Patagonia-Sonoita Creek Preserve.

Lewis's Woodpecker—Rare transient and irregularly uncommon winter visitor to deciduous groves in lower mountain canyons and valleys. Pecan groves are favored wintering areas in Southeastern Arizona. Tall dead trees or utility poles for perches seem to be an important habitat component. Most winters one or more is present at Fort Lowell and/or Reid Park in Tucson, at the Marana Pecan Grove, in the Continental area, or just upstream along Sonoita Creek from the Patons' home in Patagonia. Some winters they also occur at Fairbank on the San Pedro River and at Paradise in the Chiricahua Mountains.

Acorn Woodpecker—Common and obvious permanent resident of canyons within oak and pine-oak woodlands. Integral to Acorn Woodpecker habitat is standing dead timber in which the birds can store acorns. It's tough to miss this species in places like Bear Canyon in the Santa Catalina Mountains, Madera Canyon, Ramsey Canyon, or Cave Creek Canyon. Less common in and around Paragonia. After the 1994 Rattlesnake Fire in the Chiricahuas, Acorn Woodpeckers now summer in the burn at elevations above 9,000 feet.

Gila Woodpecker—Common resident in Saguaro forests of the Sonoran Desert and valley cottonwood groves. Almost confined to Arizona within the U.S., Gilas are a conspicuous feature of the avian landscape at the Arizona-Sonora Desert Museum, Tubac, Patagonia-Sonoita Creek Preserve, the San Pedro River, and Guadalupe Canyon.

Williamson's Sapsucker—Uncommon migrant and rare winter visitor in mountain Ponderosa Pines and major mountains canyons. Most common in the Chiricahua Mountains and in the months of September and April. Rustler and Barfoot Parks and the meadow edges along the crest in the Chiricahua Wilderness Area are the best areas. Most years one or more winter in Sawmill Canyon in the Huachucas and on Organization Ridge in the Santa Catalinas. Some winters a Williamson's Sapsucker assumes quarters in a valley grove or desert oasis such the pecan grove at Continental. These birds usually make the Tucson Audubon Society rare bird tape and the AZ/NM BirdChat Listserve.

Yellow-bellied Sapsucker—Rare winter visitor in valley groves, orchards, and lower canyon deciduous trees. Beginning with the winter of 2000–2001 a lone bird has been present at the Continental Workyard. Another was found in early 2003 over-wintering at the clubhouse at Kino Springs. In February of 2004 Yellow-bellied Sapsucker was found below Proctor Road in lower Madera Canyon, and in October 2004 one was at Peña Blanca Lake and another was upstream of Patagonia Lake. This species is easily confused with Red-naped Sapsucker, but in adult birds the throat is always heavily outlined in black. Any brown juvenile after October also belongs to this species.

Red-naped Sapsucker—Fairly common winter visitor to desert oases with deciduous trees, valley groves, and wooded mountain canyons, especially in pecan and apple orchards. Numbers peak in March and October, when it usually easy to find in the ash trees by the otter pool at the Arizona-Sonora Desert Museum, Sabino Canyon, Kino Springs, Madera Canyon, Ramsey Canyon, and anywhere in Cave Creek Canyon.

Red-breasted Sapsucker—Casual winter visitor to desert oases with deciduous trees, valley groves, and wooded mountain canyons. Recent records are from Woodland Road in Tucson, Patagonia Lake, and Whitetail Canyon in the Chiricahua Mountains. Hybrids with Red-naped Sapsucker, showing Red-naped's black facial pattern under a veneer of red, are seen every winter.

Ladder-backed Woodpecker—Fairly common permanent resident of the mesquite deserts, Soaptree Yucca valley grasslands, and the more arid oak woodlands. Usually found in pairs in such areas as Saguaro National Park, Marana Pecan Grove, Patagonia Lake, Patagonia Roadside Rest Area, San Pedro House, below Portal, and at the outlets of all of the canyons of the larger mountains.

Arizona Woodpecker—Fairly common permanent resident of the Sierra Madrean pine-oak woodlands of all the mountain ranges. Look for it at Bear Canyon in the Santa Catalinas, Madera Canyon in the Santa Ritas, Ramsey Canyon in the Huachucas, and South Fork Cave Creek in the Chiricahua Mountains. In the Chiricahuas, it is also quite common on the dry hillsides along the Trans-mountain Road between the Southwestern Research Station and Onion Saddle. In midsummer after breeding season, some move upslope into the arid oak woodlands where other Sierra Madrean specialties are not as common. During spring, listen for its sharp *peek* call note, very similar to that of a Hairy Woodpecker, in all the major canyons of the border ranges.

Northern Flicker—"Red- shafted" Flickers are common residents from foothill riparian groves up to the mountaintop coniferous forests in the border ranges, although heavy snow and severe cold probably pushes high- elevation birds down temporarily. An influx of northern migrants augments resident populations from late September through early April, and spreads into valley groves and desert oases. Northern Flickers can be found in Madera Canyon, Miller Canyon, and Cave Creek Canyon, as well as Bear Wallow in the Santa Catalina Mountains, along upper Carr Canyon Road in the Huachucas, and Rustler Park in the Chiricahua Mountains. In winter Northern Flickers visit Sweetwater Wetlands in Tucson, the Marana Pecan Grove, Kino Springs, and Patagonia Lake, where they share the habitat with Gilded Flickers. "Yellow-shafted" Northern Flickers are winter vagrants in Southeastern Arizona, primarily to lowland riparian, towns, pecan groves, and lower mountains canyons.

Gilded Flicker—Common resident in Saguaro forests and decreasingly common in valley cottonwood groves east to the upper San Pedro Valley. The easternmost birds are apt to show some hybrid characters from "Red-shafted" Northern Flickers. Gilded Flicker is easily separated in Arizona by the yellow undersurfaces on the tail and flight feathers. Perched, note that Gilded has a bright cinnamon crown. Look for Gilded Flickers at Saguaro National Park west of Tucson, San Xavier Mission, Kino Springs, the

Patagonia-Sonoita Creek Preserve, and the San Pedro House on the San Pedro River east of Sierra Vista.

Northern Beardless-Tyrannulet—Uncommon to fairly common summer resident in riparian thickets of mesquite, hackberry, and cottonwoods in foothills and canyon mouths. Rare in winter. Look—and *listen*—for it at Catalina State Park, Agua Caliente Park northeast of Tucson, Aravaipa Canyon, Florida Wash, in Sycamore Canyon and California Gulch west of Nogales, at the Patagonia Roadside Rest, and in Guadalupe Canyon. This nondescript little bird is occasionally misidentified as another small flycatcher or even as a vireo. Its bushy little crest, distinct eyebrow, and more horizontal posture should separate it from *Empidonax* flycatchers. The surest means of identification is its song, a short series of four to five loud, clear *peer* notes. Calling birds have orange mouths.

Olive-sided Flycatcher—Uncommon migrant from foothill groves up to mountain coniferous forest. Uses—and reuses—conspicuous perches, often in dead treetops. Areas that transient birds seem to favor, at least temporarily, include near the road-end in West Aravaipa Canyon, Patagonia Preserve, Patagonia Roadside Rest, the staff residence area in Ramsey Canyon, Paradise and Barfoot Junction in the Chiricahua Mountains, and Guadalupe Canyon.

Greater Pewee—Uncommon summer resident of the pines and pine-oak woodlands of the higher mountains. Rare in winter at the outlets of major canyons and in valley pecan and cottonwood groves. Its large nesting territory may include riparian woodland and adjacent slopes. Usually feeds from a tree top in typical pewee fashion, but seems to prefer taller trees than those used by the Western Wood-Pewee. Once its very distinctive and dulcet *José Maria* (*ho-SAY mah-REE-ah*) call is learned, the voice of Greater Pewee is easy to pull out of the dawn chorus in appropriate habitat. During summer listen for it in such areas as along the Catalina Highway from Bear Canyon up, one-half-mile up the Hopkins Fork of Madera Canyon, the staff residence at the end of the nature trail in Ramsey Canyon, Sawmill Campground in the upper end of Garden Canyon in the Huachucas, and at the Herb Martyr parking lot and at the Barfoot Junction on the Rustler Park Road in the Chiricahuas. The distinctive *pip* note used by overwintering pewees has led to the discovery of birds in Tucson, at the Marana Pecan Grove, lower Madera Canyon, and at Patagonia, far below the mountains where they breed.

Western Wood-Pewee—Abundant summer resident of the pines, oaks, and riparian woodlands of the mountains and river valleys. Nesting at 100-yard intervals in appropriate habitat, this bird is so common, conspicuous, and noisy that it is almost impossible to miss in the proper season, particularly in early morning and late afternoon. Look for it in Madera, Ramsey, and Cave Creek Canyons. On the other hand, Western-Wood Pewees are so nondescript they are occasionally mistaken for practically anything else.

Willow Flycatcher—Uncommon to fairly common migrant in late May and early June and again in August and September. Watch for it in dense willows, cattails, and reeds in the canal behind the Marana Pecan Grove, at Kino Springs, at the Patagonia-Sonoita Creek Preserve, at the golf course pond at Lake Cochise, and near the swimming pool at the Southwestern Research Station in the Chiricahua Mountains. Several pairs of "Southwestern" Willow Flycatchers, a federally endangered subspecies, breed along the lower San Pedro River near Dudleyville.

Hammond's Flycatcher—Fairly common spring and fall migrant through mountain canyon trees, and uncommon winter visitor in valley cottonwood groves. Look for it in migration in Madera, Ramsey, and Cave Creek Canyons. In winter watch for it at Kino Springs, Patagonia Lake, Patagonia-Sonoita Creek Preserve, and along the San Pedro River.

Gray Flycatcher—Fairly common spring and fall migrant through valley mesquite and foothill juniper stands, and uncommon winter visitor in valley thickets. Recently discovered breeding in lower Rucker Canyon of the Chiricahua Mountains. Look for it in migration and in winter at Catalina State Park, Redington Pass, Buenos Aires National Wildlife Refuge, Tubac, Patagonia Lake, Patagonia-Sonoita Creek Preserve, and the San Pedro River. This is the most common overwintering species of *Empidonax* flycatcher. Silver Creek near Portal is a good locale for this species in spring and fall only.

Dusky Flycatcher—Fairly common spring and fall migrant through mountain canyon thickets, and rare winter visitor in valley hackberry, mesquite, and elderberry thickets. Look for it in migration in Madera, Ramsey, and Cave Creek Canyons. In winter watch for it at Kino Springs, Patagonia Lake, Patagonia-Sonoita Creek Preserve, and the San Pedro River.

Pacific-slope Flycatcher—Fairly common spring and fall migrant through valley cottonwood groves and dense mesquite thickets. When "Western Flycatcher" was split into this and the species below in 1990, it created an identification problem. Positive identification of migrants is only possible if the bird is calling. Male Pacific-slope Flycatchers give a slurred, ascending *sweeet* vocalization, and male Cordilleran Flycatchers use a bi-syllabic *wee-seet!* Habitat is a good clue to the identity of yellow-throated *Empidonax* flycatchers in Southeastern Arizona. Mountain birds during the summer are Cordillerans. Most, if not all, valley birds are Pacific-slopes. Places to look and listen for Pacific-slope Flycatcher are the Marana Pecan Grove, along Arivaca Creek, Patagonia Lake, at Patagonia-Sonoita Creek Preserve, and along the San Pedro River.

Cordilleran Flycatcher—Fairly common summer resident of moist forests at higher elevations, and in deep, shady canyons. Often nests under the eaves of cabins, as in Rustler Park, or in niches in large, streamside boulders. Dependable locations include the Corkbark Fir forest on Mount Lemmon, the spring one-half mile above the end of the road in the Hopkins

Fork of Madera Canyon, the huge cliffs in Scheelite Canyon just above the one-half-mile marker, the "Bathtub" pool at the fourth stream crossing three-quarters of a mile up the South Fork Cave Creek Trail, and the USFS cabin area at Rustler Park.

Buff-breasted Flycatcher—Locally fairly common summer resident of open pine forest, primarily in the Huachuca Mountains, but a breeding enclave also exists in the Chiricahuas, and there are records for the Santa Catalina, Rincon, and Santa Rita Mountains. In favorable habitat in Mexico this bird often nests in loose colonies of four or five pairs. Two such groups exist in the Huachuca Mountains, one at the Sawmill Canyon Campground down to its outlet at the Boy Scout Cabin at the head of Garden Canyon on Fort Huachuca, and the other by the pond in lower Scotia Canyon. A similar cluster of Buff-breasteds is located near the outlet of Saulsbury Canyon in West Turkey Creek in the Chiricahua Mountains. All three of these colonies are in Chihuahua Pines. Other areas in the Huachucas where this species has been seen include lower Carr Canyon 2.2 miles from Highway 92 and at Comfort Spring one-half mile beyond the end of the same road. In the Chiricahuas Buff-breasteds breed every few years behind the Southwestern Research Station in Cave Creek Canyon, and in the burn area east of the Forest Service cabins at Rustler Park.

Black Phoebe—Common permanent resident near permanent water in deserts, valleys, and lower mountain canyons. Although ecologically tied to water, the exact form of the water may range from a horse trough to a river or a lake. Frequently nests under bridges. Has been found at all sewage ponds and recreational lakes around Tucson and throughout the southeast corner, as well as Sycamore Creek west of Nogales, the Patagonia-Sonoita Creek Preserve, San Pedro River, Willcox golf course pond, and Cave Creek Canyon in the Chiricahuas.

Eastern Phoebe—Rare but annual winter resident along wooded rivers, and in foothill canyon groves. Very rare in lower mountain canyons. Casual in spring and fall in the same habitats. Over the past decade the best place to see this species has been the outlet of Sonoita Creek into Patagonia Lake. Eastern Phoebes have also shown up sporadically in such locations as the Avra Valley Sewage Ponds, Santa Cruz River at Tumacacori Mission, Kino Springs, Patagonia-Sonoita Creek Preserve, the San Pedro River at the Highway 90 Bridge, and at Portal.

Say's Phoebe—Fairly common summer resident of deserts, valley grasslands, and artificial clearings in the mountain canyons. Most nests are placed under the eaves of buildings. More abundant and widespread in winter, when northern migrants augment the resident population. Often nests at the Kino Springs golf course, Sierra Vista Wastewater Ponds, near the clubhouse at the Willcox golf course, and under the porch of the cabins at the Southwestern Research Station in Cave Creek Canyon.

Vermilion Flycatcher—Common summer resident in weedy openings and pastures near water in deserts, valleys, and broad foothill canyons with mesquite, willow, and cottonwoods groves. Less common in winter, especially in the higher eastern sector. In summer this bird is probably more numerous along Sonoita Creek and the San Pedro River than at any other locations in the United States. It is also found at Woodland Road in northwest Tucson, Marana Pecan Grove, Aravaipa Canyon, upper Sycamore Canyon, Peña Blanca Lake, Kino Springs, Sierra Vista Wastewater Ponds, Guadalupe Canyon, and Willow Tank near Rodeo. During most winters literally dozens use the Arivaca Creek Cienaga, a few may be present at Kino Springs, and there is generally at least one pair at Reid Park in Tucson.

Dusky-capped Flycatcher—Common summer resident of Sierra Madrean pine-oak woodland canyons in all of the border foothills and mountain ranges. Very rare in winter. Its long-drawn, descending "mournful Pierre" whistle is a familiar call in Sycamore, Madera, Ramsey, and Cave Creek Canyons. It is also common at the Patagonia-Sonoita Creek Preserve. Most Dusky-caps depart from Arizona before the end of August, but a few linger into October. Recent winter records come from Patagonia Lake.

Ash-throated Flycatcher—Common summer resident of the deserts, valley grasslands, arid foothills, and lower mountain canyons. Nests in holes in Saguaros, cottonwoods, sycamores, and other trees, as well as in fence posts and steel pipes. Places to look for this bird include the Arizona-Sonora Desert Museum, Sycamore Canyon west of Nogales, Coronado National Memorial, Cochise College west of Douglas, and Silver Creek near Portal. Ash-throateds are not hard to find, but they can be difficult to separate from the Brown-cresteds if they are neither heard nor seen well. Rare in winter in the western lowlands and foothills at Peña Blanca Lake, Sycamore Canyon, Patagonia Lake, and Buenos Aires National Wildlife Refuge.

Brown-crested Flycatcher—Fairly common summer resident in desert Saguaros, valley cottonwoods, and in the sycamores of the foothills and lower mountain canyons. Can be found in Saguaro National Park, Sabino Canyon, lower Madera Canyon, the Patagonia-Sonoita Creek Preserve, along the San Pedro River, lower Cave Creek Canyon, and Guadalupe Canyon.

Nutting's Flycatcher—Vagrant from Pacific-slope dry season deciduous forest south of the border. Recorded from the Research Ranch near Elgin in July 1985 and from Patagonia Lake from mid-December 1997 through late March 1998. Other unsubstantiated sight reports are from Kino Springs from late December 1998 to mid-January 1999 and from Patagonia Lake from late December 2001 to mid-January 2002. This species resembles Ash-throated Flycatcher, but can be distinguished by its orange mouth-color and sharp *Week* call-notes. Other key field marks are a shorter bill, yellower belly, blob-like dark tail corners that do not curve inwards to form an entirely dark tail tip like an Ash-throated, and bright cinnamon edging on the flight feathers.

Observers familiar with Ash-throated will notice the smaller overall size of Nutting's Flycatcher.

Sulphur-bellied Flycatcher—Common summer resident in the sycamore canyons of the border ranges, and uncommon in Bear Canyon in the Santa Catalina Mountains. Substantial numbers do not usually arrive until mid-May. It occurs in Sycamore Canyon west of Nogales, Madera Canyon in the Santa Ritas, Harshaw Canyon near Patagonia, Garden Canyon in the Huachucas, and Cave Creek Canyon in the Chiricahuas. Both Ramsey Canyon and South Fork Cave Creek harbor about six pairs of Sulphur-bellies per mile. Listen for its diagnostic squeaky "rubber-ducky" calls.

Tropical Kingbird—Uncommon local summer resident of ponds and streams edged with cottonwoods and willows in river valleys primarily near the border. Most records are from the Santa Cruz Valley or the San Pedro Valley. Regular at Arivaca Cienaga, at Río Rico, the golf course pond at Kino Springs, and since 1993, at Kingfisher Pond near the San Pedro House. Breeding pairs reach as far north as the Marana Pecan Grove and Winkelman. Listen for the twittering *pip-pip-pip-pip* calls.

Cassin's Kingbird—Common summer resident in riparian woodlands, most abundant in river groves and lower mountain canyons, but also present at desert oases such as Sweetwater Wetlands in Tucson and the campus of Cochise College west of Douglas. Casual in winter in valleys and desert oases. Hard to miss during summer in such areas as Madera Canyon, Patagonia-Sonoita Creek Preserve, Garden Canyon, the San Pedro River, and Cave Creek Canyon. You'll soon be muttering, "It's just another Cassin's."

Thick-billed Kingbird—Locally uncommon summer resident of riparian woodlands in the foothills. Nests in sycamores or cottonwoods. Areas where it occurs regularly include Dudleyville, lower Sycamore Canyon, Arivaca Creek, the Paton home in Patagonia, Patagonia-Sonoita Creek Preserve, and the Patagonia Roadside Rest Area. It was first discovered in the U.S. in 1958 in Guadalupe Canyon, still a reliable location for it.

Western Kingbird—Common summer resident of open deserts and valley grasslands with a few trees or telephone poles for nesting. Often found perched on roadside fences or utility wires. This is the common kingbird at San Xavier Mission south of Tucson, at the Marana Pecan Grove, in the desert grasslands along the lower Madera Canyon Road, on the Buenos Aires Wildlife Refuge, in the Sonoita grasslands, on the outskirts of Sierra Vista, throughout the Sulphur Springs Valley, including Lake Cochise, and along Stateline Road east of Portal. Occasionally hundreds can be seen staging for migration on powerlines in grassy valleys in the month of September.

Rose-throated Becard—Rare and local summer resident. Nearly everyone's life bird comes from Sonoita Creek across Highway 82 from the Patagonia Roadside Rest Area. Watch for traffic as you cross this busy highway, and descend the embankment with care. *Do not cross the fence.* There are usually one or two huge, football-shaped nests hanging from the tips of sycamore branches directly over the stream in this 100-yard stretch. If you time your visit from mid-May to mid-August, there's a pretty good chance you'll see the becards entering and leaving their nests. Other recent nesting sites have been on the Patagonia-Sonoita Creek Preserve, Circle Z Ranch, Arivaca Creek, and about 3.5 miles downstream from the Sycamore Canyon parking area. A Rose-throated Becard discovered in February 2004 may have over-wintered along the Santa Cruz River behind Tumacacori Mission. This was only the third winter record for the species.

Bell's Vireo—Fairly common summer resident in dense riparian thickets in the foothills, especially in mesquite-hackberry associations. Look for it along the Santa Cruz River at Continental and Tubac, at Proctor Road in lower Madera Canyon, in the Patagonia-Sonoita Creek Preserve, at the Patagonia Roadside Rest, at Patagonia Lake, along the San Pedro River at Charleston and Hereford, along Cave Creek below Portal, either end of Aravaipa Canyon, and at the entrance to Guadalupe Canyon. This bird generally goes undetected unless its distinctive call is learned. It usually consists of two parts of three notes each: *cheedle cheedle chee—cheedle cheedle cher.* The first phrase ends with a rising inflection, as if the bird were asking a question. The second phrase, which is given after a short pause, ends with a downward turn, as if in answer to the first part. Some birds ask a lot of questions; others have mostly answers.

Gray Vireo—Rare and local summer resident of arid Pinyon Pine-juniper hillsides in the foothills. A scattering of winter records, primarily in desert mesquite. Gray Vireo is rarely seen in migration away from its breeding localities. Summer records come from Redington Pass between the Santa Catalina and Rincon Mountains, the Muleshoe Ranch in the Galiuro Mountains, and the east end of Aravaipa Canyon, especially from its Bear Canyon tributary. Some years it is also reported from Silver Creek and East Turkey Creek on the eastern flank of the Chiricahuas.

Both in song and plumage pattern, the common Plumbeous Vireo is easily mistaken for Gray Vireo. Gray Vireo, however, usually shows a single faint wingbar on a brownish wing, and the way it flicks its long tail is reminiscent of a gnatcatcher. When feeding, Gray Vireo stays low in chaparral.

Plumbeous Vireo—The gray-backed, white-bellied Plumbeous Vireo found in the Rocky Mountains is a common summer resident in mountain canyon groves, pine-oak woodland, and Ponderosa Pine forest. Plumbeous Vireo is the only species of the former Solitary Vireo complex that breeds here. Watch for Plumbeous Vireo in Bear Canyon in the Santa Catalina Mountains, the Hopkin's Fork of Madera Canyon, Garden Canyon in the Huachuca Mountains, and South Fork Cave Creek in the Chiricahua Mountains. During winter it is rare in desert oases, valley and foothill mesquite and cottonwood woodlands, and very rare in lower canyon sycamores.

Cassin's Vireo—Field separable from Plumbeous Vireo by its greenish back and yellowish flanks, Cassin's Vireo is generally an uncommon migrant through wooded habitats from desert oases up through pine forest. Sweetwater Wetlands in Tucson, the de Anza trail connecting Tubac to Tumacacori Mission, Patagonia Lake, the Patagonia-Sonoita Creek Preserve, and lower Madera, Garden, and Cave Creek Canyons in the border ranges are all known locations. In winter it is very uncommon, primarily in western valley mesquite bosques, cottonwood groves, and desert oases. Watch for over-wintering Cassin's in Tucson's Reid Park, as well as at Sweetwater Wetlands, and along the Santa Cruz River south to Nogales. Only accidental in Arizona, **Blue-headed Vireo**, which breeds in the Eastern U.S., has been reported four times, twice from the upper San Pedro River in September and November of 1987, from Sycamore Canyon in November 1998, and from Sabino Canyon in October 2004.

Hutton's Vireo—Common permanent resident of mountain oak and Sierra Madrean pine-oak woodland, especially in canyons. During summer also inhabits Ponderosa Pine forests up to Rustler Park at an elevation of 8,400 feet. Look for it in Madera Canyon in the Santa Ritas, Garden Canyon in the Huachucas, and Cave Creek Canyons in the Chiricahuas. In winter some descend to valley groves and desert oases. Watch for over-wintering Hutton's in Agua Caliente Park in Tucson, in lower Madera Canyon, at Patagonia Lake, and in Harshaw Canyon, as well as in all the major canyons. The vaguely annoyed expression of its face, deliberate foraging strategy, and lack of a black posterior wing bar, all help distinguish it from the similar Ruby-crowned Kinglet, which shares its habitat in winter. Its monotonous, bi-syllabic *zu-wee* calls are another good clue. Hutton's responds well to squeaks and owl calls.

Yellow-green Vireo—A summer vagrant to foothill cottonwood-sycamore groves along the border, primarily in June and July, occasionally into September. Five indisputable records altogether. The areas where it has been found are the Patagonia Roadside Rest, Harshaw Canyon near Patagonia, and Guadalupe Canyon. With a gray cap, distinct whitish eyebrow, dull red eye, greenish back, yellow flanks, and white underparts, seemingly this bird should not be easily confused if seen well. The bird in Harshaw Canyon in the summer of 2000, however, underscores the need for caution when identifying this species: it had virtually no yellow on its flanks, the back was only dull green, and its entire pattern was muted. Compare with Red-eyed Vireo, rare in Southeastern Arizona but more common than Yellow-green Vireo.

Jays—The three species of regularly-occurring jays found in Southeastern Arizona are largely restricted to particular habitats during summer, reducing potential competition. Steller's Jay occurs in coniferous forests and moist canyons, usually above 7,000 feet. The Mexican Jay is found in Sierra Madrean pine-oak woodland between 4,500 and 7,500 feet. Western Scrub-Jay prefers hillside chaparral below 6,000 feet. All three jays, however, may frequent riparian groves in mountain canyons, especially in winter.

Steller's Jay—Common permanent resident of mountain coniferous forests and shady, moist canyons. Usually conspicuous at Rose Canyon Lake and Ski Valley in the Santa Catalina Mountains, Reef Townsite and Ramsey Vista Campgrounds in the Huachucas, and at Rustler Park and Pinery Canyon Campgrounds in the Chiricahuas. During winter a few Steller's Jays descend to the Santa Rita Lodge in Madera Canyon, to the Visitor Center in the Ramsey Canyon Preserve, and to Stewart Campground in Cave Creek Canyon. Some winters Steller's Jays even reach the valley lowlands, such as Evergreen Cemetery or Reid Park in Tucson.

Western Scrub-Jay—Fairly common and local permanent resident of interior chaparral on dry hillsides and mixed hackberry-mesquite thickets in foothill canyons. Lower and more widespread in winter. Lack of chaparral as well as competition from the Mexican Jay makes the Western Scrub-Jay quite local in the border ranges. It is more numerous in the mountains of central Arizona, where there is more brush and there are fewer Mexican Jays. In Southeastern Arizona it can be found at Molino Basin in the Santa Catalinas, in French Joe Canyon in the Whetstone Mountains, Scheelite Canyon of the Huachucas, along the Silver Creek Road and in the Big Thicket below Portal in the Chiricahua Mountains, and in Guadalupe Canyon. Most winters a few reach the Tucson basin and the floor of the Sulphur Springs Valley.

Mexican Jay—Common resident of Sierra Madrean pine-oak woodland in all of the mountains, north sparingly to the Mogollon Rim in central Arizona. One of the noisiest birds in Bear Canyon in the Santa Catalinas, upper Sycamore Canyon in the Atascosas, Madera Canyon in the Santa Ritas, Miller Canyon in the Huachucas, and Cave Creek Canyon in the Chiricahua Mountains.

Mexican Jays travel throughout the year in a flock that averages 10 or so birds, consisting of a nucleus pair and two or more generations of offspring. One jay acts as a sentinel while the others feed. The nests are tended by three or more birds, usually including older siblings, and any member of the flock may feed the young. In this way young birds gain parenting experience that enhances their own future nesting success. A long-term research project conducted in Cave Creek Canyon by Dr. Jerram Brown has shown how altruistic behavior benefits these jays.

Pinyon Jay—Irruptive species uncommon when present during fall, winter, and spring. Years may pass between invasions, when flocks many number from two to several hundred. Major flights do not seem to be strongly correlated to the severity of the winter, droughts, or even to Pinyon Pine crop failures in central Arizona, where this jay is common. When present in Southeastern Arizona, Pinyon Jays use arid oak woodland—sometimes mixed with mesquite, and interior chaparral, as well as pinyon-juniper woodland. Locations where Pinyon Jays were found in 2002 and 2003 include Parker Canyon Lake near the Huachuca Mountains, and Cave Creek Canyon and Silver Creek in the Chiricahua Mountains.

Clark's Nutcracker—Irruptive species uncommon when present during fall, winter, and spring, some years even lingering through summer. Years may pass between invasions. Their appearance in our area may be correlated to mast crop failures in the San Francisco Peaks and the White Mountains, the nearest breeding locales for this species. When present in Southeastern Arizona, Clark's Nutcrackers are usually restricted to coniferous forests in the Huachuca and Chiricahua Mountains, although there are also records for the Santa Catalina and Santa Rita Mountains. Locations where Clark's Nutcrackers were found in 2002 and 2003 included Sawmill and Ramsey Canyons in the Huachuca Mountains and Rustler Park in the Chiricahua Mountains.

American Crow—Irruptive species uncommon in agricultural valleys when present during winter. Flocks many number from a few, as at Red Rock in the winter of 2003–2004, to several hundred, as in the Sulphur Springs Valley during the winter of 1996–1997. Probably more records come from farms around McNeal and Elfrida in the Sulphur Springs Valley than any other single location in Southeastern Arizona.

Chihuahuan Raven—Common permanent resident of valley grasslands and the Chihuahuan Desert from the Santa Cruz Valley south of Tucson eastward. Nests on tall yuccas, mesquites, windmills, and telephone poles. Easy to find at the Sierra Vista Wastewater Ponds, at Cochise College between Bisbee and Douglas, Willcox Playa, and along Stateline Road east of the Chiricahua Mountains.

Finding this bird is not difficult, but seeing the white on its neck is. Unless it is windy enough to reveal a patch of white at the base of the neck feathers, visitors to the area may not be certain if they have seen a Chihuahuan Raven or a Common. The feathering on the culmen or ridge of the upper mandible is diagnostic if well seen. Chihuahua Ravens have feathers covering 60 percent or more of the culmen. On Common Ravens the upper bill is feathered only half or less of its length. Good clues include habitat preferences and number. Typically Common Ravens prefer the mountains or the cottonwoods along the rivers, while Chihuahuans keep strictly to the open, broad, level valleys that resemble the arid plains of west Texas. Typically Commons come in twos and threes, while the social little Chihuahuan is generally in a flock of a dozen or more; during winter at Willcox flocks may number in the hundreds. The Chihuahuan's smaller size, when that can be judged, and flatter call, when heard, can also lead to a probable identification. Birders should be aware, however, that the *sinuatus* race of Common Raven breeding in the Southwest averages smaller than those in most other areas of the U.S. And, given the large vocal repertoire of both species, voice may simply be a source of confusion. Some locals swear there are actually three species present, including one that is intermediate in size and sound. This third species gets listed as "Raven spp." on Christmas Bird Counts throughout the southeast corner.

Purple Martin—Common summer resident of Saguaro stands near Tucson west to Organ Pipe Cactus National Monument. This Saguaro-nesting race is endemic to southern Arizona. A larger, coniferous forest-nesting subspecies confined to the Chiricahua Mountains was last recorded in August 1985. Purple Martins east of the Tucson area are rare in migration in May and June, and again in August and September, and are often just single birds. During late August and September, by way of contrast, Purple Martins on the periphery of Tucson join collective roosts that number in the thousands and cause utility wires to sag. Dependable locations for martins include Anklam Road west of Shannon and the intersection of Anklam Road and Speedway in west Tucson, and the Arizona-Sonora Desert Museum west of the Tucson Mountains.

Violet-green Swallow—Common summer resident of the Rocky Mountain pines and firs of the higher mountains, descending into the major canyons that drain them. Migrating Violet-greens arrive in western lowland valleys as early as January some years. This the only swallow likely in the coniferous forests. Areas to look for them include Rose Canyon Lake and Mt. Bigelow in the upper Santa Catalina Mountains, Ramsey Vista Campground and Carr Peak in the high Huachucas, and Rustler Park and Barfoot Lookout on top the Chiricahua Mountains. They also pay daily visits to all large canyons throughout the summer, and are common flying as low as the grassland at the outlet of Garden Canyon as well as the desert at the mouth of Cave Creek early in the morning.

Cave Swallow—First detected in 1979, a single bird spent most of the 1980s consorting with Cliff Swallows from mid-April through July at the Main Library at the University of Arizona in Tucson, even nesting in 1983. The most recent records were at Kino Springs in mid-August 1991, at Tucson in late-October 1991, and at Lake Cochise in mid-October 2004.

Mountain Chickadee—Fairly common permanent resident of the coniferous forests of the Santa Catalina Mountains and northward. Lower and more widespread in winter. Easiest to find along the Catalina Highway above milepost 16. Look for it at Rose Canyon, Bear Wallow, and Ski Valley. Responds well to squeaks and owl calls.

Mexican Chickadee—Fairly common permanent resident of the coniferous forest and upper Sierra Madrean pine-oak woodland of the Chiricahua Mountains. During spring Mexican Chickadee seems to descend into the major canyons to breed. At that time of year they are generally easier to find in Pinery Canyon Campground than in Rustler Park. By the onset of the rainy season in July, Mexican Chickadees are all over the crest of the Chiricahuas, including both Rustler and Barfoot Parks, and throughout the Chiricahua Wilderness Area. They are also permanent fixtures at Massai Point in Chiricahua National Monument. In the United States, Mexican Chickadee occurs on public lands only in the Chiricahua Mountains.

Bridled Titmouse—Common permanent resident of the oak and pine-oak woodlands in all mountain ranges. Less common and localized in the riparian woodlands at lower elevations. Lower and more widespread in winter. Present in Sycamore Canyon, Madera Canyon, Patagonia-Sonoita Creek Preserve, Ramsey Canyon, San Pedro River (winter only), and in Cave Creek Canyon. Responds well to squeaks and owl calls.

Juniper Titmouse—Uncommon permanent resident of One-seed Juniper and Border Pinyon Pine in the northeastern foothills of the Chiricahua Mountains and locally near the Bellota Ranch Pond in the Redington Pass area of the Santa Catalina Mountains. Lying in the rain shadow of the higher peaks, the foothills from Portal north along the eastern base of the Chiricahuas depend on winter rainfall, the same weather pattern as in the Great Basin. Along with Western Scrub-Jay and Black-chinned Sparrow, Juniper Titmouse exploits this unique Southeastern Arizona habitat. The easiest place to see this species is at feeders in Portal, or especially at the George Walker House Bed and Breakfast in Paradise, but Juniper Titmouse occurs throughout the length of Silver Creek between these two Chiricahua communities.

Verdin—Common permanent resident of desert thornscrub thickets. Locations include the Arizona-Sonora Desert Museum, Saguaro National Park, Sabino Canyon, Florida Wash below Madera Canyon, the Patagonia Roadside Rest Area, the San Pedro River, and the Big Thicket near Portal.

Bushtit—Fairly common permanent resident of canyon groves, and chaparral and oak-juniper woodlands on dry mountain slopes. Usually occurs at higher elevations than the Verdin, although wandering flocks may descend to the desert in winter. Conversely, after breeding some Bushtits ascend to the Canadian Life Zone on the 9,000-foot crest of the Chiricahua Mountains. Highly responsive to pishing, once a flock is found Bushtits are usually easy to observe. Look for them in Molino Basin, Madera Canyon, Peña Blanca Lake, Patagonia-Sonoita Creek Preserve, all canyons in the Huachuca and Chiricahua Mountains, and in Guadalupe Canyon.

Red-breasted Nuthatch—Fairly common resident in upper canyon groves and mountain coniferous forest. A few descend to valley pecan groves and desert oases in winter. Road-accessible Red-breasted Nuthatches occur at Bear Wallow in the Santa Catalinas and at the East Turkey Creek Crossing on the Trans-mountain Road in the Chiricahua Mountains, as well as at Rustler Park on top. Birders who hike will encounter this species near the one-half-mile marker in Scheelite Canyon and near the Hamburg Mine in Ramsey Canyon of the Huachuca Mountains.

Pygmy Nuthatch—Common permanent resident of the Ponderosa Pines. Prefers mature trees. Easy to find at Rose Canyon Lake and Bear Wallow in the Santa Catalina Mountains, Reef Townsite Campground in the Huachucas, and at Barfoot Junction and Rustler Park in the Chiricahua Mountains. Usually first located by its little piping call notes.

Brown Creeper—Fairly common permanent resident of riparian timber in the major mountain canyons and coniferous forest high in the mountains. Some winters can be found in Tucson. Creepers occur from Bear

Canyon up in the Santa Catalinas, Madera Canyon, Ramsey Canyon, South Fork Cave Creek, and at Rustler Park in the Chiricahua Mountains.

Cactus Wren—Common permanent resident of desert thornscrub and valley acacia and mesquite thickets. This conspicuous, noisy species can be found anywhere on the perimeter of Tucson, at the Arizona-Sonora Desert Museum, Saguaro National Park, Sabino Canyon, Florida Wash on the Madera Canyon Road, along the lower Ramsey Canyon Road, and at Portal. Cactus Wren is the Arizona State Bird.

Rock Wren—Fairly common permanent resident of arid, open, rocky areas in the foothills. Winters down to Tucson. Look for it in Aravaipa Canyon, Molino Basin, along the Ruby Road, at the Patagonia Roadside Rest Area, Harshaw Canyon, at the Lavender Pit parking area at Bisbee, along Silver Creek Road near Portal, and at Guadalupe Canyon. In winter also frequents the grounds of the Arizona-Sonora Desert Museum and the earthen dam at Whitewater Draw Wildlife Refuge.

Canyon Wren—Common permanent resident of rocky canyons and cliffs, ranging above 9,000 feet along the Chiricahua Crest Trail near Paint Rock. Its loud, descending cascade of whistles fills such rock-walled locations as Aravaipa Canyon, Sabino Canyon, Sycamore Canyon west of Nogales, Patagonia Roadside Rest Area, Scheelite Canyon, Cave Creek Canyon, and Chiricahua National Monument. In winter a bird or two ordinarily adopts the Mountain Habitat exhibit area at the Arizona-Sonora Desert Museum.

Bewick's Wren—Common permanent resident of valley and canyon groves, including mesquite bosques, and of oak and pine-oak woodlands in the foothills and lower mountains. Lower and widespread in winter, when it reaches the desert. Responds well to squeaking and owl calls. This is the most common wren in Molino Basin, Madera Canyon, Sycamore Canyon in the Atascosa Mountains, at the Patagonia-Sonoita Creek Preserve, along the San Pedro River, and throughout all lower canyons in the Huachuca and Chiricahua Mountains.

House Wren—Fairly common summer resident in mountain canyons and coniferous forest throughout the region. Common spring and fall transient in thickets in all habitats, and rare in winter in low elevation thickets in the western half of the region. Summer birds are found in the Hopkins Fork and other upper branches of Madera Canyon, Scheelite and upper Miller Canyon in the Huachuca Mountains, and near the U.S. Forest Service cabins in Rustler Park in the Chiricahua Mountains. Transients can occur anywhere from the Arizona-Sonora Desert Museum to Portal. Approximately half of the breeding birds found in the Santa Rita, Huachuca, and Chiricahua Mountains were once assigned to a separate species, "Brown-throated Wren." Now considered a subspecies only, it is characterized by having a buffy eyebrow and a soft brown throat and underparts. The western form of the

House Wren has a gray throat and an inconspicuous eyebrow. Intermediates also occur in all three border ranges.

Winter Wren—Rare winter resident in mountain and foothill canyons, very rarely in desert oases. Locations where Winter Wrens have been found in recent years include lower Sabino Canyon, upper Miller Canyon, and South Fork Cave Creek.

Marsh Wren—Fairly common transient and winter resident in reed beds and sedges at valley ponds and lakes. Easily heard scolding and occasionally seen at Sweetwater Wetlands, Patagonia Lake, Lake Cochise golf course pond, and Willow Tank on the east side of the Chiricahua Mountains.

American Dipper—Rare obligate of permanent mountains streams. Last known nest in our area was in Cave Creek at John Hands Dam in 1973. Reported some winters from Aravaipa Canyon, Sabino Canyon in the Santa Catalina Mountains, Ramsey Canyon in the Huachuca Mountains, and South Fork Cave Creek in the Chiricahua Mountains. (More common in mountain streams in central Arizona.)

Black-tailed Gnatcatcher—Fairly common permanent resident of the Sonoran desertscrub west of Tucson, uncommon in Chihuahuan desertscrub farther east. Prefers dry washes in creosote flats, but also occurs in foothill acacia and cactus thickets. Easiest to find at Tucson Mountain Park, the Arizona-Sonora Desert Museum, Saguaro National Park, and in Florida Wash. Farther east it can be found along the Charleston Road east of the San Pedro River, in Silver Creek near Portal, and in Guadalupe Canyon.

Black-capped Gnatcatcher—A very rare resident of subtropical thornscrub canyons in the border foothills. In 1981 a pair nested three times in Chino Canyon on the west side of the Santa Rita Mountains and this area has been used intermittently by Black-caps ever since. In 2003 there were sight reports from nearby Box Canyon to the north and in both 2003 and 2004 a few miles south in Montosa Canyon along the Mount Hopkins Road. Up to two pairs were found using Brown Canyon in Buenos Aires National Wildlife Refuge in 1997 and 1998. This Mexican species was first recorded in the United States in 1971 from near the Patagonia Roadside Rest Area, and there have been several documented sightings along Sonoita Creek since then, even as recently as May 1998. Just downstream of the rest area, a pair nested successfully near the upper end of Patagonia Lake in the summers of 2003 and 2004. Sycamore Canyon in the Atascosa Mountains hosted a nesting pair in 1986, and there, too, as well as in nearby California Gulch, there have been subsequent sight reports. There are also a few winter records; however, it is extremely difficult to separate Black-caps from the more numerous Blue-gray Gnatcatchers at that season. Look for the Black-capped Gnatcatcher's slightly longer bill and—compared to Blue-gray—more strongly graduated tail. While Black-capped also closely resembles

Black-tailed Gnatcatcher, the underside of its tail is largely white, similar to Blue-gray Gnatcatcher.

Eastern Bluebird—Uncommon permanent resident in grassy pine-oak woodlands and open pine forests of the border ranges from the Huachucas west to the Atascosa Mountains. Apparently disappeared as a breeding bird from the Chiricahua Mountains about 1990, but still present there in winter. The Mexican subspecies, *fulva,* sometimes called the "Azure Bluebird," is at the northern limits of its distribution in Southeastern Arizona. Look for Eastern Bluebird at Hank and Yank Spring at the head of Sycamore Canyon, in Harshaw Canyon near Patagonia, at the confluence of Sawmill and Garden Canyons in the Huachucas, and wintering in North Fork Cave Creek in the first mile above the Southwestern Research Station in the Chiricahua Mountains.

Western Bluebird—Uncommon summer resident of the Ponderosa Pines in the Santa Catalina and Chiricahua Mountains. Last breeding records for the Huachuca Mountains were in the early 1950s, but still present there in winter. Lower and usually more common in winter, when it is found in areas with abundant berries, especially junipers, hackberries, and any trees with mistletoe. In summer watch for Westerns at Rose Canyon Lake and Rustler Park. Most winters they can be found in Molino Basin, along the Ruby Road near Peña Blanca Lake, in Harshaw Canyon near Patagonia, in the oaks of the San Rafael Valley, and along the road to Paradise in the Chiricahua Mountains. During invasion winters common in agricultural areas such as the Marana Pecan Grove or Essary Hay Company in the Sulphur Springs Valley.

Mountain Bluebird—Irregular winter visitor to open valleys and open foothill scrub. Some winters Mountain Bluebirds are almost non-existent in Southeastern Arizona; other years there are flocks of hundreds. Watch for it in open deserts, pastures, and particularly in plowed fields. Locations include the Santa Cruz Flats at Western Sod Farm, Arivaca, Kino Springs, Sonoita Grasslands, Palominas Road in the San Pedro Valley, at the Essary Hay Farm in the Sulphur Springs Valley, and in the Whitetail Prairie north of Paradise in the Chiricahuas.

Townsend's Solitaire—Fairly common winter visitor, primarily to juniper woodlands and riparian groves in foothills and lower mountain canyons. Numbers vary from one year to the next. The most dependable locations include Redington Pass east of Tucson, Box Canyon on the north end of the Santa Ritas, Harshaw Canyon near Patagonia, Garden Canyon in the Huachucas, along the road to Paradise from Portal, and Guadalupe Canyon. There are a few high-elevation summer records from coniferous forest, but no evidence of breeding.

Swainson's Thrush—Uncommon and erratic migrant, primarily in the last three weeks of May and in September. Most common after dry winters and springs, when numbers of Swainson's may exceed numbers of Hermit

Thrushes for a few weeks. Prefers wet mountain and foothill canyon groves and thickets, but also found in desert oases and lush plantings in town, especially during "irruption" years. Locations include Madera Canyon, Kino Springs, Patagonia Roadside Rest, Miller Canyon, and South Fork Cave Creek.

Hermit Thrush—Common summer resident in wet mountain canyon groves and moist coniferous forest. Common migrant, primarily in well-watered mountain and foothill canyons and in moist, shady groves and oases in the lowlands. In most winters common below the snowline in mountain canyons, foothill canyons, valley groves, and desert oases. Bear Wallow in the Santa Catalinas, Madera Canyon, Miller Canyon above Beatty's Guest Ranch, South Fork Cave Creek, and Rustler Park are all reliable summer locations. In winter check Sweetwater Wetlands, Molino Basin, lower Madera Canyon below the Santa Rita Lodge, the Patagonia Roadside Rest Area, the Upper Picnic Area in Garden Canyon, the San Pedro River, Cave Creek Canyon, and Guadalupe Canyon.

Rufous-backed Robin—Rare and reclusive winter visitor from Mexico in damp, dense valley, foothill, and lower mountain canyon thickets. This bird may infrequently mingle with flocks of American Robins, but skulks in the background. Recent sightings are from the Arizona-Sonora Desert Museum, Florida Canyon Work Station, Kino Springs, Patagonia Lake, the Patagonia-Sonoita Creek Preserve, Harshaw Canyon, Ramsey Canyon, and along the San Pedro River at Hereford and Palominas. There are only four summer records: one from Madera Canyon, one from Sonoita, another from Whitetail Canyon in the Chiricahuas, and one from Guadalupe Canyon. Consult the Tucson Audubon Society rare bird tape or AZ/NM BirdChat on the web for news of recent sightings.

Aztec Thrush—Very rare summer visitor to wet canyon riparian woods in the border ranges. There is one winter record from January 1991 of a bird feasting on Pyracantha berries at Portal in the Chiricahua Mountains. Since the first Aztec Thrush was discovered in Madera Canyon in May 1978, there have been many sightings, especially in August. However, there were no reports at all from 1997–1999. Madera Canyon has produced more records than any other location, but Aztecs have also been observed in Huachuca, Garden, upper Carr near Comfort Spring, and Ramsey Canyons in the Huachucas, and from South Fork Cave Creek in the Chiricahuas. Inexperienced birders may confuse a black-and-white juvenile Spotted Towhee for an Aztec Thrush, but the bill shape should be diagnostic. Watch for a nervous adult Spotted Tow- hee in close proximity. (If it feeds the youngster in question, that's a clue.) When present, Aztec Thrush is one species that always makes the Tucson Audubon Society rare bird tape and the AZ/NM BirdChat Listserve.

Sage Thrasher—Uncommon winter visitor in sparse vegetation in the deserts, valley mesquite grasslands, and open foothills. Sometimes common in migration. Most often found at San Xavier Mission, Redington Pass, along

Mile Wide Road in Avra Valley, Box Canyon Road near Madera Canyon, Harshaw Canyon near Patagonia, Charleston Road east of the San Pedro River, Double Adobe Road in the Sulphur Springs Valley, and Paradise Road in the Chiricahua Mountains.

Bendire's Thrasher—Uncommon to fairly common resident in desert mesquite and valley mesquite grasslands, especially in hedgerows along fence-lines. Easiest to see when singing in January and February. Good locations include Thornydale Road in northwest Tucson, San Xavier Mission, the Santa Cruz Flats, along Central Highway in the Sulphur Springs Valley, Stateline Road near Rodeo, and along the Guadalupe Canyon Road. Bendire's has a lemon-yellow eye, arrow-shaped spots on the chest, and a straight bill with a pale spot at the base.

Curve-billed Thrasher—Very common permanent resident of both Sonoran and Chihuahuan Deserts, and of valley mesquite grasslands. Unlike other members of its clan, this thrasher is not shy. It is often seen perched in the top of trees or utility poles, giving a sharp, human-like *Whit-wheet!* whistle, as if to attract attention. Easy to find at the Arizona-Sonora Desert Museum, Tucson Mountain Park, Saguaro National Park, along the Santa Cruz and San Pedro Rivers, at the Patagonia Roadside Rest Area, in patches of Chihuahuan Desert near Sierra Vista, Tombstone, and Douglas, and at Portal. This is the thrasher that inhabits Tucson and all other towns in Southeastern Arizona. While immature Curve-bills may resemble Bendire's, their bills lack the pale spot at the base.

Crissal Thrasher—Fairly common but usually difficult-to-see permanent resident of dense thickets along dry washes in the deserts, valley mesquite grasslands, and in interior chaparral in the foothills. Crissals are almost as bold as Curved-bills from January through March, when birds tee up on the tallest brush in their territories to sing their long-drawn ballads that end with *Chee-ry! chee-ry!, toit toit.* Watch for this species at San Xavier Mission, Molino Basin, McCleary Wash, on desert terraces along the San Pedro River, in Silver Creek and the Big Thicket near Portal, and in Guadalupe Canyon.

Le Conte's Thrasher—Very rare, irregular, and local resident of open, sandy creosote flats in the Colorado River division of the Sonoran Desert west and north of Tucson. Always rare, this retiring bird is easiest to see when singing in January and February. Responds well to recordings of its call, particularly in late winter, but beware—Crissal Thrashers also respond to Le Conte's Thrasher tapes. Although there are no recent records, locations in Avra Valley where Le Conte's has been at least sporadic include south on the dirt track from the end of Mile Wide Road, and west on Emigh Road from its junction with Sandario Road at Marana High School. Watch for this pale thrasher to run between the shrubs, rather than fly. (The nearest reliable location is outside the range of this book at the junction of Baseline Road and Salome Highway west of Phoenix.)

Blue Mockingbird—Casual winter visitor to hackberry groves in foothill riparian canyons along the Mexican border. There are at least two Arizona records, the first from the Circle Z Ranch south of the Patagonia-Sonoita Creek Sanctuary from late December 1991 through early March 1992, and the second from lower Cave Creek near Portal from January through early April 1995. Neither bird was particularly shy and both vocalized fairly frequently as they foraged thrasher-style under shrubs or clambered around small trees searching for dried fruits. Calls include a rich, inquisitive *querp?* and a burbling, well-spaced series of characteristic mimic-thrush notes. A third bird was seen briefly in desertscrub in Tucson in late September 1992, but that bird may have been an escapee. Blue Mockingbird is known to use thorn forest streams just 125 miles south in Sonora; deeper into the Sierra Madre it follows deciduous growth up watercourses into pine-oak woodlands.

Sprague's Pipit—Rare winter visitor to tall, valley grasslands. Its distinctive flight style, an abrupt climb followed by a plummeting descent back into the grass, is probably the best give-away to its presence. It may also give a loud *squeet* alarm note at take-off. Most birders looking for this species in Southeastern Arizona gravitate to the San Rafael Grasslands. Other proven locations are on the Buenos Aires National Wildlife Refuge, in the Sonoita Grasslands, and near McNeal off Leslie Canyon Road in the Sulphur Springs Valley.

Phainopepla—Common permanent resident of desert mesquites, river valley elderberries, and foothill canyons with juniper, especially where the trees are laden with mistletoe. Uncommon in the eastern sector in winter. Easy to find in the desert at the Arizona-Sonora Desert-Museum, the west unit of Saguaro National Park, Kino Springs, Patagonia Lake, Patagonia-Sonoita Creek Preserve, along the San Pedro River, and in Guadalupe Canyon.

Olive Warbler—Fairly common summer resident of mountain coniferous forests. Rare in winter in canyon riparian, occasionally descending to valley groves. This bird can be hard to spot as it feeds deliberately among the needles at the top of a pine. Good locations include Rose Canyon Lake and Bear Wallow in the Santa Catalina Mountains, Sawmill and Ramsey Vista Campgrounds in the Huachuca Mountains, and Barfoot Junction on the road to Rustler Park in the Chiricahua Mountains. One of the best places to see this bird is the Chiricahua Crest Trail to Barfoot Lookout, which offers tree-top-level views of the canopy. Olive Warblers belong to a monotypic family and its exact taxonomic relationship to the wood-warblers below is uncertain.

Migrant Warblers—Because of the mild weather in Southeastern Arizona, as well as its geographic position as a land bridge midway between tropical and temperate latitudes, large concentrations of migrant warblers are uncommon. They occur almost anywhere from the mesquite thickets in the deserts, to the cottonwood groves along the valley rivers, to the wooded canyons and coniferous forests of the mountains. A few of the spots that are often visited by the local birders during early spring are Sweetwater Wetlands, the Marana Pecan Grove, Lower Madera Canyon, Kino Springs, Patagonia Lake, Patagonia-Sonoita Creek Preserve, Highway 90 Bridge and Charleston on the San Pedro River, and Guadalupe Canyon. By May warblers and other migrant landbirds are as likely to be found in mountain canyons as in the desert oases. Sycamore, Madera, French Joe, Ramsey, and Cave Creek Canyons are all famous as late spring vagrant traps. During the fall migration from late July through October, the sequence reverses: most migrants move through the mountains early in the season and then, gradually, numbers increase in foothill and valley locations as the mountains cool.

Reasonably common, regularly-occurring warblers found here only as migrants are Nashville, Northern Parula, Townsend's, Hermit, Northern Waterthrush, Louisiana Waterthrush, MacGillivray's, and Wilson's. These are treated below in the species accounts. There are also records for many Eastern vagrants, including Blue-winged, Golden-winged, Tennessee, Black-and-white, Magnolia, Black-throated Blue, Chestnut-sided, Pine, Prairie, American Redstart, Prothonotary, Worm-eating, Ovenbird, Kentucky, and Hooded, as well as others.

Nashville Warbler—Uncommon spring and fairly common fall migrant in thickets from desert oases up to upper mountain canyons. Most common in mid-elevation areas such as Madera Canyon in the Santa Rita Mountains, Garden Canyon in the Huachuca Mountains, and Cave Creek Canyon in the Chiricahua Mountains. Most years Nashvilles are particularly abundant in August and September in French Joe Canyon in the Whetstone Mountains, when flocks of transient Nashvilles may outnumber all other warblers of all other species combined.

Virginia's Warbler—Fairly common summer resident of interior chaparral and oak-juniper woodland on dry hillsides in the mountains as well as coniferous forest mixed with Gambel Oak. Often comes down to canyon bottoms on brushy slopes. Look for it in Bear Canyon in the Santa Catalina Mountains, Madera Canyon in the Santa Ritas, Scheelite Canyon in the Huachucas, and in South Fork Cave Creek and along the road between Onion Saddle and Rustler Park in the Chiricahua Mountains.

Lucy's Warbler—Common summer resident in dense stands of mesquite and hackberry in desert washes and in valley cottonwood groves. Some good locations are Catalina State Park, Florida Wash, Kino Springs, the lower hillside along Patagonia Roadside Rest, the San Pedro River, and Portal. Nests in tree cavities. The first summer warbler to arrive and to depart, Lucy's is largely silent and more difficult to find from the beginning of July to the end of September. The Marana Pecan Grove is an excellent fall location for Lucy's Warbler.

Crescent-chested Warbler—Mexican vagrant to wet canyons within Sierra Madrean pine-oak woodland in the Huachuca and Santa Rita Mountains, and cottonwood groves in the Patagonia-Sonoita Creek Preserve, which lies in between those two ranges. After making its U.S. debut in Garden Canyon in the Huachucas in early September 1983, a pair appeared in Ramsey Canyon the following spring from late April to mid-May 1984. No further Crescent-chesteds were seen until a bird was discovered at the Patagonia-Sonoita Creek Preserve in mid-September 1992. This bird entertained hundreds of birders throughout the winter, and it—or a wandering kinsman—returned to Patagonia from mid-November 1993 through mid-January 1994. Another briefly appeared at Bog Springs in the Santa Rita Mountains in late May through early June 2001 and a Crescent-chested was in the Hopkin's Fork of Madera in late April 2003. Arizona Crescent-chested Warblers are nearly always found in a mixed flock with Bridled Titmice and Yellow-rumped Warblers.

Northern Parula—A rare annual visitor to desert oases, valley groves, and canyon riparian, primarily in spring, but records span the year. Locations with recent sightings include Sweetwater Wetlands in Tucson, Patagonia Roadside Rest Area, and Cave Creek in the Chiricahua Mountains.

Tropical Parula—There are only two Southeastern Arizona records of this Mexican vagrant. The first was a male that summered in Madera Canyon from mid-July through mid-September 1984. It was possibly accompanied by a female for a single day soon after it arrived. More recently a male sang tirelessly in Miller Canyon from late June through mid-July 2001, working its way up-canyon from Beatty's Guest Ranch to the first stream crossing above the Tombstone Water Supply. Tropical Parulas use subtropical thorn forest and lower pine-oak woodland canyons in southern Sonora. They can be separated from Northern Parulas, which are rare annual migrants through the same habitats, by the lack of white eye crescents and more extensive yellow on the lower face and lower belly.

Yellow-rumped Warbler—The "Audubon's" form breeds in coniferous forest in all of the higher mountain ranges. Places to look for it include Bear Wallow in the Santa Catalinas, the upper Carr Canyon Road in the Huachuca Mountains, and Barfoot Junction and Rustler Park in the Chiricahua Mountains. "Audubon's" form is also the most abundant wintering warbler in valley, foothill, and lower mountain canyon riparian groves. Literally hundreds winter along the Santa Cruz River in Tucson. Other winter locations include Sweetwater Wetlands, Avra Valley Ponds, Arivaca, Patagonia Lake, the Patagonia-Sonoita Creek Preserve, Kingfisher Pond on the San Pedro River, Portal, and Guadalupe Canyon. The "Myrtle" form is found with wintering flocks of "Audubon's," and is seemingly rare until early spring, when Yellow-rumps molt into nuptial plumage. In April "Myrtle" Yellow-rumped Warblers become uncommon to fairly common, depending on the year.

Black-throated Gray Warbler—Common summer resident in oak, pine-oak, and pinyon-juniper woodlands in the mountains. Uncommon migrant through the lowlands and rare in winter in valley and foothill riparian groves. Locations include Molino Basin, Sycamore Canyon, Madera Canyon, Ramsey Canyon Preserve, and Cave Creek Canyon. This bird feeds in oaks on sun-drenched slopes. Responds well to squeaks and owl toots. Given the amount of appropriate habitat, Black-throated Gray may be the most abundant warbler summering in Southeastern Arizona.

Townsend's Warbler—Fairly common spring and common fall transient, primarily through mountain coniferous forest, but also in mountain canyons—especially on oaks with newly emergent leaves, and rarely in foothill and valley riparian groves, as well as desert oases. Reliable during migration periods in Bear Canyon in the Santa Catalinas, Madera Canyon, Sawmill Canyon, South Fork Cave Creek, and Rustler Park. Most common along the crests of the Santa Catalina, Santa Rita, Huachuca, and Chiricahua Mountains. Rare in winter in any area with trees at lower elevations.

Hermit Warbler—Fairly common spring and common fall transient, primarily through mountain coniferous forest, but also in mountain canyons—especially on oaks with newly emergent leaves, and rarely in foothill and valley riparian groves, as well as sporadically at desert oases. Reliable during migration periods in Bear Canyon in the Santa Catalinas, Madera Canyon, Sawmill Canyon, South Fork Cave Creek, and Rustler Park. Often in mixed flocks with Townsend's Warblers. Accidental in winter. At most locations Townsend's outnumber migrant Hermit Warblers.

Grace's Warbler—Fairly common summer resident of tall Sierra Madrean pine-oak woodland and Ponderosa Pine forest in the mountains. Follows the conifers down canyon bottoms, and usually found gleaning among the needles at the top of a pine tree. Sings its accelerating trill frequently. Look for it at Bear Canyon and Bear Wallow in the Santa Catalinas, above the end of the road in the Hopkin's Fork of Madera Canyon, at Sawmill Canyon and Ramsey Vista Campgrounds in the Huachucas, and in South Fork Cave Creek and Rustler Park in the Chiricahuas.

Northern Waterthrush—Very uncommon spring and fall migrant on the wooded margins of ponds, rivers, streams, and springs, usually below an elevation of 6,000 feet. There is also a handful of winter records. While Northern Waterthrush can occur at almost any riparian area, some of the sites where its appearance is expected on an almost annual basis include Kino Springs, Patagonia-Sonoita Creek Preserve, the San Pedro River anywhere between Escapule Canyon and Palominas, Cave Creek between Portal and the Southwestern Research Station, and Willow Tank on the east side of the Chiricahua Mountains. Partially because their preferred habitats overlap, Northern and Louisiana Waterthrushes are occasionally confused. Northern's dotted throat separates this species from Louisiana, but its tapering or even-width eyebrow and lack of contrasty buffy flanks are also good clues.

Louisiana Waterthrush—Rare but annual winter visitor to wooded valley river edges and foothill stream margins. Casual at other times of the year in the same riparian habitats, and least apt to be seen in spring. A Louisiana Waterthrush is ordinarily present all winter in the first half-mile of Sonoita Creek above Patagonia Lake. Other areas which occasionally harbor wintering Louisianas include lower Madera Canyon near Proctor Road, the Santa Cruz River behind Tumacacori Mission, and Sycamore Canyon west of Nogales. Louisiana Waterthrush tends to be less common in the eastern half of the region, but individuals have been discovered—especially as early fall transients in late July and August—in Ramsey Canyon, Cave Creek Canyon, and Guadalupe Canyon. Use caution separating this species from Northern. Look for an unmarked white throat, a white eyebrow that tends to broaden or flare behind the eye, and buffy flanks that contrast with the white ground color of the breast.

MacGillivray's Warbler—Fairly common spring and fall migrant through thickets and dense brush at all elevations from desert oases to high mountain springs. Look for it at Sweetwater Wetlands in Tucson, Marana Pecan Grove, Aravaipa Canyon, Palo Duro Pond, Patagonia-Sonoita Creek Preserve, Scheelite Canyon, along the San Pedro River, and Silver Creek Spring near Portal. Accidental in winter.

Wilson's Warbler—Common spring and fall migrant, especially April through mid-May and mid-August through September, but some migrants are seen from March through November. Found in all habitats from desert through coniferous forest, but primarily in the lowlands during cooler months. Very rare during winter. Locations include Sweetwater Wetlands, Arizona-Sonora Desert Museum, Madera Canyon, Patagonia Lake, Patagonia Roadside Rest, Sawmill Canyon, San Pedro River, South Fork Cave Creek, and Rustler Park.

Red-faced Warbler—Fairly common summer resident of Gambel Oak and aspen groves within mountain coniferous forest, and upper canyons with maples or other deciduous trees. Occurs lower in major wet canyons during migration periods in April and August. Nests on the ground under a small tree or grass clump. This handsome bird can be found at Rose Canyon Lake, Bear Wallow, and at Ski Valley in the Santa Catalinas; usually one-half-mile or higher above the road end in the Hopkins Fork of Madera Canyon; at the one-half-mile marker and above in Scheelite Canyon, upper Ramsey Canyon, upper Miller Canyon, and at Comfort Spring in the Huachucas; and at Pinery Canyon Campground, Rustler Park, and beginning about two miles up South Fork Cave Creek in the Chiricahua Mountains. Responds well to owl toots.

Painted Redstart—Common summer resident in Sierra Madrean pine-oak woodlands in the mountains, most common along streams. A few winter in mountain canyons, especially at canyon homes with sugar-water feeders for hummingbirds. Easy to find in Bear Canyon in the Santa Catalina Mountains, Sycamore Canyon in the Atascosas, Madera Canyon in the Santa Ritas,

Ramsey Canyon in the Huachucas, and Cave Creek Canyon and South Fork Cave Creek in the Chiricahuas. Researchers speculate that by flashing its white outer tail feathers it startles potential insect prey out of hiding. Responds well to owl toots. Although it is common, you will never get to the point of saying, "It's just a redstart."

Slate-throated Redstart—A vagrant from below the border, the only definite records came from pine-oak woodland canyon thickets in Miller Canyon of the Huachuca Mountains in mid-April 1976 and Madera Canyon in late May 1996. There are additional sight reports from Portal in May 1978, Sawmill Canyon in the Huachucas in July 1988, and from South Fork Cave Creek in the Chiricahuas in March 1993. This species can be readily distinguished from the common Painted Redstart by the absence of a white crescent under eye, lack of white markings on the wings, and reduced white in the tail.

Fan-tailed Warbler—Mexican vagrant to shady, cliff-walled canyon thickets, usually near water, within Sierra Madrean pine-oak woodland in the border ranges. The first record for both Arizona and the U.S. came from Baker Canyon, a tributary of Guadalupe Canyon, in late May 1961. The next sighting was in Scheelite Canyon in May 1983, followed by an observation in nearby Garden Canyon in May 1984. A Fan-tail discovered in Sycamore Canyon in the Atascosa Mountains was seen by numerous birders in June and July 1987. A sighting in Guadalupe Canyon in September 1990 is supported by photographs. Additional, albeit brief, observations include one at French Joe Canyon in late May 1995 and another tape-recorded at the Patagonia Roadside Rest in late May 1997. Fan-tails forage near or on the ground, expressively fanning a long, white-tipped tail, especially in response to pygmy-owl toots. (They are known to have nested approximately 10 miles south of Guadalupe Canyon in Cajón Bonito, Sonora.)

Rufous-capped Warbler—Mexican summer vagrant to cliff-walled canyon thickets within Sierra Madrean pine-oak woodland in the border ranges. The first Arizona record was of a female that nested unsuccessfully midway between Sunnyflat Campground and the Southwestern Research Station in Cave Creek Canyon of the Chiricahuas in May 1977. Probably the same bird returned to this location in April 1978. Rufous-caps have since been observed at Coronado National Memorial in August 1983, Comfort Spring in the Huachuca Mountains in April 1985, from California Gulch in July 1993 and Sycamore Canyon in the Atascosa Mountains from mid-March through June 1994. Since 1995 Rufous-capped Warblers have been resident in French Joe Canyon in the Whetstone Mountains, where they have successfully nested every summer since 2000. Other recent records include a winter bird on the San Pedro near Hereford in November and December 1998, another in Sycamore Canyon in December of the same year, and a late September 2000 record from Carr Canyon in the Huachuca Mountains. In 2004 Rufous-caps were found in South Fork Cave Creek in late April and in Sycamore Canyon in late July. Both the long, cocked tail and the behavior of this understory species are reminiscent of a Bewick's Wren.

Hepatic Tanager—Fairly common summer resident of canyon groves, pine-oak woodlands, and pine forests in the mountains. Rarely winters in Southeastern Arizona, with recent reports from the Patagonia-Sonoita Creek Preserve, Madera and Sycamore Canyons. Rose Canyon Lake, Sycamore Canyon, Madera Canyon, Scheelite Canyon in the Huachucas, and South Fork Cave Creek are all proven summer locations for Hepatic Tanagers. Compared to the brilliant scarlet of a Summer Tanager, the male Hepatic is dull brick red. Both sexes have blackish bills and gray cheek patches that serve to distinguish them from either sex of the Summer. Their call notes are also distinctive. The Hepatic utters a single *chuck* note, while the Summer gives a tri-syllabic *Kit-ty-tuck!*

Summer Tanager—Common summer resident of valley and foothill riparian groves, particularly in cottonwoods. Can be found at Kino Springs, Patagonia-Sonoita Creek Preserve, the San Pedro River, and Portal.

Scarlet Tanager—An Eastern vagrant that is most likely to visit river valley, foothill canyon, and lower mountain canyon groves in fall, although a sprinkling of reports span the calendar. Most of the nearly 20 records involve immatures, females, or winter-plumaged males, but a richly colored, full adult male was feasting on mulberry fruits at the Patons' home in Patagonia in May of 2002.

Western Tanager—Fairly common summer resident in mountain coniferous forests. During the prolonged spring and fall migrations Western Tanagers are common in virtually all Southeastern Arizona habitats, including town parks, desert washes, valley cottonwoods, and canyon sycamores. Ski Valley in the Santa Catalina Mountains, Reef Townsite Campground in the Huachucas, and Rustler Park in the Chiricahuas are breeding areas. In migration Western Tanagers are common at such lowland locations as the Arizona-Sonora Desert Museum, Marana Pecan Grove, Kino Springs, Patagonia Roadside Rest, and the San Pedro River.

Flame-colored Tanager—Very rare summer resident of tall canyon timber within Sierra Madrean pine-oak woodland in the border ranges. After the first U.S. record of a male in South Fork Cave Creek from mid-April through mid-July 1985, there was a seven-year hiatus until March 1992, when Flame-colored Tanagers appeared in both Madera Canyon and the Ramsey Canyon Preserve. A report from Miller Canyon in May 1994 expanded the areas where they are known to occur. Beginning with the South Fork bird that mated with a Western Tanager (and successfully fledged two hybrid young), Flame-colored Tanagers have attempted to nest in Whitetail Canyon in the Chiricahuas, the Ramsey Canyon Preserve and Miller Canyon in the Huachucas, and Madera Canyon in the Santa Rita Mountains. In 2003 seemingly-pure male Flame-colored Tanagers were found in both Miller and

Madera Canyons. The Madera Canyon pair returned again in the summer of 2004, and there are now perhaps 20 records of this species in Southeastern Arizona.

Like Western Tanager—and unlike Hepatic or Summer—Flame-colored Tanager has wing-bars. Flame-colored also has large white spots on the tertial tips and pure white tail corners. In addition to these features, it can usually be separated from Western by its large, charcoal-colored bill and dark-bordered cheek patch. The stripes on its back are always diagnostic—if they are visible. From March through May, first-year males have flecks of orange on the face; as they mature the orange-red coloration spreads back over the entire body. Females of any age are bright yellow. They can be separated from female Westerns by their dark bill, dark ear outline, thick white wingbars, and streaked back. Because at least some hybrid crosses with Western Tanagers have occurred in the border ranges, it is important to note whether males have well-defined streaks on the back—not the solid black rear mantle of a Western hybrid, and a dull yellow rump—not the bright yellow rump of a male Western Tanager. Females with Western ancestry may not be field separable from pure Flame-colored Tanager females.

Green-tailed Towhee—Common migrant and uncommon winter visitor to desert and valley field hedgerows and thickets, and dense brush in foothill canyons. Numbers fluctuate from year to year. Green-tailed Towhees can be found at Sweetwater Wetlands, Marana Pecan Grove, Florida Wash, Kino Springs, Patagonia-Sonoita Creek Preserve, the San Pedro River at Fairbank, and Portal.

Spotted Towhee—Fairly common permanent resident in foothill and mountain thickets within all vegetation types in the Upper Sonoran Life Zone, and less common but still present up to 9,000 feet in the Transition Life Zone. A few descend into desert and valley thickets during winter. Locations to look for Spotted Towhees include Bear Canyon in the Santa Catalinas, Madera Canyon in the Santa Ritas, Miller Canyon in the Huachucas, and Cave Creek in the Chiricahua Mountains.

Canyon Towhee—Fairly common permanent resident of the thickets in deserts, valleys, foothills, and lower mountain canyons. This bird may not be colorful, but it is confiding. Often seen about cabins, picnic areas, and parking lots. Easy to find at San Xavier Mission, Molino Basin, Florida Wash, Peña Blanca Lake, Patagonia Roadside Rest Area, San Pedro House, and Portal. If you miss it at any of these spots, check under your car before you drive off.

Abert's Towhee—Fairly common permanent resident of the undergrowth in valley mesquite thickets and riparian woodlands, usually near permanent water. Abert's has one of the smallest ranges of any species that lives primarily in the U.S. Can be found at Sweetwater Wetlands, Marana Pecan Grove, Kino Springs, Patagonia-Sonoita Creek Preserve, the San Pedro

House, and—since the early 1990s—just downstream from Portal along Cave Creek.

Rufous-winged Sparrow—Uncommon and local permanent resident of desertscrub and desert grasslands mixed with cholla near the Santa Rita Mountains, on the Tohono O'Odham Nation lands, and in the Tucson area. Search for this species at the Shannon-Broadway Desert or at the junction of Speedway and Anklam west of Tucson, on Wilmot Road about a half-mile north of Interstate 10 in Tucson, Continental, Florida Wash, Amado Roadside Rest Area, and both Chino and Montosa Canyons. Some summers Rufous-winged Sparrow expands its range all the way up the Santa Cruz River to the first pond at Kino Springs.

Cassin's Sparrow—Fairly common summer resident July through September when its song can be heard in valley mesquite grasslands. In wet years it also sings from March to mid-May. Rare at other seasons. Cassin's occurs in the same areas and sings its poignant song in the same season—fortunately, for identification purposes—as the similar Botteri's Sparrow. Proven locations include Florida Wash, Nogales Airport, Highway 82 east of Sonoita, lower Garden Canyon Road in the Huachuca Mountains, the San Pedro House, Davis Road west of Tombstone, and—especially in wet years—at Lake Cochise and at the junction of the San Simon and Portal Roads.

Botteri's Sparrow—Fairly common summer resident of valley mesquite grasslands, especially in stands of tall Sacaton Grass. Difficult to find and to identify except when it sings its "bouncing ball" song in May (some years) and during the rainy season from July through September. Has been found along the Box Canyon Road below Madera Canyon, along the lower Madera Canyon Road, at the Nogales Airport, the Research Ranch near Elgin, the grassland below Garden Canyon in the Huachucas, at the San Pedro House, in fields west of Rodeo, and along the Guadalupe Canyon Road.

Rufous-crowned Sparrow—Fairly common permanent resident on rocky slopes in the foothills and in interior chaparral in the mountains. Fairly easy to find in such areas as Sycamore Canyon, Peña Blanca Lake, Florida Wash, Patagonia Roadside Rest Area, French Joe Canyon, Scheelite Canyon and Coronado National Memorial in the Huachucas, Chiricahua National Monument, Silver Creek near Portal, and Guadalupe Canyon.

Five-striped Sparrow—Rare summer resident of subtropical scrub in steep-walled foothill canyons along the Mexican border. Occasional in winter. Since the first U.S. record of a lone bird in 1957 in lower Madera Canyon, breeding populations of Five-stripes have been found in a few south-draining canyons of the Atascosa Mountains west of Nogales. Most birders try California Gulch four miles south of the Ruby Road. The road into California Gulch is rough, but it is only a half-mile walk down to the sparrow. Sycamore Canyon, beginning about three miles south of the trailhead, is another location. Here intrepid birders simply follow the canyon bed down to the sparrows without the benefit of an established trail. There are also old records from both Chino Canyon on the west side of the Santa Ritas, and along Sonoita Creek below the Patagonia Roadside Rest Area.

Brewer's Sparrow—Common to abundant winter visitor in desert, weedy fields, valley mesquite grasslands, and lower canyon outlets. Fairly easy to find off Sandario Road in Avra Valley west of Tucson, Marana Pecan Grove, Kino Springs, Palominas Road west of the San Pedro River, Cochise College in the Sulphur Springs Valley, and along Portal Road.

Black-chinned Sparrow—Uncommon permanent resident of interior chaparral in the Santa Catalina Mountains, the Whetstone Mountains, the Mule Mountains above Bisbee, and the northeastern quarter of the Chiricahua Mountains. In winter uses mesquite thickets in desert washes and foothills. Summer locations are Molino Basin in the Santa Catalinas, French Joe Canyon, and Silver Creek in the Chiricahuas. In winter Black-chins can be found in King Canyon across Kinney Road from the entrance to the Arizona-Sonora Desert Museum, McCleary Wash, and usually in good numbers between Portal and USFS boundary in Cave Creek. Some winters they are also at Catalina State Park and below Proctor Road in lower Madera Canyon. Given its usual habitat preferences, the most bizarre winter location in Southeastern Arizona for Black-chinned Sparrow is in the reeds along the shoreline of Patagonia Lake, where it is occasional.

Black-throated Sparrow—Common permanent resident in both Sonoran and Chihuahuan desert scrub. Easy to find in the desert surrounding Tucson, Florida Wash, along the San Pedro River at Charleston, in the desert between Portal and Rodeo, and along the road into Guadalupe Canyon.

Sage Sparrow—Uncommon to fairly common, depending on the winter, in open mesquite and saltbush flats. Locations include Avra Valley, the Santa Cruz Flats, Picacho Reservoir, Sulphur Springs Valley—especially near Whitewater Draw, and the San Simon Valley. Seldom flies, prefers to run on the ground.

Lark Bunting—Common to abundant winter visitor to open desert flats and valley fields and grasslands. Flocks of Lark Buntings arrive in August and the final birds do not depart till early June. Fields along the Santa Cruz River at Sweetwater Wetlands, Sierra Vista Wastewater Ponds, Willcox golf course, Highway 191 between Sunizona and Elfrida, Central Highway west of Cochise College in the Sulphur Springs Valley, and along the Stateline Road near Rodeo usually host dozens, if not hundreds, of buntings.

Grasshopper Sparrow—Fairly common resident of dense grasslands from Arivaca east to the entrance road to Guadalupe Canyon. The Sonoita Grasslands, San Rafael Valley, the entrance road to Garden Canyon in the Huachuca Mountains, and along Highway 80 south of Apache are regular locations. During winter, more widespread and possible to encounter in pastures and grassy swales in Avra Valley west of Tucson as well as in all open valleys.

Baird's Sparrow—Uncommon but rarely seen winter visitor to high valley grasslands along the border. Seems to prefer areas where the grass is fairly tall or mixed with a few weeds on rolling hills. Most Tucson birders look for Baird's in the San Rafael Valley. It also occurs in the Sonoita grasslands, along the Palominas Road in the upper San Pedro Valley, and east of McNeal off Leslie Canyon Road in the Sulphur Springs Valley.

Yellow-eyed Junco—Common permanent resident of grassy areas within mountain coniferous forests. Easy to find in summer at Rose Canyon Lake in the Santa Catalinas, at the Ramsey Vista Campground in the Huachucas, and at Rustler Park in the Chiricahua Mountains. When populations are high Yellow-eyed Junco also breeds in grassy areas of major canyons such as Madera, Ramsey, and South Fork Cave Creek. Look for it at the Santa Rita Lodge, Ramsey Canyon Preserve, Portal, Paradise and other canyon outlets during winter, especially at seed-feeding stations.

McCown's Longspur—Rare winter visitor in bare valley fields, stubble, and sparse grasses. This hard-to-see species has been found in the Sonoita Grasslands, San Rafael Valley, at the Sierra Vista Wastewater fields, and in fields along Highway 191 north of Elfrida on the Essary Hay, Zuck Farm, and at Seven Leagues Ranch. Look for it amid flocks of Horned Larks.

Chestnut-collared Longspur—Fairly common winter visitor in tall valley grasslands near Sonoita, in the San Rafael Valley, in the Sulphur Springs Valley at Zuck Farm and Essary Hay, and irregularly at Willow Tank near Rodeo. Sometimes abundant in migration.

Northern Cardinal—Common permanent resident of thickets and riparian woodlands in deserts, valley mesquite grasslands, and foothill canyons. Usually easy to find at San Xavier Mission, Saguaro National Park, Kino Springs, Patagonia-Sonoita Creek Preserve, San Pedro River at the San Pedro House, and Portal.

Pyrrhuloxia—Fairly common to common permanent resident in thickets and riparian woodlands in deserts, valley mesquite grasslands, and foothill canyons. More common from the San Pedro Valley westward to about Ajo. Pyrrhuloxias have the peculiar habit of moving up in elevation into the canyon outlets of the border ranges during winter. Locations include San Xavier Mission, Marana Pecan Grove, Tubac, Patagonia-Sonoita Creek Preserve, the lower Ramsey Canyon Road, Sulphur Springs Valley, the Big Thicket below Portal, and—during winter—Portal.

Yellow Grosbeak—Approximately 15 summer records of this Mexican vagrant since its first appearance in the United States near Patagonia in 1971. Most records are of "one-day wonders." Virtually all records fall in either June or July, but the most recent occurrence was an adult male that spent nearly a week in late May 2004 at the Arizona-Sonora Desert Museum. It seems to prefer major sycamore canyons with streams in the border ranges, and river valley cottonwood groves with permanent water. Madera Canyon has had the most records, but it has also been reported from the Patagonia Roadside Rest Area, Sycamore Canyon, Ramsey Canyon Preserve, the San Pedro River at Fairbank, and Cave Creek Canyon at the Southwestern Research Station. Yellow Grosbeak is sure to get top billing on the Tucson Audubon Society rare bird tape on on the AZ/NM Birdchat Listserve if one strays into the Southeastern corner.

Black-headed Grosbeak—Common summer resident of canyon riparian, pine-oak woodland, and open Ponderosa Pine forest in the mountains. Migrates through desert oases and valley groves. Easy to find at Rose Canyon Lake, and Sycamore, Madera, Ramsey, and Cave Creek Canyons. Common during migration at the Arizona-Sonora Desert Museum, Patagonia-Sonoita Creek Preserve, and along the San Pedro River.

Blue Grosbeak—Common summer resident of mesquite valley grassland and foothill canyon thickets, but arriving later than most other migrants. Very rare in winter. Probably reaches its greatest density in the weedy edges of irrigated fields. Reliable locations are Kino Springs, Patagonia-Sonoita Creek Preserve, San Pedro River, Cochise College campus in the Sulphur Springs Valley, Stateline Road near Rodeo, and the big mesquite thicket between Portal and USFS boundary. In late August large numbers pour through the Altar, Santa Cruz, Sonoita Creek, and San Pedro Valleys.

Lazuli Bunting—Common spring and fall migrant in valley riparian thickets, tall weeds on the edge of irrigated fields and ponds, and foothill canyon thickets. Uncommon winter visitor. Rare in summer. Can be found at the Marana Pecan Grove, Kino Springs, Patagonia-Sonoita Creek Preserve, Sierra Vista Wastewater Ponds, San Pedro House, Willcox golf course pond, and Portal. Most winters easiest to see at the Patons' home in Patagonia.

Indigo Bunting—Uncommon and local summer resident, primarily in the Sonoita Creek area, but breeding enclaves have occurred, at least intermittently, in Silver Creek in the Chiricahua Mountains and in Guadalupe Canyon. From mid-April through May and again in August and the first half of September migrant Indigo Buntings are uncommon in weedy river valleys, foothill canyons, and lower mountain canyons, often with Lazuli Buntings. Casual at the same locations in winter. Aside from in and around Patagonia, other areas to check include Arivaca Cienaga, Kino Springs, the San Pedro House, and Portal.

Varied Bunting—Fairly common local summer resident in foothill canyon mesquite thickets and thornscrub, arriving later than most other migrants. Proven locations are California Gulch and lower Sycamore Canyon west of Nogales, Florida Wash and Proctor Road on the road into Madera Canyon, the bridge on the Box Canyon Road, the first pond at Kino Springs, Patagonia Roadside Rest Area, Fairbank on the San Pedro River, Sulphur Draw one mile west of Willow Tank near Rodeo, and the entrance area at

Guadalupe Canyon. Varied Buntings arrived on the grounds of the Arizona-Sonora Desert Museum in 2003, and returned in 2004.

Painted Bunting—Rare to uncommon late summer visitor to rank undergrowth in valley, foothill, and lower canyon ponds, streams, and riparian groves. Casual at other times of the year. Formerly almost all birds were greenish immatures and females, but in recent years adult males are also well represented. Some locations Painted Bunting seem to turn up annually include the Arivaca Cienaga, Kino Springs, Patagonia-Sonoita Creek Preserve, Kingfisher Pond on the San Pedro River, Whitewater Draw, and Portal. They also show up sporadically at sewage ponds from Avra Valley to Sierra Vista.

Eastern Meadowlark—Common permanent resident of valley grasslands from Arivaca and the Santa Rita Mountains eastward. Less common westward and in winter. Easy to find near Sonoita, in the San Rafael Valley, at the San Pedro House, lower Ramsey Canyon Road, Essary Hay and Whitewater Draw Wildlife Refuge in the Sulphur Springs Valley, and along the Portal Road. The race of Eastern Meadowlark that breeds in Southeastern Arizona, *lilianae,* has virtually pure white outer tail feathers, slightly whiter than those of Western Meadowlark. The most useful visible field character is a distinct blackish post-ocular stripe that contrasts with *lilianae's* pale cheek. In Western Meadowlark the stripe behind the eye blurs into a dark-streaked cheek. Voice is always preferable to nuances of plumage when separating the two meadowlark species.

Western Meadowlark—Fairly common winter resident of valley grasslands and irrigated fields near Tucson and west of the Santa Rita Mountains. In winter can usually be found near Avra Valley Sewage Ponds, in the fields adjacent to the Marana Pecan Grove, or in the Santa Cruz Flats. Less common farther east during winter at such locations as the Sierra Vista Wastewater fields and at Essary Hay Company fields in the Sulphur Springs Valley. Western Meadowlarks are rare and irregular breeders on the Santa Cruz River near Tucson and in Avra Valley during exceptionally wet years. The last documented nest in the Sulphur Springs Valley was found in 1941.

Yellow-headed Blackbird—Common to abundant winter visitor and uncommon summer resident near permanent water with tall reeds in the valleys. Also winters at cattle pens and in irrigated fields. The most reliable sites are at Sweetwater Wetlands, Picacho Reservoir, Sierra Vista Wastewater Ponds, farm ponds and fields along the Hereford Road east of the San Pedro River, and the Willcox golf course pond, Whitewater Draw Wildlife Refuge, and Willow Tank on the east side of the Chiricahua Mountains. Huge numbers of Yellow-heads are easiest to see when they come in to roost on late winter afternoons.

Great-tailed Grackle—Common permanent resident in cities, on farms, and at tree-lined ponds in the deserts and valleys. The first record of this bird in Southeastern Arizona was in 1935 at Safford. Now it is common in every city and town below 4,500 feet in elevation.

Bronzed Cowbird—Fairly common summer resident of irrigated fields, golf courses, and lawns, and uncommon in mountain canyons with sycamores. Uncommon in winter at livestock pens in the Santa Cruz Valley. In summer some good locations include the Arizona-Sonora Desert Museum, Madera Canyon, Kino Springs golf course club house, the Patagonia city park, and Portal. In winter, Bronzed Cowbirds can usually be found at cattle feedlots in the Tucson area. This species was first recorded in Arizona at Tucson in 1909.

Black-vented Oriole—Mexican vagrant in spring and possibly summer to canyon riparian in foothills and mountains along the border. This beautiful oriole is superficially similar to Scott's, but it lacks any white in the wing and has an all-black tail, including the undertail coverts. The only accepted record is from Patagonia Lake State Park on April 18, 1991. There is another possibly valid record from Cave Creek Canyon dating back to July 1971.

Orchard Oriole—Rare spring and fall migrant, and accidental winter visitor to desert oases, valley river, foothill canyon, and lower mountain canyon groves, often to feeders at private residences. Most birds are females or immatures. Recent records are from the Santa Cruz River north of the Ina Road Bridge, residential Tucson, and the George Walker House in Paradise in the Chiricahua Mountains.

Hooded Oriole—Fairly common summer resident in desert oases, valley groves, and sycamore canyons in foothills and lower mountains. Increasingly common in the cities, particularly around hummingbird feeders. Occasionally winters in Tucson. Nests in palm trees in the cities, and in walnuts, sycamores, and cottonwoods elsewhere. Can be found in Agua Caliente Park in Tucson, at the Arizona-Sonora Desert Museum, Sycamore Canyon, Madera Canyon, Patagonia Roadside Rest Area, San Pedro House, and at Portal.

Streak-backed Oriole—Very rare Mexican resident along the lower San Pedro and the lower Santa Cruz River Valleys. Nearly annual now at Dudleyville. Nesting pairs successfully fledged young at Dudleyville in 1993 1994, 1998, and 2002, and there were two pairs at Dudleyville in 1997 and 1998. Another pair has twice nested unsuccessfully at the Marana Pecan Grove in 1994 and 1995. In Sonora, Mexico it is found in river valley riparian woodland, where it builds large pendulous nests on the ends of dangling limbs. Has wintered sporadically in Tucson, Green Valley, and Arivaca. This bird usually tops the Tucson Audubon Society rare bird tape and the AZ/NM Birdchat Listserve when it is present.

Bullock's Oriole—Fairly common summer resident in desert oases, valley groves, and sycamore canyons in foothills and lower mountains. Winters sporadically in Tucson. Proven locations include the Santa Rita Lodge in

Madera Canyon, Patagonia-Sonoita Creek Preserve, San Pedro House on the San Pedro River, and along main street in Portal.

Baltimore Oriole—Casual spring visitor to lower canyon groves and foothill residences in the Chiricahua Mountains, especially near Portal, and to Tucson. Accidental in fall. Almost all records pertain to males, perhaps because of the difficulty separating female Baltimore from female Bullock's Oriole. Not reported most years.

Scott's Oriole—Fairly common summer resident of upper valley yucca grasslands, foothill oak savanna, and mountain pine-oak woodlands. Very rare in winter at feeders in the Santa Cruz Valley and lower mountain canyons. Usually nests in yucca, but occasionally in small trees. Can be found in Molino Basin, in the agaves along Highway 82 just east of Sonoita, in the yuccas along Highway 92 south of Sierra Vista, along Highway 181 west of Chiricahua National Monument, and in the mountain canyons such as Madera, Ramsey, Miller, and Cave Creek. Visits canyon hummingbird feeders in Madera Canyon, Ramsey Canyon, and at Portal in the spring, but much less often in summer. Somewhat regular but very rare during winter at private residence feeders in Tucson and Nogales, and in Ash and Stump Canyons near Sierra Vista.

Purple Finch—Irregular migrant and winter visitor to desert oases, valley, foothill canyon, and mountain canyon groves, primarily to private feeding stations. There is one mid-June record from Portal, as well as a record from Ponderosa Pine forest in the Santa Catalina Mountains. Most records only involve a single bird. Recent reports are from Madera Canyon and from the Patons' home in Patagonia.

Cassin's Finch—Irregular but sometimes fairly common winter visitor in canyon riparian groves and in open pine forest. During major invasions occasionally descends to Tucson, where it shows a preference for groves of introduced pines in parks and cemeteries. Cassin's quickly becomes a habitué of seed-feeding stations in major canyons such as Sonoita Creek, Madera, Ramsey, and Cave Creek, as well as at summer homes in the Ponderosa Pine forest in the Santa Catalina Mountains. In 1990 Cassin's Finches summered in Portal, and there are a few other summer records of one to a few birds from both Portal and Paradise.

House Finch—Abundant permanent resident in cities, farms, deserts, valleys, and wet canyons in the foothills and lower mountains. Flocks of this species almost monopolize feeders in towns such as Patagonia and Portal, and at the Santa Rita Lodge in Madera Canyon, Ash Canyon, Portal, and Paradise.

Red Crossbill—Uncommon and irregular resident of major canyons with tall pines and mountain coniferous forests. Some winters crossbills descend to Tucson parks and cemeteries with conifers, where they have even been recorded breeding and lingering into summer. Sporadic, but possible, at Bear Canyon and Rose Canyon Lake in the Santa Catalinas, upper Madera

Canyon in the Santa Ritas, Sawmill Canyon in the Huachucas, and at Rustler Park in the Chiricahuas. Some years there is a flock between the Southwestern Research Station and Herb Martyr Recreation Site in Cave Creek Canyon.

Lesser Goldfinch—Common resident of oases and river groves in the deserts, valleys, foothills, and mountain canyon outlets. Can be found at Aravaipa Canyon, the Marana Pecan Grove, Arivaca Creek, Kino Springs, Patagonia-Sonoita Creek Preserve, Upper Picnic Area in Garden Canyon in the Huachuca Mountains, Kingfisher Pond on the San Pedro River, and at Portal. Sporadic in summer in mountain meadows and grassy burns within coniferous forests. The great preponderance of male Lesser Goldfinches in Arizona have green backs, but very rarely a male with a black back is seen.

Lawrence's Goldfinch—Irregular and uncommon fall and winter visitor in desert and river valley weedy fields, pecan groves, and riparian woodlands. Most common in the lowlands and agricultural areas near Tucson. Proven locations are along the Santa Cruz River anywhere between Sweetwater Wetlands and Cortaro Road Bridge, the Marana Pecan Grove, Tanque Verde Wash east of Tucson, Continental Workyard, Tubac, and Arivaca Creek. Every three to ten years there are invasions as far east as the upper San Pedro River at Hereford, and—very infrequently—to Portal.

American Goldfinch—Fairly common but local winter resident of riparian thickets, pecan orchards, and river groves in valleys, foothills, and mountain canyon outlets. Numbers fluctuate from winter to winter. Feeding stations such as the Patons' home in Patagonia, Ballator's home in Ash Canyon, Jensens' home in Portal, or the George Walker House in Paradise are usually reliable. Other areas include the Marana Pecan Grove, Kino Springs, Patagonia-Sonoita Creek Preserve, Upper Picnic Area in Garden Canyon in the Huachuca Mountains, Kingfisher Pond on the San Pedro River, and Cave Creek Canyon in the Chiricahua Mountains.

Evening Grosbeak—Irregular and uncommon summer resident in mountain coniferous forests, usually near deciduous trees such as maples and Box Elders. Unpredictable but often found near Bear Wallow in the Santa Catalina Mountains, in Sawmill Canyon in the Huachucas, and at Rustler Park in the Chiricahuas. Usually rare in winter, at canyon feeders such as the Santa Rita Lodge in Madera Canyon, Ramsey Canyon Preserve, and in Portal. Over 400 Evening Grosbeaks were recorded, however, on the Portal Christmas Bird Count during the invasion winter of 1996–1997.

BIRDS OF SOUTHEASTERN ARIZONA

BAR GRAPHS

All of the birds that have occurred in Southeastern Arizona through October 2004 are represented in the following graphs. The "Specialties" section, which precedes the bar graphs, provides a fuller picture of the status of the avian specialties found in Southeastern Arizona that are of particular interest to out-of-area birders, as well as species—often locally rare—of special interest to birdwatchers who live within the area.

The abundance definitions used here (see page 287) strike a balance between the probability of finding (seeing or hearing) a species and its actual abundance. In 2000 ABA adopted a set of standard definitions for the bar graphs used in the ABA Birdfinding Guide Series. The aim was to create sensible, easily understood definitions for the abundance and "findability" of birds which would be useful not only within ABA, but also for the whole of the North American birding community. ABA encourages widespread use of these abundance definitions; no specific permission is necessary.

HABITAT CATEGORIES

The habitat categories on the left half of each species' bar graph are designed to tell you where to look for any regularly occurring bird. Of the ten different habitats included, four are riparian, underscoring the importance of water and its associated plants in determining bird distribution and abundance in Southeastern Arizona. The role of elevation and topography in shaping the vegetative community also limits the species of birds that may occur in any given location. In the habitat chart the elevational limits of the habitats are indicated in feet.

Seasonal "pie charts" indicate the times of the year when each species is most likely to be found in any given habitat. Yellow-rumped Warblers, for example, breed in the coniferous forest on the mountain peaks during summer, and they winter in desert and foothill habitats. The bar graph represents them only as common year round. Using the seasonal pie charts in conjunction with the habitat checklist should enable you to predict exactly where you ought to invest your time and energy when searching for any given species.

The following locations within each habitat type are described in the text. They are listed with those nearest to Tucson first, followed by those progressively farther away. Remember that the locations cited below are *not* comprehensive; there are other possible areas within each habitat category that may be equally productive. Also remember that birds are the most mobile of all wildlife. Most birds can and do occur outside of their "preferred" habitats.

Rivers, Ponds, and Lakes: Open water with or without associated marsh vegetation is the most limited habitat in Southeastern Arizona. Yet all of the

Willcox Playa/Lake Cochise　　　Richard Cachor Taylor

pelagic and near-shore birds, herons and egrets, waterfowl, shorebirds, and gulls and terns in this region are dependent on it. With few exceptions, all large bodies of water in this area lie below 4,000 feet in elevation. Areas to visit to see open-water and marsh birds are: Sweetwater Wetlands, Avra Valley Sewage Ponds, Picacho Reservoir, Nogales Sewage Ponds, Palo Duro Pond, Aguirre Lake at Buenos Aires National Wildlife Refuge, Peña Blanca Lake, Big Pond at Sells, Kino Springs, Patagonia Lake, Parker Canyon Lake, Sierra Vista Wastewater Ponds, Kingfisher Pond, Lake Cochise at Willcox, and Willow Tank east of Portal.

Desertscrub: Two distinct arid land biomes meet at elevations below 4,500 feet in Southeastern Arizona: the Sonoran and the Chihuahuan Deserts. Most desert birds, however, occur in both. Cactus Wren and Curve-billed Thrasher are examples of species which range across the lowlands of the entire area. Areas which harbor typical

Desert Bighorn Sheep, Aravaipa Canyon
Richard Cachor Taylor

desert species include: Tucson, Sabino Canyon, the Arizona-Sonora Desert Museum, Saguaro National Park, the west entrance of Aravaipa Canyon, Sells, Fairbank on the San Pedro River, Douglas, and the Big Thicket east of Portal.

Valley Grassland and Desert Fields: This habitat includes vast tracts of unbroken savanna as well as the enormous fields at agricultural developments, also usually below 4,500 feet in elevation. Grasshopper Sparrows and Eastern Meadowlarks share this habitat with wintering Mountain Plovers and Chestnut-collared Longspurs. The best grasslands are those at the Buenos Aires National Wildlife Refuge, the Sonoita Grassland, the San Rafael

Sonoita Grassland with Santa Rita Mountains in the background.
Richard Cachor Taylor

Grassland, near Palominas in the San Pedro Valley, the Sulphur Springs Valley, and the upper San Bernardino Valley southeast of the Chiricahuas. Major agricultural areas are found in Avra Valley west of Tucson, near Picacho Reservoir, Kansas Settlement near Willcox, and in the southern Sulphur Springs Valley surrounding Elfrida.

Valley Groves and Pecan Farms: Tall groves of Fremont Cottonwoods and isolated stands of pecans in Southeastern Arizona's broad, arid valleys are magnets for breeding birds, migrants, and rarities that are often far out of range. Gray Hawks and Tropical Kingbirds are among the birds that prefer this habitat. Some of the areas to check for these species include city parks in Tucson, the Marana Pecan Grove, Tubac, the Patagonia-Sonoita Creek Preserve, Arivaca Cienaga, Dudleyville, Kino Springs,

Sonoita Creek   Richard Cachor Taylor

San Pedro House, Kingfisher Pond, and the San Bernardino National Wildlife Refuge.

Foothill Groves: Ordinarily, foothill groves occur at slightly higher elevations than valley groves, usually between 3,500 and 4,500 feet. Sycamore trees intertwine with cottonwoods in the canopy that shades foothill streams. They also have steep canyon walls that create a completely different "edge habitat" from the ecotone that separates river valley groves from the adjacent deserts, grassland, or agricultural fields. Many species are shared with valley groves, but many others are not. Highly-restricted Thick-billed Kingbirds and Rose-throated Becards are good symbols for this habitat. Some of the foothill grove locations discussed in the text include: Patagonia Roadside Rest Area, Harshaw Creek, Arivaca Creek, Aravaipa Canyon, Sycamore Canyon, Muleshoe Ranch Preserve, and Guadalupe Canyon.

Aravaipa Creek
Richard Cachor Taylor

Foothill Thornscrub: A subtropical thicket of spiny shrubs grows on sunny slopes above some foothill groves, generally between the same elevations of 3,500 and 4,500 feet. This limited habitat attracts a group of species that are more common in arid situations on the Pacific slope of western Mexico. Buff-collared Nightjar, Varied Bunting, and Five-striped Sparrow represent these species. Some areas with foothill thornscrub are Sutherland Wash in Catalina State Park, McCleary Wash below Madera Canyon, Chino and Montosa Canyons, Patagonia Roadside Rest Area, the west entrance of Aravaipa Canyon, Sycamore Canyon

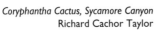

Coryphantha Cactus, Sycamore Canyon
Richard Cachor Taylor

and California Gulch in the Atascosa Mountains, and Guadalupe Canyon on the Arizona/New Mexico border.

Mountain Interior Chaparral: Where nights are too cold for the frost-sensitive species that characterize foothill thornscrub, normally between elevations of 4,500 and 6,500 feet, a structurally similar set of plants covers the slopes. In Southeastern Arizona, the primary plant constituents are frequently manzanita and Mountain Mahogany. Where soils are deeper, however, and there is adequate precipitation, a short woodland of Pinyon Pine and One-seed Juniper replaces the chaparral, but the birds are much the

Heart of Rocks, Chiricahua National Monument
Richard Cachor Taylor

same. Breeding species include Western Scrub-Jay and Virginia's Warbler. Mountain Interior Chaparral and pinyon-juniper woodland can be found at Molino Basin in the Santa Catalina Mountains, in Scheelite Canyon in the Huachuca Mountains, in Coronado National Memorial, at Chiricahua National Monument, and in Silver Creek near Portal.

Mountain Pine-oak Woodland: Sierra Madrean pine-oak woodland is the largest single habitat type in Mexico. Here it reaches its northernmost

outposts in the Border Ranges at mid-elevations between 5,000 and 7,000 feet. Dominant plants include a variety of spring deciduous oaks, Alligator Juniper, and both Chihuahua and Apache Pines. Arizona Woodpecker and Mex-

Mt. Wrightson, Santa Rita Mountains　　Richard Cachor Taylor

ican Jay are typical in this habitat. Areas with mountain pine-oak woodland include slopes adjacent to Madera Canyon, Sycamore Canyon (well below its usual altitudinal limits), Garden, Ramsey, and Miller Canyons in the Huachucas, and Cave Creek and South Fork Canyons in the Chiricahua Mountains.

Mountain Canyon Groves: Owing to the presence of permanent water near or on the surface, strands of Arizona Sycamore flourish in some can-

yons between 5,000 and 6,500 feet. Tall conifers follow the water and the cool-air drainage down these narrow defiles. Elegant Trogon is perhaps the most eloquent symbol of this habitat along the border in Southeastern Arizona, but this is also the center of abundance for Sul-

Cave Creek Canyon, Chiricahua Mountains
Richard Cachor Taylor

phur-bellied Flycatcher and Painted Redstart. Locations with Mountain Canyon Groves include the actual canyon beds of Madera Canyon, Sycamore Canyon, Garden, Ramsey, and Miller Canyons in the Huachucas, and Cave Creek and South Fork Canyons in the Chiricahua Mountains.

Mountain Coniferous Forest: The high ranges above 7,000 feet in Southeastern Arizona have isolated stands of Ponderosa

Barfoot Park and Peak, Chiricahua Mountains
Richard Cachor Taylor

Pine, Douglas-fir, and other trees typical of the Rocky Mountains farther north. With them come Hairy Woodpecker, Steller's Jay, and Red-breasted Nuthatch. In Southeastern Arizona there is paved access to the high Santa Catalina Mountains, and dirt roads climb to the forests of the Huachuca and Chiricahua Mountains. Trails provide access to this habitat type in the upper Santa Rita and Galiuro Mountains.

BAR GRAPH ABUNDANCE CODES

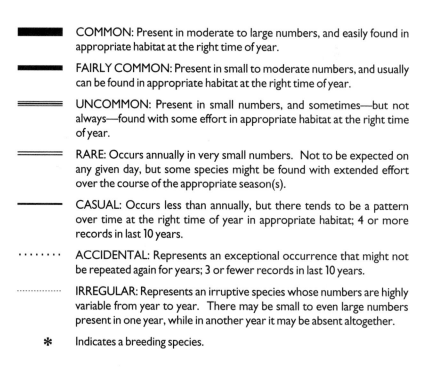

COMMON: Present in moderate to large numbers, and easily found in appropriate habitat at the right time of year.

FAIRLY COMMON: Present in small to moderate numbers, and usually can be found in appropriate habitat at the right time of year.

UNCOMMON: Present in small numbers, and sometimes—but not always—found with some effort in appropriate habitat at the right time of year.

RARE: Occurs annually in very small numbers. Not to be expected on any given day, but some species might be found with extended effort over the course of the appropriate season(s).

CASUAL: Occurs less than annually, but there tends to be a pattern over time at the right time of year in appropriate habitat; 4 or more records in last 10 years.

ACCIDENTAL: Represents an exceptional occurrence that might not be repeated again for years; 3 or fewer records in last 10 years.

IRREGULAR: Represents an irruptive species whose numbers are highly variable from year to year. There may be small to even large numbers present in one year, while in another year it may be absent altogether.

* Indicates a breeding species.

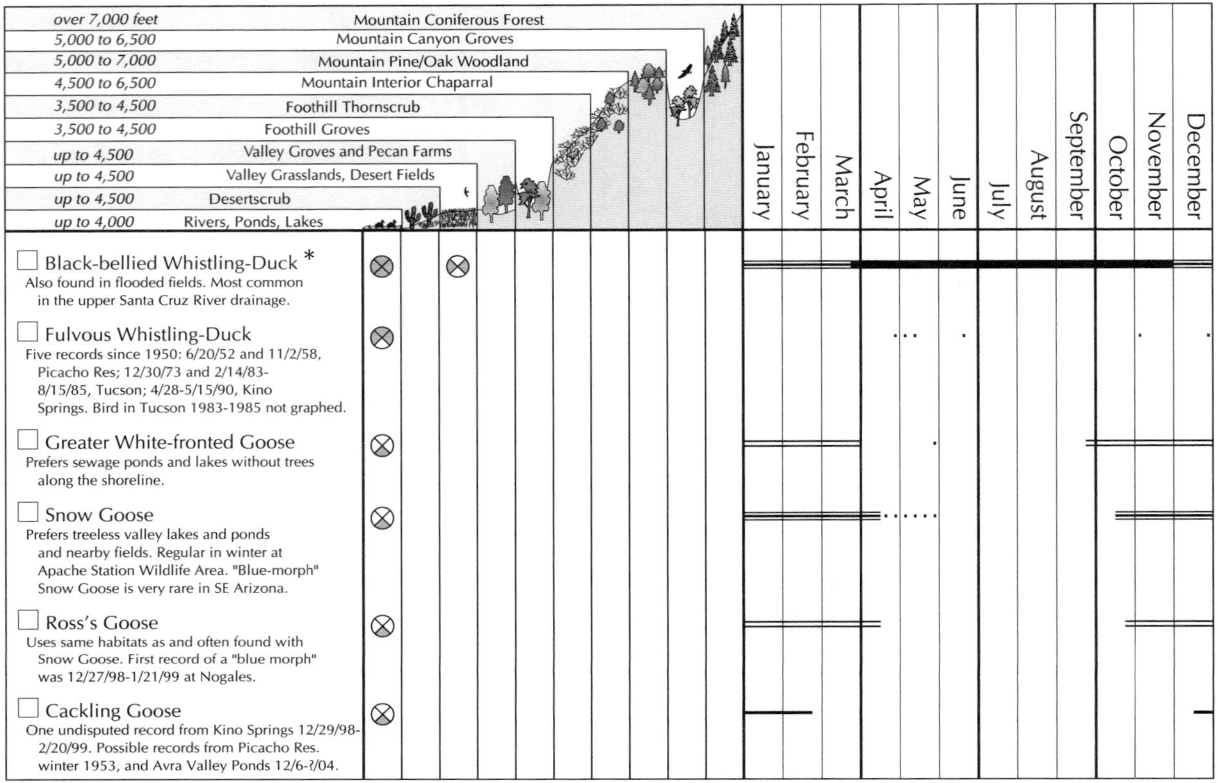

	December	November	October	September	August	July	June	May	April	March	February	January

Habitat legend (left column, bottom to top):

- over 7,000 feet — Mountain Coniferous Forest
- 5,000 to 6,500 — Mountain Canyon Groves
- 5,000 to 7,000 — Mountain Pine/Oak Woodland
- 4,500 to 6,500 — Mountain Interior Chaparral
- 3,500 to 4,500 — Foothill Thornscrub
- 3,500 to 4,500 — Foothill Groves
- up to 4,500 — Valley Groves and Pecan Farms
- up to 4,500 — Valley Grasslands, Desert Fields
- up to 4,500 — Desertscrub
- up to 4,000 — Rivers, Ponds, Lakes

Species:

☐ **Black-bellied Whistling-Duck** *
Also found in flooded fields. Most common in the upper Santa Cruz River drainage.

☐ **Fulvous Whistling-Duck**
Five records since 1950: 6/20/52 and 11/2/58, Picacho Res; 12/30/73 and 2/14/83-8/15/85, Tucson; 4/28-5/15/90, Kino Springs. Bird in Tucson 1983-1985 not graphed.

☐ **Greater White-fronted Goose**
Prefers sewage ponds and lakes without trees along the shoreline.

☐ **Snow Goose**
Prefers treeless valley lakes and ponds and nearby fields. Regular in winter at Apache Station Wildlife Area. "Blue-morph" Snow Goose is very rare in SE Arizona.

☐ **Ross's Goose**
Uses same habitats as and often found with Snow Goose. First record of a "blue morph" was 12/27/98-1/21/99 at Nogales.

☐ **Cackling Goose**
One undisputed record from Kino Springs 12/29/98-2/20/99. Possible records from Picacho Res. winter 1953, and Avra Valley Ponds 12/6-?/04.

Canada Goose
A lone goose summered at Willcox in 2002.

Brant
Two records: 12/29-30/72, Tucson;
5/29/93, Willcox.

Trumpeter Swan
One record: 12/19/94-1/2/95 at Willow Tank,
San Simon Valley, and 1 dead bird
recovered at Gleeson, Sulphur Springs Valley
1/1/98.

Tundra Swan

Wood Duck
Prefers wooded ponds and rivers.

Gadwall *
Has nested at Palo Duro Pond.

Eurasian Wigeon
Usually found with large flocks of American
Wigeon at golf course ponds or sewage ponds.

American Wigeon
Most abundant on golf courses and golf
course ponds.

Mallard *

Mallard "Mexican Duck" *
Most common in San Pedro and Sulphur Springs
Valleys. Pure "Mexican Duck" drakes, lacking
curly black tail feathers, are rare.

Blue-winged Teal

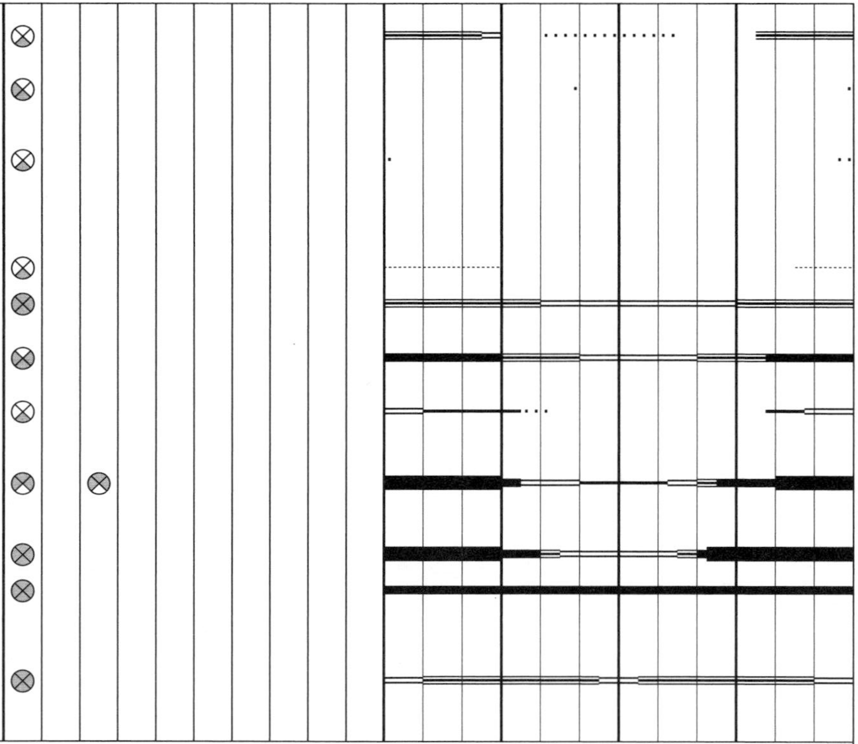

Spring Summer Fall Winter

* Nesting

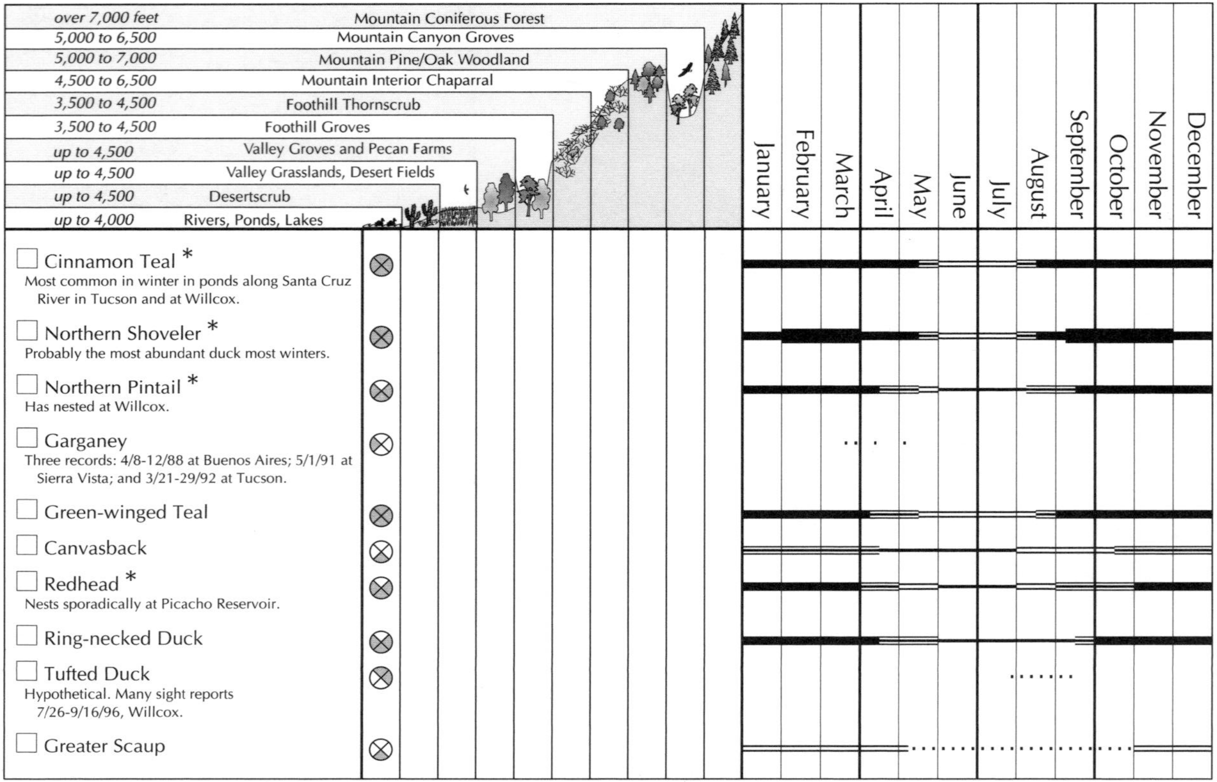

	December	November	October	September	August	July	June	May	April	March	February	January

over 7,000 feet — Mountain Coniferous Forest
5,000 to 6,500 — Mountain Canyon Groves
5,000 to 7,000 — Mountain Pine/Oak Woodland
4,500 to 6,500 — Mountain Interior Chaparral
3,500 to 4,500 — Foothill Thornscrub
3,500 to 4,500 — Foothill Groves
up to 4,500 — Valley Groves and Pecan Farms
up to 4,500 — Valley Grasslands, Desert Fields
up to 4,500 — Desertscrub
up to 4,000 — Rivers, Ponds, Lakes

Cinnamon Teal *
Most common in winter in ponds along Santa Cruz
River in Tucson and at Willcox.

Northern Shoveler *
Probably the most abundant duck most winters.

Northern Pintail *
Has nested at Willcox.

Garganey
Three records: 4/8-12/88 at Buenos Aires; 5/1/91 at
Sierra Vista; and 3/21-29/92 at Tucson.

Green-winged Teal

Canvasback

Redhead *
Nests sporadically at Picacho Reservoir.

Ring-necked Duck

Tufted Duck
Hypothetical. Many sight reports
7/26-9/16/96, Willcox.

Greater Scaup

Lesser Scaup

Harlequin Duck
One record 12/3/95 at a Tucson golf course pond.

Surf Scoter
Vagrant, primarily in fall.

White-winged Scoter
Vagrant, primarily in November.

Black Scoter
Two records: 11/3-4/75, Tucson; 12/30/78, Nogales.

Long-tailed Duck
Five records since 1990 from Tucson, Avra Valley
Sewage Ponds, Apache Station Wildlife
Area, and Sierra Vista Wastewater Ponds.

Bufflehead
A female summered at Lake Cochise
in 2003 and 2004.

Common Goldeneye

Barrow's Goldeneye
Two records: 3/29/73, Tucson;
1/24-2/21/82, Willcox.

Hooded Merganser

Common Merganser
Larger lakes.

Red-breasted Merganser
Larger lakes.

Ruddy Duck *

Spring   Summer   Fall   Winter

* Nesting

	December	November	October	September	August	July	June	May	April	March	February	January

Mountain Coniferous Forest
5,000 to 6,500 — Mountain Canyon Groves
5,000 to 7,000 — Mountain Pine/Oak Woodland
4,500 to 6,500 — Mountain Interior Chaparral
3,500 to 4,500 — Foothill Thornscrub
3,500 to 4,500 — Foothill Groves
up to 4,500 — Valley Groves and Pecan Farms
up to 4,500 — Valley Grasslands, Desert Fields
up to 4,500 — Desertscrub
up to 4,000 — Rivers, Ponds, Lakes

over 7,000 feet

☐ **Blue Grouse**
Hypothetical. All observations occurred in
Chiricahua Mtns from 1973-1985.

☐ **Wild Turkey** *
"Mexican" race turkeys occur in Huachuca Mtns;
rarely San Pedro River, Sonoita Creek, and
Guadalupe Canyon. Forty-four "Mexican" race
turkeys were introduced in Chiricahua Mtns.
in 2003 and 2004.

☐ **Scaled Quail** *
Primarily Chihuahuan Desert grassland.

☐ **Elegant Quail**
Hypothetical. While known to breed within 60
miles of border, origins are unknown for a lone
bird present at a private residence in Douglas
12/6/97-4/12/98 and 10/10/98-3/28/99.

☐ **Gambel's Quail** *

☐ **Northern Bobwhite** *
Extirpated in 1897; efforts at reintroduction of the
"Masked Bobwhite" subspecies began
at Buenos Aires NWR in 1974.

□ **Montezuma Quail** *
Grassy glades from oak savannah to top of Chiricahua Peak.

□ **Pacific Loon**
Recent records are from Parker Canyon Lake and Lake Cochise at Willcox.

□ **Common Loon**
Usually on larger lakes such as Parker Canyon.

□ **Least Grebe**
A lone Least Grebe has been present at Sweetwater Wetlands in Tucson since June 2000, and another was found in a Tucson park in April 2003. Probably nested in 1962 east of Arivaca.

□ **Pied-billed Grebe** *

□ **Horned Grebe**

□ **Eared Grebe** *
Nesting at Willcox since 1992.

□ **Western Grebe**
Most common at Patagonia Lake.

□ **Clark's Grebe**
Occasionally winters at Patagonia Lake. Often found with Western Grebes.

□ **Least Storm-Petrel**
Hypothetical. Sight report 8/24/92, Patagonia Lake.

□ **Red-billed Tropicbird**
Three records: 9/15/27 at Apache Pass on north end of Chiricahua Mtns; 6/29/90 near Tucson; and 5/22/92 in Green Valley.

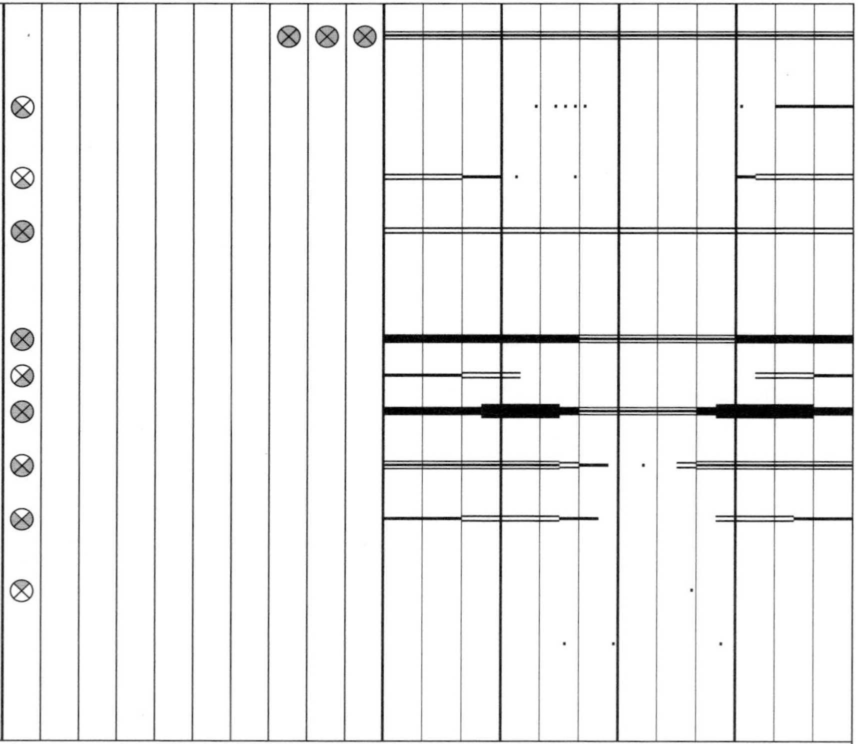

* Nesting

⊗ Spring   ⊗ Summer   ⊗ Fall   ⊗ Winter

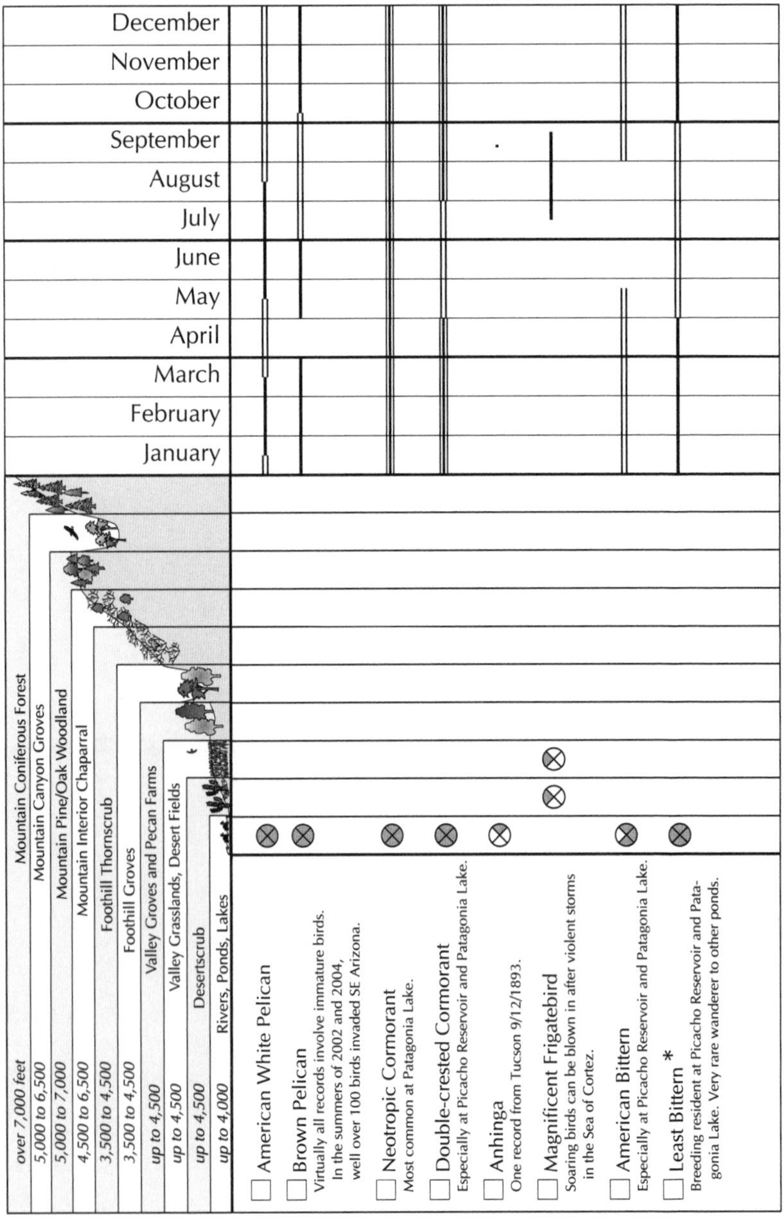

Months (top axis):
December
November
October
September
August
July
June
May
April
March
February
January

Habitat/Elevation categories (vertical labels):

over 7,000 feet — Mountain Coniferous Forest
5,000 to 6,500 — Mountain Canyon Groves
5,000 to 7,000 — Mountain Pine/Oak Woodland
4,500 to 6,500 — Mountain Interior Chaparral
3,500 to 4,500 — Foothill Thornscrub
3,500 to 4,500 — Foothill Groves
up to 4,500 — Valley Groves and Pecan Farms
up to 4,500 — Valley Grasslands, Desert Fields
up to 4,500 — Desertscrub
up to 4,000 — Rivers, Ponds, Lakes

Species:

☐ American White Pelican

☐ Brown Pelican
Virtually all records involve immature birds.
In the summers of 2002 and 2004,
well over 100 birds invaded SE Arizona.

☐ Neotropic Cormorant
Most common at Patagonia Lake.

☐ Double-crested Cormorant
Especially at Picacho Reservoir and Patagonia Lake.

☐ Anhinga
One record from Tucson 9/12/1893.

☐ Magnificent Frigatebird
Soaring birds can be blown in after violent storms
in the Sea of Cortez.

☐ American Bittern
Especially at Picacho Reservoir and Patagonia Lake.

☐ Least Bittern *
Breeding resident at Picacho Reservoir and Patagonia Lake. Very rare wanderer to other ponds.

Great Blue Heron *

Great Egret
Consistent at Reid Park in Tucson, Picacho Reservoir, and Whitewater Draw when the lake is full.

Snowy Egret
Nested at Picacho Reservoir in 1973. Also fairly common at Whitewater Draw when there is water in lake.

Little Blue Heron

Tricolored Heron
Prefers valley ponds with nearby trees.

Reddish Egret
Five records: Avra Valley Sewage Ponds from 8/7-19/96, 7/13/98, and 6/28-7/6/04; Picacho Reservoir 10/21-11/22/01; and Lakeside Park, Tucson,10/11-12/03.

Cattle Egret
Prefers irrigated fields and farm ponds, e.g., Whitewater Draw when there is water in the lake.

Green Heron *
Prefers valley ponds and rivers with nearby trees.

Black-crowned Night-Heron *
Aggregations of over 20 birds are occasionally seen in spring and summer.

Yellow-crowned Night-Heron
Four records: 5/26/68 at Tucson; 5/8-6/16/84 and 6/26-7/12/85 at Dudleyville; and 5/31/92 at Picacho Reservoir.

⊗ Spring   ⊗ Summer   ⊗ Fall   ⊗ Winter

* Nesting

	December							
	November							
	October							
	September							
	August							
	July							
	June							
	May							
	April							
	March							
	February							
	January							

over 7,000 feet	Mountain Coniferous Forest
5,000 to 6,500	Mountain Canyon Groves
5,000 to 7,000	Mountain Pine/Oak Woodland
4,500 to 6,500	Mountain Interior Chaparral
3,500 to 4,500	Foothill Thornscrub
3,500 to 4,500	Foothill Groves
up to 4,500	Valley Groves and Pecan Farms
up to 4,500	Valley Grasslands, Desert Fields
up to 4,500	Desertscrub
up to 4,000	Rivers, Ponds, Lakes

☐ White Ibis
Three records: 6/22-9/14/86 at Picacho Reservoir, 8/1/88 on Santa Cruz River in Tucson, and 7/5-9/15/99 at Nogales.

☐ White-faced Ibis
Also found in flooded fields and shoulder-deep in alfalfa.

☐ Roseate Spoonbill
Graph represents flock of 33 at Picacho Reservoir in 1973. Three records since: one bird at Nogales Sewage Ponds 7/22-23/96; one at Picacho Reservoir 9/25-10/4/97; and one at Rio Rico 8/23-9/21/04.

☐ Wood Stork
Four records since 1950: 6/20/52 at Picacho Reservoir; 5/15/55 at Tucson; 12/24/72 at Tombstone; and 7/30/75 at Patagonia.

☐ Black Vulture *
Most sightings from Patagonia, Nogales, and the Sells area.

☐ Turkey Vulture *
Uncommon in winter primarily at Nogales and on Tohono O'odham Nation lands.

California Condor
Extirpated. Last recorded in Chiricahua Mtns 3/7/1881. Reintroduced to Grand Canyon and Vermilion Cliffs in northern Arizona 12/12/1996.

Osprey
Can occur in any habitat during migration.

Swallow-tailed Kite
Hypothetical. Sight report, Dudleyville 8/2-3/80.

White-tailed Kite *
Presently Marana, Buenos Aires, and San Rafael Grassland are the best areas.

Mississippi Kite *
San Pedro River, especially near Dudleyville and St. David.

Bald Eagle
San Rafael and Sulphur Springs Valleys.

Northern Harrier *

Sharp-shinned Hawk *

Cooper's Hawk *
Fairly common resident in Tucson residential areas.

Northern Goshawk *
Some winters a few goshawks invade lowlands.

Great Black-Hawk
Hypothetical. One sight report 7/27/87 on upper San Pedro River.

Gray Hawk *
More common in valley cottonwood groves.

* Nesting   Spring   Summer   Fall   Winter

December	
November	
October	
September	
August	
July	
June	
May	
April	
March	
February	
January	

over 7,000 feet — Mountain Coniferous Forest
5,000 to 6,500 — Mountain Canyon Groves
5,000 to 7,000 — Mountain Pine/Oak Woodland
4,500 to 6,500 — Mountain Interior Chaparral
3,500 to 4,500 — Foothill Thornscrub
3,500 to 4,500 — Foothill Groves
up to 4,500 — Valley Groves and Pecan Farms
up to 4,500 — Valley Grasslands, Desert Fields
up to 4,500 — Desertscrub
up to 4,000 — Rivers, Ponds, Lakes

☐ Common Black-Hawk *
Aravaipa, Redfield, and Bass Canyons in Galiuro
Mtns, and near Winkelman on San Pedro River.

☐ Harris's Hawk *
Always a breeding pair at Roger Rd Sewage Ponds
in Tucson; fairly common north of Tucson.

☐ Red-shouldered Hawk
Vagrant. Records from July through early February.

☐ Broad-winged Hawk
Vagrant. Most records from Huachucas, Chiricahuas

☐ Short-tailed Hawk *
Since 2001 regular but rare in summer at Barfoot
Park in Chiricahua Mtns. Also recorded from
Huachuca Mtns, and sight reports in 2004
from Santa Catalina Mtns.

☐ Swainson's Hawk *

☐ White-tailed Hawk
Hypothetical. Two sight records: 12/64-1/65, Avra
Valley; 1/5-2/8/71 in San Rafael Grassland.

☐ Zone-tailed Hawk *
Has wintered in Tucson in recent years.

	Red-tailed Hawk *
	Harlan's form is extremely rare in winter.
	Ferruginous Hawk
	Fairly common in Sulphur Springs Valley; light-morph outnumber dark-morph birds by 20:1.
	Rough-legged Hawk
	Golden Eagle *
	Soars over all habitats; nests primarily on foothill and mountain cliffs.
	Crested Caracara *
	Tohono O'odham Nation lands; rare in winter in Avra Valley and near Green Valley.
	American Kestrel *
	Hunts open areas, fields, meadows, and burns.
	Merlin
	Aplomado Falcon
	Extirpated. Last record in Sulphur Springs Valley was 11/13/39 near McNeal; last record in San Pedro Valley was 10/7/40 near St. David.
	Peregrine Falcon *
	Prefers areas adjacent to cliffs in summer, and river valley areas in winter.
	Prairie Falcon *
	Prefers areas adjacent to cliffs in summer, and open valleys in winter.
	Black Rail
	Hypothetical. Two sight records: 4/23/1881 at Tucson and 4/18-19/1977 at Willcox.

* Nesting

⊗ Spring ⊗ Summer ⊗ Fall ⊗ Winter

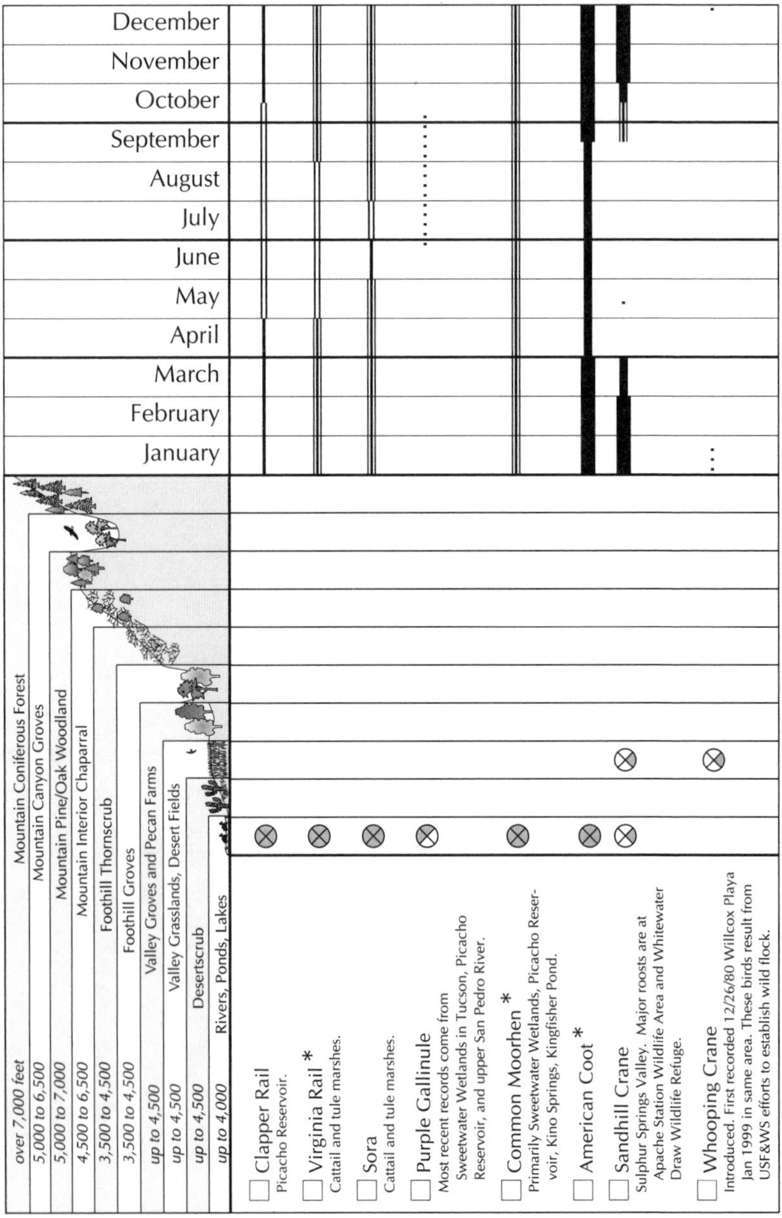
December
November
October
September
August
July
June
May
April
March
February
January
over 7,000 feet
Mountain Coniferous Forest
5,000 to 6,500
Mountain Canyon Groves
5,000 to 7,000
Mountain Pine/Oak Woodland
4,500 to 6,500
Mountain Interior Chaparral
3,500 to 4,500
Foothill Thornscrub
3,500 to 4,500
Foothill Groves
up to 4,500
Valley Groves and Pecan Farms
up to 4,500
Valley Grasslands, Desert Fields
up to 4,500
Desertscrub
up to 4,000
Rivers, Ponds, Lakes
Clapper Rail
Picacho Reservoir.
Virginia Rail *
Cattail and tule marshes.
Sora
Cattail and tule marshes.
Purple Gallinule
Most recent records come from Sweetwater Wetlands in Tucson, Picacho Reservoir, and upper San Pedro River.
Common Moorhen *
Primarily Sweetwater Wetlands, Picacho Reservoir, Kino Springs, Kingfisher Pond.
American Coot *
Sandhill Crane
Sulphur Springs Valley. Major roosts are at Apache Station Wildlife Area and Whitewater Draw Wildlife Refuge.
Whooping Crane
Introduced. First recorded 12/26/80 Willcox Playa Jan 1999 in same area. These birds result from USF&WS efforts to establish wild flock.

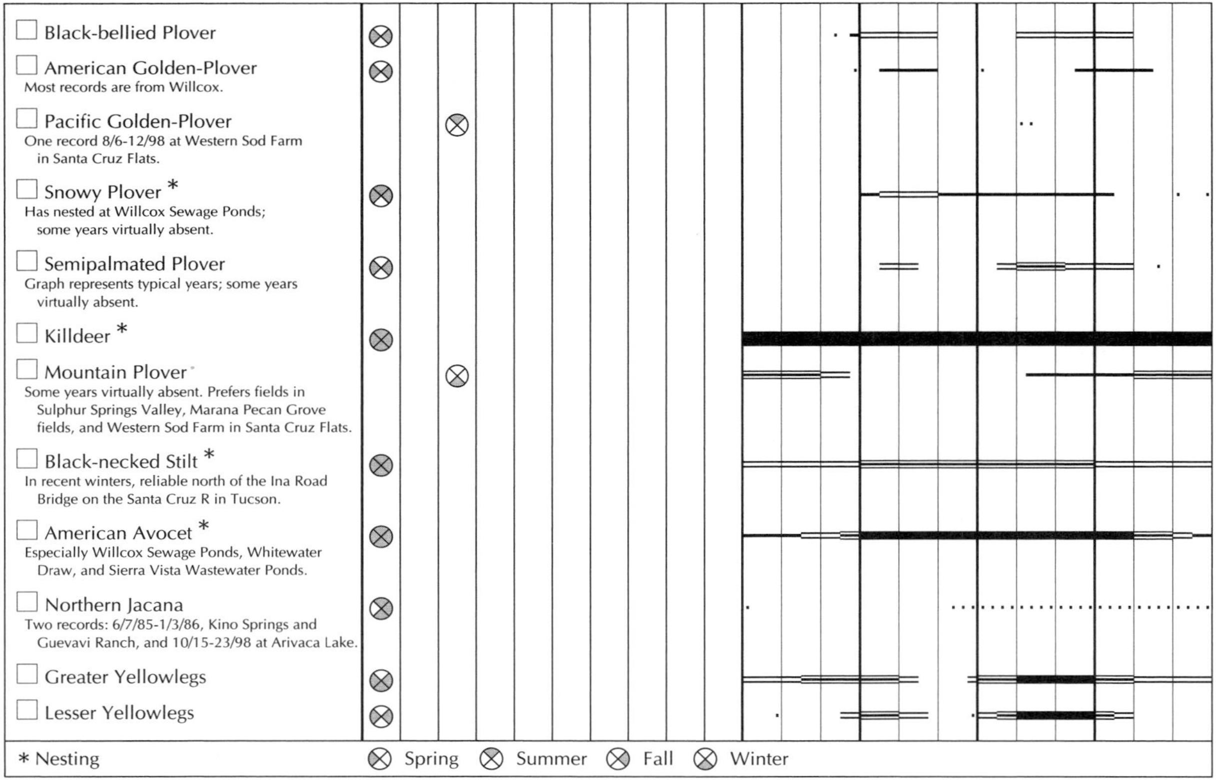

☐ Black-bellied Plover

☐ American Golden-Plover
Most records are from Willcox.

☐ Pacific Golden-Plover
One record 8/6-12/98 at Western Sod Farm
in Santa Cruz Flats.

☐ Snowy Plover *
Has nested at Willcox Sewage Ponds;
some years virtually absent.

☐ Semipalmated Plover
Graph represents typical years; some years
virtually absent.

☐ Killdeer *

☐ Mountain Plover
Some years virtually absent. Prefers fields in
Sulphur Springs Valley, Marana Pecan Grove
fields, and Western Sod Farm in Santa Cruz Flats.

☐ Black-necked Stilt *
In recent winters, reliable north of the Ina Road
Bridge on the Santa Cruz R in Tucson.

☐ American Avocet *
Especially Willcox Sewage Ponds, Whitewater
Draw, and Sierra Vista Wastewater Ponds.

☐ Northern Jacana
Two records: 6/7/85-1/3/86, Kino Springs and
Guevavi Ranch, and 10/15-23/98 at Arivaca Lake.

☐ Greater Yellowlegs

☐ Lesser Yellowlegs

* Nesting   ⊗ Spring   ⊗ Summer   ⊗ Fall   ⊗ Winter

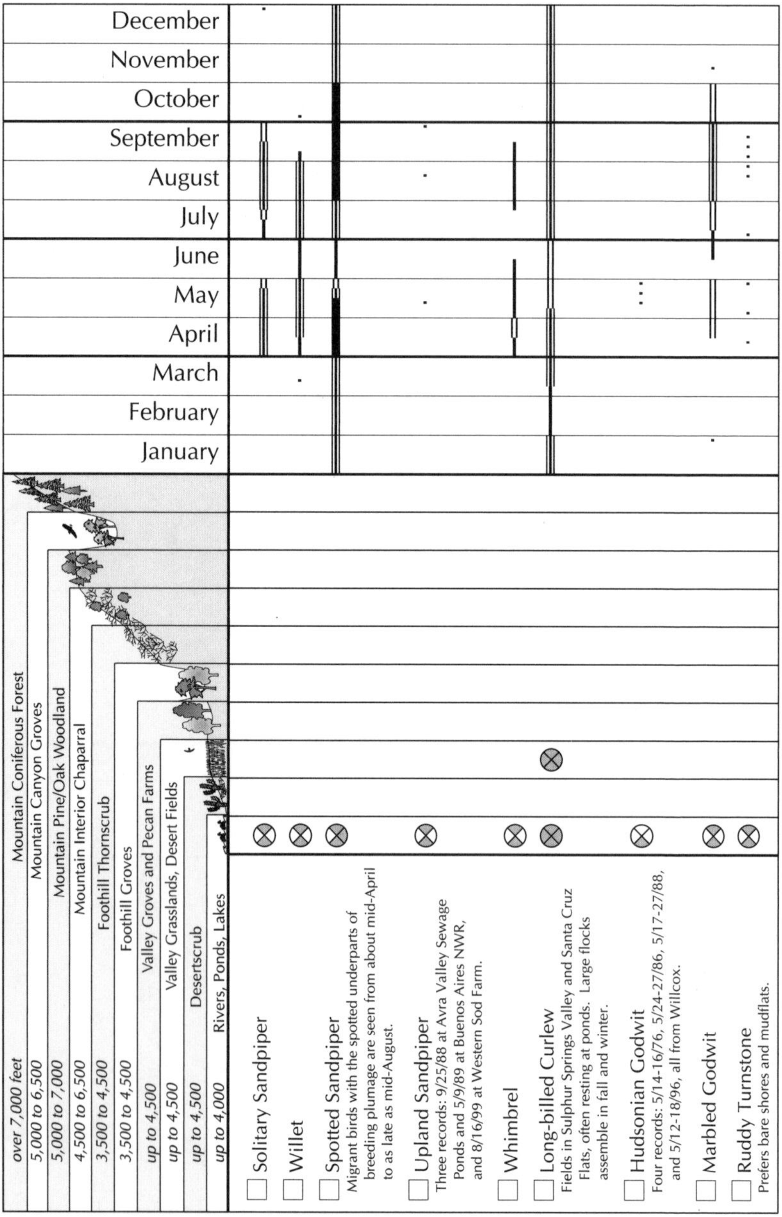

December
November
October
September
August
July
June
May
April
March
February
January
over 7,000 feet
Mountain Coniferous Forest
5,000 to 6,500
Mountain Canyon Groves
5,000 to 7,000
Mountain Pine/Oak Woodland
4,500 to 6,500
Mountain Interior Chaparral
3,500 to 4,500
Foothill Thornscrub
3,500 to 4,500
Foothill Groves
up to 4,500
Valley Groves and Pecan Farms
up to 4,500
Valley Grasslands, Desert Fields
up to 4,500
Desertscrub
up to 4,000
Rivers, Ponds, Lakes
Solitary Sandpiper
Willet
Spotted Sandpiper
Migrant birds with the spotted underparts of breeding plumage are seen from about mid-April to as late as mid-August.
Upland Sandpiper
Three records: 9/25/88 at Avra Valley Sewage Ponds and 5/9/89 at Buenos Aires NWR, and 8/16/99 at Western Sod Farm.
Whimbrel
Long-billed Curlew
Fields in Sulphur Springs Valley and Santa Cruz Flats, often resting at ponds. Large flocks assemble in fall and winter.
Hudsonian Godwit
Four records: 5/14-16/76, 5/24-27/86, 5/17-27/88, and 5/12-18/96, all from Willcox.
Marbled Godwit
Ruddy Turnstone
Prefers bare shores and mudflats.

☐ Red Knot
Prefers bare shores and mudflats.

☐ Sanderling

☐ Semipalmated Sandpiper
Most fall records are of juveniles.

☐ Western Sandpiper
Most winter records from Santa Cruz Valley in
Tucson or Avra Valley Sewage Ponds.

☐ Least Sandpiper
Common in winter along Santa Cruz River
in Tucson.

☐ White-rumped Sandpiper
Seven records from Willcox, Whitewater Draw,
Buenos Aires NWR, and Sierra Vista.

☐ Baird's Sandpiper
Numbers fluctuate. Some years common in fall.

☐ Pectoral Sandpiper

☐ Dunlin
Has wintered on Santa Cruz River in Tucson and
at Picacho Reservoir.

☐ Stilt Sandpiper

☐ Ruff
Hypothetical. Two sight records:10/13/86 in
Tucson, and 10/3/97, Picacho Reservoir.

☐ Short-billed Dowitcher
Easily confused with and far outnumbered by
next species; use call notes.

* Nesting

Spring   Summer   Fall   Winter
⊗   ⊗   ⊗   ⊗

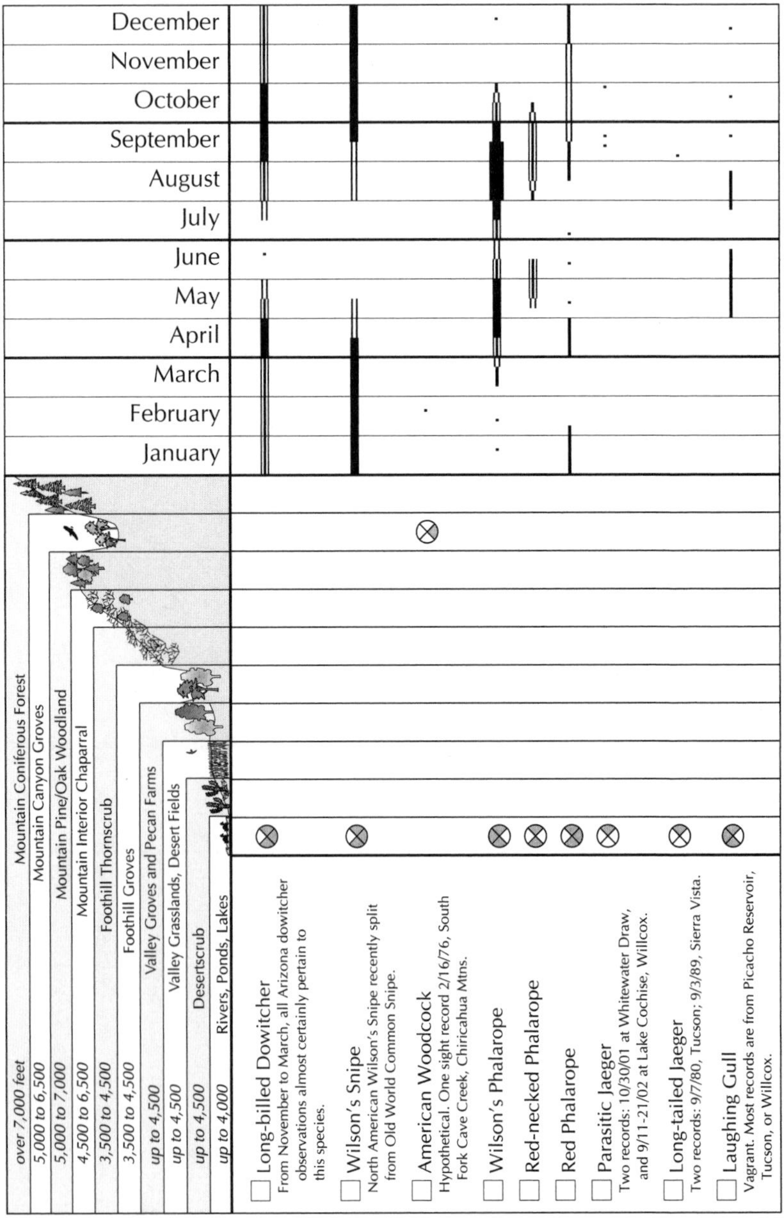

	December	November	October	September	August	July	June	May	April	March	February	January

over 7,000 feet — Mountain Coniferous Forest
5,000 to 6,500 — Mountain Canyon Groves
5,000 to 7,000 — Mountain Pine/Oak Woodland
4,500 to 6,500 — Mountain Interior Chaparral
3,500 to 4,500 — Foothill Thornscrub
3,500 to 4,500 — Foothill Groves
up to 4,500 — Valley Groves and Pecan Farms
up to 4,500 — Valley Grasslands, Desert Fields
up to 4,500 — Desertscrub
up to 4,000 — Rivers, Ponds, Lakes

Long-billed Dowitcher
From November to March, all Arizona dowitcher observations almost certainly pertain to this species.

Wilson's Snipe
North American Wilson's Snipe recently split from Old World Common Snipe.

American Woodcock
Hypothetical. One sight record 2/16/76, South Fork Cave Creek, Chiricahua Mtns.

Wilson's Phalarope

Red-necked Phalarope

Red Phalarope

Parasitic Jaeger
Two records: 10/30/01 at Whitewater Draw, and 9/11-21/02 at Lake Cochise, Willcox.

Long-tailed Jaeger
Two records: 9/7/80, Tucson; 9/3/89, Sierra Vista.

Laughing Gull
Vagrant. Most records are from Picacho Reservoir, Tucson, or Willcox.

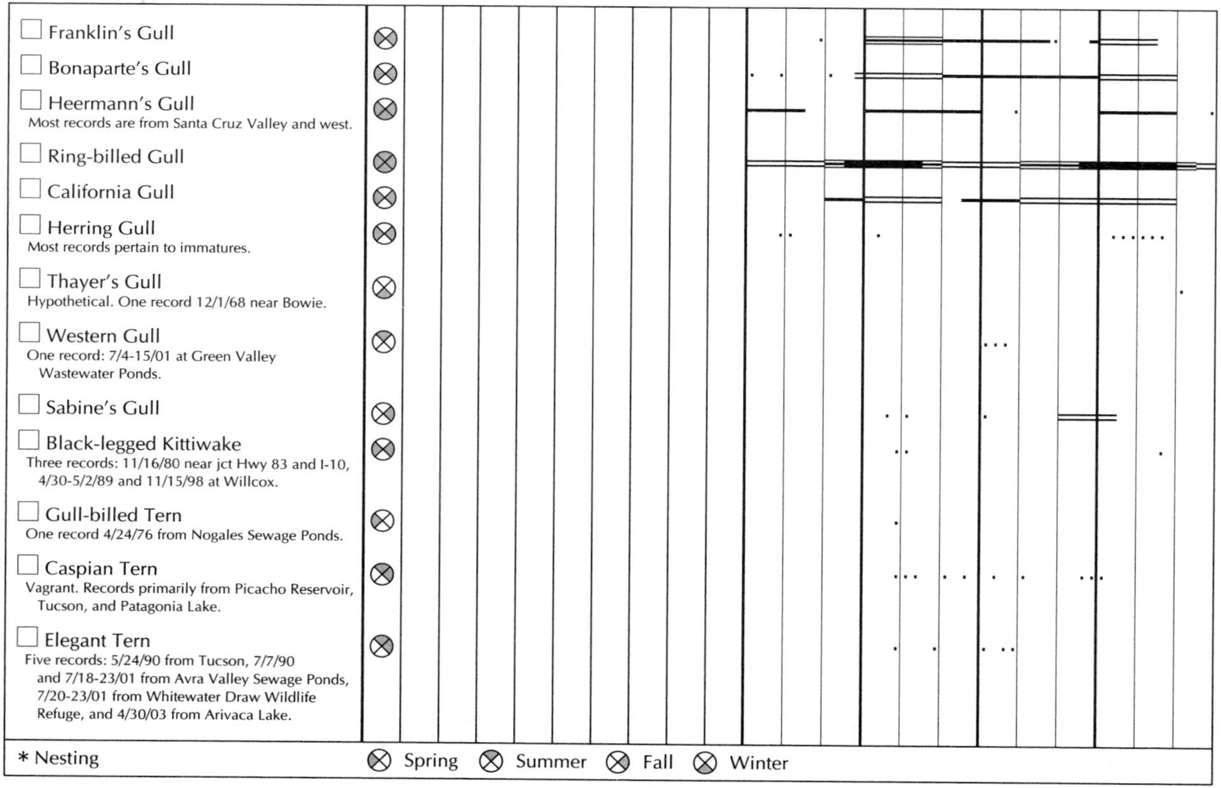

Franklin's Gull

Bonaparte's Gull

Heermann's Gull
Most records are from Santa Cruz Valley and west.

Ring-billed Gull

California Gull

Herring Gull
Most records pertain to immatures.

Thayer's Gull
Hypothetical. One record 12/1/68 near Bowie.

Western Gull
One record: 7/4-15/01 at Green Valley
Wastewater Ponds.

Sabine's Gull

Black-legged Kittiwake
Three records: 11/16/80 near jct Hwy 83 and I-10,
4/30-5/2/89 and 11/15/98 at Willcox.

Gull-billed Tern
One record 4/24/76 from Nogales Sewage Ponds.

Caspian Tern
Vagrant. Records primarily from Picacho Reservoir,
Tucson, and Patagonia Lake.

Elegant Tern
Five records: 5/24/90 from Tucson, 7/7/90
and 7/18-23/01 from Avra Valley Sewage Ponds,
7/20-23/01 from Whitewater Draw Wildlife
Refuge, and 4/30/03 from Arivaca Lake.

Spring Summer Fall Winter

* Nesting

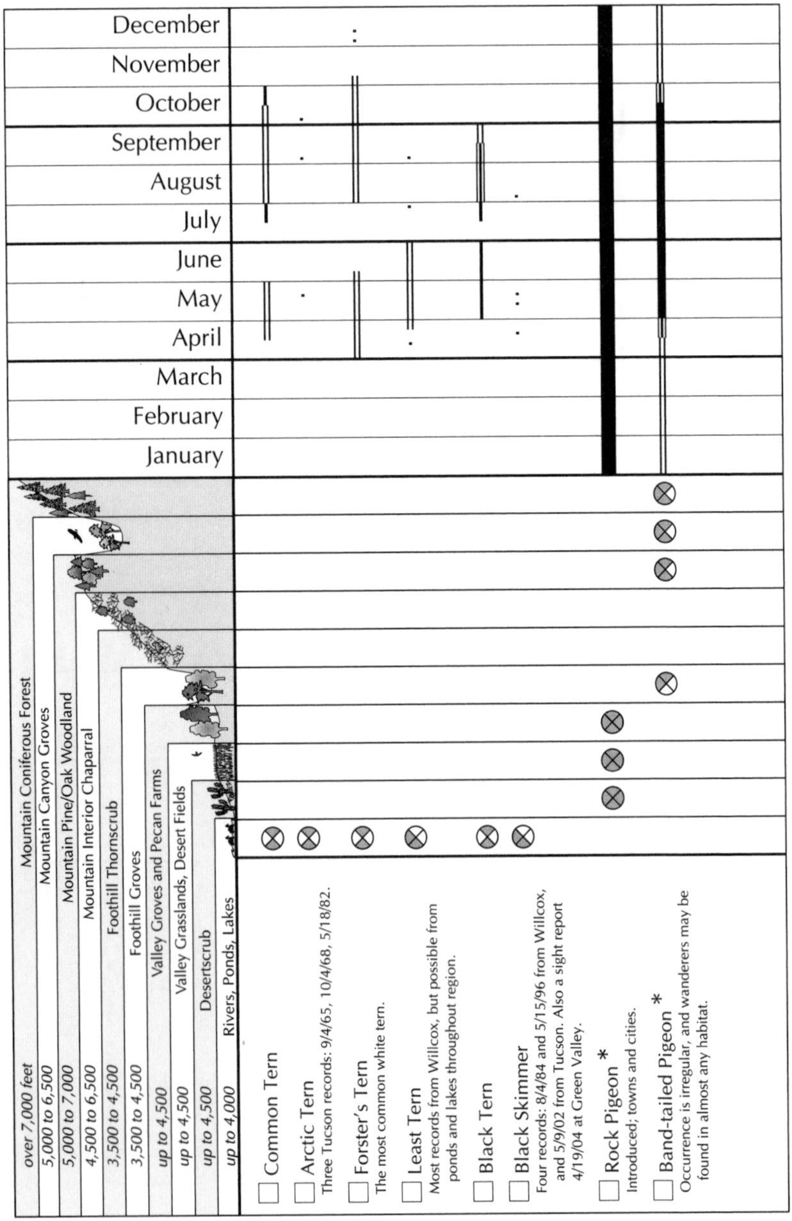

December
November
October
September
August
July
June
May
April
March
February
January

over 7,000 feet — Mountain Coniferous Forest
5,000 to 6,500 — Mountain Canyon Groves
5,000 to 7,000 — Mountain Pine/Oak Woodland
4,500 to 6,500 — Mountain Interior Chaparral
3,500 to 4,500 — Foothill Thornscrub
3,500 to 4,500 — Foothill Groves
up to 4,500 — Valley Groves and Pecan Farms
up to 4,500 — Valley Grasslands, Desert Fields
up to 4,500 — Desertscrub
up to 4,000 — Rivers, Ponds, Lakes

☐ Common Tern

☐ Arctic Tern
Three Tucson records: 9/4/65, 10/4/68, 5/18/82.

☐ Forster's Tern
The most common white tern.

☐ Least Tern
Most records from Willcox, but possible from ponds and lakes throughout region.

☐ Black Tern

☐ Black Skimmer
Four records: 8/4/84 and 5/15/96 from Willcox, and 5/9/02 from Tucson. Also a sight report 4/19/04 at Green Valley.

☐ Rock Pigeon *
Introduced; towns and cities.

☐ Band-tailed Pigeon *
Occurrence is irregular, and wanderers may be found in almost any habitat.

☐ **Eurasian Collared-Dove**
First discovered in Arizona in 2000. Still local, but breeding enclaves at Red Rock and Benson, and reported from most small valley towns.

☐ **White-winged Dove** *
Wintering birds are usually confined to towns and ranches along Sonoita Creek and the Santa Cruz River south of Tucson, as well as in Douglas. In summer stays below 5,500'.

☐ **Mourning Dove** *
Decreases in abundance with increased elevation.

☐ **Inca Dove** *
Most common in urban areas.

☐ **Common Ground-Dove** *
Scaly head and red-based bill always separate Common from the rare Ruddy Ground-Dove.

☐ **Ruddy Ground-Dove**
Usually found with Common Ground-Doves and/or Inca Doves. Summered at Red Rock in 2003 and 2004.

☐ **Thick-billed Parrot**
Extirpated. See Specialties section. Graph represents movements of reintroduced birds, 1986-1989.

☐ **Black-billed Cuckoo**
Five records: 10/11/66 at Pena Blanca Lake, 8/26/72 at Patagonia, 10/2/84 at Silver Creek near Portal, 9/23/00 at Bisbee, and 10/7/84 in Pinery Canyon, Chiricahua Mtns.

Spring   Summer   Fall   Winter

* Nesting

	December
	November
	October
	September
	August
	July
	June
	May
	April
	March
	February
	January

over 7,000 feet — Mountain Coniferous Forest
5,000 to 6,500 — Mountain Canyon Groves
5,000 to 7,000 — Mountain Pine/Oak Woodland
4,500 to 6,500 — Mountain Interior Chaparral
3,500 to 4,500 — Foothill Thornscrub
3,500 to 4,500 — Foothill Groves
up to 4,500 — Valley Groves and Pecan Farms
up to 4,500 — Valley Grasslands, Desert Fields
up to 4,500 — Desertscrub
up to 4,000 — Rivers, Ponds, Lakes

☐ Yellow-billed Cuckoo *
Typically, this is the last breeding species to arrive in our area. Migrating cuckoos are seen annually in mountain canyon groves, and sporadically in almost any habitat.

☐ Greater Roadrunner *
While typically confined to deserts and open valleys, roadrunners occasionally penetrate chaparral and pine-oak woodland to elevations of 7,000 feet.

☐ Groove-billed Ani
Some years not recorded.

☐ Barn Owl *
Rare in other habitats up to Ponderosa Pine forest.

☐ Flammulated Owl *
Difficult to find after mid-summer when not calling.

☐ Western Screech-Owl *
Difficult to find after mid-summer when not calling. Prefers more open habitat than Whiskered Screech-Owl.

☐ Whiskered Screech-Owl *
Difficult to find after mid-summer when not calling. Ordinarily at higher elevations than Western.

Great Horned Owl *

Northern Pygmy-Owl *
Difficult to find after mid-summer when not calling.
Likes large juniper trees.

Ferruginous Pygmy-Owl *
Western part of area only. The "Cactus Ferruginous
Pygmy-Owl" is a federally endangered subspecies.

Elf Owl *
Difficult to find after mid-summer when not calling.

Burrowing Owl *
Local. Large tracts of appropriate habitat
unoccupied.

Spotted Owl *
Usually found near cliffs. The "Mexican Spotted
Owl" is a federally threatened subspecies.

Long-eared Owl *
Has nested in sparse oak woodland.

Short-eared Owl
Farmlands and marshes. Present winter of 1998-
1999 at Whitewater Draw Wildlife Refuge, and
since 2000 in the San Rafael Valley.

Northern Saw-whet Owl *
Most sightings occur between March 10 and June
10 when birds are calling, or during winter when
an individual's roost is found in town or at
a desert oasis, such as the Desert Museum.

Lesser Nighthawk *
Often near ponds, rivers, streetlights, and large
parking areas.

* Nesting

⊗ Spring   ⊗ Summer   ⊗ Fall   ⊗ Winter

Elevation	Habitat
over 7,000 feet	Mountain Coniferous Forest
5,000 to 6,500	Mountain Canyon Groves
5,000 to 7,000	Mountain Pine/Oak Woodland
4,500 to 6,500	Mountain Interior Chaparral
3,500 to 4,500	Foothill Thornscrub
3,500 to 4,500	Foothill Groves
up to 4,500	Valley Groves and Pecan Farms
up to 4,500	Valley Grasslands, Desert Fields
up to 4,500	Desertscrub
up to 4,000	Rivers, Ponds, Lakes

Habitat columns (left to right): Rivers Ponds Lakes, Desertscrub, Valley Grasslands Desert Fields, Valley Groves and Pecan Farms, Foothill Groves, Foothill Thornscrub, Mountain Interior Chaparral, Mountain Pine/Oak Woodland, Mountain Canyon Groves, Mountain Coniferous Forest

Species	Rivers/Ponds/Lakes	Desertscrub	Valley Grasslands	Valley Groves	Foothill Groves	Foothill Thornscrub	Mtn Interior Chaparral	Mtn Pine/Oak	Mtn Canyon Groves	Mtn Coniferous
☐ Common Nighthawk * Sonoita, San Rafael Grassland, near Huachuca Mtns, and western base of Chiricahua Mtns.		⊗								
☐ Common Poorwill * Occasionally heard on still nights in winter.	⊗	⊗		⊗	⊗					
☐ Buff-collared Nightjar * Recent observations are from California Gulch area.				⊗	⊗					
☐ Whip-poor-will * The typical subspecies in SE Arizona is the "Mexican Whip-poor-will," with a unique vocalization that sounds like "purple-whip!"							⊗	⊗	⊗	
☐ Black Swift Hypothetical. Almost all observations near cliffs in upper Cave Creek Canyon in Chiricahua Mtns.									⊗	
☐ Chimney Swift Almost all records from Univ. of Arizona in Tucson. No records since 1985.	⊗									
☐ Vaux's Swift Aerial.	⊗	⊗	⊗	⊗	⊗	⊗	⊗	⊗	⊗	

☐ White-throated Swift *
Cliffs in summer; widespread in winter. These swifts return to the higher mountains in March, early or late depending on the year.

☐ Broad-billed Hummingbird *
More common west of San Pedro.

☐ White-eared Hummingbird *
Annual since 1989 at Ramsey Canyon and since mid-1990s at Miller Canyon.

☐ Berylline Hummingbird *
Has fledged young as late as mid-September. Hybrids with Magnificent Hummingbird characters are frequently observed in Miller and Ramsey Canyons. A probable hybrid with Broad-billed Hummingbird was in Ash Canyon in 2003.

☐ Cinnamon Hummingbird
One record 7/21-23/92, Patagonia. See Specialties.

☐ Violet-crowned Hummingbird *
Especially at Patagonia. Has wintered at feeders from Tucson to Portal.

☐ Blue-throated Hummingbird *
Some winter at feeders in mountain canyons, rarely in Tucson.

☐ Magnificent Hummingbird *
Some winter at feeders in mountain canyons.

☐ Plain-capped Starthroat
Primarily near flowering agaves; enters pine-oak and mountain canyon groves only below 6,000 feet.

* Nesting

⊗ Spring   ⊗ Summer   ⊗ Fall   ⊗ Winter

	December
	November
	October
	September
	August
	July
	June
	May
	April
	March
	February
	January

over 7,000 feet — Mountain Coniferous Forest
5,000 to 6,500 — Mountain Canyon Groves
5,000 to 7,000 — Mountain Pine/Oak Woodland
4,500 to 6,500 — Mountain Interior Chaparral
3,500 to 4,500 — Foothill Thornscrub
3,500 to 4,500 — Foothill Groves
up to 4,500 — Valley Groves and Pecan Farms
up to 4,500 — Valley Grasslands, Desert Fields
up to 4,500 — Desertscrub
up to 4,000 — Rivers, Ponds, Lakes

☐ Lucifer Hummingbird *
Wooded canyons and agave slopes near Mexican border.

☐ Black-chinned Hummingbird *
Almost all males depart by mid-September.

☐ Anna's Hummingbird *
More common w of San Pedro and below 6,000 ft.

☐ Costa's Hummingbird *
Most common w of San Pedro and below 5,000 ft. Year round at Arizona-Sonora Desert Museum.

☐ Calliope Hummingbird
Males precede females and immatures; most adult males pass through in fall by August 15.

☐ Bumblebee Hummingbird
One record of two females 7/2/1896, Ramsey Canyon. Identity of specimens may be in error. See Specialties.

☐ Broad-tailed Hummingbird *
Also migrates through lowlands.

☐ Rufous Hummingbird
Males precede females and immatures; most adult males pass through in fall by Aug. 15.

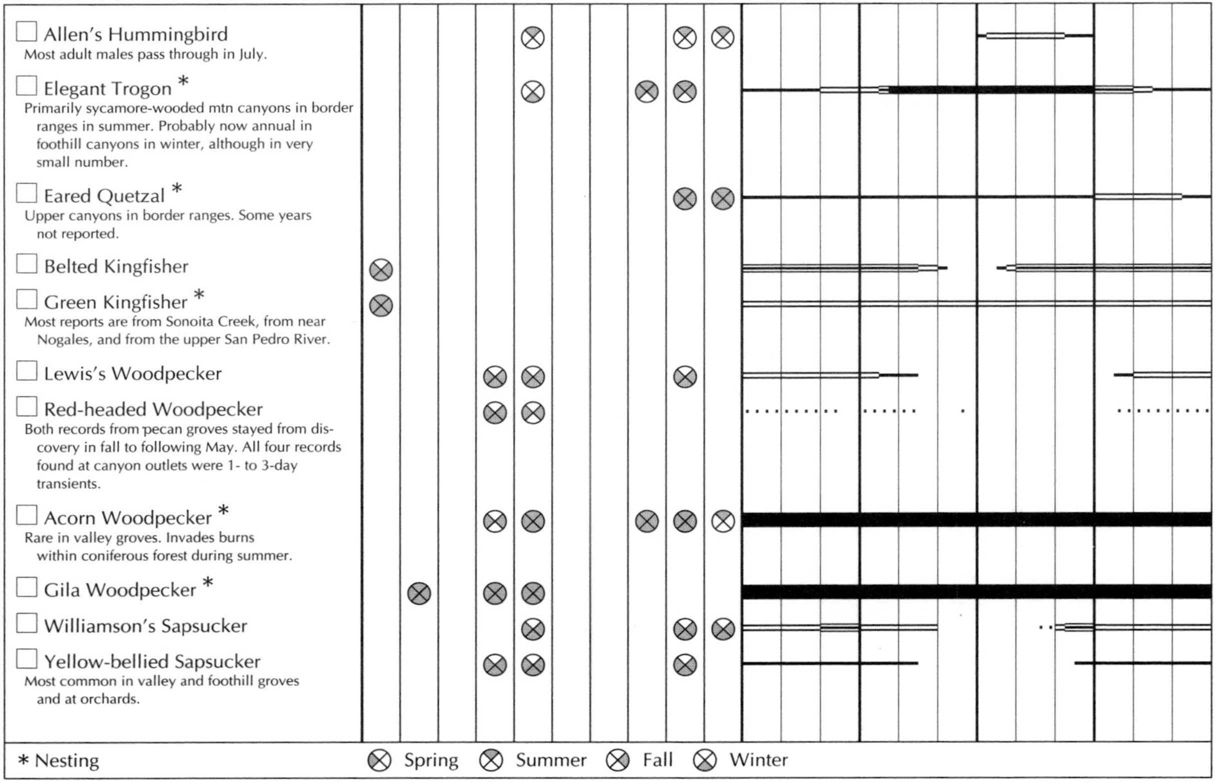

☐ Allen's Hummingbird
Most adult males pass through in July.

☐ Elegant Trogon *
Primarily sycamore-wooded mtn canyons in border
ranges in summer. Probably now annual in
foothill canyons in winter, although in very
small number.

☐ Eared Quetzal *
Upper canyons in border ranges. Some years
not reported.

☐ Belted Kingfisher

☐ Green Kingfisher *
Most reports are from Sonoita Creek, from near
Nogales, and from the upper San Pedro River.

☐ Lewis's Woodpecker

☐ Red-headed Woodpecker
Both records from pecan groves stayed from discovery in fall to following May. All four records
found at canyon outlets were 1- to 3-day
transients.

☐ Acorn Woodpecker *
Rare in valley groves. Invades burns
within coniferous forest during summer.

☐ Gila Woodpecker *

☐ Williamson's Sapsucker

☐ Yellow-bellied Sapsucker
Most common in valley and foothill groves
and at orchards.

Spring   Summer   Fall   Winter

* Nesting

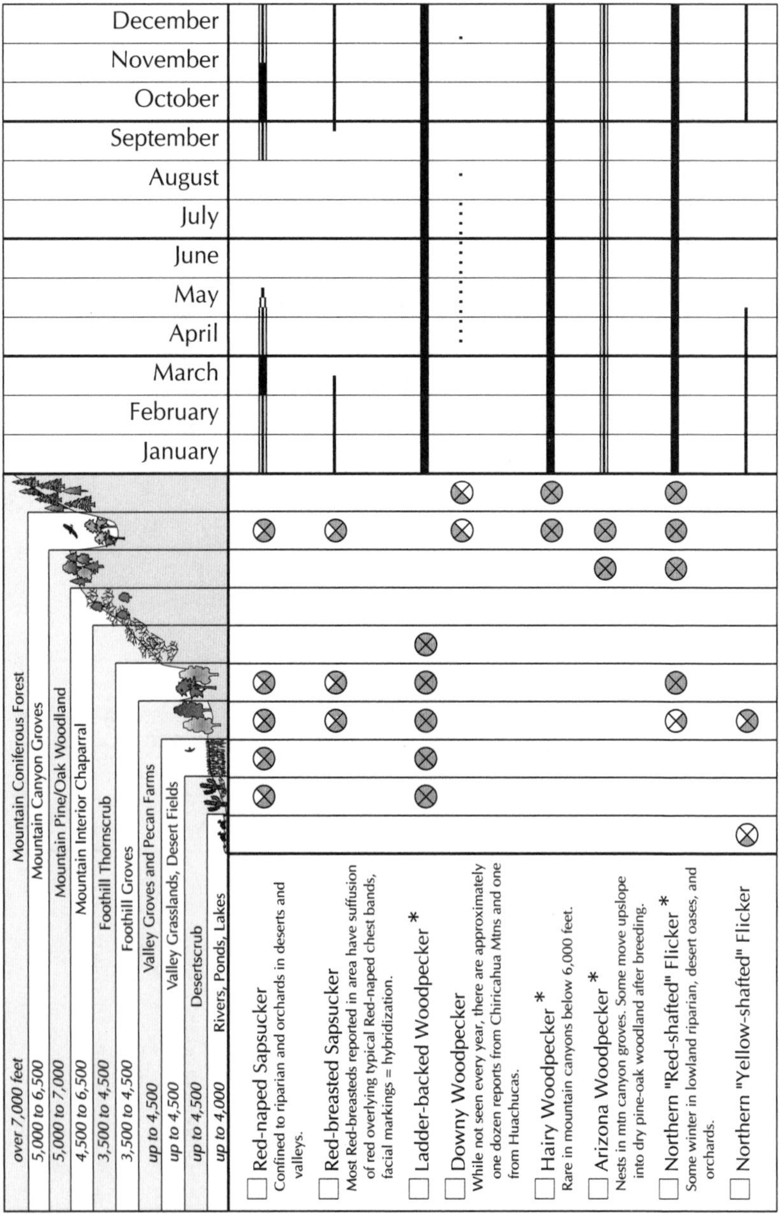

December
November
October
September
August
July
June
May
April
March
February
January

Elevation / Habitat

- over 7,000 feet — Mountain Coniferous Forest
- 5,000 to 6,500 — Mountain Canyon Groves
- 5,000 to 7,000 — Mountain Pine/Oak Woodland
- 4,500 to 6,500 — Mountain Interior Chaparral
- 3,500 to 4,500 — Foothill Thornscrub
- 3,500 to 4,500 — Foothill Groves
- up to 4,500 — Valley Groves and Pecan Farms
- up to 4,500 — Valley Grasslands, Desert Fields
- up to 4,500 — Desertscrub
- up to 4,000 — Rivers, Ponds, Lakes

Species

Red-naped Sapsucker
Confined to riparian and orchards in deserts and valleys.

Red-breasted Sapsucker
Most Red-breasteds reported in area have suffusion of red overlying typical Red-naped chest bands, facial markings = hybridization.

Ladder-backed Woodpecker *

Downy Woodpecker
While not seen every year, there are approximately one dozen reports from Chiricahua Mtns and one from Huachucas.

Hairy Woodpecker *
Rare in mountain canyons below 6,000 feet.

Arizona Woodpecker *
Nests in mtn canyon groves. Some move upslope into dry pine-oak woodland after breeding.

Northern "Red-shafted" Flicker *
Some winter in lowland riparian, desert oases, and orchards.

Northern "Yellow-shafted" Flicker

Gilded Flicker *
Sonoran desert Saguaro stands and western cottonwood riparian only.

Northern Beardless-Tyrannulet *
Prefers mesquite thickets.

Olive-sided Flycatcher
Perches on dead treetops.

Greater Pewee *
Often perches on dead treetops in spring; a few winter in valley groves and orchards.

Western Wood-Pewee *
Migrates through lowlands.

Eastern Wood-Pewee
Seven records: 10/7/53, Tucson; 9/16/56 near Portal; 10/15/72 at Nogales; 5/1-31/80 in Cave Creek; 5/15/98 near Portal; 6/23-8/15/98 in Madera Canyon; and 6/13/01 on San Pedro River.

Yellow-bellied Flycatcher
Two records: 9/22/56 at Tucson and 12/20/92-2/28/93 at Patagonia.

Acadian Flycatcher
One record: 5/24/1886 from Tucson.

Willow Flycatcher *
Prefers more open habitats than Hammond's or Dusky. Several pairs breed near Dudleyville. This form, "Southwest Willow Flycatcher," is federally listed as endangered.

Least Flycatcher
Hypothetical. Five sight records from Chiricahuas, upper San Pedro River, Arivaca Lake, and Tucson Mtns.

Spring | Summer | Fall | Winter

* Nesting

Elevation / Habitat zones (left axis):

Elevation	Habitat
over 7,000 feet	Mountain Coniferous Forest
5,000 to 6,500	Mountain Canyon Groves
5,000 to 7,000	Mountain Pine/Oak Woodland
4,500 to 6,500	Mountain Interior Chaparral
3,500 to 4,500	Foothill Thornscrub
3,500 to 4,500	Foothill Groves
up to 4,500	Valley Groves and Pecan Farms
up to 4,500	Valley Grasslands, Desert Fields
up to 4,500	Desertscrub
up to 4,000	Rivers, Ponds, Lakes

Months (top axis): January, February, March, April, May, June, July, August, September, October, November, December

☐ Hammond's Flycatcher
Uncommon transient in higher mountains to about 8,000 feet. Rare in lower mountain canyons in winter (most winter in foothill groves).

☐ Gray Flycatcher *
Mesquite thickets and arid juniper hillsides. Breeds in lower Rucker Canyon, Chiricahua Mtns.

☐ Dusky Flycatcher
Very rare in lower mountain canyon groves in winter. Some years a common migrant.

☐ Pacific-slope Flycatcher
Most, if not all, "Western Flycatchers" migrating through valleys are this species.

☐ Cordilleran Flycatcher *
Nest sites include boulders in upper canyons and under roof eaves in mountain coniferous forest.

☐ Buff-breasted Flycatcher *
Most easily found in the Huachuca Mtns.

☐ Black Phoebe *
Uses foothill groves and lower mountain canyon groves only when permanent water is present.

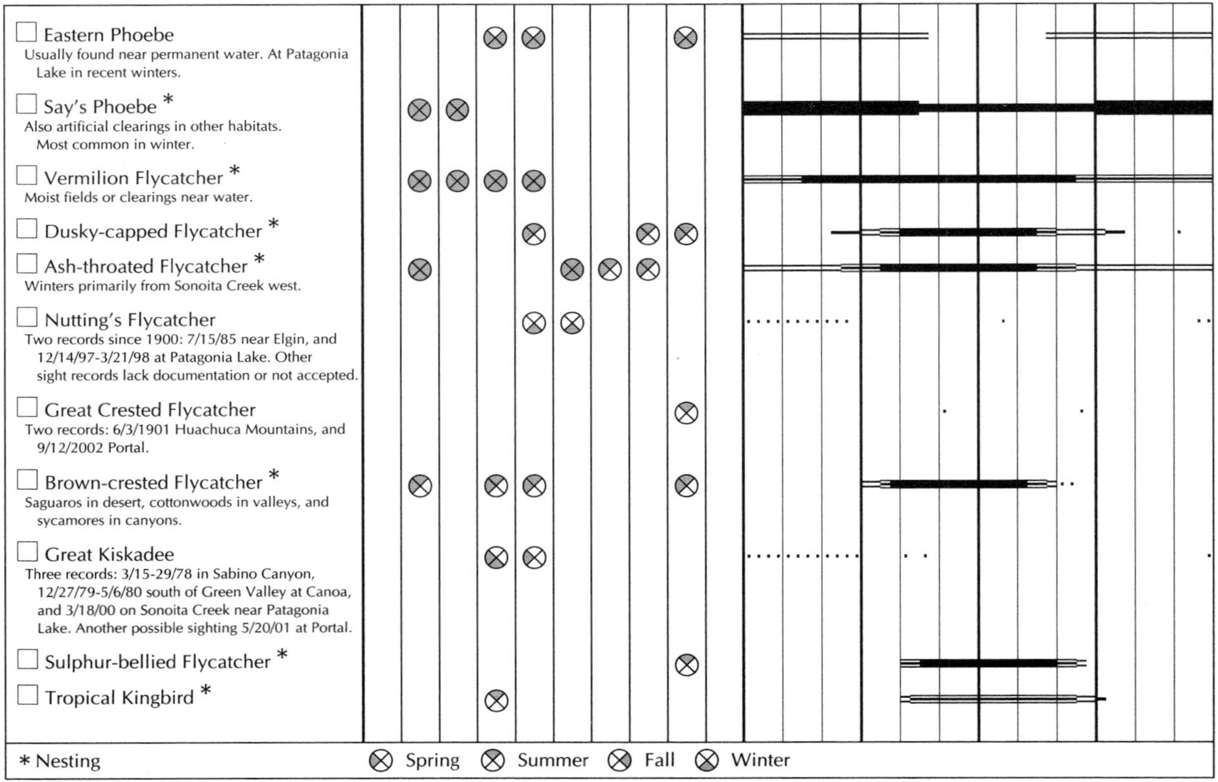

Eastern Phoebe
Usually found near permanent water. At Patagonia
Lake in recent winters.

Say's Phoebe *
Also artificial clearings in other habitats.
Most common in winter.

Vermilion Flycatcher *
Moist fields or clearings near water.

Dusky-capped Flycatcher *

Ash-throated Flycatcher *
Winters primarily from Sonoita Creek west.

Nutting's Flycatcher
Two records since 1900: 7/15/85 near Elgin, and
12/14/97-3/21/98 at Patagonia Lake. Other
sight records lack documentation or not accepted.

Great Crested Flycatcher
Two records: 6/3/1901 Huachuca Mountains, and
9/12/2002 Portal.

Brown-crested Flycatcher *
Saguaros in desert, cottonwoods in valleys, and
sycamores in canyons.

Great Kiskadee
Three records: 3/15-29/78 in Sabino Canyon,
12/27/79-5/6/80 south of Green Valley at Canoa,
and 3/18/00 on Sonoita Creek near Patagonia
Lake. Another possible sighting 5/20/01 at Portal.

Sulphur-bellied Flycatcher *

Tropical Kingbird *

* Nesting

Spring   Summer   Fall   Winter

December
November
October
September
August
July
June
May
April
March
February
January

Mountain Coniferous Forest — over 7,000 feet
Mountain Canyon Groves — 5,000 to 6,500
Mountain Pine/Oak Woodland — 5,000 to 7,000
Mountain Interior Chaparral — 4,500 to 6,500
Foothill Thornscrub — 3,500 to 4,500
Foothill Groves — 3,500 to 4,500
Valley Groves and Pecan Farms — up to 4,500
Valley Grasslands, Desert Fields — up to 4,500
Desertscrub — up to 4,500
Rivers, Ponds, Lakes — up to 4,000

☐ Cassin's Kingbird *
Generally higher elevations and more heavily wooded habitats than Western Kingbird.

☐ Thick-billed Kingbird *
Enclaves in foothill riparian woodlands near Mexican border. Very rarely at the mouths of mountain canyons.

☐ Western Kingbird *
Northern migrants augment summer residents in September as they stage to move south, and Western Kingbirds may number in the thousands in the valleys.

☐ Eastern Kingbird
Open woodlands and riparian edges.

☐ Scissor-tailed Flycatcher
Most strays are during rainy season; August is peak month.

☐ Rose-throated Becard *
Foothill riparian woodland near Mexican border adjacent to thornscrub. Patagonia Roadside Rest is usually the location with best access.

☐ Loggerhead Shrike *
In winter, migrants augment resident population.

☐ Northern Shrike
Five records: 12/15/74-3/22/75 at Elgin; 12/30/76 below Portal; 1/28/78 near Continental; 12/17/88-2/16/89 near Palominas; and 12/2/89 at Empire-Cienaga RCA.

☐ White-eyed Vireo
Approximately 10 records.

☐ Bell's Vireo *

☐ Black-capped Vireo
Hypothetical. One record 4/4/70, Tanque Verde Guest Ranch east of Tucson.

☐ Gray Vireo *
Pinyon-juniper hillsides in Redington Pass and east end Aravaipa Canyon.

☐ Yellow-throated Vireo
Almost all mtn foothill canyon records are in May or June. Valley grove records span May-Sep.

☐ Plumbeous Vireo *
Within desertscrub prefers dense mesquite thickets.

☐ Cassin's Vireo
Within desertscrub prefers dense mesquite thickets.

☐ Blue-headed Vireo
Four records: 9/26/87 and 11/16/87 from upper San Pedro, 11/30/98 from Sycamore Canyon, and 10/23/04 from Sabino Canyon.

☐ Hutton's Vireo *
Rare in valley riparian in winter.

☐ Warbling Vireo *
Common migrant through all wooded habitats, desert oases.

⊗ Spring   ⊗ Summer   ⊗ Fall   ⊗ Winter

* Nesting

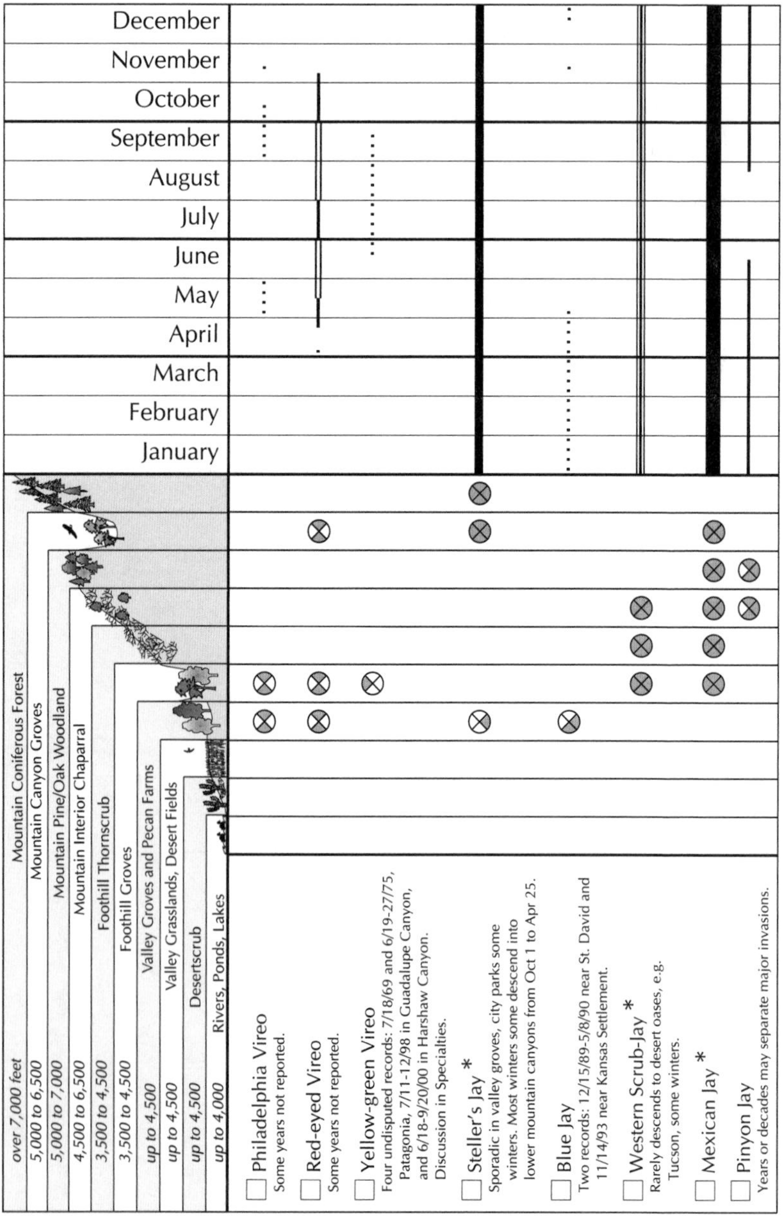

	December	November	October	September	August	July	June	May	April	March	February	January

Elevation labels (left axis):
- over 7,000 feet — Mountain Coniferous Forest
- 5,000 to 6,500 — Mountain Canyon Groves
- 5,000 to 7,000 — Mountain Pine/Oak Woodland
- 4,500 to 6,500 — Mountain Interior Chaparral
- 3,500 to 4,500 — Foothill Thornscrub
- 3,500 to 4,500 — Foothill Groves
- up to 4,500 — Valley Groves and Pecan Farms
- up to 4,500 — Valley Grasslands, Desert Fields
- up to 4,500 — Desertscrub
- up to 4,000 — Rivers, Ponds, Lakes

☐ **Philadelphia Vireo**
Some years not reported.

☐ **Red-eyed Vireo**
Some years not reported.

☐ **Yellow-green Vireo**
Four undisputed records: 7/18/69 and 6/19-27/75, Patagonia, 7/11-12/98 in Guadalupe Canyon, and 6/18-9/20/00 in Harshaw Canyon. Discussion in Specialties.

☐ **Steller's Jay** *
Sporadic in valley groves, city parks some winters. Most winters some descend into lower mountain canyons from Oct 1 to Apr 25.

☐ **Blue Jay**
Two records: 12/15/89-5/8/90 near St. David and 11/14/93 near Kansas Settlement.

☐ **Western Scrub-Jay** *
Rarely descends to desert oases, e.g. Tucson, some winters.

☐ **Mexican Jay** *

☐ **Pinyon Jay**
Years or decades may separate major invasions.

☐ Clark's Nutcracker
Years or decades may separate invasions. During invasions usually not found in summer.

☐ American Crow
Agricultural areas only, especially Safford, St. David, Elfrida. Not recorded some winters.

☐ Chihuahuan Raven *
Prefers open habitats. See discussion in Specialties.

☐ Common Raven *
Prefers wooded habitats and mountains.

☐ Horned Lark *
Primarily valley grasslands and fields. Within desertscrub, only in large flat openings.

☐ Purple Martin *
Saguaro stands and formerly forest openings in Chiricahuas; flocks of 100s, occasionally 1000s mass on N and W sides of Tucson in Sept.

☐ Tree Swallow
Most common at valley ponds and rivers.

☐ Violet-green Swallow *
Migrates through lowlands, especially near water.

☐ Northern Rough-winged Swallow *
Especially near ponds and rivers.

☐ Bank Swallow
Especially near ponds.

☐ Cliff Swallow *
Nests at Univ. of Arizona, Tucson, and Cochise College near Douglas.

⊗ Spring   ⊗ Summer   ⊗ Fall   ⊗ Winter

* Nesting

| | December | November | October | September | August | July | June | May | April | March | February | January |

Elevation / Habitat zones:

over 7,000 feet	Mountain Coniferous Forest
5,000 to 6,500	Mountain Canyon Groves
5,000 to 7,000	Mountain Pine/Oak Woodland
4,500 to 6,500	Mountain Interior Chaparral
3,500 to 4,500	Foothill Thornscrub
3,500 to 4,500	Foothill Groves
up to 4,500	Valley Groves and Pecan Farms
up to 4,500	Valley Grasslands, Desert Fields
up to 4,500	Desertscrub
up to 4,000	Rivers, Ponds, Lakes

☐ **Cave Swallow**
Three recent records: 8/17/91, Kino Springs; 10/27/91 from Tucson; and 10/20/04 from Lake Cochise at Willcox. One bird nested at Univ. Arizona in Tucson 1979-1987.

☐ **Barn Swallow** *
In the desert, only at ponds and irrigated fields.

☐ **Mountain Chickadee** *
Breeds in Santa Catalina and Rincon Mtns only. Very rarely wanders to Chiricahua Mtns.

☐ **Mexican Chickadee** *
Chiricahua Mtns only.

☐ **Bridled Titmouse** *
Less common in valley riparian.

☐ **Juniper Titmouse** *
Chiricahua, Rincon, and Santa Catalina Mtns only.

☐ **Verdin** *

☐ **Bushtit** *
Wanders down to desert washes, up to coniferous forest after breeding.

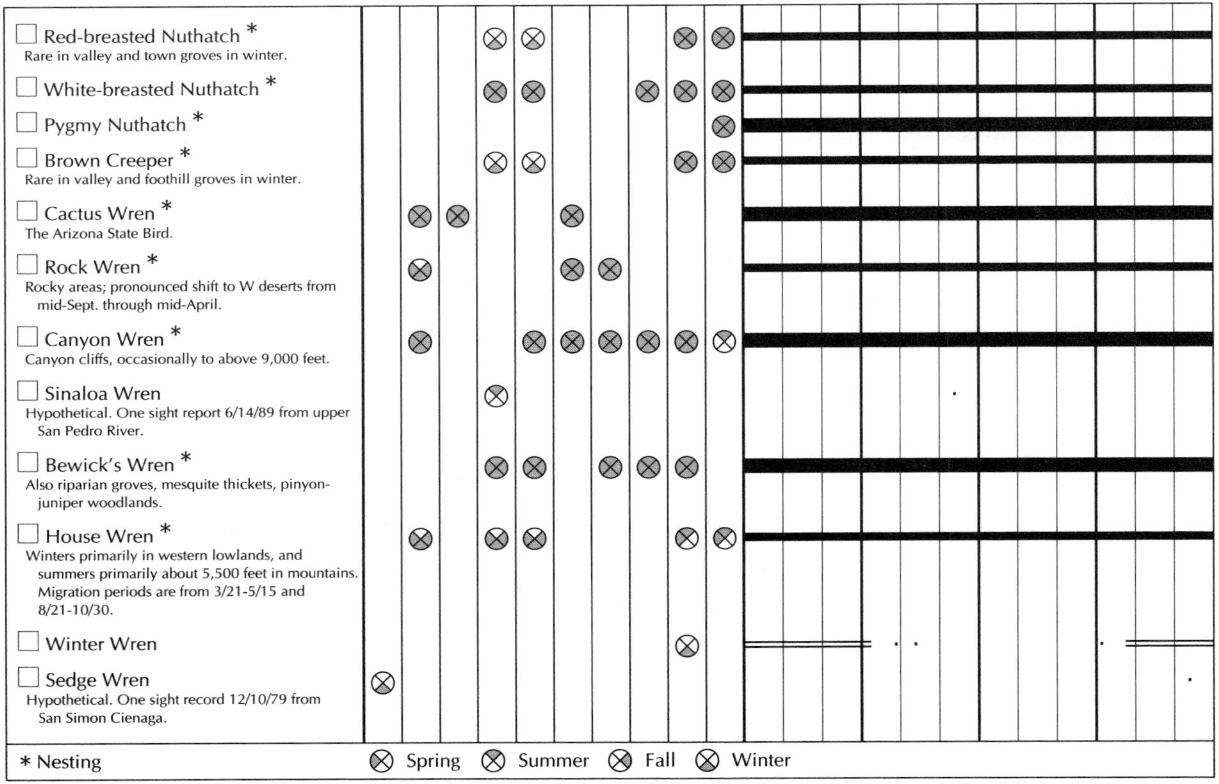

□ Red-breasted Nuthatch *
Rare in valley and town groves in winter.

□ White-breasted Nuthatch *

□ Pygmy Nuthatch *

□ Brown Creeper *
Rare in valley and foothill groves in winter.

□ Cactus Wren *
The Arizona State Bird.

□ Rock Wren *
Rocky areas; pronounced shift to W deserts from mid-Sept. through mid-April.

□ Canyon Wren *
Canyon cliffs, occasionally to above 9,000 feet.

□ Sinaloa Wren
Hypothetical. One sight report 6/14/89 from upper San Pedro River.

□ Bewick's Wren *
Also riparian groves, mesquite thickets, pinyon-juniper woodlands.

□ House Wren *
Winters primarily in western lowlands, and summers primarily about 5,500 feet in mountains. Migration periods are from 3/21-5/15 and 8/21-10/30.

□ Winter Wren

□ Sedge Wren
Hypothetical. One sight record 12/10/79 from San Simon Cienaga.

* Nesting   Spring ⊗ Summer ⊗ Fall ⊗ Winter

	Mountain Coniferous Forest
over 7,000 feet	Mountain Coniferous Forest
5,000 to 6,500	Mountain Canyon Groves
5,000 to 7,000	Mountain Pine/Oak Woodland
4,500 to 6,500	Mountain Interior Chaparral
3,500 to 4,500	Foothill Thornscrub
3,500 to 4,500	Foothill Groves
up to 4,500	Valley Groves and Pecan Farms
up to 4,500	Valley Grasslands, Desert Fields
up to 4,500	Desertscrub
up to 4,000	Rivers, Ponds, Lakes

Marsh Wren
Emergent marsh vegetation.

American Dipper *
Mtn streams. Last nest reported 1973 in Chiricahuas.

Golden-crowned Kinglet *
Resident upper Santa Catalina and Chiricahua Mtns; descends into canyons and rarely to desert groves during extreme winter weather.

Ruby-crowned Kinglet
Numbers peak in March when a wave of migrants passes through. There is no evidence this species breeds in either the Santa Catalina or Chiricahua Mtns.

Blue-gray Gnatcatcher *
Western deserts from mid-Sept. through March.

Black-tailed Gnatcatcher *
More common in western part of region.

Black-capped Gnatcatcher *
Recently at Brown Canyon, Chino Canyon, Montosa Canyon, Box Canyon, and Patagonia Lake. Discussion in Specialties.

☐ Northern Wheatear
One record 10/29/96 from Marana Pecan Grove.

☐ Eastern Bluebird *
Confined to the southern tier of Mexican border ranges. No recent summer records from Chiricahua Mtns.

☐ Western Bluebird *
Breeds only in Santa Catalina and Chiricahua Mtns. Winters throughout region in Upper Sonoran Life Zone. During invasion years, flocks also occur in desert Oct. 15-March 15.

☐ Mountain Bluebird *
Graph represents invasion year; some winters almost none present. Nested once in Sonoita in 1981.

☐ Townsend's Solitaire
Numbers fluctuate. Vagrant to coniferous forest in summer.

☐ Veery
Two records: 5/15/84, Portal; and 5/25/89, Fairbank. At least a handful of sight records by reliable observers for early May 1999.

☐ Gray-cheeked Thrush
One record 9/11/32 from Cave Creek near Portal.

☐ Swainson's Thrush
Most common during drought years, primarily in foothills and mountain canyon groves. Also city thickets, ranch yards, and desert oases.

Spring   Summer   Fall   Winter

* Nesting

	December	November	October	September	August	July	June	May	April	March	February	January

over 7,000 feet — Mountain Coniferous Forest
5,000 to 6,500 — Mountain Canyon Groves
5,000 to 7,000 — Mountain Pine/Oak Woodland
4,500 to 6,500 — Mountain Interior Chaparral
3,500 to 4,500 — Foothill Thornscrub
3,500 to 4,500 — Foothill Groves
up to 4,500 — Valley Groves and Pecan Farms
up to 4,500 — Valley Grasslands, Desert Fields
up to 4,500 — Desertscrub
up to 4,000 — Rivers, Ponds, Lakes

☐ **Hermit Thrush** *
All breeding birds depart their mountain homes, usually above 6,000 feet, between 9/15 and 11/15 and they return between 3/7 and 5/7. Most wintering birds are below 6,000 feet, and they originate from Canada and Alaska.

☐ **Wood Thrush**
Most years not reported. Approximately a dozen records.

☐ **Rufous-backed Robin**
Most recent sightings are from the Patagonia, Patagonia Lake, and Nogales areas. See discussion in Specialties.

☐ **American Robin** *
Not in lowlands in summer. Occasional flocks in excess of 100 birds seen in winter. Northern migrants arrive 10/15 and most depart by 5/15.

☐ **Varied Thrush**
Dense riparian groves; not reported some winters.

☐ **Aztec Thrush**
Also one winter record: Portal 1/26–2/4/91. Presence of immature birds in late summer suggests nesting. Not recorded from 1997 through 1999.

Gray Catbird
Also city parks and desert oases.

Northern Mockingbird *
Invades lower mountain canyons from 3/7 to 8/30.

Sage Thrasher
Graph represents average winter; some years fairly common.

Brown Thrasher
Found primarily 10/1 to 5/7, but has summered in Portal.

Bendire's Thrasher *
Hedgerows and mesquite thickets in flat, broad, and open valleys. Sings mid-Jan through Mar.

Curve-billed Thrasher *

Crissal Thrasher *
Dense thickets; sings January through March.

Le Conte's Thrasher *
Open Creosote Bush desert in Avra Valley. Not recorded most years.

Blue Mockingbird
Two records: 12/21/91–3/22/92 below Patagonia; 1/4–4/12/95 at Portal. A third record from Tucson 9/23/92 was perhaps an escapee. Discussion in Specialties.

European Starling *
Towns, farms, and ranches.

Spring   Summer   Fall   Winter

* Nesting

December
November
October
September
August
July
June
May
April
March
February
January

over 7,000 feet — Mountain Coniferous Forest
5,000 to 6,500 — Mountain Canyon Groves
5,000 to 7,000 — Mountain Pine/Oak Woodland
4,500 to 6,500 — Mountain Interior Chaparral
3,500 to 4,500 — Foothill Thornscrub
3,500 to 4,500 — Foothill Groves
up to 4,500 — Valley Groves and Pecan Farms
up to 4,500 — Valley Grasslands, Desert Fields
up to 4,500 — Desertscrub
up to 4,000 — Rivers, Ponds, Lakes

☐ Red-throated Pipit
Hypothetical. One sight report 5/2/89 from Avra Valley Sewage Ponds. Flight call heard by experienced observers 10/26/91 at Marana Pecan Grove.

☐ American Pipit
Pond and stream edges, open fields, golf courses.

☐ Sprague's Pipit
Tall grasses. Most reports from Sonoita Grasslands and San Rafael Valley.

☐ Bohemian Waxwing
Three records: 2/10–3/10/32 in e. Baboquivari Mtns; 12/5/48 at Benson; 5/6/74 in Carr Canyon.

☐ Cedar Waxwing
Also exploits Pyracantha plantings, mulberries, and tall trees in towns. Numbers fluctuate.

☐ Phainopepla *
Especially near trees with mistletoe. Range extends only to lower mtn canyon groves. Very common in western Sonoran Desert mesquite in winter.

☐ Olive Warbler *
In winter a few birds descend to lower mountain canyon and river groves.

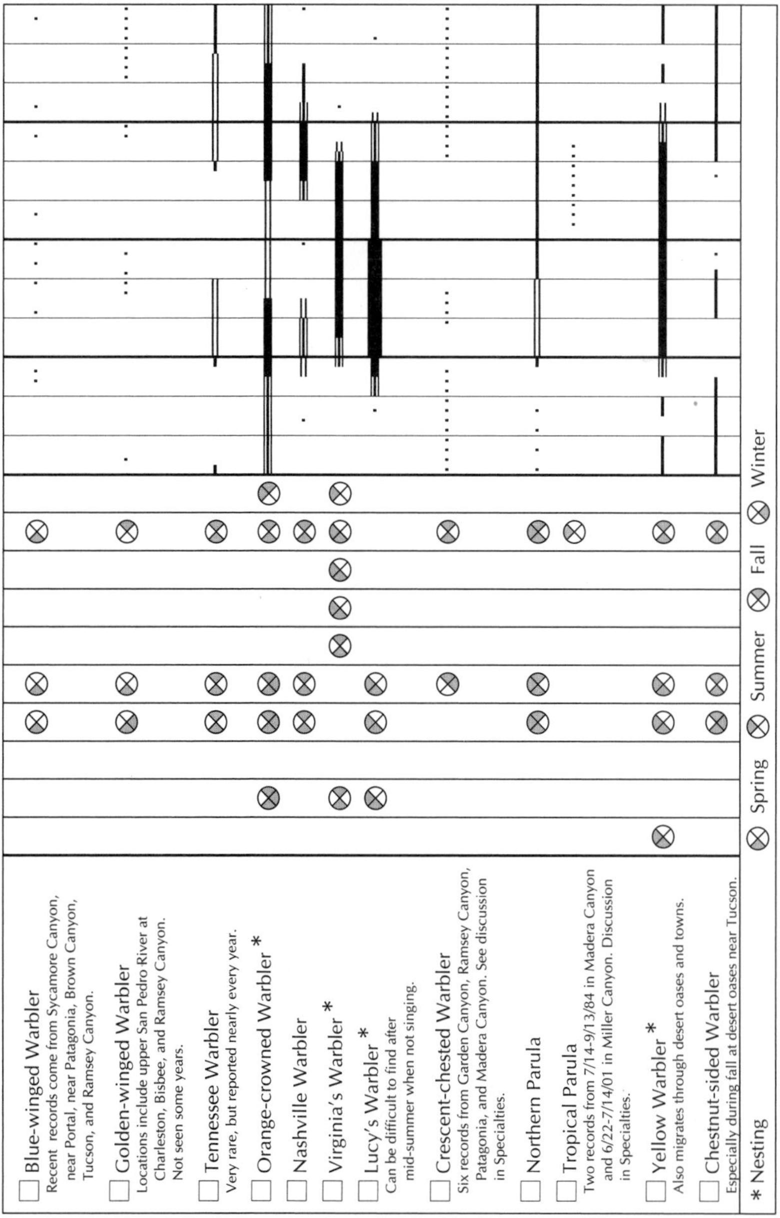

□ Blue-winged Warbler
Recent records come from Sycamore Canyon, near Portal, near Patagonia, Brown Canyon, Tucson, and Ramsey Canyon.

□ Golden-winged Warbler
Locations include upper San Pedro River at Charleston, Bisbee, and Ramsey Canyon. Not seen some years.

□ Tennessee Warbler
Very rare, but reported nearly every year.

□ Orange-crowned Warbler *

□ Nashville Warbler

□ Virginia's Warbler *

□ Lucy's Warbler *
Can be difficult to find after mid-summer when not singing.

□ Crescent-chested Warbler
Six records from Garden Canyon, Ramsey Canyon, Patagonia, and Madera Canyon. See discussion in Specialties.

□ Northern Parula

□ Tropical Parula
Two records from 7/14-9/13/84 in Madera Canyon and 6/22-7/14/01 in Miller Canyon. Discussion in Specialties.

□ Yellow Warbler *
Also migrates through desert oases and towns.

□ Chestnut-sided Warbler
Especially during fall at desert oases near Tucson.

⊗ Spring   ⊗ Summer   ⊗ Fall   ⊗ Winter

* Nesting

| | December |
| November |
| October |
| September |
| August |
| July |
| June |
| May |
| April |
| March |
| February |
| January |

over 7,000 feet — Mountain Coniferous Forest
5,000 to 6,500 — Mountain Canyon Groves
5,000 to 7,000 — Mountain Pine/Oak Woodland
4,500 to 6,500 — Mountain Interior Chaparral
3,500 to 4,500 — Foothill Thornscrub
3,500 to 4,500 — Foothill Groves
up to 4,500 — Valley Groves and Pecan Farms
up to 4,500 — Valley Grasslands, Desert Fields
up to 4,500 — Desertscrub
up to 4,000 — Rivers, Ponds, Lakes

Magnolia Warbler
Not recorded most years.

Cape May Warbler
Has wintered in Tucson.

Black-throated Blue Warbler
Once detected, individuals often remain in area
for a full month.

Yellow-rumped "Audubon's"
Warbler *
First appears in lowlands in mid-September;
last seen in lowlands in late May.

Yellow-rumped "Myrtle" Warbler
Usually associates with "Audubon's".

Black-throated Gray Warbler *

Black-throated Green Warbler

Townsend's Warbler
Abundance decreases with elevation.

Hermit Warbler
Abundance decreases with elevation.

☐ Blackburnian Warbler
Not recorded most years.

☐ Yellow-throated Warbler
Recently, 11/15-12/7/97 at Tucson, and 7/30/04 at Ramsey Canyon. Not recorded most years.

☐ Grace's Warbler *
Always associated with pines.

☐ Pine Warbler
At least two different birds in winters of 1997-1998 and 1998-1999 in Tucson. Record of 3/26-31/91 in Cave Creek Canyon. Not recorded some years.

☐ Prairie Warbler
Six records, most from Tucson. The spring record is from Madera Canyon.

☐ Palm Warbler
Some years not reported.

☐ Bay-breasted Warbler
Not recorded most years.

☐ Blackpoll Warbler
Not recorded most years.

☐ Cerulean Warbler
Two records: 5/28/70 in Cave Creek Canyon and 5/18-20/79 in Madera Canyon.

☐ Black-and-white Warbler
Some years, winters in western lowland groves.

☐ American Redstart

☐ Prothonotary Warbler
Valley groves, lower mountain canyons only, usually near areas of permanent water.

⊗ Spring   ⊗ Summer   ⊗ Fall   ⊗ Winter

* Nesting

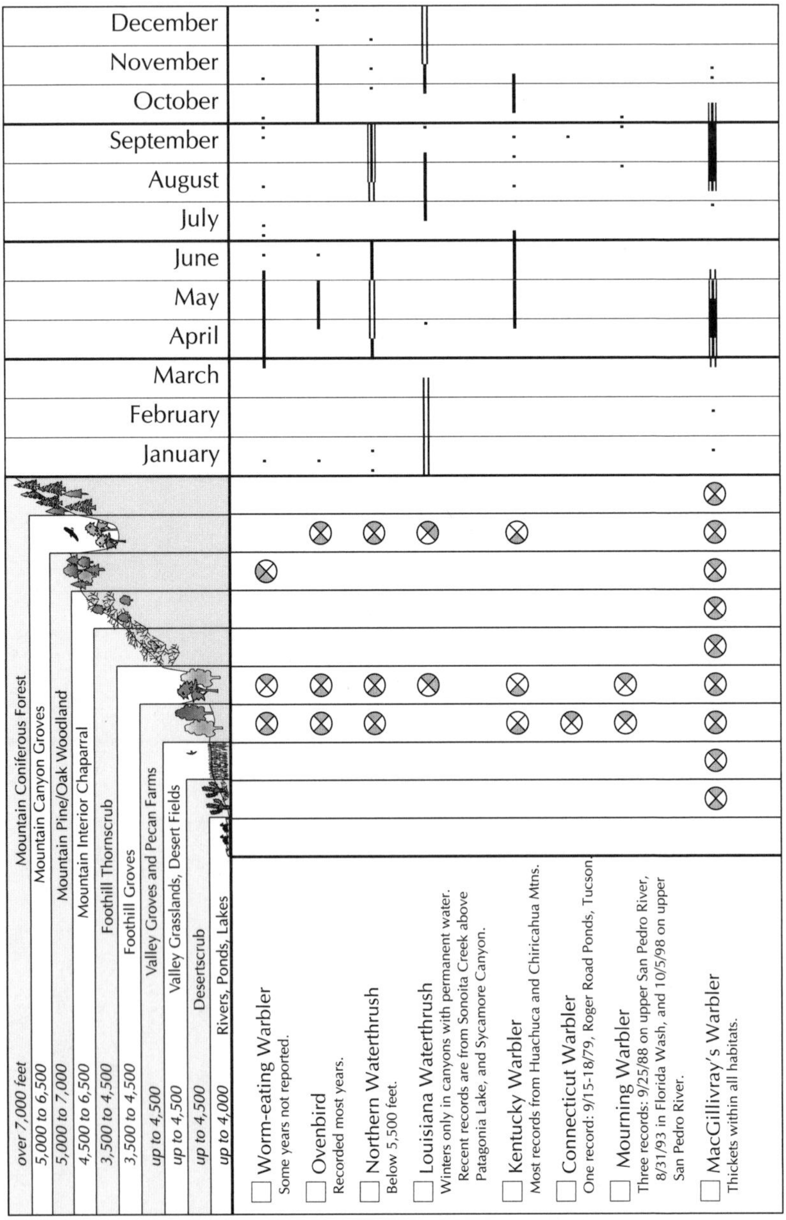

Months (vertical axis): December, November, October, September, August, July, June, May, April, March, February, January

Habitat / elevation labels:

Elevation	Habitat
over 7,000 feet	Mountain Coniferous Forest
5,000 to 6,500	Mountain Canyon Groves
5,000 to 7,000	Mountain Pine/Oak Woodland
4,500 to 6,500	Mountain Interior Chaparral
3,500 to 4,500	Foothill Thornscrub
3,500 to 4,500	Foothill Groves
up to 4,500	Valley Groves and Pecan Farms
up to 4,500	Valley Grasslands, Desert Fields
up to 4,500	Desertscrub
up to 4,000	Rivers, Ponds, Lakes

Worm-eating Warbler
Some years not reported.

Ovenbird
Recorded most years.

Northern Waterthrush
Below 5,500 feet.

Louisiana Waterthrush
Winters only in canyons with permanent water. Recent records are from Sonoita Creek above Patagonia Lake, and Sycamore Canyon.

Kentucky Warbler
Most records from Huachuca and Chiricahua Mtns.

Connecticut Warbler
One record: 9/15-18/79, Roger Road Ponds, Tucson.

Mourning Warbler
Three records: 9/25/88 on upper San Pedro River, 8/31/93 in Florida Wash, and 10/5/98 on upper San Pedro River.

MacGillivray's Warbler
Thickets within all habitats.

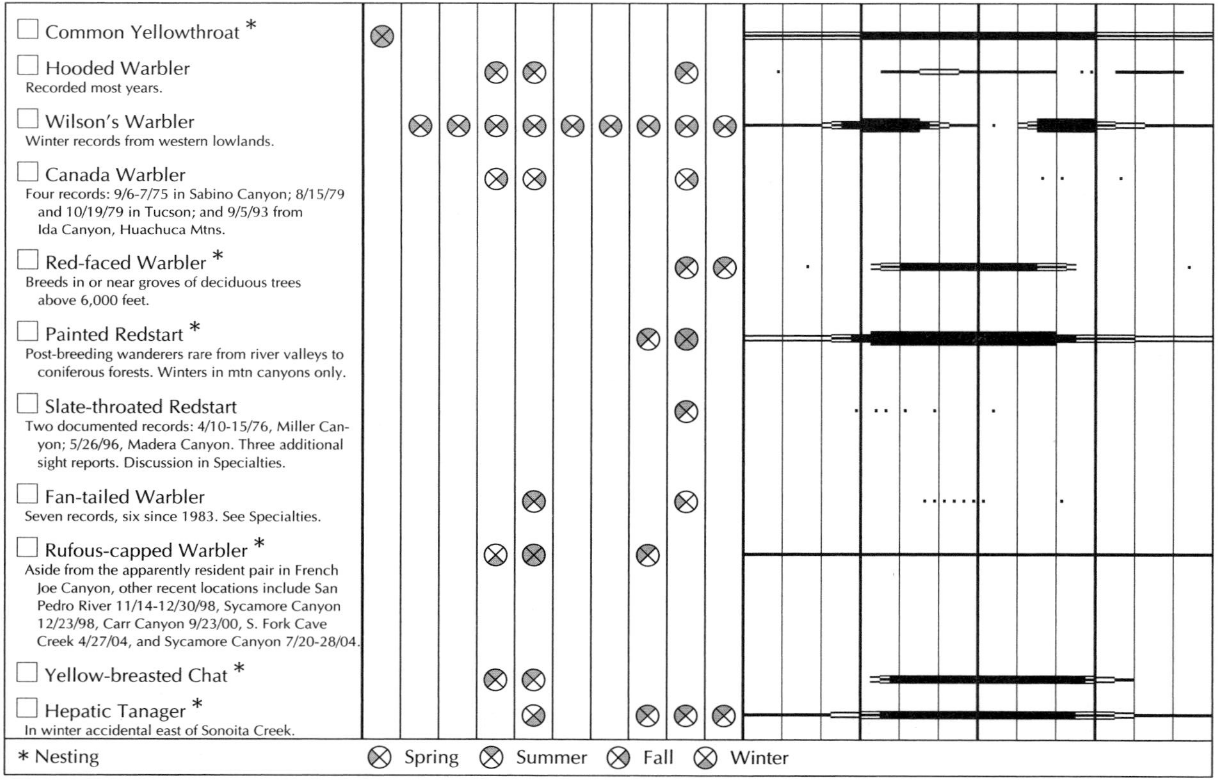

☐ Common Yellowthroat *

☐ Hooded Warbler
Recorded most years.

☐ Wilson's Warbler
Winter records from western lowlands.

☐ Canada Warbler
Four records: 9/6–7/75 in Sabino Canyon; 8/15/79
and 10/19/79 in Tucson; and 9/5/93 from
Ida Canyon, Huachuca Mtns.

☐ Red-faced Warbler *
Breeds in or near groves of deciduous trees
above 6,000 feet.

☐ Painted Redstart *
Post-breeding wanderers rare from river valleys to
coniferous forests. Winters in mtn canyons only.

☐ Slate-throated Redstart
Two documented records: 4/10–15/76, Miller Canyon; 5/26/96, Madera Canyon. Three additional
sight reports. Discussion in Specialties.

☐ Fan-tailed Warbler
Seven records, six since 1983. See Specialties.

☐ Rufous-capped Warbler *
Aside from the apparently resident pair in French
Joe Canyon, other recent locations include San
Pedro River 11/14–12/30/98, Sycamore Canyon
12/23/98, Carr Canyon 9/23/00, S. Fork Cave
Creek 4/27/04, and Sycamore Canyon 7/20–28/04.

☐ Yellow-breasted Chat *

☐ Hepatic Tanager *
In winter accidental east of Sonoita Creek.

* Nesting

⊗ Spring ⊗ Summer ⊗ Fall ⊗ Winter

	December	November	October	September	August	July	June	May	April	March	February	January

over 7,000 feet — Mountain Coniferous Forest
5,000 to 6,500 — Mountain Canyon Groves
5,000 to 7,000 — Mountain Pine/Oak Woodland
4,500 to 6,500 — Mountain Interior Chaparral
3,500 to 4,500 — Foothill Thornscrub
3,500 to 4,500 — Foothill Groves
up to 4,500 — Valley Groves and Pecan Farms
up to 4,500 — Valley Grasslands, Desert Fields
up to 4,500 — Desertscrub
up to 4,000 — Rivers, Ponds, Lakes

☐ Summer Tanager *
In winter known only from western sector.

☐ Scarlet Tanager
Some years not reported.

☐ Western Tanager *
Primarily in breeding areas in coniferous forest in late June to early July. Migrates through almost all habitats.

☐ Flame-colored Tanager *
Frequently hybridizes with Western Tanager in SE Arizona. See discussion in Specialties.

☐ White-collared Seedeater
Hypothetical. Two records: 8/24/97 at Kino Springs, 1/2-16/98 at Patagonia Sewage Ponds. Nearest breeding pop. 500 miles S in northern Sinaloa where sometimes kept as cage bird.

☐ Green-tailed Towhee
Numbers fluctuate from year to year.

☐ Spotted Towhee *
Brushy habitats.

☐ Eastern Towhee
One record: 1/3-3/14/00 on Sonoita Creek near Patagonia.

☐ Canyon Towhee *
Below 5,500 feet.

☐ Abert's Towhee *
Dense thickets along rivers, streams and ponds. Common at Sweetwater Wetlands, Marana Pecan Grove in Tucson, and San Pedro River at Hwy 92 bridge.

☐ Rufous-winged Sparrow *
Local. See discussion in Specialties.

☐ Cassin's Sparrow *
Usually heard before seen. Most easily found during summer rainy season and in spring after wet winters. See Specialties.

☐ Botteri's Sparrow *
Usually heard before seen. Most easily found during summer rainy season and in spring after wet winters. See Specialties.

☐ Rufous-crowned Sparrow *
Prefers arid slopes. See Specialties.

☐ Five-striped Sparrow *
Easiest to find in California Gulch and Sycamore Canyon. Probably some winter, but more research needed.

☐ Chipping Sparrow *
A few winter birds first appear in lowlands in early August; last few birds do not depart lowlands until late May.

* Nesting

⊗ Spring ⊗ Summer ⊗ Fall ⊗ Winter

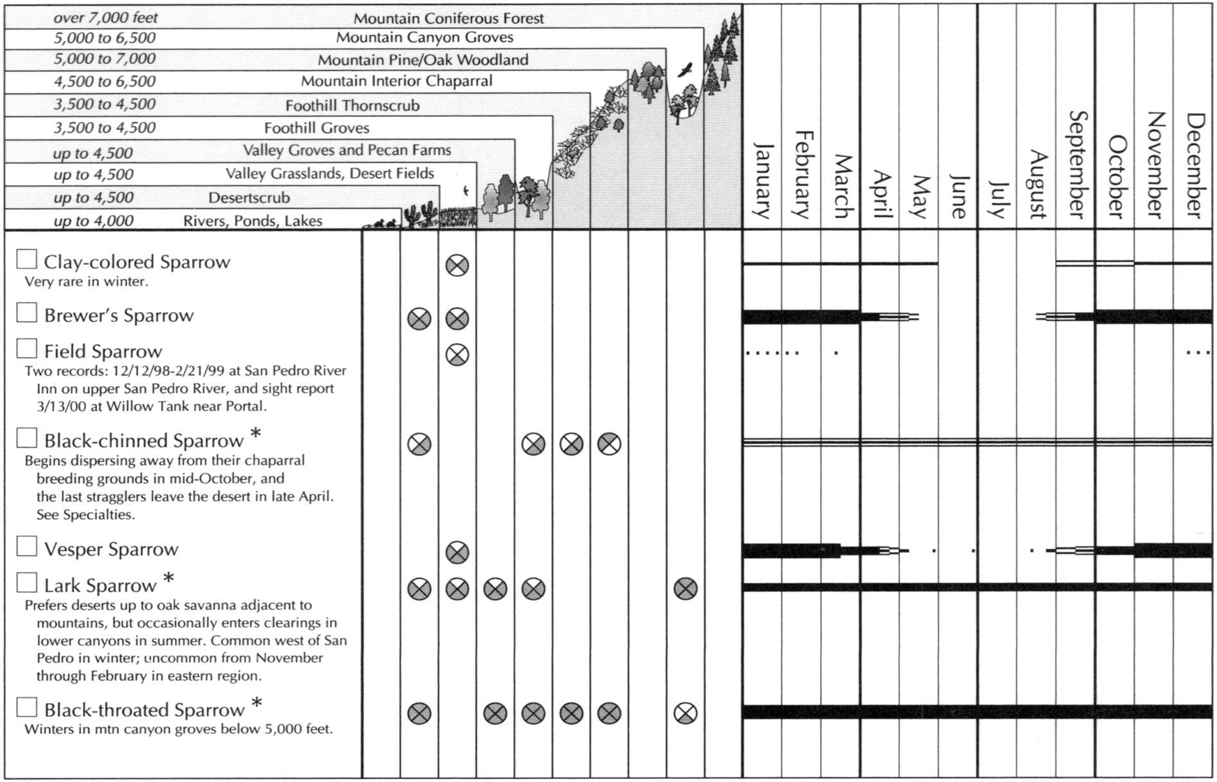
over 7,000 feet
Mountain Coniferous Forest
5,000 to 6,500
Mountain Canyon Groves
5,000 to 7,000
Mountain Pine/Oak Woodland
4,500 to 6,500
Mountain Interior Chaparral
3,500 to 4,500
Foothill Thornscrub
3,500 to 4,500
Foothill Groves
up to 4,500
Valley Groves and Pecan Farms
up to 4,500
Valley Grasslands, Desert Fields
up to 4,500
Desertscrub
up to 4,000
Rivers, Ponds, Lakes
January
February
March
April
May
June
July
August
September
October
November
December
Clay-colored Sparrow
Very rare in winter.
Brewer's Sparrow
Field Sparrow
Two records: 12/12/98-2/21/99 at San Pedro River Inn on upper San Pedro River, and sight report 3/13/00 at Willow Tank near Portal.
Black-chinned Sparrow *
Begins dispersing away from their chaparral breeding grounds in mid-October, and the last stragglers leave the desert in late April. See Specialties.
Vesper Sparrow
Lark Sparrow *
Prefers deserts up to oak savanna adjacent to mountains, but occasionally enters clearings in lower canyons in summer. Common west of San Pedro in winter; uncommon from November through February in eastern region.
Black-throated Sparrow *
Winters in mtn canyon groves below 5,000 feet.

Sage Sparrow
Numbers fluctuate, especially in eastern half of area. Most winters found in Avra Valley, Picacho Reservoir, and Frontier Road and Whitewater Draw in Sulphur Springs Valley.

Lark Bunting
Numbers fluctuate. Most winters is the most abundant species on Portal Christmas Count, but not recorded at all in 1996.

Savannah Sparrow

Grasshopper Sparrow *
Within desertscrub confined to grassy flats. Best areas include Sonoita Grasslands, San Rafael Valley, lower Garden Canyon Rd, and Apache area along Hwy 80. Northern migrants largely replace breeding birds October-March.

Baird's Sparrow
Tall and dense grasslands. See discussion in Specialties.

Le Conte's Sparrow
One record from Santa Cruz River in Tucson 12/19-?/04.

Nelson's Sharp-tailed Sparrow
Arizona's first record came from Avra Valley Sewage Ponds 10/7-8/03.

Fox Sparrow
Most birds belong to the "Slate-colored" race of the Rocky Mtns. Far more rare are "Red" race birds that breed in the far north and that have stripes on the back. "Sooty" race from the Pacific NW is dark overall.

Spring Summer Fall Winter

* Nesting

	December	November	October	September	August	July	June	May	April	March	February	January

over 7,000 feet — Mountain Coniferous Forest
5,000 to 6,500 — Mountain Canyon Groves
5,000 to 7,000 — Mountain Pine/Oak Woodland
4,500 to 6,500 — Mountain Interior Chaparral
3,500 to 4,500 — Foothill Thornscrub
3,500 to 4,500 — Foothill Groves
up to 4,500 — Valley Groves and Pecan Farms
up to 4,500 — Valley Grasslands, Desert Fields
up to 4,500 — Desertscrub
up to 4,000 — Rivers, Ponds, Lakes

☐ **Song Sparrow** *
This resident of riparian undergrowth is joined by migrants which occupy dense thickets up to lower mountain canyon groves, as well as along most pond edges, from mid-September through end of April.

☐ **Lincoln's Sparrow**

☐ **Swamp Sparrow**

☐ **White-throated Sparrow**
Probably easiest to find at Patons' and at Patagonia-Sonoita Creek Preserve.

☐ **Harris's Sparrow**
Usually associates with White-crowned Sparrows.

☐ **White-crowned Sparrow**
Usually one of the most abundant wintering birds.

☐ **Golden-crowned Sparrow**
Usually associates with White-crowned Sparrows.

☐ **Dark-eyed Junco, "Slate-colored"**
Usually only a handful are reported from SE Arizona in the average winter. Associates with other juncos.

☐ Dark-eyed Junco, "Oregon"
This subspecies is usually the most abundant race
of Dark-eyed Junco below 5,000 feet,
especially in valleys.

☐ Dark-eyed Junco, "Gray-headed"
This subspecies is usually the most abundant race
of Dark-eyed Junco above 5,000 feet.

☐ Dark-eyed Junco, "Pink-sided"
Usually found in hedgerows when in valley farm
areas. Usually associates with "Oregon" Junco.

☐ Dark-eyed Junco, "Red-backed"
This subspecies breeds in Central Arizona.
Usually associates with other juncos. Not
reported some years.

☐ Dark-eyed Junco, "White-winged"
Three records: 12/19/00 - 3/6/01 at Evergreen
Cemetery in Tucson, 12/24/00 in Whitetail
Canyon, Chiricahua Mtns, and 3/9-
11/01 in Molino Basin, Santa Catalina Mtns.

☐ Yellow-eyed Junco *
See discussion in Specialties.

☐ McCown's Longspur
Usually found among flocks of Horned Larks.
See Specialties.

☐ Lapland Longspur
Not recorded most years. Locations include near
McNeal in Sulphur Springs Valley, Arivaca
Cienaga, Avra Valley Sewage Ponds, and San
Rafael Grassland. Often associates with
Horned Larks and McCown's Longspurs.

* Nesting

Spring   Summer   Fall   Winter

December
November
October
September
August
July
June
May
April
March
February
January

over 7,000 feet — Mountain Coniferous Forest
5,000 to 6,500 — Mountain Canyon Groves
5,000 to 7,000 — Mountain Pine/Oak Woodland
4,500 to 6,500 — Mountain Interior Chaparral
3,500 to 4,500 — Foothill Thornscrub
3,500 to 4,500 — Foothill Groves
up to 4,500 — Valley Groves and Pecan Farms
up to 4,500 — Valley Grasslands, Desert Fields
up to 4,500 — Desertscrub
up to 4,000 — Rivers, Ponds, Lakes

☐ Smith's Longspur *
Hypothetical. One observed 11/3/86, upper San Pedro River near Charleston.

☐ Chestnut-collared Longspur
Flocks visit stock tanks and corrals. See Specialties.

☐ Northern Cardinal *
In mountain canyon groves below 5,500 feet.

☐ Pyrrhuloxia *
Some winter in mountain canyon groves below 5,500 feet. Valley birds form flocks in winter.

☐ Yellow Grosbeak
Approximately 15 records through spring 2004.

☐ Rose-breasted Grosbeak
Reported annually multiple times and locations; this is perhaps the most "common" Eastern vagrant

☐ Black-headed Grosbeak *
Migrates through all habitats with trees.

☐ Blue Grosbeak *
Most common in mesquite grassland.

Lazuli Bunting
Especially weedy fields. Migrants more abundant during drought years.

Indigo Bunting *
Often with Lazuli Buntings. Non-breeding birds migrate from mid-April through May and from August through September.

Varied Bunting *
Although enclaves of Varied Buntings exist throughout, most easily seen from Patagonia west in foothill canyons with thornscrub on the hillsides. See Specialties.

Painted Bunting
Most birds are greenish females or immatures. Below 5,500 feet in mountain canyon groves.

Dickcissel
Marana Pecan Grove and Lake Cochise, Willcox have produced most recent records. Birds usually heard before seen.

Bobolink
More common in fall, usually at sewage ponds.

Red-winged Blackbird *
Uses desert and valley feedlots and pastures.

Eastern Meadowlark *
The race in SE Arizona, lilianae, can usually be separated from wintering Western Meadowlarks by its black post-ocular stripe contrasting with a pale cheek. See Specialties.

Western Meadowlark *
Has bred after wet winters. See Specialties.

Spring   Summer   Fall   Winter

* Nesting

December
November
October
September
August
July
June
May
April
March
February
January

over 7,000 feet — Mountain Coniferous Forest
5,000 to 6,500 — Mountain Canyon Groves
5,000 to 7,000 — Mountain Pine/Oak Woodland
4,500 to 6,500 — Mountain Interior Chaparral
3,500 to 4,500 — Foothill Thornscrub
3,500 to 4,500 — Foothill Groves
up to 4,500 — Valley Groves and Pecan Farms
up to 4,500 — Valley Grasslands, Desert Fields
up to 4,500 — Desertscrub
up to 4,000 — Rivers, Ponds, Lakes

☐ Yellow-headed Blackbird
Also uses desert and valley feedlots and
pastures. Winter populations fluctuate.

☐ Rusty Blackbird
Not reported some years. Primarily at sewage
ponds and wet pastures.

☐ Brewer's Blackbird
Also feedlots, farms, and towns.

☐ Common Grackle
Arrived in southeast Arizona in the 1980s, but
still not reported most years.

☐ Great-tailed Grackle *
First arrived in Arizona at Safford in 1935, and
in Tucson in 1937. Primarily farms, ranches,
and towns.

☐ Bronzed Cowbird *
Average arrival date in Tucson is mid-March;
average arrival date in Portal and Paradise in
the Chiricahua Mtns is the first week of May.
Some winter in Tucson feedlots. See Specialties.

☐ Brown-headed Cowbird *
Disperses into foothills and lower mountain canyons from mid- to late April; rejoins valley birds in last week of July to last week of August. Winter birds concentrate at valley feedlots and corrals.

☐ Black-vented Oriole
One documented record 4/18/91 at Patagonia Lake; one sight record from Portal 7/17-25/71. See Specialties.

☐ Orchard Oriole
Some years not reported.

☐ Hooded Oriole *
Graph represents lowlands. Dates in lower mountain canyons average from mid-April to late August. Most winter records from Tucson feeders. See Specialties.

☐ Streak-backed Oriole *
Has nested near Marana Pecan Grove and Dudleyville. See Specialties.

☐ Bullock's Oriole *
Graph represents lowlands. Dates in lower mountain canyons average from mid-April to late August. Most winter records from Tucson feeders. See Specialties.

☐ Baltimore Oriole
Not recorded most years.

☐ Scott's Oriole *
Most winter records from canyon and valley feeders.

⊗ Spring   ⊗ Summer   ⊗ Fall   ⊗ Winter

* Nesting

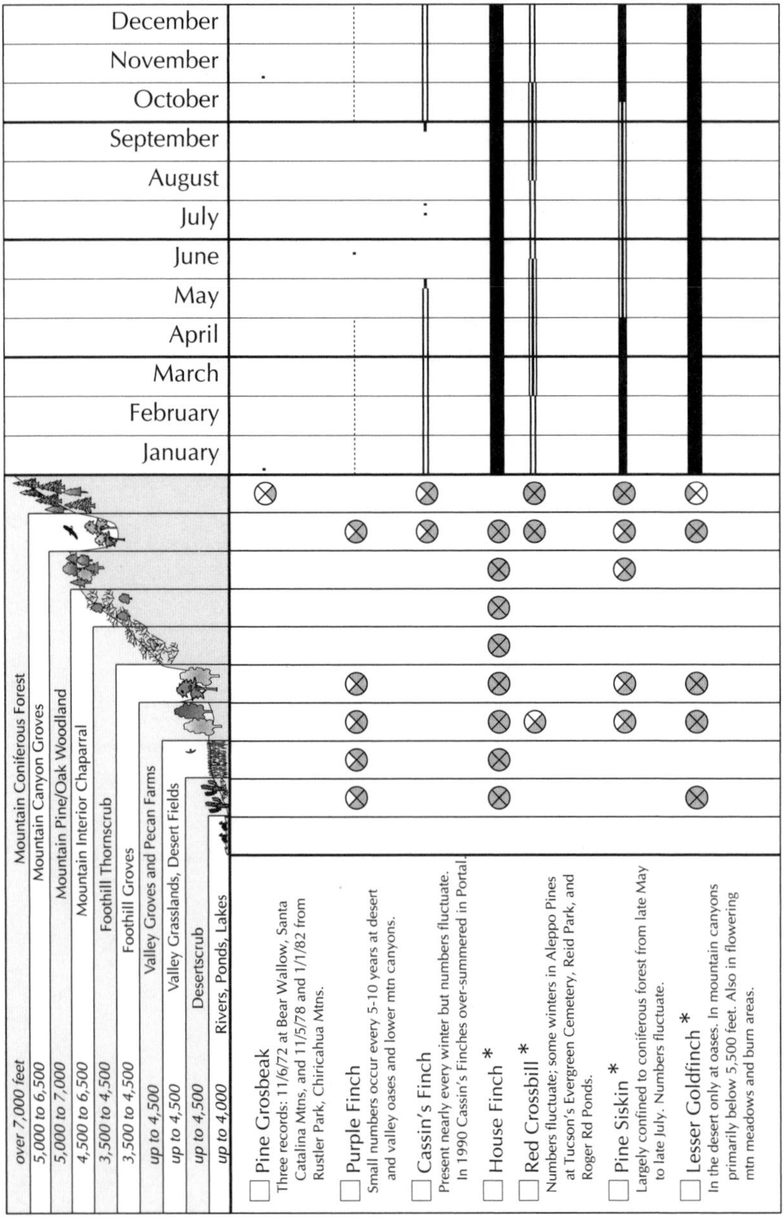

December
November
October
September
August
July
June
May
April
March
February
January

over 7,000 feet — Mountain Coniferous Forest
5,000 to 6,500 — Mountain Canyon Groves
5,000 to 7,000 — Mountain Pine/Oak Woodland
4,500 to 6,500 — Mountain Interior Chaparral
3,500 to 4,500 — Foothill Thornscrub
3,500 to 4,500 — Foothill Groves
up to 4,500 — Valley Groves and Pecan Farms
up to 4,500 — Valley Grasslands, Desert Fields
up to 4,500 — Desertscrub
up to 4,000 — Rivers, Ponds, Lakes

☐ Pine Grosbeak
Three records: 11/6/72 at Bear Wallow, Santa Catalina Mtns, and 11/5/78 and 1/1/82 from Rustler Park, Chiricahua Mtns.

☐ Purple Finch
Small numbers occur every 5-10 years at desert and valley oases and lower mtn canyons.

☐ Cassin's Finch
Present nearly every winter but numbers fluctuate. In 1990 Cassin's Finches over-summered in Portal.

☐ House Finch *

☐ Red Crossbill *
Numbers fluctuate; some winters in Aleppo Pines at Tucson's Evergreen Cemetery, Reid Park, and Roger Rd Ponds.

☐ Pine Siskin *
Largely confined to coniferous forest from late May to late July. Numbers fluctuate.

☐ Lesser Goldfinch *
In the desert only at oases. In mountain canyons primarily below 5,500 feet. Also in flowering mtn meadows and burn areas.

☐ Lawrence's Goldfinch
Fields and desert oases; numbers fluctuate, but more common in western valleys.

☐ American Goldfinch
Wet fields and riparian trees. In mountain canyons below 5,500 feet.

☐ Evening Grosbeak *
Numbers fluctuate; descends into mtn canyons from mid-Oct. through mid-May.

☐ House Sparrow *
Towns, farms, and ranches below 5,000 feet.

Spring Summer Fall Winter

* Nesting

AMPHIBIANS AND REPTILES
OF SOUTHEASTERN ARIZONA

Most desert and foothill snakes are nocturnal and are seldom seen unless a special effort is made to find them. Those unexpectedly found during the day frequently give both the observer and the animal quite a fright. As a rule, the best way to find amphibians and snakes with minimal stress to either their or your nervous system is to drive backcountry roads at night—particularly after rains. The best roads are those that have vegetation growing close to the edges. The following appendix is complete. You'll be fortunate to find even a small fraction of the species listed, and it's entirely possible to bird Southeastern Arizona for a week or a month without seeing a snake at all, let alone a rattler.

SALAMANDER

Arizona Tiger Salamander Rare; oak woodland streams. The only native salamander in Arizona. Parker and Scotia Canyons in the Huachuca Mountains. Perhaps owing to introductions, now found in Avra Valley Sewage Ponds, Lake Cochise, and other wastewater treatment facilities.

FROGS and TOADS

Western Barking Frog Rare; rocky hillsides in canyons, Santa Rita and Pajarito Mountains. Found after summer rains.

Couch's Spadefoot Abundant after first summer rains; deserts and grasslands .

Southern Spadefoot Abundant after summer rains; primarily desert.

Plains Spadefoot Abundant after summer rains; Upper Sonoran grasslands.

Sonoran Desert Toad Along tributaries of the Río Yaqui (San Bernardino Ranch and Guadalupe Canyon) and the Río de la Concepción (Sycamore Canyon).

Southwestern Woodhouse's Toad Permanent streams and irrigation ditches, mostly Lower Sonoran.

Red-spotted Toad Localized; pools and seeps in rocky canyons. Upper Sonoran.

Great Plains Toad Irrigation ditches and rain-pools of the deserts and grasslands, Lower and Upper Sonoran.

Green Toad Abundant after summer rains; grasslands, Cochise and Santa Cruz Counties.

Sonoran Green Toad Breeds after the summer rains in deserts west of Tucson.

Canyon Treefrog Common; rocky streams from the desert to the pines.

Mountain Treefrog Known only from Miller Canyon, Huachuca Mountains, where last sighted in 1970.

Tarahumara Frog Possibly now locally extirpated. Formerly found in the United States only along the tributaries of the Río de la Concepción (Sycamore, Peña Blanca, and Alamo Canyons) and Josephine Canyon in the Santa Rita Mountains. Reintroduction efforts began in 2004.

Chiricahua Leopard Frog Rocky streams in oak and pine-oak woodlands.

Plains Leopard Frog Ponds and pools in the Sulphur Springs Valley and West Turkey Creek in the Chiricahua Mountains.

Lowland Leopard Frog Desert and foothill ponds and streams in the Santa Rita and Atascosa Mountains.

Subaquatic Singing Leopard Frog Accorded species status in 1993, this interesting species sings its courtship songs only underwater in pools in Miller, Ramsey, and Brown Canyons in the Huachuca Mountains.

Bullfrog Introduced, primarily in valley ponds and lakes.

Sinaloa Narrow-mouthed Toad Rare; found after summer rains in pools and streams, Pajarito and Patagonia Mountains.

TURTLES

Yellow Mud Turtle Streams and ponds in the grasslands, Cochise and Pima Counties.

Sonoran Mud Turtle Streams of the Gila River drainage, chiefly in the woodlands.

Western Box Turtle Grasslands, mainly Cochise County.

Desert Tortoise Sonoran Desert from near Benson westward.

Spiny Softshell Introduced; now established in ponds and streams in the Santa Cruz and San Pedro watersheds.

Red-eared Slider Introduced; now established at Sweetwater Wetlands.

LIZARDS

Tucson Banded Gecko Rocky areas protected from frost and around houses, Lower Sonoran.

Mediterranean Gecko Introduced in Tucson.

Desert Iguana Creosote flats in the Sonoran Desert west of Tucson.

Arizona Chuckwalla Rocky outcrops in the Sonoran Desert west of Avra Valley.

Lesser Earless Lizard Grasslands and areas of low brush, Upper Sonoran.

Greater Earless Lizard Washes and streambeds in areas of low brush and open oak woodlands, Lower and Upper Sonoran.

Zebra-tailed Lizard Sandy plains, and deserts, Lower Sonoran.

Common Collared Lizard Rocky areas of deserts and foothills.

Large-spotted Leopard Lizard Brush grasslands and deserts, Lower Sonoran.

Bunch Grass Lizard Grassy slopes in coniferous forests of the border ranges.

Mountain Spiny Lizard Cliffs, rocky areas, and talus slopes in oak and coniferous forests of the border ranges and up to the tops of the highest peaks.

Northern Crevice Spiny Lizard Rocky areas in Guadalupe Canyon, Peloncillo Mountains.

Desert Spiny Lizard Desertscrub, mesquite thickets, cottonwood groves, and rocky areas, Lower Sonoran. Usually on the ground.

Clark's Spiny Lizard Mainly in wooded areas along streams on the slopes of the border ranges, Upper Sonoran. Usually found in trees.

Southern Prairie Lizard Many habitats, Upper Sonoran and Transition.

Striped Plateau Lizard Wooded streams within pine-oak woodland in the Chiricahua Mountains.

Side-blotched Lizard Many habitats, deserts and grasslands, Lower and Upper Sonoran.

Tree Lizard Trees and large rocks, from the deserts to the pines.

Texas Horned Lizard Plains with scrubby vegetation, Chihuahuan Desert in Cochise County.

Short-horned Lizard Primarily mountains up to the summits of the highest peaks. Not a desert species.

Round-tailed Horned Lizard Plains with scrubby vegetation, Chihuahuan Desert in Cochise County.

Regal Horned Lizard Rocky areas of desert foothills, Sonoran Desert in Pima and Santa Cruz Counties.

Great Plains Skink Under rocks and litter along water-courses, from the deserts to the mountains.

Mountain Skink Under rocks and litter in wooded areas of the border ranges.

Giant Spotted Whiptail Dense brush along water-courses, from the deserts and grasslands into the oak woodlands up to 4,500 feet.

Little Striped Whiptail Grasslands; known only from vicinity of Willcox Playa in Cochise County.

Desert Grassland Whiptail Plains and slopes of deserts and mesquite grasslands, Lower and Upper Sonoran.

Chihuahuan Spotted Whiptail Canyon bottoms in oak and oak-pine woodlands and in riparian woodlands and rocky areas of grasslands and deserts, mostly Upper Sonoran.

Sonoran Spotted Whiptail Oak woodland along the border.

Gila Spotted Whiptail Upper Sonoran chaparral and woodland in the Santa Catalina and Chiricahua Mountains.

Arizona Desert Whiptail Many habitats, but usually fairly open areas. From the deserts to the lower oak woodlands up to 4,500 feet.

Checkered Whiptail From creosote brush to Pinyon Pine. Known only from Peloncillo Mountains.

Madrean Alligator Lizard Under rocks and litter, primarily in pine-oak woodlands; rarely in coniferous forest or riparian woodlands in the deserts.

Gila Monster Rare; rocky areas from the deserts to lower edge of oak woodlands. Venomous.

SNAKES

Western Blind Snake Deserts and arid grasslands, Sonoran and Chihuahuan Deserts, Lower Sonoran.

Texas Blind Snake Deserts and grasslands, particularly in moist areas. Chihuahuan Deserts and surrounding grasslands.

Regal Ring-necked Snake Moist areas in oak grasslands and riparian woodlands, mostly Upper Sonoran.

Western Hog-nosed Snake Mainly grasslands, Upper Sonoran.

Spotted Leaf-nosed Snake Sandy soils, west of Tucson; nocturnal.

Saddled Leaf-nosed Snake Rocky soils, west of Tucson.

Coachwhip Many habitats, deserts and grasslands. Often very pink, leading to local name of "Red Racer."

Sonoran Whipsnake From the brushy deserts to the oak-pine woodlands.

Western Patch-nosed Snake Open scrub of deserts, Lower Sonoran.

Graham Patch-nosed Snake Open oak and pine-oak woodlands, Upper Sonoran.

Green Rat Snake Rare; canyons of the border ranges.

Glossy Snake Many habitats, deserts and grasslands; nocturnal.

Sonoran Gopher Snake Many habitats, from the deserts to the mountains. Probably the most commonly seen snake.

Common Kingsnake Many habitats in the deserts and grasslands. A black form with few or no light dorsal markings may be found south of Tucson.

Sonoran Mountain Kingsnake Scrub, woodlands, and coniferous forests of the mountains. Similar to Arizona Coral Snake, but has distinct head.

Western Long-nosed Snake Deserts and grasslands; nocturnal.

Western Black-necked Garter Snake Streams from the desert to the pines.

Mexican Garter Snake Streams, mainly on the grasslands.

Checkered Garter Snake Usually along streams and ponds in the deserts and grasslands.

Western Ground Snake Sandy plains and rocky hillsides of the deserts and grasslands.

Banded Sand Snake Sandy soils, Sonoran Deserts from lower San Pedro Valley westward.

Chihuahuan Hook-nosed Snake Known only from the deserts and grasslands in Cochise County.

Thornscrub Hook-nosed Snake Known only from the grasslands of Santa Cruz County.

Southwestern Black-headed Snake Under rocks and litter from the desert canyons to the oak woodlands.

Plains Black-headed Snake Under rocks and litter in the grasslands. Usually in moist areas.

Huachuca Black-headed Snake Rare; under rocks and litter in the grasslands and oak woodlands of the Huachuca, Santa Rita, and Patagonia Mountains.

Yaqui Black-headed Snake Streamside woodlands in the Chiricahua, Mule, and Atascosa Mountains.

Brown Vine Snake Rare; brush and trees along canyon bottoms. Known only from the area west of Nogales in the headwater tributaries of the Río de la Concepción.

Sonoran Lyre Snake Rocky canyons and hillsides from the deserts to the pines.

Night Snake Many habitats, from the desert to the oak woodlands.

Arizona Coral Snake Rare; arid habitats, from the deserts to the lower oak woodlands. Tiny head. Venomous.

Massasauga Rare; grasslands of Cochise County. Venomous.

Western Diamond-backed Rattlesnake Many habitats, from the deserts and grasslands to the lower oak woodlands. The most common valley rattlesnake. Venomous.

Banded Rock Rattlesnake Rocky areas of the oak and pine-oak woodlands of the border ranges. Pink and green color morphs. Venomous.

Black-tailed Rattlesnake Rocky areas from the deserts to the pines. The most common rattlesnake in the mountains. Venomous.

Tiger Rattlesnake Rocky areas, Sonoran Desert west of Tucson. Venomous.

Western "Arizona Black" Rattlesnake Many habitats, from the foothills to the pines. Found only in the Rincon and Santa Catalina Mountains and northward. Venomous.

Mojave Rattlesnake Non-rocky plains of the open deserts and grasslands; rarely in the mountains. Venomous.

Twin-spotted Rattlesnake Rocky areas within the coniferous forests of the border ranges. Venomous.

Ridge-nosed Rattlesnake Rare; rocky areas in wooded canyons in the Santa Rita and Huachuca Mountains; two reports from the Chiricahua Mountains. Venomous.

MAMMALS OF SOUTHEASTERN ARIZONA

Virginia "Sonoran" Opossum Possibly introduced: primarily in valley farming areas, but also recorded in canyons of the Huachuca Mountains.

Vagrant Shrew Meadows and grassy areas in the higher mountains.

Desert Shrew River woodlands at lower elevations.

Leaf-chinned Bat Known only from mines in Santa Cruz County.

California Leaf-nosed Bat Mines and caves at lower elevations.

Mexican Long-tongued Bat Small groups in mines, caves, and abandoned buildings at mid to high elevations in mountains. Endangered.

Lesser Long-nosed Bat Moist caves and mines. Colonial roosts. Endangered.

Yuma Myotis Mines, caves, tree hollows.

Cave Myotis Caves at lower elevations.

Southwestern Myotis Primarily in Ponderosa Pine and dense canyon woodlands.

Fringed Myotis Caves and buildings at higher elevations.

Long-legged Myotis Open forests at higher elevations.

California Myotis Caves and hollows; all elevations.

Small-footed Myotis Mines, caves, hollows; all elevations.

Silver-haired Bat Solitary; forested areas in the mountains.

Western Pipistrelle Crevices and buildings; all elevations.

Big Brown Bat Buildings and caves; all elevations.

Red Bat Solitary; forested areas in the mountains.

Southern Yellow Bat Roosts in Washington Fan Palms near Tucson, and probably sycamores and hackberry trees farther east.

Hoary Bat Solitary; hangs in trees, forested areas.

Allen's Lappet-browed Bat Usually at mid to high elevations in mountains.

Townsend's Western Big-eared Bat Caves, usually at higher elevations.

Mexican Big-eared Bat Colonial in mines and caves in the oak woodlands.

Pallid Bat Many habitats, all elevations.

Mexican Free-tailed Bat Mines, caves, buildings, low to mid elevations.

Pocketed Free-tailed Bat Mines and caves at lower elevations.

Big Free-tailed Bat Mines and caves at lower elevations.

Western Mastiff Bat Rock crevices at lower elevations.

Underwood's Mastiff Bat Rock crevices at lower elevations in the Baboquivari Mountains, primarily seen over ponds in the evenings.

Grizzly Bear Locally extirpated about 1901; formerly primarily in oak and pine-oak woodlands.

Black Bear Higher mountains. Crosses valleys from one mountain range to the next.

Ring-tail Rocky areas at all elevations; nocturnal.

Raccoon Streams at all elevations.

Coati Fairly common in oak and pine-oak woodlands.

Long-tailed Weasel Many habitats; all elevations.

Badger Valley grasslands and deserts.

Western Spotted Skunk Woodlands; all elevations.

Striped Skunk Many habitats; all elevations.

Hooded Skunk Common, brush and woodlands, Lower and Upper Sonoran.

Hog-nosed Skunk Common, brush and woodlands, Lower and Upper Sonoran.

Coyote Many habitats; all elevations.

Mexican Gray Wolf Probably extirpated; formerly throughout. Last recorded in 1971.

Kit Fox Desertscrub.

Gray Fox Scrub, Upper and Lower Sonoran.

Jaguar Straggler from Mexico, primarily in foothill canyons. Recorded in the Dos Cabezas Mountains near Willcox in 1987 after a 49-year hiatus. Another Jaguar was photographed in the Pedregosa Mountains in 1996, and since then, Arizona Game and Fish Department automatic cameras established that there were minimally two Jaguars roaming the border ranges in 2004.

Mountain Lion Mountains, mid- to high elevations.

Ocelot One definite record from near Patagonia in 1960 and a sight record from Cave Creek in the Chiricahua Mountains in 1982. Usually found near foothill streams.

Jaguarundi Hypothetical; one seen in March 1938 in Canelo Hills. Scrub or deserts and lower mountain slopes.

Bobcat Primarily mountain and foothill edges, especially along water-courses.

Spotted Ground-Squirrel Grasslands, Sulphur Springs and San Pedro Valleys.

Rock Squirrel Rocky areas, Lower and Upper Sonoran.

Harris's Antelope Ground-Squirrel Deserts and grasslands.

Round-tailed Ground-Squirrel Deserts, lower elevations.

Cliff Chipmunk Scrub and woodlands, mountains. Not in Huachuca or Santa Rita Mountains.

Black-tailed Prairie-Dog Locally extirpated about 1938; formerly in valley grasslands surrounding the Chiricahua and Huachuca Mountains.

Abert's Tassel-eared Squirrel Introduced from Central Arizona into the Catalina Mountains.

Arizona Gray Squirrel Oaks and pines in all the mountains in the southeast corner except the Chiricahuas; also in the Patagonia-Sonoita Creek Preserve. Taxonomically, the Arizona Gray Squirrel is a true fox squirrel closely related to the Apache Fox Squirrel.

Apache Fox Squirrel Primarily pine-oak woodlands, but also regular in coniferous forest on the summit of Fly Peak at 9,666 feet elevation; in the U.S. endemic to the Chiricahua Mountains.

Southern Pygmy Pocket-Gopher Meadows and stream-banks, from Huachuca Mountains westward, Upper Sonoran.

Valley Pocket-Gopher Meadows and valleys, all elevations.

Bailey Pocket-Gopher Meadows at high elevations in the Huachuca and Chiricahua Mountains.

Silky Pocket-Mouse Grasslands, Upper Sonoran.

Arizona Pocket-Mouse Deserts, south and west of Tucson.

Bailey's Pocket-Mouse Deserts, south and west of Tucson.

Desert Pocket-Mouse Deserts and grasslands, Lower Sonoran.

Rock Pocket-Mouse Lava flows and rocky areas, Lower Sonoran.

Hispid Pocket-Mouse Grasslands, Upper Sonoran.

Banner-tailed Kangaroo-Rat Grasslands, Upper Sonoran.

Merriam's Kangaroo-Rat Deserts and grasslands, Lower Sonoran.

Ord's Kangaroo-Rat Grassland, Upper Sonoran.

Beaver Extirpated by 1900; formerly in cottonwood groves along the upper Santa Cruz and San Pedro Rivers.

Northern Pygmy-Mouse Grasslands, Upper Sonoran.

Southern Grasshopper-Mouse Weedy fields and grasslands, Lower Sonoran.

Plains Harvest-Mouse Grasslands, Cochise County.

Western Harvest-Mouse Weedy fields and grasslands, Lower and Upper Sonoran.

Fulvous Harvest-Mouse Grasslands, western Cochise and Santa Cruz Counties.

Pygmy Mouse Grasslands, Upper Sonoran.

Cactus Mouse Cactus, Lower Sonoran.

Merriam's Mouse Deserts, Pinal, Pima, and Santa Cruz Counties.

Deer Mouse Many habitats; all elevations.

White-footed Mouse Brush and woodlands; all elevations.

Brush Mouse Scrub; all elevations.

Pinyon Mouse Rocky pinyon-juniper areas, Chiricahua Mountains.

Rock Mouse Rocky areas, Chiricahua Mountains.

Hispid Cotton-Rat Open riparian and grassy areas, Lower Sonoran.

Least Cotton-Rat Grasslands, Lower and Upper Sonoran.

Yellow-nosed Cotton-Rat Foothills and mountains, Cochise and Santa Cruz Counties.

White-throated Woodrat Cactus and scrub, Lower and Upper Sonoran.

Mexican Woodrat Rocky scrub, Upper Sonoran.

Norway Rat Introduced; cities.

House Mouse Introduced; cities.

Porcupine Mesquite and cottonwood woods and aspen groves within coniferous forests, Lower Sonoran through Canadian.

Antelope Jackrabbit Brush, grasslands, foothills of the Santa Rita Mountains.

Black-tailed Jackrabbit Open deserts and grasslands, Lower and Upper Sonoran.

Eastern Cottontail Woodlands, Chiricahua Mountains.

Desert Cottontail Deserts and brush lands, Lower Sonoran.

Collared Peccary Deserts and oak woodlands, Lower and Upper Sonoran.

Merriam's Elk Extirpated from the Chiricahua Mountains in 1906. This race extinct.

Rocky Mountain "Desert" Mule Deer Desertscrub, foothills, and valley edges.

Coues White-tailed Deer River-bottom groves, all woodlands and forested mountains.

Pronghorn Extirpated before 1900; present populations stem from re-introductions since 1949. Grasslands on the Buenos Aires Wildlife Refuge, near Sonoita, in the San Rafael Valley, on Fort Huachuca, in the upper Sulphur Springs Valley, and the San Bernardino Valley southeast of the Chiricahua Mountains harbor approximately 500 Pronghorns altogether, according to Arizona Game and Fish Department estimates in 2004.

Desert Bighorn Sheep Rocky, cliff-walled mountains in the Sonoran Desert north and west of Tucson. Aravaipa Canyon is the best area in which to see this reclusive species. The Arizona Game and Fish Department estimated that the total population in Southeastern Arizona was approximately 250-300 wild sheep in 2004.

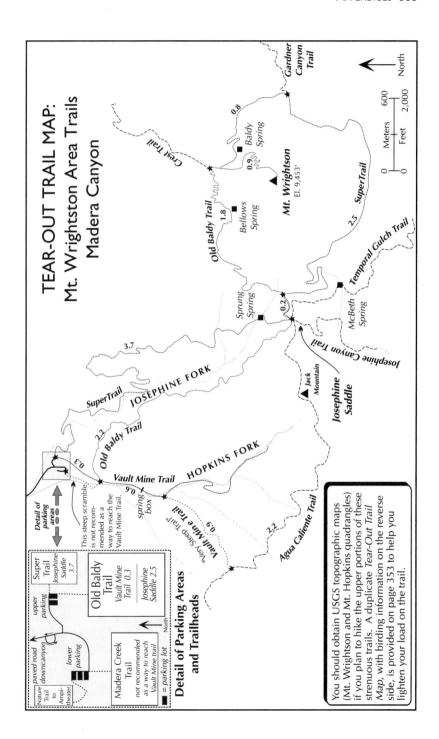

TEAR-OUT TRAIL MAP:
Mt. Wrightston Area Trails
Madera Canyon

North

Meters   0   600
Feet   0   2,000

Gardner Canyon Trail

Crest Trail

0.8

Baldy Spring

0.9

Mt. Wrightson
El. 9,453'

SuperTrail

Old Baldy Trail

1.8

Bellows Spring

2.5

Sprung Spring

Temporal Gulch Trail

0.2

McBeth Spring

Josephine Canyon Trail

Jack Mountain

Josephine Saddle

3.7

SuperTrail

JOSEPHINE FORK

Old Baldy Trail

2.2

0.3

HOPKINS FORK

Vault Mine Trail

0.6

spring box

"Very Steep Trail"

Vault Mine Trail

0.9

2.2

Agua Caliente Trail

Detail of parking areas

This steep scramble is not recommended as a way to reach the Vault Mine Trail.

Detail of Parking Areas and Trailheads

Nature Trail to Amphitheater

paved road down canyon

upper parking

lower parking

Super Trail
Josephine Saddle 3.7

Old Baldy Trail
Vault Mine Trail 0.3
Josephine Saddle 2.5

North

Madera Creek Trail
not recommended as a way to reach Vault Mine trail

■ = parking lot

You should obtain USGS topographic maps (Mt. Wrightson and Mt. Hopkins quadrangles) if you plan to hike the upper portions of these strenuous trails. A duplicate Tear-Out Trail Map, with birding information on the reverse side, is provided on page 353 to help you lighten your load on the trail.

The **Hopkins Fork** of Madera Canyon is both the best and the most popular destination for birders who care to hike. To reach the trailhead, it is recommended that you turn left just beyond the oval to reach the uppermost Josephine Fork parking area. A cable on the right, uphill end of the lot marks the easiest point of access for Hopkins Fork. An abandoned dirt road contours 0.3 mile across the ridge that divides Josephine Fork from the Hopkins Fork of upper Madera Canyon. It joins the Hopkins Fork at the beginning of the Old Baldy (an alternative, unofficial name for Mt. Wrightson) Trail in 0.3 mile. This very steep short-cut to Josephine Saddle is 2.2 miles long (instead of the 3.7-mile alternative "Super Trail"). Birders should ignore the Old Baldy Trail and take the route continuing straight up the bottom of Hopkins Fork.

The most reliable area for Elegant Trogons in the Hopkins Fork has traditionally been in the basin one-quarter mile farther up canyon. The trail follows the left side of the stream a couple hundred yards, then climbs a steep and rocky hill. Links of an old pipeline are frequent up to a concrete spring box on the right side of the path. This marks the lower end of the trogon nesting zone, although pairs patrol the whole length of Hopkins. Other summering species that share the big Silverleaf Oak and Alligator Juniper in the shady basin include Cooper's Hawk, Flammulated Owl, Magnificent Hummingbird, Greater Pewee, Cordilleran, Dusky-capped, and Sulphur-bellied Flycatchers, Plumbeous and Hutton's Vireos, Hermit Thrush, Grace's Warbler, Painted Redstart, and Hepatic Tanager. In migration, Warbling Vireo, Swainson's Thrush, and Western Tanager are all usually common. One or two Red-faced Warblers are often here in April and May. Look for a nesting pair of Painted Redstarts near a permanent spring that cascades between a pair of slab-like boulders just 100 yards above the spring box. Two Aztec Thrushes were discovered using the stretch of Hopkins Fork above the spring box in August 1994, and another was in this area in August of 2000. A Crescent-chested Warbler in late April 2003 was at the ford just up the trail.

The trail crosses the streambed in 0.25 mile and divides 200 yards beyond. The Vault Mine Trail to the Agua Caliente Trail is the "very steep trail" mentioned on the sign at the lower trail junction. (It leads one-half mile to the abandoned Vault Mine, over 600 feet above. The Vault Mine Trail above this junction is not recommended.) Birders who have still not seen the trogon should veer left another 200 yards up the bottom of Hopkins Fork to where the trail disappears into the rocks of the stream channel itself. The quarter-mile stretch above the stream crossing to where the trail ends in the streambed is just as good for trogons as the quarter-mile stretch below the stream crossing. If the trogons are nesting, you may have to wait all morning for a nest exchange before a bird passes by. *Under no circumstances should you disturb or knowingly approach an active nest tree.* From here back to the Josephine Fork parking area is 0.9 mile.

The eight-mile-long Super Trail to Mount Wrightson begins at the left end of the **Josephine Fork** parking lot. If you have plenty of stamina, this scenic path is great for birding. Don't forget to carry plenty of water. At first, you will be in the oak belt and the birds will be about the same as those which occupy the middle canyon near the Santa Rita Lodge. Elegant Trogons occasionally nest in sycamores along the stream approximately one mile up Josephine. A male Tropical Parula was using this area of Josephine from mid-July to mid-September 1984. A possible female Tropical Parula was seen with the male one day only in late July.

After one mile the trail makes a sharp switchback to the left and climbs a dry hillside. Hutton's Vireo, Black-throated Gray Warbler, and Scott's Oriole are the typical birds. Approximately three miles above the Josephine parking area, the trail enters a Ponderosa Pine forest, the home of Greater Pewee, Grace's Warbler, and Yellow-eyed Junco. Watch for Red-faced Warbler at Sprung Spring (3.8 miles above the parking area). This is about as low as the Red-faced Warbler is found in the nesting season. The first Eared Quetzal ever recorded in the Santa Rita Mountains was sighted here in July 1991. Josephine Saddle is only 0.2 mile beyond. Elevation change between the 5,400-foot-high parking area and elevation 7,100 foot Josephine Saddle is 1,700 feet.

In forested glades along the remaining four miles on the Super Trail to the 9,453-foot-high summit of Mt. Wrightson, you should find a community of Transition and Canadian Life Zone birds which includes Broad-tailed Hummingbird, Hairy Woodpecker, Steller's Jay, Red-breasted and Pygmy Nuthatches, Brown Creeper, House Wren, Yellow-rumped, Grace's, Red-faced, and Olive Warblers, Hepatic and Western Tanagers, Yellow-eyed Junco, Red Crossbill (irregular), and Pine Siskin. The Baldy Saddle area (elevation 8,800 feet; 0.9 mile below Mt. Wrightson) is a particularly good location for most of these species. In May 1993 a Buff-breasted Flycatcher was also reported from the saddle.

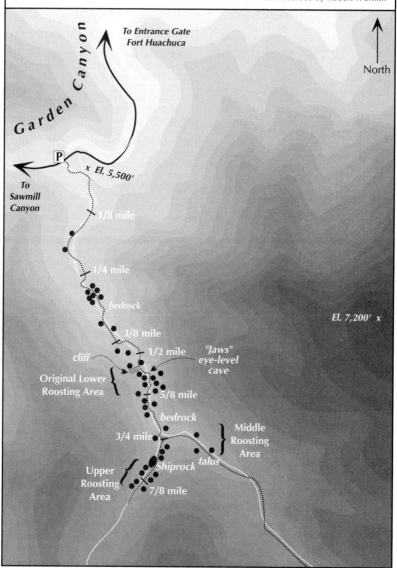

TEAR-OUT TRAIL MAP:
Scheelite Canyon, Fort Huachuca

● = Spotted Owl sighting locations since 1978   Contour Interval: 100 feet
······ = foot trail

From data recorded by Robert T. Smith

To Entrance Gate
Fort Huachuca

North

Garden Canyon

P
x El. 5,500'

To
Sawmill
Canyon

1/8 mile

1/4 mile

bedrock

El. 7,200' x

3/8 mile

1/2 mile   "Jaws"
eye-level
cliff   cave

Original Lower
Roosting Area   5/8 mile

bedrock
Middle
Roosting
Area
3/4 mile

Upper
Roosting   *Shiprock* *talus*
Area   7/8 mile

The trail up **Scheelite Canyon** is steep and mined with rolling rocks. *There is no drinking water in the canyon.* Robert T. Smith, "Smitty" to the 6,000-plus birders whom he led up the canyon from 1978 until his death in 1998, should be credited as the protector of the Spotted Owls of Scheelite.

Scheelite is most famous for its Spotted Owls, but it is also a good location for an impressive array of other pine-oak woodland birds. Watch for Bridled Titmouse, Virginia's Warbler (summer), and Rufous-crowned Sparrow in the lower canyon. This is also the best stretch for Montezuma Quail, Hammond's and Dusky Flycatchers (migration), Dusky-capped Flycatcher (summer), Western Scrub-Jay (screeching on the brushy slopes above), Hutton's Vireo, Black-throated Gray Warbler (summer), and Canyon Towhee.

Some years a pair of Elegant Trogons nests in the dense riparian area midway between the canyon entrance and "Jaws," a rock formation on the left side of the trail set amidst tall timber. Listen here for the distinctive vocalizations of Northern Pygmy-Owl, Whip-poor-will (occasionally even in the daytime during summer), Red-breasted Nuthatch, House Wren, and Hepatic Tanager (summer).

After one-half mile the trail (the indefatigable Smitty painted these useful mileage markers) approaches an area with a towering cliff on the right side. This is the start of the "lower area" commonly used by the owls for roosting (although they can occur as low as the first one-quarter mile). Canyon Wrens generally sound the alarm as you approach. In summer Painted Redstarts are invariably here, and often a pair of Red-faced Warblers. Summering Cordilleran Flycatchers also nest in this cool, shady zone.

Ordinarily the Spotted Owls take perches under 20 feet in height, usually on a major limb in the lower half of a tree. In large oaks they may park well out on a bough, but look for them to sit near the trunk in small trees and conifers. The pair is often side by side, and almost always within 100 feet of one another if both are present. The code of self-restraint Smitty asked birders to exercise is simple:
- *do not approach within 50 feet of the birds;*
- *do not talk loudly; do not point at the birds or wave your arms;*
- *photographers should not use flash or make noise to get the birds' attention;*
- *do not use tape recordings or try to imitate the calls of Spotted Owls. Spotted Owl calls are specifically prohibited on Fort Huachuca.*

Approximately 100 yards beyond the 5/8-mile marker, Scheelite narrows to a rocky chute with a small spring, except in extremely dry years. The platter-sized pools may attract up to three species of warblers (Virginia's, Black-throated Gray, or Red-faced bathing in a single puddle. White-throated Swifts (summer) zoom overhead and an occasional Golden Eagle floats across the narrow slit of sky. Check here for Greater Pewee (summer) and Plumbeous Vireo (summer). Mexican Jays occur throughout Scheelite, but above the chute Steller's Jays are also common. At mile marker 3/4, approximately 150 paces beyond the seep, Scheelite splits into two major canyons. Elevation here is 6,350, 600 feet above the parking area.

The main trail continues up the left fork another 2.8 miles, climbing steeply 2,000 more feet before it joins the Crest Trail. The Spotted Owls sometimes roost near the junction—and infrequently in the first 200 yards up the left fork, but usually—when not in the lower area—the birds are up the unmaintained track ascending the right-hand fork. Look for them in dense stands of maple or oak, especially 200 yards above the junction to about 3/8 mile up the canyon. The trail peters out 200 or so yards beyond "Shiprock," a prow-shaped boulder in the center of the dry creek bed.

Take your time on the trip downcanyon, and stay quiet until you are back at your vehicle.

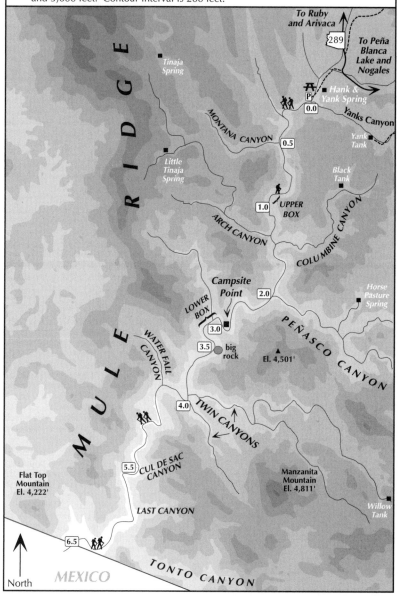

TEAR-OUT TRAIL MAP: Sycamore Canyon

The darker the shading, the higher the elevation.
The darkest areas have elevations above 4,800 feet.
The lightest areas have elevations between 3,400
and 3,600 feet. Contour interval is 200 feet.

To Ruby
and Arivaca

289

To Peña
Blanca
Lake and
Nogales

Tinaja
Spring

Hank &
Yank Spring

P

0.0

Yanks Canyon

MONTANA CANYON

0.5

Yank
Tank

Little
Tinaja
Spring

Black
Tank

1.0   UPPER
BOX

ARCH CANYON

COLUMBINE CANYON

R I D G E

Campsite
Point   2.0

Horse
Pasture
Spring

LOWER
BOX

3.0

PEÑASCO CANYON

WATER FALL CANYON

3.5   big
rock

El. 4,501'

M U L E

4.0   TWIN CANYONS

Flat Top
Mountain
El. 4,222'

5.5   CUL DE SAC
CANYON

Manzanita
Mountain
El. 4,811'

LAST CANYON

Willow
Tank

6.5

North

MEXICO

TONTO CANYON

No one should attempt to hike down **Syca-more Canyon** *without water.* From April through October, plan on hauling three or four quarts per person. Unless you depart before sunrise — which is recommended — carry lunch, too. Because there is no trail for most of the way, a spill is entirely probable, so add a first aid kit to your knapsack. If at all possible, bird Sycamore with a companion who could go for assistance in the advent of a severe sprain or broken leg.

The route begins at the ruins of Hank and Yank Bartlett's 1870s homestead. After wet winters, huge patches of Parry Penstemon along a trail-of-use that leads to the stream are frequented by Costa's Hummingbird in April and May. Broad-billed and Black-chinned Hummingbirds (summer) are the common species after the trail drops into the streambed. Ferruginous Pygmy-Owls used an area just above Montana Canyon in the spring and summers of 1979, 1981, and 1986. The big ash trees at the confluence of Montana Canyon (0.5 mile) on the right (west) side of Sycamore ordinarily mark the upper limits for Elegant Trogons.

Slightly over one mile downstream from the Hank and Yank parking area, the canyon twists around a small waterfall — best negotiated by climbing over a small spur on the left (east) side — and the first scrawny sycamores appear. A pair of Sulphur-bellied Flycatchers nests here. The waterfall signals the beginning of the Upper Box area of Sycamore. For the next 0.25 mile the water threads its way through a tortuous stone vise. At the bottom end of the Upper Box the stream plunges across polished granite through a gap only 10-feet-wide. Unless you are very sure of your footing, plan on getting wet. Acrobatic birders may be able to pass this pool by spidering along the right (west) wall of the stream.

A series of plunge pools carved out of solid rock, locally called tinajas, on the right (west) side immediately below the Upper Box indicate the confluence of Arch Canyon. A short distance beyond a little brook trimmed with Golden Columbine trickles into Sycamore from the left (east) side. This is Columbine Canyon. Stay on the right side of Sycamore Canyon to negotiate the next few canyon bends and boulder fields. The canyon will suddenly widen and sycamore trees will spread their delicious shade across the canyon floor the remaining 0.25 mile to the Peñasco Canyon tributary, which joins Sycamore from the left (east) side.

It's worth the time to pause here to bird. All of the Madrean pine-oak woodland species of the border ranges occur in this area of Sycamore, many a full thousand feet below their usual altitudinal limits. Some of the summering species to watch for include Montezuma Quail, Zone-tailed Hawk, Band-tailed Pigeon, Elegant Trogon, Arizona Woodpecker, Northern "Red-shafted" Flicker, Western Wood-Pewee, Dusky-capped, Brown-crested, and Sulphur-bellied Flycatchers, Cassin's Kingbird, Violet-green Swallow, Mexican Jay, Bridled Titmouse, Bushtit, White-breasted Nuthatch, Bewick's Wren, Hermit Thrush, Plumbeous Vireo, Painted Redstart, Hepatic and Summer Tanagers, Black-headed Grosbeak, Spotted and Canyon Towhees, Rufous-crowned Sparrow, Hooded, Bullock's, and Scott's Orioles, House Finch, and Lesser Goldfinch. In migration these are joined by Warbling Vireos and Western Tanagers, and in winter by Red-naped Sapsuckers and Yellow-rumped Warblers. Watch for Louisiana Waterthrush (very rare) from mid-July through mid-March.

A trail-of-use generally hugs the base of the left (east) wall of Sycamore Canyon all the way down to Campsite Point, a spur with a natural flat top about 15 feet above the stream level that projects into the canyon from the right (west) side at about mile 3.0.

Just behind "Big Rock," a huge boulder on the left (east) side of the canyon at mile 3.5, a Fan-tailed Warbler set up housekeeping in 1987. The mile or so of Sycamore below Big Rock is probably more apt to shelter an overwintering trogon (or two) than any other area in Arizona. During summer Varied Bunting is common below Big Rock.

Two canyon outlets only a few yards apart coming in from the left (east) side of Sycamore at approximately mile 4.0, identify the upper end of the Rose-throated Becard, Thick-billed Kingbird, and Five-striped Sparrow zone of Sycamore. Researchers call this double confluence "Twin Canyons." One or two football-shaped becard nests typically overhang the creek in the next 200 yards below a sharp elbow in the stream—when they are in residency. Some summers no becards are detected in Sycamore Canyon.

The Five-stripes, however, are probably present every year. While the population fluctuates, in an average summer there are about 50 adults. Listen for their songs on the steep hillsides above the stream from mid-April through August. The slopes of lower Sycamore used by the sparrows are those matted with impenetrable thickets of thornscrub. The males usually sing from exposed perches.

The trip back to your car will take at least as long as the hike down, even without birding. Watch your footing!

AMERICAN BIRDING ASSOCIATION

PRINCIPLES OF BIRDING ETHICS

Everyone who enjoys birds and birding must always respect wild-life, its environment, and the rights of others. In any conflict of interest between birds and birders, the welfare of the birds and their environment comes first.

CODE OF BIRDING ETHICS

1. Promote the welfare of birds and their environment.

1(a) Support the protection of important bird habitat.

1(b) To avoid stressing birds or exposing them to danger, exercise restraint and caution during observation, photography, sound recording, or filming.

Limit the use of recordings and other methods of attracting birds, and never use such methods in heavily birded areas or for attracting any species that is Threatened, Endangered, or of Special Concern, or is rare in your local area.

Keep well back from nests and nesting colonies, roosts, display areas, and important feeding sites. In such sensitive areas, if there is a need for extended observation, photography, filming, or recording, try to use a blind or hide, and take advantage of natural cover.

Use artificial light sparingly for filming or photography, especially for close-ups.

1(c) Before advertising the presence of a rare bird, evaluate the potential for disturbance to the bird, its surroundings, and other people in the area, and proceed only if access can be controlled, disturbance can be minimized, and permission has been obtained from private land-owners. The sites of rare nesting birds should be divulged only to the proper conservation authorities.

1(d) Stay on roads, trails, and paths where they exist; otherwise keep habitat disturbance to a minimum.

2. Respect the law and the rights of others.

2(a) Do not enter private property without the owner's explicit permission.

2(b) Follow all laws, rules, and regulations governing use of roads and public areas, both at home and abroad.

2(c) Practice common courtesy in contacts with other people. Your exemplary behavior will generate goodwill with birders and non-birders alike.

3. **Ensure that feeders, nest structures, and other artificial bird environments are safe.**

3(a) Keep dispensers, water, and food clean and free of decay or disease. It is important to feed birds continually during harsh weather.

3(b) Maintain and clean nest structures regularly.

3(c) If you are attracting birds to an area, ensure the birds are not exposed to predation from cats and other domestic animals, or dangers posed by artificial hazards.

4. **Group birding, whether organized or impromptu, requires special care.**

Each individual in the group, in addition to the obligations spelled out in Items #1 and #2, has responsibilities as a Group Member.

4(a) Respect the interests, rights, and skills of fellow birders, as well as those of people participating in other legitimate outdoor activities. Freely share your knowledge and experience, except where code 1(c) applies. Be especially helpful to beginning birders.

4(b) If you witness unethical birding behavior, assess the situation and intervene if you think it prudent. When interceding, inform the person(s) of the inappropriate action and attempt, within reason, to have it stopped. If the behavior continues, document it and notify appropriate individuals or organizations.

Group Leader Responsibilities [amateur and professional trips and tours].

4(c) Be an exemplary ethical role model for the group. Teach through word and example.

4(d) Keep groups to a size that limits impact on the environment and does not interfere with others using the same area.

4(e) Ensure everyone in the group knows of and practices this code.

4(f) Learn and inform the group of any special circumstances applicable to the areas being visited (e.g., no tape recorders allowed).

4(g) Acknowledge that professional tour companies bear a special responsibility to place the welfare of birds and the benefits of public knowledge ahead of the company's commercial interests. Ideally, leaders should keep track of tour sightings, document unusual occurrences, and submit records to appropriate organizations.

PLEASE FOLLOW THIS CODE
DISTRIBUTE IT AND TEACH IT TO OTHERS.

Additional copies of the Code of Birding Ethics can be obtained from: ABA, PO Box 6599, Colorado Springs, CO 80934-6599. Phone 800/850-2473 or 719/578-1614; fax 800/247-3329 or 719/578-1480; e-mail: member@aba.org

This ABA Code of Birding Ethics may be reprinted, reproduced, and distributed without restriction. Please acknowledge the role of ABA in developing and promoting this code.

ABA BIRDFINDING GUIDE SERIES

A Birder's Guide to Michigan
Allen T. Chartier and Jerry Ziarno
A Birder's Guide to Washington
Hal Opperman
A Birder's Guide to Alaska
George C. West
A Birder's Guide to the Rio Grande Valley
Mark W. Lockwood, William B. McKinney, James N. Paton, Barry R. Zimmer
A Birder's Guide to Metropolitan Areas of North America
Paul Lehman
A Birder's Guide to the Bahamas
Anthony R. White
A Birder's Guide to Virginia
David Johnston
A Birder's Guide to Southern California
Brad Schram
A Birder's Guide to Colorado
Harold R. Holt
A Birder's Guide to Florida
Bill Pranty
A Birder's Guide to New Hampshire
Alan Delorey
Birdfinder: A Birder's Guide to Planning North American Trips
Jerry A. Cooper
A Birder's Guide to Southeastern Arizona
Richard Cachor Taylor
A Birder's Guide to Arkansas
Mel White
A Birder's Guide to Eastern Massachusetts
Bird Observer
A Birder's Guide to the Texas Coast
Harold R. Holt
A Birder's Guide to Wyoming
Oliver K. Scott

OTHER RECENT ABA PUBLICATIONS

Birding on Borrowed Time   Attu: Birding on the Edge
Phoebe Snetsinger   *Charles E. Osgood*
ABA Checklist: Birds of the Continental United States and Canada
ABA Checklist Committee

ABA SALES — 800-634-7736
www.americanbirding.org/abasales

REPORT TO ARIZONA BIRD COMMITTEE
DOCUMENTATION OF UNUSUAL BIRD SIGHTING

Species: Date Observed:

Age: Sex: Number:

Location: Exact address or specific details, such as distance and direction from the nearest landmark:

County: City: Elevation:

Time: Duration of Observation:

Distance to Bird: Light Conditions:

Habitat:

Optical Equipment:

Observer:

Initial Observer and others who independently identified this bird:

Detailed Description: include size, shape, plumage characters, eye color, legs, bill, and any other unique features:

Vocalizations:

Behavior:

Describe the specific features that led to your conclusion. What other species were considered? How were these eliminated?

What experience have you had with this and the similar species?

Significance of the occurrence for this date and place:

Notes were made ____ At the time of the sighting OR ____ Later (when?)
            ____Before OR ____After consulting field guides

How well was the bird seen? ___Very well ___Moderately well ___OK
            ___ Poorly

Books, illustrations and advice consulted; how did these influence your description and conclusion?

Additional documentation: attach and label notes, drawings, photos, recordings, etc.

Include your name, the date, and location on the materials!

   Signature_____ Date Prepared_____

   Address, e-mail address, and phone number:

Send to: Arizona Bird Committee, Gary Rosenberg, Secretary, PO Box 91856, Tucson, AZ 85752-1856 OR Email to: ghrosenberg@comcast.net

Reference: "How To Document Rare Birds", *Birding* 24(3):145

The original of this form is available on the Arizona Bird Committee website,
http://ghrosenberg.home.comcast.net/index.html

REFERENCES

BIRDS

Brown, David E. 1985. *Arizona Wetlands and Waterfowl.* University of Arizona Press.

_____. 1989. *Arizona Game Birds.* University of Arizona Press and the Arizona Game and Fish Department.

Monson, Gale, and Allan R. Phillips. 1981. *Annotated Checklist of the Birds of Arizona.* University of Arizona Press.

Phillips, Alan, Joe Marshall, and Gale Monson. 1964. *The Birds of Arizona.* University of Arizona Press.

Rosenberg, Gary H., and Dave Stejskal. 2002. *Field Checklist of the Birds of Arizona.* Arizona Bird Committee.

Taylor, Richard Cachor. 1997. *Location Checklist to the Birds of the Chiricahua Mountains.* Borderland Productions.

_____. 1995. *Location Checklist to the Birds of the Huachuca Mountains and the Upper San Pedro River.* Borderland Productions.

_____. 1994. *Trogons of the Arizona Borderlands.* Treasure Chest Publications.

Tucson Audubon Society Publications Committee. 2004. *Davis and Russell's Finding Birds in Southeastern Arizona.* Tucson Audubon Society.

GEOLOGY AND HISTORY

Chronic, Halka. 1994. *Roadside Geology of Arizona.* Mountain Press Publishing Company.

Trimble, Marshall. 1994. *Roadside History of Arizona,* Mountain Press Publishing Company.

PLANTS

Arnberger, Leslie P. 1982. *Flowers of the Southwest Uplands.* Southwest Parks and Monuments Association.

Bowers, Janice. 1993. *Shrubs and Trees of the Southwest Deserts.* Southwest Parks and Monuments Association.

Brown, David E., editor. 1994. *Biotic Communities of the Southwest United States & Northwest Mexico.* University of Utah Press.

Dodge, Natt. 1985. *Flowers of the Southwest Deserts.* Southwest Parks and Monuments Association.

Elmore, Frances, and Jeanne Janish. 1976. *Shrubs and Trees of the Southwest Uplands.* Southwest Parks and Monuments Association.

Epple, Anne Orth. 1995. *A Field Guide to the Plants of Arizona.* Globe Pequot Press.

Niehaus, Theodore F. 1998. *A Field Guide to Southwestern and Texas Wildflowers.* Peterson Field Guide No. 31. Houghton Mifflin Company.

Quinn, Meg. 2000. *Wildflowers of the Desert Southwest.* Rio Nuevo Publishers.

_____. 2001. *Cacti of the Desert Southwest.* Rio Nuevo Publishers.

_____. 2003. *Wildflowers of the Mountain Southwest.* Rio Nuevo Publishers.

INSECTS

Bailowitz, Richard A., and James P. Brock. 1991. *Butterflies of Southeastern Arizona,* Sonoran Arthropod Studies.

_____ and Douglas Danforth. 1997. *70 Common Butterflies of the Southwest.* Southwest Parks and Monuments Association.

Stewart, Bob, Priscilla Brodkin, and Hank Brodkin. 2001. *Butterflies of Arizona, A Photographic Guide.* West Coast Lady Press.

Werner, Floyd, and Carl Olsen. 1994. *Insects of the Southwest.* Fisher Books.

REPTILES

Lowe, Charles, Cecil Schwalbe, and Terry Johnson. 1989. *The Venomous Reptiles of Arizona.* Arizona Game and Fish Department.

Stebbins, Robert C. 2003. *A Field Guide to Western Reptiles and Amphibians.* Peterson Field Guide. Houghton Mifflin Company.

MAMMALS:

Cockrum, E. Lendell, and Yar Petryszyn. 1992. *Mammals of the Southwest.* Treasure Chest Publications.

Hoffmeister, Donald F. 1986. *Mammals of Arizona.* University of Arizona Press and the Arizona Game and Fish Department.

NATIVE AMERICANS

Arnold, Elliot. 1979. *Blood Brother.* University of Nebraska Press. (novel)

Opler, Morris Edward. 1965. *An Apache Life-Way.* University of Chicago Press.

Preston, Douglas. 1992. *Cities of Gold.* Simon and Schuster.

Spicer, Edward H. 1976. *Cycles of Conquest.* University of Arizona Press.

NATURAL HISTORY

Heald, Weldon. 1993. *The Chiricahua Sky Island.* Marguerite Bantlin Publishing.

Krutch, Joseph Wood. 1952. *The Desert Year.* University of Arizona Press.

Nabhan, Gary Paul. 1987. *Gathering the Desert.* University of Arizona Press.

Phillips, Steven J., and Patricia Wentworth Comus, editors. 2000. *A Natural History of the Sonoran Desert.* Arizona-Sonora Desert Museum.

HIKING

Cowgill, Pete, and Eber Glendening. 1998. *Trail Guide to the Santa Catalina Mountains.* Rainbow Expeditions.

Leavengood, Betty. 1991. *Tucson Hiking Guide.* Pruett Publishing Company.

_____ and Mike Liebert. 1994. *Hiker's Guide to the Santa Rita Mountains.* Pruett Publishing Company.

Taylor, Leonard. 1991. *Hiker's Guide to the Huachuca Mountains.* Thunder Peak Productions.

Taylor, Richard Cachor. 1977. *Hiking Trails and Wilderness Routes of the Chiricahua Mountains.* Rainbow Expeditions.

NEWSLETTER

Tucson Audubon Society. *The Vermilion Flycatcher* (monthly bulletin). 300 E. University Blvd., #120, Tucson, AZ 85705.

AUDIO

Keller, Geoffrey A. 2001. *Bird Songs of Southeastern Arizona and Sonora, Mexico.* Cornell Laboratory of Ornithology. (two CDs)

VIDEO

Gates, Larry and Terri. 1993. *Birds of Southeastern Arizona.* Portal Productions.

INDEX

Southeastern Arizona Mileage Chart

Locations (listed along the diagonal of the chart):

1. Amado/Arivaca Jct.
2. Arivaca
3. Aravaipa East
4. Aravaipa West
5. Ariz.-Sonora Desert Museum
6. Bisbee
7. Buenos Aires NWR HQ
8. Chiricahua National Monument
9. Coronado National Memorial
10. Douglas
11. Dudleyville
12. Elfrida
13. Green Valley
14. Madera Canyon
15. Muleshoe Ranch Preserve
16. Nogales
17. Patagonia
18. Picacho Reservoir
19. Portal
20. Ramsey Canyon Visitor Center
21. Rustler Park
22. Sabino Canyon House
23. San Pedro House
24. San Simon
25. Sierra Vista
26. Ski Valley, Santa Catalina Mtns
27. Sonoita
28. Sycamore Canyon, Atascosa Mtns
29. Tombstone
30. Tucson: I-10 and I-19
31. Willcox

Triangular mileage grid (each row lists distances from that location to the preceding locations, read left to right):

Location	Distances to preceding locations
Arivaca	23
Aravaipa East	185 | 208
Aravaipa West	101 | 124 | 139
Ariz.-Sonora Desert Museum	40 | 73 | 169 | 78
Bisbee	129 | 152 | 159 | 164 | 112
Buenos Aires NWR HQ	41 | 19 | 212 | 128 | 57 | 156
Chiricahua National Monument	144 | 167 | 103 | 179 | 128 | 65 | 171
Coronado National Memorial	119 | 142 | 162 | 110 | 19 | 154 | 84 | 61
Douglas	154 | 177 | 160 | 197 | 146 | 24 | 189 | 61 | 43
Dudleyville	93 | 116 | 122 | 16 | 70 | 156 | 27 | 171 | 154 | 189
Elfrida	138 | 161 | 115 | 165 | 121 | 38 | 154 | 120 | 46 | 23 | 164
Green Valley	11 | 34 | 177 | 90 | 39 | 133 | 81 | 115 | 112 | 177 | 82 | 189
Madera Canyon	22 | 45 | 190 | 104 | 51 | 145 | 78 | 112 | 95 | 190 | 95 | 132 | 12
Muleshoe Ranch Preserve	143 | 166 | 97 | 178 | 127 | 61 | 170 | 61 | 65 | 97 | 61 | 73 | 125 | 124
Nogales	37 | 60 | 186 | 138 | 87 | 127 | 92 | 79 | 82 | 155 | 82 | 132 | 48 | 60 | 144
Patagonia	51 | 74 | 168 | 127 | 76 | 74 | 97 | 74 | 64 | 170 | 64 | 117 | 101 | 101 | 60 | 18
Picacho Reservoir	94 | 117 | 213 | 109 | 75 | 157 | 121 | 172 | 155 | 190 | 165 | 83 | 190 | 130 | 101 | 131 | 126
Portal	174 | 197 | 141 | 166 | 117 | 81 | 209 | 26 | 57 | 30 | 209 | 171 | 185 | 171 | 165 | 185 | 131 | 210
Ramsey Canyon Visitor Center	110 | 133 | 152 | 153 | 102 | 30 | 145 | 113 | 16 | 54 | 145 | 72 | 55 | 99 | 145 | 87 | 99 | 189 | 15
Rustler Park	161 | 184 | 120 | 196 | 145 | 82 | 188 | 17 | 72 | 52 | 188 | 186 | 189 | 158 | 180 | 186 | 143 | 15 | 146 | 17
Sabino Canyon House	50 | 73 | 157 | 70 | 30 | 101 | 61 | 109 | 99 | 134 | 55 | 39 | 78 | 72 | 87 | 55 | 78 | 154 | 27 | 138 | 143
San Pedro House	108 | 131 | 150 | 99 | 36 | 142 | 109 | 26 | 57 | 61 | 115 | 57 | 52 | 66 | 64 | 44 | 115 | 65 | 10 | 45 | 116 | 52
San Simon	155 | 178 | 190 | 139 | 129 | 182 | 52 | 132 | 83 | 163 | 72 | 144 | 85 | 144 | 158 | 136 | 72 | 93 | 119 | 136 | 183 | 93 | 72
Sierra Vista	101 | 124 | 143 | 143 | 92 | 29 | 135 | 102 | 19 | 53 | 135 | 62 | 50 | 59 | 101 | 45 | 59 | 110 | 10 | 104 | 119 | 45 | 12 | 119
Ski Valley, Santa Catalina Mtns	79 | 102 | 186 | 111 | 59 | 130 | 106 | 145 | 128 | 163 | 138 | 56 | 163 | 104 | 104 | 116 | 183 | 43 | 93 | 104 | 183 | 26 | 107 | 183 | 107
Sonoita	39 | 62 | 156 | 114 | 63 | 62 | 109 | 115 | 52 | 86 | 106 | 71 | 29 | 36 | 70 | 59 | 12 | 107 | 200 | 30 | 26 | 59 | 62 | 136 | 89 | 200
Sycamore Canyon, Atascosa Mtns	40 | 63 | 212 | 143 | 92 | 118 | 105 | 171 | 108 | 142 | 135 | 128 | 63 | 62 | 26 | 44 | 26 | 143 | 99 | 12 | 170 | 69 | 62 | 200 | 132 | 99 | 121
Tombstone	105 | 128 | 132 | 135 | 94 | 24 | 128 | 90 | 35 | 48 | 128 | 60 | 33 | 67 | 76 | 81 | 89 | 107 | 73 | 26 | 128 | 85 | 17 | 69 | 24 | 126 | 182 | 80
Tucson: I-10 and I-19	33 | 56 | 152 | 68 | 17 | 96 | 60 | 111 | 94 | 129 | 60 | 104 | 22 | 36 | 110 | 70 | 59 | 85 | 128 | 17 | 149 | 61 | 82 | 156 | 46 | 33 | 75 | 46 | 68
Willcox	113 | 136 | 72 | 148 | 97 | 70 | 140 | 31 | 90 | 88 | 140 | 51 | 102 | 95 | 30 | 114 | 96 | 141 | 69 | 80 | 48 | 80 | 78 | 42 | 114 | 109 | 84 | 140 | 60 | 80